T0257520

Intelligent Network Design Driven by Big Data Analytics, IoT, AI and Cloud Computing

Other volumes in this series:

Intelligent Network Design Driven by Big Data Analytics, IoT, AI and Cloud Computing

Edited by
Sunil Kumar, Glenford Mapp and Korhan Cengiz

The Institution of Engineering and Technology

Published by The Institution of Engineering and Technology, London, United Kingdom

The Institution of Engineering and Technology is registered as a Charity in England & Wales (no. 211014) and Scotland (no. SC038698).

The Institution of Engineering and Technology
Futures Place
Kings Way, Stevenage
Herts, SG1 2UA, United Kingdom

www.theiet.org

British Library Cataloguing in Publication Data
A catalogue record for this product is available from the British Library

ISBN 978-1-83953-533-8 (hardback)
ISBN 978-1-83953-534-5 (PDF)

Typeset in India by Exeter Premedia Services Private Limited
Printed in the UK by CPI Group (UK) Ltd, Croydon
Cover Image: Yuichiro Chino via Getty Images

Contents

13 Image Processing for medical images on the basis of intelligence and biocomputing 279

M. Mohammed Mustafa, S. Umamaheswari, and Korhen Cengiz

About the Editors

Sunil Kumar is an associate professor of Computer Science and Engineering at Amity University, Noida campus, India. His research interests include computer networks, distributed systems, wireless sensor networks, SDN, and big data. He is industry CCNA & CCNP certified. He is a member of the IET, CSTA, IAER, IAENG. He holds a PhD in energy optimization in distributed wireless sensor networks from Amity University, Noida India.

Glenford Mapp is an associate professor at Middlesex University, London, UK. His primary expertise is in the development of new technologies for mobile and distributed systems such as service platforms, cloud computing, network addressing and transport protocols for local environments. He had previously worked for AT&T Cambridge Laboratories for ten years. He received his PhD in computer science from the University of Cambridge, UK.

Korhan Cengiz is an assistant professor of electrical and electronics engineering at Trakya University, Turkey. His research interests include computer networks, big data, wireless sensor networks, wireless communications, routing protocols, statistical signal processing, indoor positioning systems, power electronics and machine learning. He is an associate editor of *Interdisciplinary Sciences: Computational Life Sciences,* handling editor of *Microprocessors and Microsystems*, and associate editor of *IET Electronics Letters, IET Networks*, amongst others.

Chapter 1

Introduction to intelligent network design driven by big data analytics, IoT, AI and cloud computing

Sunil Kumar[1], Glenford Mapp[2], and Korhan Cengiz[3]

Preface

As enterprise access networks evolve with more mobile users, diverse devices and cloud-based applications, managing user performance on an end-to-end basis has become next to impossible. Recent advances in big data network analytics, combined with AI and cloud computing are being leveraged to tackle this growing problem. The book focuses on how new network analytics platforms are being used to ingest, analyze and correlate a myriad of infrastructure data across the entire network stack with the goal of finding and fixing the quality of service network performance problems.

This book presents new upcoming technologies in the field of networking and telecommunication. It addresses major new technological developments and reflects on industry needs, current research trends and future directions. The authors focus on the development of AI-powered mechanisms for future wireless networking applications and architectures which will lead to more performant, resilient and valuable ecosystems and automated services. The book is a primary readership and is a "must-read" for researchers, academicians, engineers and scientists involved in the design and development of protocols and AI applications for wireless communication devices and wireless networking technologies.

All chapters presented here are the product of extensive field research involving applications and techniques related to data analysis in general, and to big data, AI, IoT and network technologies in particular.

[1]Department of Computer Science & Engineering, Amity University, India
[2]Faculty of Science & Technology, Department of Computer Science, Middlesex University, London, UK
[3]Department of Electrical-Electronics Engineering, Trakya University, Edirne, Turkey

Chapter 2: Role of automation, Big Data, AI, ML IBN, and cloud computing in intelligent networks

There are more smart devices in our world today than individuals. A growing number of people are linked to the Internet 24 hours a day, in some form or another. A growing number of people own three, four, or more smart devices and rely on them. Smartphones, fitness and health trackers, e-readers, and tablets are just a few examples. It is forecast that on average there will be 3.4 smart devices or connections for every person on earth [1, 2]. The Internet of Things (IoT) is relevant to many industries. IoT systems contribute to the environmental controls, retail, transportation, healthcare, and agriculture industries among many others. According to Statista, the number of IoT devices that are in use across all relevant industries is forecast to grow to more than 8 billion by 2030 [3, 4]. As for consumers, important growth areas are the Internet and digital media devices, which include smartphones. This area is also predicted to grow to more than 8 billion by 2030 [5]. Other applications with more than 1 million connected devices are connected and autonomous vehicles, IT infrastructure, asset management, and electric utility smart grid [6].

All of this is made possible through intelligent networks. The planet is rapidly becoming covered in networks that allow digital devices to communicate and interconnect. Consider the network mesh as a digital skin that surrounds the earth. Mobile devices, electronic sensors, electronic measuring equipment, medical gadgets, and gauges can all link with this digital skin. They keep track of, communicate with, analyze, and, in some situations, automatically adjust to the data collected and transmitted [7, 8].

Keywords: AI, ML, cloud computing, IBN, Big Data, IoT, automation, virtualization, intelligent networks.

Chapter 3: An intelligent verification management approach for efficient VLSI computing system

Any masterpiece is conjoined with all works of engineering, which includes the field of computer science or an electrical and electronics or mixture of both computer and electronics. Today, this gives the industry to understand research, evolve and develop into newer technology unfolding many scriptures behind the engineering works. In the similar manner, this chapter unfolds the prominent works involved in the verification of the designs involved in VLSI domain. Considering machine learning (ML), neural networks and artificial intelligence (AI) concepts and applying these to a wide range of verification approaches are quite interesting. The specific kinds of Register Transfer Level (RTL) design require rigorous verification which is targeted over any type of Field Programmable Gate Array (FPGA) or application-specific integrated circuits (ASICs). The verification process should be closed with testing all possible scenarios that too with intelligent verification methods. This chapter in the following pages brings the unique way of verification procedure involved in the RTL development methodologies using hardware description languages. With the help of system Verilog language, the developed reusable testbench is used for verification. The injected inputs to the testbench are randomized with constraints, such that the design should produce accurate output. To unify the verification language there is a dedicated methodology commonly known as Universal Verification Methodology (UVM); by this, the article is extended to experience the readers also through the coverage-based formal verification. For continuous functional verification, an intelligent regression model is also developed with the help of ML and scripting. With this repeated injection of various test cases is possible in order to verify the functionality. Thus, with the adoption of the presented verification environment and distinctive approach, one can affirm that the design is ready to be deployed over the targeted semiconductor chips. As the verification is an unignorable procedure, this can be used to classify the algorithms developed in ML for data clustering, data encoding and its accurate analysis. More importantly, this chapter allows us to understand an intelligent verification model for testing the design with regression run with the corresponding set-up and the pass/failure analysis steps. This structure may result in a significant reduction of the simulation time for a VLSI verification engineer.

Keywords: VLSI, verification, intelligent, ASIC.

Chapter 4: Evaluation of machine learning algorithms on academic big dataset by using feature selection techniques

Identifying the most accurate methods for forecasting students' academic achievement is the focus of this research. Globally, all educational institutions are concerned about student attrition. The goal of all educational institutions is to increase the student's retention and graduation rates and this is only possible if at-risk students are identified early. Due to inherent classifier constraints and the incorporation of fewer student features, most commonly used prediction models are inefficient and incur. Different data mining algorithms like classification, clustering, regression, and association rule mining are used to uncover hidden patterns and relevant information in student performance big datasets in academics. Naïve Bayes, random forest, decision tree, multilayer perceptron (MLP), decision table (DT), JRip, and logistic regression (LR) are some of the data mining techniques that can be applied. A student's academic performance big dataset comprises many features, none of which are relevant or play a significant role in the mining process. So, features with a variance close to 0 are removed from the student's academic performance big dataset because they have no impact on the mining process. To determine the influence of various attributes on the class level, various feature selection (FS) techniques such as the correlation attribute evaluator (CAE), information gain attribute evaluator (IGAE), and gain ratio attribute evaluator (GRAE) are utilized. In this study, authors have investigated the performance of various data mining algorithms on the big dataset, as well as the effectiveness of various FS techniques. In conclusion, each classification algorithm that is built with some FS methods improves the performance of the classification algorithms in their overall predictive performance.

Keywords: data mining, classification, Big Data; feature selection, correlation attribute evaluator, information gain attribute evaluator, gain ratio attribute evaluator.

Chapter 5: Accurate management and progression of Big Data analysis

Statistical investigations are concerned with circumstances including arranging, information assortment, association of data, and scrutiny of compiled data, conversion, and exposure in a clear and chosen procedure. To do so, research techniques can be distinguished in two different ways: conclusion overviews and statistical surveying. In assessments of public sentiment, the primary objective is to assemble data about deciding subjects dependent on close-to-home meetings. Statistical surveying is directed through the market investigation of a specific item. Assortment, association, depiction of information, estimation, and translation of coefficients have a place with descriptive statistics, while investigation and understanding of information, related to an edge of vulnerability, is the obligation of the inductive or inferential statistics, additionally called the proportion of vulnerability or techniques that depend on likelihood hypothesis [9, 10]. The utilization of tables and charts is visited in statistics. The tables serve to arrange and classify the information, and the illustrations pass on the data with lucidity and straightforwardness, adding to a goal pursuing.

Keywords: Big data analysis, scheduling, statistics, machine learning, enormous information, cybercrime, Internet of things (IoT).

Chapter 6: Cram on data recovery and backup cloud computing techniques

The present digital world technology is evolving at a rapid pace. To store, manage and protect the digital information, it is necessary to back up and recover the data with utmost efficiency. As a solution, cloud computing that offers customers a wide range of services can be used [11, 12]. Storage-as-a-Service (SaaS) is one of the cloud platform's services, in which a large volume of digital data is maintained in the cloud database. Enterprise's most sensitive data are stored in the cloud, ensuring that it is secure and accessible at all times and from all locations. At times, information may become unavailable due to natural disasters such as windstorms, rainfall, earthquakes, or any technical fault and accidental deletion. To ensure data security and availability under such circumstances, it is vital to have a good understanding of the data backup and recovery strategies. This chapter examines a variety of cloud computing backup and recovery techniques.

Keywords: cloud computing, data backup, data recovery, advantage, disadvantage.

Chapter 7: An adaptive software defined networking (SDN) for load balancing in cloud computing

The Internet of Things (IoT) can be perceived as a collection of millions of devices that are connected among each other and with the Internet as a connectivity backbone to acquire and share real-time data for providing intelligent services. The tremendous rise in the number of devices requires an adequate network infrastructure to remotely deal with data orchestration. To overcome this issue, a new approach of infrastructure sharing over the cloud among service providers has transpired, with the goal of lowering excessive infrastructure deployment costs. The software-defined networking (SDN) is a networking architecture that enables network operators and users to monitor and manage the network devices remotely and more flexibly by using software that runs on external servers. As SDN and cloud integration improves reliability, scalability, and manageability, this paper combines cloud infrastructure with SDN. Although SDN-based cloud networks have numerous advantages as mentioned above, there still exist certain challenges that draw the attention of researchers like energy efficiency, security, load balancing, and so on. The work carried out in this chapter is an attempt to address one of the challenging tasks, namely the load balancing, by developing a new multiple-controller load-balancing strategy. The proposed strategy effectively balances the load even if one or more super controllers fail. Furthermore, results are simulated and compared under different operational environments, both with and without the Modified Bully algorithm. The comparison results ensure that the introduced technique exhibits better performance with metrics such as packet loss, packet transmission ratio, and throughput.

Keywords: SDN, load balancing, IoT, controller, packet loss, transmission ratio, throughput.

Chapter 8: Emerging security challenges in cloud computing: An insight

Cloud computing has been evolved as a new computing prototype with the aim of providing reliability, quality of service and cost-effective with no location barrier. More massive databases and applications are relocated to an immense centralized data center known as the cloud. Cloud computing has enormous benefits of no need to purchase physical space from a separate vendor instead of using the cloud, but these benefits have security threats [13, 14]. The resource virtualization, the data and the machine are physically absent in the cloud; the storage of data in the cloud causes security issues. An unauthorized person can penetrate through the cloud security and can data manipulation, data loss or theft might take place. This chapter has described cloud computing and various security issues and challenges that are present in different cloud models and cloud environment. It also gives an idea of different threat management techniques available to encounter security issues and challenges. The RSA algorithm implementation has been described in detail, and the Advance Encryption Standard policy, along with its implementation, has also been discussed. For better clarification, several reviews are conducted on the existing models.

Keywords: security, cloud computing, saas, pass, iaas, cryptography.

Chapter 9: Factors responsible and phases of speaker recognition system

The method of identifying a speaker based on his or her speech is known as automatic speaker recognition. Speaker/voice recognition is a biometric sensory device that recognizes people by their voices. Most speaker recognition systems nowadays are focused on spectral information, which means they use spectral information derived from speech signal segments of 10–30 ms in length. However, if the received speech signal contains some noise, the cepstral-based system's output suffers. The primary goal of the study is to see the various factors responsible for improved performance of the speaker recognition systems by modeling prosodic features, and phases of speaker recognition system. Furthermore, in the presence of background noise, the analysis focused on a text-independent speaker recognition system.

Keywords: voice recognition, signals, noise, quality.

Chapter 10: IOT-based water quality assessment using fuzzy logic controller

Water is an essential resource that we use in our daily life. The standard of the water quality must be observed in real time to make sure that we obtain a secured and clean supply of water to our residential areas. A water quality-monitoring and decision-making system (WQMDMS) is implemented for this purpose based on Internet of Things (IoT) and fuzzy logic (FLC) to decide the usage of water (drinking or tap water) in a common water tank system. The physical and chemical properties of data are obtained through continuous monitoring of sensors. The work describes in detail the design of a fuzzy logic controller for a water quality measurement system, to determine the quality of water by decision-making, and accordingly, the usage of water is decided. The WQMDM system measures the physico-chemical characteristics of water like pH, turbidity, and temperature by the use of corresponding analog and digital sensors. The values of the parameters obtained are used to detect the presence of water contaminants and accordingly, the quality of water is determined. The measurements from the sensor are handled and processed by Esp32 and these refined values follow the rules determined by the fuzzy inference system. The output highlights the water quality that is categorized as very poor, poor, average, good. The usage of the water will be determined by the results obtained using the FLC and as per the percentage of water quality, the water is decided as drinking water or tap water.

Keywords: WQMDMS, IoT, controller, fuzzy logic.

Chapter 11: Design and analysis of wireless sensor network for intelligent transportation and industry automation

Wireless sensor networks (WSNs) are dense networks and combination of various distributed heterogeneous sensor nodes in terms of battery power, data storage and computational capacity. WSNs are very useful in industry automation-Internet of things (IOT), agriculture, economic, commercial and various monitoring applications in digital world. Energy is limited in wireless devices and in many conditions, it is not a replaceable or chargeable resource. One of the most characteristics of WSNs is that they are strongly coupled with their application. This chapter is based on the design and analysis of WSN for intelligent transportation and industry automation. Proposed work has been validated in NS2 and compared to other existing protocols. The simulation results are based on throughput, PDR, and delay parameters.

Keywords: WSN, Wi-Max, NS2, sensors.

Chapter 12: A review of edge computing in healthcare Internet of Things: theories, practices, and challenges

The pandemic has forced industries to move immediately their critical workload to the cloud in order to ensure continuous functioning. As cloud computing expansions pace and organisations strive for methods to increase their network, agility and storage, edge computing has shown to be the best alternative. The healthcare business has a long history of collaborating with cutting-edge information technology, and the Internet of Things (IoT) is no exception. Researchers are still looking for substantial methods to collect, view, process, and analyze data that can signify a quantitative revolution in healthcare as devices become more convenient and smaller data become larger. To provide real-time analytics, healthcare organisations frequently deploy cloud technology as the storage layer between system and insight. Edge computing, also known as fog computing, allows computers to perform important analyses without having to go through the time-consuming cloud storage process [15, 16]. For this form of processing, speed is key, and it may be crucial in constructing a healthcare IoT that is useful for patient interaction, inpatient treatment, population health management and remote monitoring. We present a thorough overview to highlight the most recent trends in fog computing activities related to the IoT in healthcare. Other perspectives on the edge computing domain are also offered, such as styles of application support, techniques and resources [17]. Finally, necessity of edge computing in era of Covid-19 pandemic is addressed.

Keywords: edge computing, fog computing, cloud computing, IOT, machine learning, healthcare.

Chapter 13: Image processing for medical images on the basis of intelligence and bio computing

Intelligence in medical imaging explores how intelligent computing can create large number of changes to existing technology in the field of medical image processing. The book presents various algorithms, techniques and models toward integrating medical image processing with artificial intelligence and biocomputing. Bioinformatics solutions lead to an effective method for processing the image data for the purpose of retrieving the information of interest and to collect various data sources for extracting the knowledge. Moreover, image processing methods and techniques help the scientists and physicians in medical field for diagnosis and therapies. It describes evolutionary optimization techniques, support vector machines (SVMs), fuzzy logic, a Bayesian probabilistic framework, a reinforcement learning-based multistage image segmentation algorithm, a machine learning (ML) approach. It discusses how these techniques are used for image classification, image formation, image visualization, image analysis, image management, and image enhancement. The term "medical image processing" illustrates the provision of digital image processing particularly for medicine. Medical imaging intends to identify internal structures hidden in the human body. It helps to find out abnormalities in the body. Digital images can be processed effectively, also evaluated and utilized in many circumstances concurrently with help of suitable communication protocols.

Keywords: image processing, machine learning, CNN, deep learning, medical images.

Chapter 14: IoT-based architecture for smart health-care systems

Internet of Things (IoT) provides a pathway for connecting physical entities with digital entities using devices and communication technologies. The rapid growth of IoT in recent days has made a significant influence in many fields. Healthcare is one of those fields which will be hugely benefited by IoT. IoT can resolve many challenges faced by patients and doctors in healthcare. Smart health-care applications allow the doctor to monitor the patient's health state without human intervention. Sensors collect and send the data from the patient. Recorded data are stored in a database that enables medical experts to analyze those data. Any abnormal change in the status of the patient can be notified to the doctor. This paperwork aims to study different research works made on IoT-based health-care systems that are implemented using basic development boards. Various hardware parameters of health-care systems and sensors used for those parameters are explored. A basic Arduino-based health-care application is proposed using sensors and global system for mobile communication (GSM) module.

Keywords: IoT, smart healthcare, patient monitoring.

Chapter 15: IoT-based heart disease prediction system

In India, around 80 per cent of people who die due to heart disease do not receive proper treatment. This is a daunting task for doctors as they often do not diagnose patients properly. The treatment of this disease is very costly. The purpose system improves the cost-effective treatment using data mining technology to simplify the Decision Support System. Most hospitals employee a hospital management system to manage the care of their patients. Unfortunately, many of these programs do not use big clinical data to extract important information. As these systems generate a large quantity of data in various embodiment in spite of the data being rarely looked upon and remains unused. Therefore, in this process, much effort is required to make wise decisions. This project helps diagnose a disease using various data mining techniques. Currently, diagnosing a disease involves identifying various symptoms and features of a disease.

Keywords: heart disease prediction, data mining, deep learning.

Chapter 16: DIAIF: detection of interest flooding using artificial intelligence-based framework in NDN android

In today's world, information-centric networking (ICN) is a brand-new next-generation network for distributing multimedia content. ICN focuses on sharing content across the network rather than obtaining content from a single fixed server. In-network caching aids in the dissemination of content from the network, and the ICN also includes a number of intrusive security mechanisms. Despite the ICN network's many security measures, several attacks, especially interest flooding attacks (IFA), continue to wreak havoc on the network's distribution capability. In order to address security threats, the literature includes a number of mitigating procedures. However, legitimate users' requests are misclassified as an attack in an emergency circumstance, affecting the network's QoS. In this chapter, Detection of Interest Flooding Attack using Artificial Intelligence Framework (DIAIF) is proposed in ICN. DIAIF seeks to lighten the load on ICN routers by removing the source of the attack without interfering with legitimate user requests. DIAIF depends on router feedback to assign a beneficial value (BV) to each piece of content and to block dangerous users based on the BV. The ICN testbed was designed to assess the proposed DIAIF's performance in terms of QoS during severe flood scenarios, responding with malicious content without interfering with genuine user requests, and identifying the source of attack in a communication scenario.

Keywords: Information centric networking, QoS, attacks, flooding attacks, security threats.

Chapter 17: Intelligent and cost-effective mechanism for monitoring road quality using machine learning

Nowadays, one of the most significant components of road infrastructure is monitoring road surface conditions, which leads to better driving conditions and reduces the chance of a road accident. Traditional road condition monitoring systems are incapable of gathering real-time information concerning road conditions. In previous generations, road surface condition monitoring was done for fixed roadways and vehicles travelling at a constant pace. Several systems have presented a method for exploiting the sensors installed in automobiles. However, this method will not assist in forecasting the precise placement of potholes, speed bumps, or staggered roads.

As a result, smartphone-based road condition evaluation and navigation are becoming increasingly popular. We propose exploring several machine learning techniques to accurately assess road conditions using accelerometer, gyroscope, and Global Positioning System (GPS) data collected from cellphones. We also recorded footage of the roadways in order to reduce noise in the data. This two-pronged approach to data collection will aid in the exact positioning of potholes, speed bumps and staggered roads. This method of data collection will aid in the classification of road conditions into numerous features such as roads with smooth surfaces, potholes, speed bumps and staggered highways using machine learning algorithms. This method of data collection will aid in the classification of road conditions into numerous features; machine learning algorithms are used to create characteristics such as smooth roads, potholes, speed breakers, and staggered highways. The user will receive this information via the map, which will classify the various road conditions. Accelerometers and gyroscope sensors will analyse multiple features from all three axes of the sensors in order to produce a more precise location of designated routes. To classify the road conditions, we investigate the performance utilising support vector machine (SVM), random forest, neural network and deep neural network. As a result, our findings demonstrate that models trained using a dual data gathering strategy will produce more accurate outcomes. Data classification will be substantially more accurate when neural networks are used. The methods described here can be used on a broader scale to monitor roads for problems that pose a safety concern to commuters and to give maintenance data to appropriate authorities.

Keywords: SVM, machine learning, GPS data, accelerometer data, android, road quality, smartphone.

References

[1]   Kumar S., Ranjan P., Ramaswami R. 'EMEEDP: enhanced multi-hop energy efficient distributed protocol for heterogeneous wireless sensor network'. *Fifth International Conference on Communication Systems and Network Technologies*; Gwalior, India, IEEE, 2015. pp. 194–200.

[2]   Kumar S., Rao A.L.N., Ramaswani R. 'Energy optimization technique for distributed localized wireless sensor network'. *International Conference*

on *Issues and Challenges in Intelligent Computing Techniques (ICICT)*; Ghaziabad, India, IEEE, 2014. pp. 350–55.

[3] Chauhan R., Kumar S. 'Packet loss prediction using artificial intelligence unified with big data analytics, internet of things and cloud computing technologies'. *5th International Conference on Information Systems and Computer Networks (ISCON)*; Mathura, India; 2021. pp. 01–6.

[4] Sudhakaran S., Kumar S., Ranjan P., Tripathy M.R. 'Blockchain-based transparent and secure decentralized algorithm'. *International Conference on Intelligent Computing and Smart Communication 2019. Algorithms for Intelligent Systems*; Springer, Singapore: THDC Institute of Hydropower Engineering and Technology Tehri Uttarakhand, 2020. pp. 327–36.

[5] Kumar S., Trivedi M.C., Ranjan P., Punhani A. *Evolution of Software-Defined Networking Foundations for IoT and 5G Mobile Networks*. IGI Publisher; 2020.

[6] Kumar S., Ranjan P., Radhakrishnan R., Tripathy M.R. 'Energy efficient multichannel MAC protocol for high traffic applications in heterogeneous wireless sensor networks'. *Recent Advances in Electrical & Electronic Engineering*. 2017, vol. 10(3), pp. 223–32.

[7] Kumar S., Ranjan P., Ramaswami R., Tripathy M.R. 'Resource efficient clustering and next hop knowledge based routing in multiple heterogeneous wireless sensor networks'. *International Journal of Grid and High Performance Computing*. 2017, vol. 9(2), pp. 1–20.

[8] Kumar S., Cengiz K., Vimal S., Suresh A. 'Energy efficient resource migration based load balance mechanism for high traffic applications IoT'. *Wireless personal communications*. 2021, vol. 10(3), pp. 1–14.

[9] Singh P., Bansal A., Kamal A.E., Kumar S. 'Road Surface Quality Monitoring Using Machine Learning Algorithm' in Reddy A.N.R., Marla D., Favorskaya M.N., Satapathy S.C. (eds.). *Intelligent Manufacturing and Energy Sustainability. Smart Innovation, Systems and Technologies*. 265. Singapore: Springer; 2022.

[10] Kumar S., Ranjan P., Radhakrishnan R., Tripathy M.R. 'Energy aware distributed protocol for heterogeneous wireless sensor network'. *International Journal of Control and Automation*. 2015, vol. 8(10), pp. 421–30.

[11] Kumar S., Ranjan P., Singh P., Tripathy M.R. 'Design and implementation of fault tolerance technique for internet of things (iot)'. *Proceedings - 12th International Conference on Computational Intelligence and Communication Networks*; Bhimtal, India, IEEE, 2020. pp. 154–59.

[12] Singh P., Bansal A., Kumar S. 'Performance analysis of various information platforms for recognizing the quality of Indian roads'. *Proceedings of the Confluence - 10th International Conference on Cloud Computing*; Noida, India; 2020.

[13] Reghu S., Kumar S. 'Development of robust infrastructure in networking to survive a disaster'. *4th International Conference on Information Systems and Computer Networks*; Mathura, India, 2019. pp. 250–55.

[14] Chauhan R., Kumar S. 'Packet loss prediction using artificial intelligence uni-fied with big data analytics, internet of things and cloud computing technolo-gies'. *5th International Conference on Information Systems and Computer Networks (ISCON)*; Mathura, India, IEEE, 2021. pp. 01–06.

[15] Haidar M., Kumar S. 'Smart healthcare system for biomedical and health care applications using aadhaar and blockchain'. *2021 5th International Conference on Information Systems and Computer Networks, ISCON 2021*; Mathura, India, IEEE, 2022. pp. 1–5.

[16] Punhani A., Faujdar N., Kumar S. 'Design and evaluation of cubic Torus Network-on-Chip architecture'. *International Journal of Innovative Technology and Exploring Engineering*. 2019, vol. 8(6), pp. 2278–3075.

[17] Dubey G., Kumar S., Kumar S., Navaney P. 'Extended opinion lexicon and ML-based sentiment analysis of tweets: a novel approach towards accurate classifier'. *International Journal of Computational Vision and Robotics*. 2020, vol. 10(6), pp. 505–21.

Chapter 2

Role of automation, Big Data, AI, ML IBN, and cloud computing in intelligent networks

Sunil Kumar[1] and Priya Ranjan[2]

There are more smart devices in our world today than individuals. A growing number of people are linked to the Internet 24 hours a day, in some form or another. A growing number of people own three, four, or more smart devices and rely on them. Smartphones, fitness and health trackers, e-readers, and tablets are just a few examples. It is forecast that on average there will be 3.4 smart devices or connections for every person on earth. The Internet of Things (IoT) is relevant to many industries. IoT systems contribute to the environmental controls, retail, transportation, healthcare, and agriculture industries among many others. According to Statista, the number of IoT devices that are in use across all relevant industries is forecast to grow to more than 8 billion by 2030. As for consumers, important growth areas are the Internet and digital media devices, which include smartphones. This area is also predicted to grow to more than 8 billion by 2030. Other applications with more than 1 million connected devices are connected and autonomous vehicles, IT infrastructure, asset management, and electric utility smart grid.

All of this is made possible through intelligent networks. The planet is rapidly becoming covered in networks that allow digital devices to communicate and interconnect. Consider the network mesh as a digital skin that surrounds the earth. Mobile devices, electronic sensors, electronic measuring equipment, medical gadgets, and gauges can all link with this digital skin. They keep track of, communicate with, analyze, and, in some situations, automatically adjust to the data collected and transmitted.

2.1 Evolution of networks: everything is connected

Hundreds of trillions of gigabytes of data are generated by 30 billion things. How can they collaborate to help us make better decisions and improve our lives and

[1]Department of Computer Science & Engineering, Amity University, Uttar Pradesh, India
[2]Department of Electronics & Communication Engineering, SRM University, Andhra Pradesh, India

businesses? The networks that we utilize daily enable these relationships [1]. The Internet and the digitized world are built on the foundation of intelligent networks. The methods we use to communicate are constantly changing. Breakthroughs in wireless and digital technology have substantially extended the reach of our communications, which were formerly limited by wires and plugs [2]. Through their connectivity to the Internet, networks in businesses and large organizations can supply products and services to clients. Networks can also be used on a larger scale to consolidate, store, and offer access to data on network servers [3].

The Internet is the world's largest network, and it serves as the "electronic skin" that protects the globe. The Internet is a collection of private and public networks that are linked together. The Internet is accessible to businesses, small office networks, and residential networks. The data collected, retained, and analyzed by sensors benefit a wide range of companies. Businesses now have a better understanding of the things they sell and who is buying them. They can streamline production and target their marketing and advertising to specific areas or audiences using this type of data, encouraging the development of new business opportunities, and marketing ideas [4].

2.1.1   Intelligent devices

The Internet of Things (IoT) is the Internet-connected network of millions of smart devices and sensors. Many organizations can use and evaluate the data collected and shared by these linked devices and sensors. Businesses, cities, governments, hospitals, and individuals are among these organizations. The IoT has been made possible in part by the availability of low-cost CPUs and wireless networks. Inanimate objects such as doorknobs and light bulbs can now be fitted with an intelligent sensor that collects and transmits data to a network [5, 6].

In 2025, researchers predict that 38.6 billion IoT devices will be connected to the Internet, with 50 billion by 2030. Every month, 190 million new linked devices are added! Computers, smartphones, tablets, and smart TVs will account for about a third of all connected devices. Sensors, actuators, and newly designed intelligent gadgets that monitor, regulate, analyze, and optimize our reality will make up the remaining two-thirds. Smart doorbells, garage doors, thermostats, sports wearables, pacemakers, traffic lights, parking spots, and other intelligent connected sensors are just a few examples. Only human imagination limits the number of potential objects that could become sentient sensors [7].

2.1.2   Intelligent devices connection with networks

The obtained data must be stored and shared; hence an intelligent device must be connected to a network. A wired ethernet connection or a wireless link to a controller is required. Low-power alternatives such as Bluetooth LE, Zigbee, or LoRa are more practical than wireless ethernet. Sensor data are collected by controllers, while network or Internet access is provided by controllers. Controllers may be able to make judgments right away or send data to a more powerful computer for study. This more powerful computer may be on the same LAN as the controller, or it could only be reached via the Internet [8, 9].

Actuators are frequently used in conjunction with intelligent devices. Actuators are devices that accept electrical input and convert it into physical action. For example, if a smart device senses excessive heat in a room, the temperature reading is sent to the microcontroller. The data can be sent from the microcontroller to an actuator, which will then switch on the air conditioner. The majority of new devices such as fitness wearables, implanted pacemakers, air meters in a mine shaft, and water meters in a farm field all require wireless connectivity. Because many sensors are "out in the field" and are powered by batteries or solar panels, consideration must be given to power consumption. Low-powered connection options must be used to optimize and extend the availability of the sensor [10–12].

2.2   Huge volume of data generation by intelligent devices

Data are collected from a variety of sources, including individuals, photographs, text, sensors, and online sites. Cell phones, PCs, kiosks, tablets, routers, switches, firewalls, and cash registers all contribute data. The volume of data created by intelligent gadgets has recently increased dramatically. Intelligent gadgets are currently found in an increasing number of places and items. Security cameras, traffic lights, intelligent cars, thermometers, and even grape plants are among them. Big Data refer to a large amount of data, but how large is a large amount of data? No one can say with certainty whether data from a company are considered "Big Data." The following are three indicators that suggest a company is dealing with Big Data:

- They have a significant amount of data that require more storage space as time goes on (volume).
- They are dealing with an ever-increasing amount of data (velocity).
- They have information in a number of formats (variety).

How much data do intelligent devices collect? Here are some estimated examples. For comparison, assume that the average MP3 song is about 3 megabytes.

- Intelligent devices in one smart connected home can produce as much as 1 gigabyte (GB) of information a week, or the equivalent of 333 MP3 songs.
- Intelligent devices in one autonomous car can generate 4,000 gigabits (Gb) of data per day. That is, 500 gigabytes (GB) of data, which is the equivalent of about 167,000 MP3 songs.
- Safety intelligent devices in mining operations can generate up to 2.4 terabits (TB) of data every minute. That is, 300 GB or about 100,000 MP3 songs.
- An Airbus A380 Engine generates 1 petabyte (PB) of data on a flight from London to Singapore. That is, 1 million GB or about 334 million MP3 songs.

2.2.1   Issues and challenges of Big Data Analytics

The World Economic Forum predicts that the amount of data generated daily will be 463 exabytes (EB) globally. One EB is equal to 1 billion gigabytes! To put this into context, according to Statista, every minute of every day:

- 500 hours of YouTube videos uploaded daily by different devices.
- 69 million instant messages shared by different devices.
- Over 347,000 GB of Netflix video uploaded and shared daily.
- 198 million emails sent on a daily basis.
- Over 60,000 Instagram images shared by devices daily.

The rapid growth of data can be an advantage or an obstacle when it comes to achieving business goals. To be successful, enterprises must be able to easily access and manage their data assets. With this enormous amount of data being constantly created, traditional technologies and data warehouses cannot keep up with storage needs. Even with cloud storage services from firms such as Amazon, Google, Microsoft, and others, the security of stored data becomes a significant issue. To prevent data loss, Big Data systems must be safe, have high fault tolerance, and use replication. It is not only about storing data; when it comes to Big Data storage, it is also about managing and securing it [13–15].

2.2.2   Storage of Big Data

Big Data are typically stored on multiple servers, usually housed within data centers. The information is generally spread and replicated on numerous servers in different data centers for security, accessibility, and redundancy [16].

2.2.2.1   Edge computing

Edge computing (Figure 2.1) is an architecture that utilizes end-user clients or devices at the edge of the network to do a substantial amount of the preprocessing and storage required by an organization. Edge computing was designed to keep the data closer to the data source for preprocessing. Intelligent device data, in particular, can be preprocessed closer to where it was collected. The information gained from that preprocessed analysis can be fed back into companies' systems to modify processes if required. Because the sensor data are preprocessed by end devices within the company system, communications to and from the servers and devices are quicker. This requires less bandwidth than constantly sending raw data to the cloud [17, 18]. After the data have been preprocessed, it is often shipped off for long-term storage, backup, or deeper analysis within the cloud [19].

2.2.2.2   Cloud and computing

The cloud is a collection of data centers or group of connected servers. Access to software, storage, and services available on the servers is obtained through the Internet via a browser interface [20, 21]. Cloud services are provided by many large

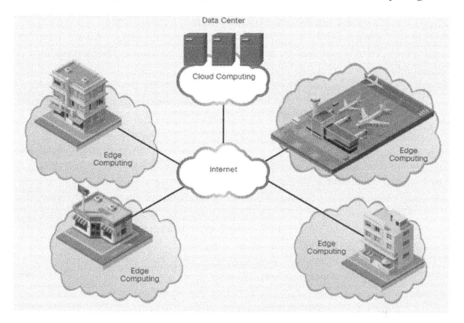

Figure 2.1   Edge computing

companies such as Google, Microsoft, and Apple. Cloud storage services are provided by different vendors such as Google Drive, Apple iCloud, Microsoft OneDrive, and Dropbox. From an individual's perspective, using the cloud services allows you:

- to access various programs instead of downloading them onto your local device
- to save all of your data, such as images, music, movies, and emails, freeing up local hard disc space
- to be able to access your data and applications from any location, at any time, and on any device

One of the disadvantages of using the cloud is that your data could fall into the wrong hands. Your data are at the mercy of the security robustness of your chosen cloud provider. From the perspective of an enterprise, cloud services and computing support a variety of data management issues.

2.2.2.3   Distributed processing

From a data management perspective, analytics were simple when only humans created data. The amount of data was manageable and relatively easy to sift through. However, with the explosion of business automation systems and the exponential growth of web applications and machine-generated data, analytics is becoming increasingly more difficult to manage. In fact, 90 percent of the data on the planet now were created in the last 2 years. Exponential growth is characterized by an increase in volume over a short period of time. This high volume of data is difficult to process and analyze within a reasonable amount of time. Rather than large data-bases being processed by big and powerful mainframe computers and stored in giant disk arrays (vertical scaling), distributed data processing takes the large volume of data and breaks it into smaller pieces. These smaller data volumes are dispersed over multiple sites to be processed by a large number of computers with less powerful CPUs. Each computer in the distributed architecture examines its own piece of the Big Data puzzle (horizontal scaling).

Most distributed file systems are designed to be invisible to client programs. The distributed file system locates files and moves data, but the users have no way of knowing that the files are distributed among many different servers or nodes. The users access these files as if they were local to their own computers. All users see the same view of the file system and are able to access data concurrently with other users. Hadoop was built to deal with these massive amounts of data. The Hadoop project began with two components: MapReduce is a distributed, fault-tolerant file system based on Hadoop Distributed File System, which is a distributed way to process data. Hadoop has now evolved into a very comprehensive ecosystem of software for Big Data management. Hadoop is open-source software enabling the distributed processing of large data sets that can be terabytes in size and that are stored in clusters of computers. Hadoop is designed to scale up from single servers to thousands of machines where they offer computation and storage. To make it more efficient, Hadoop can be installed and run on many virtual machines (VMs). These VMs can all work together in parallel to process and store the data.

Hadoop uses scalability and fault tolerance as two important features:

- Scalability: With Hadoop, cluster size can easily scale from a 5-node cluster to a 1,000-node cluster without excessively increasing the administrative burden.
- Fault tolerance: Hadoop creates many replicated files automatically and pro-vides backup to ensure that data will not be lost. If a disk, node, or a whole rack fails, the data are safe.

2.3   Need of data analysis by business

Every organization must become more efficient and innovative to stay competitive and relevant in the digitized world. The IoT is an integral part of achieving that effi-ciency and innovation. Many companies want to collect and analyze large amounts of new product usage data in order to acquire valuable insights. Businesses can use data analytics to better evaluate the impact of their products and services, alter their processes and aims, and give better products to their consumers faster. The ability to gain new insights from their data brings value to the business.

To businesses, data are the new oil. Like crude oil, it is valuable, but if it is unrefined, it cannot be easily used. Crude oil has to be changed to gasoline, plastic, chemicals, and other substances to create a valuable product. It is the same with data. Data must be broken down and analyzed for it to have value. Transactional and analytical data are the two main types of processed data that provide value. As events occur, transactional data are recorded and processed. Daily sales reports and production schedules are analyzed using transactional data to decide how much inventory to keep on hand. Managerial analysis such as assessing whether the company should establish a new manufacturing plant or hire more salespeople is aided by analytical data.

2.3.1   Sources of information

The source of data in the large data sets is varied. Apart from sensor data, other data originate from anything that has been scanned, entered, and released into the Internet from sources such as:

- Social media sites: Facebook, YouTube, WhatsApp, WeChat, TikTok, and Instagram
- HTTP, content search, net surfing data
- Archived data
- Metadata that is attached to emails, transmitted documents, and pictures
- Medical forms, insurance forms, and tax forms
- Genomics research using DNA

Even if data are considered structured, different applications create files in different formats that are not necessarily compatible with one another. Structured data may need to be manipulated into a common format such as CSV. Comma-separated value (CSV) files are a type of plaintext file that uses commas to separate columns in a table of data and the carriage return character to separate rows. Each row is a record. Although they are commonly used for importing and exporting in traditional databases and spreadsheets, there is no specific standard. Data formatting techniques such as JSON and XML are also plaintext file types that use a standard way of representing data records. These file formats are compatible with a wide range of applications.

Unstructured data require different tools to prepare data for processing or analysis. The following are two examples:

Web pages are created to provide data to humans, not machines. "Web scraping" tools automatically extract data from HTML pages. This is similar to a Web Crawler or spider of a search engine. It explores the web to extract data and creates a database to respond to the search queries. The web scraping software may use Hypertext Transfer Protocol or a web browser to access the World Wide Web. Typically, web scraping is an automated process that uses a bot or web crawler to do data mining. Specific data are gathered and copied from the web to a database or spreadsheet. The data can then be easily analyzed.

Many large web service providers such as Facebook provide standardized interfaces to collect the data automatically using application programming interfaces (APIs). The most common approach is to use RESTful APIs. RESTful APIs use HTTP as the communication protocol and JSON structure to encode the data.

Internet websites such as Google and Twitter gather large amounts of static and time-series data. Knowledge of the APIs for these sites allows data analysts and engineers to access the large amount of data that are constantly being generated on the Internet.

2.3.2   Data visualization

The mined data must be analyzed by intelligent tools and techniques and should be presented to managers and decision-makers to be of value with minimum errors. There are many different visualizations that can be used to present the value in the data. Determining the best chart to use will vary based on the following:

- Number of variables to show
- Number of data points in each variable
- Is the data representing a timeline?
- Items that require comparisons
- Some of the most popular chart types are line, column, bar, pie, and scatter.

2.3.3   Analyzing Big Data for effective use of business

Big Data is just that – BIG! It is most helpful to analyze it to get value out of it. Analyzing big data typically requires tools and applications created for this purpose. These analysis tools have been designed to provide businesses with detailed information, patterns, and valuable insights.

Before beginning any analysis, it is critical to know what problem the business is trying to solve or what information the business is looking for. Are they interested in customer behavior in specific states, energy consumption patterns in different city quadrants, or the number of Facebook "likes" based on age? There are many desktop Big Data Analytics tools that businesses could select such as Knime, OpenRefine, Orange, and RapidMiner. Cloud-based analytics tools include Google's Big Query, IBM Cognos Analytics, TIBCO Spotfire, and Board.

2.3.4   Intelligent devices thinking intelligently

Can things think? Can a device learn from its environment? In this context, there are many definitions of "think." One possible definition is the ability to connect a series of related pieces of information together and then use them to alter a course of action. For example, when we are young, we have no concept that fire is hot and that placing our hand in the fire will cause pain. A fire may appear visually pleasing and actually encourage one to try and touch the flames. We quickly learn that the fire can cause injury. We then start to associate the image of the fire with the pain it can cause. From this point onward, we start to think about the results of touching the fire and base our actions on this acquired information.

Many products now include smart technology that allows them to change their behavior in particular situations. This can be as basic as a smart appliance that reduces its power consumption during peak demand periods or as complex as a self-driving car. When a gadget makes a choice or takes a course of action based on information from the outside world, it is referred to as a smart device. The word "smart" now appears in the titles of many of the devices with which we interact. This suggests that the device can change its behavior in response to its surroundings.

2.4   Artificial intelligence and machine learning in networking

Machine intelligence is referred to as artificial intelligence (AI). Natural intelligence, on the other hand, is the intelligence demonstrated by living beings. AI employs intelligent agents who are able to assess their surroundings and make actions that increase the likelihood of achieving a given goal or purpose. AI refers to systems that replicate cognitive functions such as learning and problem-solving that are traditionally associated with human minds. Autonomous cars, intelligent routing in content delivery networks, strategic game playing, and military simulations are some of the jobs that are now considered to require some level of AI.

Many of the tasks that once required AI have become ordinary as technology advances. Many of these tasks have shifted from AI to machine learning (ML). ML is a branch of AI that employs statistical techniques to enable computers to "learn" from their surroundings. This allows computers to improve at a task without having to be properly trained for it. This is especially useful when designing and programming specific algorithms is difficult or infeasible. One objective of learning is to be able to generalize based on experience. For machines, this involves the ability to perform accurately on new, previously unseen tasks after gaining experience with a learning data set. The training data set must come from data that is representative of the larger data pool. This data pool enables the machine to build a general model about this data, which would help it make accurate predictions.

2.4.1   Role of ML in networks

One of the features of the IoT is that it enables the collection of huge pools of data that can "teach" programs how to respond to certain conditions. Some of the more common uses of ML technology include the following.

2.4.1.1   Speech recognition

Many different companies now offer digital assistants which allow you to use speech to communicate with a computer system. Apple, Microsoft, Google, and Amazon all offer this service. These companies not only allow commands to be given verbally but also offer speech-to-text capabilities.

2.4.1.2   Product recommendation

Systems build up a customer profile and recommend products or services based on previous patterns. Users of Amazon and eBay receive recommendations on products. Organizations such as LinkedIn, Facebook, and GooglePlus recommend users you may wish to connect with.

2.4.1.3   Credit card fraud detection

A profile is constructed about the purchasing patterns of a client. Any deviation from these patterns triggers an alert and the system automatically takes action. This action ranges from denying the transaction to notifying the authorities. Some of the events that are detected and could indicate a fraudulent transaction include purchasing products not normally purchased, purchases in a different geographical area, rapidly purchasing many different products, and purchasing large-ticket items.

2.4.1.4   Facial recognition

Security cameras are everywhere, from stores and streets to airports and transportation hubs. These cameras continually scan the crowds, normally watching for dangerous or illegal activities, but they can also be used to identify and track individuals. The system builds a pattern of specific facial features and then watches for a match to these facial patterns triggering some action.

2.4.1.5   Anomaly detection

In manufacturing, mining, transportation, and other areas, ML can be used to learn about normal operating conditions in mechanical systems. This makes it possible to detect unusual operating conditions that could signal that something is ready to break. Over time, ML not only detects anomalies but also suggests what the most likely cause of the anomaly may be. Anomaly detection is commonly used in preventive maintenance but can also be used to detect other unusual conditions that could signal safety or security issues in other types of systems such as data networks.

2.5   Intent-based networking

For a business to survive, it must be agile and respond quickly to the needs and demands of its customers. Businesses are increasingly dependent on their digital resources to meet customer demands, so the underlying IT network must also be responsive enough to quickly adapt to these requirements. This normally involves adjustments to many systems and processes. These adjustments may include changes to security policies and procedures, business services and applications, and operational policies. With traditional networks, many different components must be manually adjusted to meet ever-changing business requirements. This requires different technicians and engineers to ensure that the systems are changed to allow them to work together to accomplish their goals. This sometimes results in errors and delays and often in suboptimal network performance.

In order to be nimble, responsive, and business-relevant, the new business network must seamlessly and securely incorporate IoT devices, cloud-based services, and remote offices. The network must also protect these new digital activities from the constantly evolving threat landscape. To meet this demand, the IT industry has begun to develop a systematic strategy to link infrastructure management to business goals. Intent-based networking is the name given to this method. The diagram depicts the general concept of intent-based networking. Business needs are automatically and continuously converted into IT infrastructure implementation under this new paradigm.

2.6   Role of programming

It is usual for programmers to write the first draft of a program in a programming language that they are unfamiliar with. These language-independent programs, which are typically referred to as algorithms, are centered on logic rather than syntax. A flowchart is a visual representation of an algorithm. System software and application software are the two most popular types of computer software. Application software programs are designed to perform a certain task or set of tasks. Cisco Packet Tracer, for example, is a network simulation application that allows users to model complicated networks and ask "what if" network behavior questions. System software connects the hardware of the computer to the application program. The system software is responsible for controlling the computer hardware and allowing application programs to run. Linux, Apple OSX, and Microsoft Windows are all instances of system software. A programming language is used to construct both system and application software. A programming language is a set of rules for writing programs that send instructions to computer hardware. Algorithms are self-contained, step-by-step sets of operations to be done, and these programs implement them. Some programming languages compile their code into a collection of machine instructions. C++ is an example of a computer language that is compiled. Others do not compile these instructions into machine code before interpreting them. An interpreted programming language such as Python is an example. The process of creating a program can begin once the programming language has been decided and the process has been diagrammed in a flowchart. Program architectures are similar in most computer languages.

2.6.1   Basic programming using Blockly

Blockly is a visual programming tool created to help beginners understand the concepts of programming. By using a number of block types, Blockly allows a user to create a program without entering any lines of code. Blockly implements visual programming by assigning different programming structures to colored blocks. The blocks also contain slots and spaces to allow programmers to enter values required by the structure. Programmers can connect programming structures together by dragging and attaching the appropriate blocks. Programming structures such as conditionals, loops, and variables are all available for use.

Creating a new variable in Blockly is a simple matter of dragging the variable block onto the workspace and filling in the value slot. It is also possible to change the contents of a variable as the program is being executed. Blockly also supports functions. Similar to the variables, Blockly has specific blocks to represent functions. Also similar to variables, programmers simply select and drag function blocks to the workspace and fill in the required slots. The blocks are available such as an IF-THEN block, a WHILE block, and a FOR block. There are also blocks specifically for sensors and actuators. Blockly can translate its block-based code into Python or JavaScript. This is very useful to beginner programmers.

2.6.2   Blockly games

Google offers a number of free and open-source instructional games to aid programming learning. Blockly Games is the name of the game series.

Visit https://blockly.games to discover more about Blockly Games or to give it a try.

To assist you to get started, there are several stages to accomplish. Blockly may appear to be a toy, but it is a fantastic tool for honing your logical reasoning skills, which is one of the fundamentals of computer programming. The first part of this session covered how to use basic programming to support IoT devices. Flowcharts are diagrams that show how processes work. System software and application software are the two most popular types of computer software. Application software is designed to complete a certain task.

Variables in programming can be divided into two groups:

- Local variables: Variables that are contained within a program, function, or process.
- Global variables: These are variables that are in scope during the execution of the program. Any section of the program can retrieve them.

IF-THEN, FOR Loops, and WHILE Loops are the most frequent logic constructs.

Blockly is a visual programming tool designed to assist novices in learning programming fundamentals. Blockly uses colored blocks to implement visual programming by assigning different programming structures to them.

Python is a widely used programming language that is intended to be simple to learn and write. Python is an interpreted language, so parsing and executing Python code necessitates the use of an interpreter.

2.7   Role of technology to design a model

Technology helps to have design, electrical, and physical/mechanical skills while prototyping in the IoT (working with your hands to put things together). Skills in networking and programming are also incredibly useful. IoT developers also benefit from understanding cloud computing as well as network and device security. Because the IoT is still in its early stages, there are still unknown tasks to be discovered. This is an excellent time to create anything that is connected to the IoT. Because the IoT connects people, processes, data, and things, the number of inventions that the IoT can help generate and subsequently include is limitless.

- Is totally working but not without flaws.
- Is a fully functional version of the product.
- Is used to assess product performance and make improvements.

- Has a fully functional interior and exterior.
- The cost of production may be high.
- Is frequently utilized as a technology demonstration in the IoT.

How do you create a prototype? There are several options for getting started. The Google Glass was created by a team at Google using the "Rapid Prototyping Method." To see a video regarding Google's approach to prototyping, look up "google glass quick prototype TED talk" on the Internet. Google, of course, has plenty of cash to pay for the people and materials involved in prototyping. Most of us will require financial assistance to bring our ideas from our thoughts to a proto-type. There is crowdfunding for us. Kickstarter, Indiegogo, and Crowdfunder are just three of the several online crowdfunding platforms available. Look for "Pebble Time Kickstarter Video" on the Internet.

Of course, the Internet is a good place to start. People have been exchanging ideas for millennia, but the Internet has taken it to a whole new level. People who have never met in person are able to interact and work together now. There are a number of websites where you may connect with other creators. Maker Media is a global platform that brings together makers to share projects and ideas. Makers can also use the platform to find and purchase products for their projects. Make a search for Makezine on the Internet for further information.

2.7.1   Electronic toolkits

Computer programs cannot function without the use of a computer. While you can write programs for practically any computer, there are several platforms that are specifically meant for beginners. Some of the most popular platforms are listed here. Arduino is an open-source physical computing platform that consists of a simple microcontroller board and a software development environment. You may create interactive objects that operate lights, motors, and other physical things using input from a variety of switches or sensors. Go to http://arduino. cc to learn more about Arduino. While the Arduino is not designed to be used as a computer, its low power consumption allows it to effectively control other devices.

The Raspberry Pi is a low-cost, credit-card sized computer that connects to a computer monitor or television. A regular keyboard and mouse are used to oper-ate it. It can do all of the functions of a computer, including accessing the Internet and watching high-definition videos, as well as spreadsheets, word processing, and game play. Go visit http://www.raspberrypi.org to learn more about Raspberry Pi. In terms of size, power consumption, and application, the Beaglebone is quite simi-lar to the Raspberry Pi. Because the Beaglebone has more computing capability than the Raspberry Pi, it is a superior choice for applications that demand more processing. Go to http://beagleboard.org to learn more about Beaglebone. Finally, Adafruit is a great place to start with IoT projects.

2.7.2 *Programming resources*

Programming is essential in the IoT. When designing an IoT solution, bespoke code is really handy. Blockly and Python have already been introduced to you. There are plenty of other free tools available to assist you in honing your programming skills.

MIT OpenCourseWare (OCW) is a web-based repository of nearly all MIT course materials. OCW is an excellent site to learn about computer programming for free because it is open to the entire world. http://ocw.mit.edu/courses/intro-programming/ contains OCW programming-related courses.

- Another wonderful resource is Code Academy. It focuses on interactivity to aid learning.

See? I told you! It does not have to be tough to learn basic programming. It is possible to have a good time! You now have some very powerful starting tools after creating a process flowchart and using Blockly and Python. What do you think you could make for the IoT? How could a small prototype help you get started? It can be entertaining, such as programming a remote-controlled toy to play with your cat while you are away. Programming a heat sensor for a newborn's bed, for example, may be lifesaving. I am willing to wager that once you have had some experience prototyping in the IoT, you will begin to see things differently.

2.8 Relation of AI, ML, and IBN

Aim-based networking uses automation, AI, and ML to regulate the function of a network in order to achieve a certain goal or intent. With intent-based networking, the IT team can explain exactly what they want the network to do in plain English, and the network will make it happen. The network can convert the intent into policies and then automate the deployment of the necessary configurations across the network.

The intent-based network employs AI and ML to verify that any services delivered satisfy the specified service level. The intent-based network can send alerts and make ideas for improvement if they do not achieve the service level. The intent-based network may be able to automatically alter the network to meet the service levels in some instances.

2.9 Business challenges and opportunities

The IoT has a lot of advantages, but it also has a lot of drawbacks. We are now faced with an ever-expanding collection of new technologies that we must learn since the IoT is a transformational technology. The IoT is transforming our lives in every way.

This is not the first time we have seen a technical advancement with such ramifications. Farm mechanization enhanced the productivity of accessible farmland and triggered a population shift from rural to urban areas. The invention of the vehicle allowed for improved workforce mobility and recreational pursuits. Many mundane operations could be automated with greater precision and efficiency thanks to the personal computer. On a worldwide scale, the Internet began to break down geographical barriers and enhance equality among people. These are only a few examples of transformative innovations that have occurred in recent years. Each of these technologies brought significant changes to an established culture and was initially received with fear and apprehension. The underlying benefits were apparent when the first dread of the unknown was overcome and the technology was accepted. Each perceived problem brings with it a slew of new possibilities.

Can you imagine how different your life would be if you did not have a car, a computer, or Internet access?

2.9.1   The evolving job market

The IoT is transforming the work market. Jobs that are built to embrace this new environment and all it has to offer are replacing traditional jobs. Opportunities in IT may be limited to edge computing, the development of new processes, or a specialty in a field that has yet to be realized. In the following domains, these jobs represent abilities from a variety of fields, including computer science, computer engineering (a combination of computer science and electrical engineering), and software engineering:

- Collaboration
- Enterprise Networks
- Data Center and Virtualization
- AI
- Application Development
- IoT Program Developer
- IoT Security Specialist

Not all of the jobs created by the IoT are IT-related. The IoT should be viewed as an enabling technology with applications in all industries and elements of our daily life. Within its sphere, the IoT has spawned a plethora of work opportunities. These positions are available across the design, development, and implementation of the IoT. There are a few major categories that describe the various career options available in today's digital world:

- Enablers: These positions are responsible for developing and implementing the underlying technology.
- Engagers: These professionals plan, develop, integrate, and provide IoT services to customers.
- Enhancers: These positions create their own value-added services in addition to Engagers' services, which are unique to the IoT.

The IoT is also creating a need for a new type of IT expert. These are people who have the knowledge and abilities needed to create new IoT-enabled goods and analyze the data they collect.

A workforce with expertise in both information science and software or computer engineering is required. With addition, in the IoT, operational and information technologies are merging. People must interact and learn from one another in order to comprehend the things, networks, and procedures that exploit the IoT's boundless potential.

We must stay current in order to harness the full potential of what the IoT has to offer, given the ever-changing landscape of the digitized world. As new technologies emerge, the work sector will continue to offer additional opportunities. At the same time, the skill sets required for these positions will evolve, necessitating the need for lifelong learning.

2.10   Security

Many companies' data have been accessed by hackers over the years. The outcome has been the leaking of millions of users' data on the Internet, which has had a tremendous impact. Login passwords and other personal data linked to more than one million Yahoo and Gmail accounts are purportedly being sold on the dark web marketplace, according to recent reporting. Usernames, emails, and unencrypted passwords are purportedly included in the online accounts for sale on the Dark Web. The accounts are considered to be the result of numerous big cyberattacks rather than a single data leak.

In July 2017, hackers broke into Equifax (EFX), one of the largest credit bureaus, and stole the personal information of 145 million people. Because of the amount of sensitive information revealed, including Social Security numbers, it was deemed one of the greatest data breaches of all time. Two months later, the business revealed the hack. Because the stolen data could be exploited for identity fraud, it could have a long-term impact. In 2018, the company's food and nutrition app, MyFitnessPal, was hacked, affecting an estimated 150 million subscribers. According to the inquiry, usernames, email addresses, and hashed passwords may have been compromised.

2.10.1   *Challenges to secure device and networks*

IoT devices are developed with the necessary network connectivity capabilities but often do not implement strong network security. Network security is a critical factor when deploying IoT devices. Methods must be taken to ensure the authenticity, integrity, and security of the data, the path from the sensor to the collector, and the connectivity to the device.

The number of networked sensors and smart devices is rapidly expanding, posing a greater risk of assault. Sensors and smart devices are often small devices with a variety of operating systems, CPU kinds, and memory capacities. Many of these items will be low-cost, single-purpose gadgets with basic network connectivity.

Some IoT devices that are connected to the Internet can interact with the physical environment. They have found their way into gadgets, automobiles, our bodies, and our houses. Sensors could collect information from the refrigerator or heating system. They could also be found mounted to tree trunks or in city lampposts. Physical security is difficult or impossible to achieve in many nontraditional locations.

Sensor-enabled IoT devices may be positioned in inaccessible or remote areas, making human intervention or configuration nearly impossible. The devices are frequently built to last far longer than ordinary high-tech equipment. Some IoT devices are purposely created without the capacity to be upgraded, or they may be placed in locations where reconfiguring or upgrading is difficult or impossible. Every day, new vulnerabilities are discovered. If a device cannot be upgraded, the vulnerability will remain for the duration of its life. If a gadget may be upgraded, the average consumer may not have a technical background; hence the upgrading procedure should be automated or simple enough for a layperson to complete.

2.10.1.1 Wi-Fi security

Because they are simple to set up and operate, wireless networks are popular in all types and sizes of enterprises. The organization must provide a wireless experience that is both mobile and secure for both employees and visitors. Hackers within range can access and infiltrate a wireless network if it is not properly secured.

2.10.1.2 End-user devices should be protected

The source or destination of data delivered via the network is referred to as an end device. Any user device, such as computers, tablets, or phones, is considered an end device. Servers and printers are examples of equipment that users can access or send data to.

The following are some of the most frequent methods for securing end devices:

i. Activate the firewall

   To prevent hackers from accessing your personal or commercial data, turn on and update your firewall, whether it is a software firewall or a hardware firewall on your router.

ii. Manage your browser and operating system

   Hackers are continually looking for methods to exploit flaws in your operating systems and web browsers. Set the security settings on your computer and browser to medium or higher to secure your machine and data. Regularly download and install the newest software patches and security updates from the vendors as well as your computer's operating system and web browsers.

iii. Antivirus and antispyware software should be used

Viruses, Trojan horses, worms, ransomware, and spyware are
all examples of malicious software that is placed on your computer without your consent in order to get access to your data and
machine. Viruses can corrupt your data, slow down your computer,
or even take control of it. To avoid downloading viruses and malware in the first place, only download software from reputable
websites. Antivirus software is designed to detect and remove
viruses from your computer and incoming email. Antispyware is
sometimes included with antivirus software. To safeguard your
computer against the latest harmful software, keep your software
up to date.

iv. Safeguard all of your devices

To prevent unwanted access, password-protect your computing
equipment, whether they be routers, PCs, laptops, tablets, or cellphones. Encryption should be used to store data, especially sensitive or confidential information. Only keep vital information on
mobile devices in case they are stolen or lost while you are away
from home. If one of your devices is hacked, thieves could gain
access to all of your data via your cloud storage service, such as
iCloud or Google Drive.

2.10.1.3   Needs for safety

The categories of data were first discussed in this module. Individually identifiable
information (PII) or sensitive personal information (SPI) is any data on a live person that can be used alone or in combination with other data to identify, contact, or
find that person. Legitimate businesses have agreements (Terms and Conditions or
Terms of Service) that allow them to use the information they acquire about you to
improve their business. Companies that utilize sensors on their own equipment or
vehicles are also legitimate users of our data. Governments and communities that
have put environmental sensors on trains, buses, or traffic signals have a right to the
data they collect.

2.10.1.4   Defending the corporate world

The module then went through security best practices. Physically guarding the outside and inside perimeters of places where data are housed, such as data centers, is
part of security. Because of the large number of IoT devices, their position in nontraditional settings, and the fact that many of them cannot be upgraded, securing
them is difficult. A hat in Black Hackers takes advantage of available Wi-Fi on a

regular basis. You can take a number of steps to safeguard your company's wireless network. Keep your firewall set on, manage your operating system and browser, and use antivirus and antispyware to keep your devices safe.

If you are utilizing a public or unsecured Wi-Fi hotspot, observe these safety guidelines: Do not access or transfer any sensitive personal information over a public wireless network.

2.10.1.5   Personal data and devices must be kept safe

We are increasing the potential for security vulnerabilities as we install more and more smart sensors in our houses. Sensors are frequently connected to the same network as our home or small business equipment, allowing a breach on one device to spread to all connected devices.

2.11   Summary

In this chapter, we discussed the latest technologies in the field of intelligent networks. We also discussed the roles and relationships of AI, ML, Big Data, IBN, and cloud computing to improve the performance and QoS of networks.

References

[1] Kumar S., Ranjan P., Ramaswami R., Tripathy M.R. 'EMEEDP: enhanced multi-hop energy efficient distributed protocol for heterogeneous wireless sensor network'. *Proceedings of the 5th International Conference on Communication Systems and Network Technologies, CSNT 2015*; 2015. pp. 194–200.

[2] Kumar S., Ramaswami R., Rao A.L.N. 'Energy optimization in distributed localized wireless sensor networks'. *Proceedings of the International Conference on Issues and Challenges Intelligent Computing Technique (ICICT)*; Ghaziabad, India, IEEE, 2014. pp. 350–55.

[3] Chauhan R., Kumar S. 'Packet loss prediction using artificial intelligence unified with big data analytics, internet of things and cloud computing technologies'. *2021 5th International Conference on Information Systems and Computer Networks (ISCON), 2021*; Mathura, India, IEEE, 2021. pp. 1–6.

[4] Sudhakaran S., Kumar S., Ranjan P., Tripathy M.R. 'Blockchain-based transparent and secure decentralized algorithm'. *International Conference on Intelligent Computing and Smart Communication 2019. Algorithms for Intelligent Systems*; Singapore: Springer; 2020.

[5] Kumar S., Trivedi M.C., Ranjan P. *Evolution of software-defined networking foundations for iot and 5G mobile networks*. IGI USA: IGI Publisher; 2020. pp. 1–235. Available from https://www.igi-global.com/book/evolution-software-defined-networking-foundations/244540

[6]   Kumar S., Ranjan P., Radhakrishnan R., Tripathy M.R. 'Energy efficient multichannel MAC protocol for high traffic applications in heterogeneous wireless sensor networks'. *Recent Advances in Electrical & Electronic Engineering.* 2017, vol. 10(3), pp. 223–32.

[7]   Kumar S., Ranjan P., Ramaswami R., Tripathy M.R. 'Resource efficient clustering and next hop knowledge based routing in multiple heterogeneous wireless sensor networks'. *International Journal of Grid and High Performance Computing.* 2017, vol. 9(2), pp. 1–20.

[8]   Kumar S., Cengiz K., Vimal S., Suresh A. 'Energy efficient resource migration based load balance mechanism for high traffic applications IoT'. *Wireless personal communications.* 2022, vol. 10(3), pp. 1–14.

[9]   Haidar M., Kumar S. 'Smart healthcare system for biomedical and health care applications using aadhaar and blockchain'. *5th International Conference on Information Systems and Computer Networks, ISCON 2021*; GLA University, Mathura, 22–23 October 2021; 2022. pp. 1–5.

[10] Punhani A., Faujdar N., Kumar S. 'Design and evaluation of cubic torus network-on-chip architecture'. *International Journal of Innovative Technology and Exploring Engineering.* 2019, vol. 8(6), pp. 2278–3075.

[11] Dubey G., Kumar S., Kumar S., Navaney P. 'Extended opinion lexicon and ML-based sentiment analysis of tweets: a novel approach towards accurate classifier'. *International Journal of Computational Vision and Robotics.* 2020, vol. 10(6), pp. 505–21.

[12] Singh P., Bansal A., Kamal A.E., Kumar S. 'Road surface quality monitoring using machine learning algorithm' in Reddy A.N.R., Marla D., Favorskaya M.N., Satapathy S.C. (eds.). *Intelligent Manufacturing and Energy Sustainability. Smart Innovation, Systems and Technologies.* 265. Singapore: Springer; 2022.

[13] Kumar S., Ranjan P., Radhakrishnan R., Tripathy M.R. 'Energy aware distributed protocol for heterogeneous wireless sensor network'. *International Journal of Control and Automation.* 2015, vol. 8(10), pp. 421–30.

[14] Kumar S., Ranjan P., Tripathy M.R. 'A utility maximization approach to MAC layer channel access and forwarding'. *Progress in Electromagnetics Research Symposium*; PIERS 2015 Prague, Czech Republic, 2015. pp. 2363–67.

[15] Kumar S., Ranjan P., Ramaswami R., Tripathy M.R. 'An NS3 implementation of physical layer based on 802.11 for utility maximization of WSN'. *Proceedings of the International Conference on Computational Intelligence and Communication Networks*; Jabalpur, India, IEEE, 2016. pp. 79–84.

[16] Sharma A., Awasthi Y., Kumar S. 'The role of blockchain, AI and iot for smart road traffic management system'. *2020 IEEE India Council International Subsections Conference (INDISCON), 2020*; Visakhapatnam, India, IEEE, 2020. pp. 289–96.

[17] Singh P., Bansal A., Kumar S. 'Performance analysis of various information platforms for recognizing the quality of indian roads'. *2020 10th International Conference on Cloud Computing, Data Science & Engineering (Confluence), 2020*; Noida, India, IEEE, 2020. pp. 63–76.

[18] Kumar S., Ranjan P., Singh P., Tripathy M.R. 'Design and implementation of fault tolerance technique for internet of things (iot)'. *2020 12th International Conference on Computational Intelligence and Communication Networks (CICN), 2020*; Bhimtal, India, IEEE, 2020. pp. 154–59.

[19] Singh P., Bansal A., Kumar S. 'Performance analysis of various information platforms for recognizing the quality of indian roads'. *2020 10th International Conference on Cloud Computing, Data Science & Engineering (Confluence), 2020*; Noida, India, IEEE, 2020. pp. 63–76.

[20] Reghu S., Kumar S. 'Development of robust infrastructure in networking to survive a disaster'. *2019 4th International Conference on Information Systems and Computer Networks (ISCON), 2019*; Mathura, India, IEEE, 2019. pp. 250–55.

[21] Chauhan R., Kumar S. 'Packet loss prediction using artificial intelligence unified with big data analytics, internet of things and cloud computing technologies'. *IEEE*; Mathura, India, 2021. pp. 1–6.

Chapter 3

An intelligent verification management approach for efficient VLSI computing system

Konasagar Achyut[1], Swati K Kulkarni[2], Akshata A Raut[3], Siba Kumar Panda[4], and Lakshmi Nair[5]

Any masterpiece is conjoined with all works of engineering, which includes the field of computer science or an electrical and electronics or mixture of both computer and electronics. Today, this gives the industry to understand research, evolve and develop into newer technology unfolding many scriptures behind the engineering works. In the similar manner, this chapter unfolds the prominent works involved in the verification of the designs involved in VLSI domain. Considering machine learning (ML), neural networks and artificial intelligence (AI) concepts and applying these to a wide range of verification approaches are quite interesting. The specific kinds of Register Transfer Level (RTL) design require rigorous verification which is targeted over any type of Field Programmable Gate Array (FPGA) or application-specific integrated circuits (ASICs). The verification process should be closed with testing all possible scenarios that too with intelligent verification methods. This chapter in the following pages brings the unique way of verification procedure involved in the RTL development methodologies using hardware description languages. With the help of system Verilog language, the developed reusable testbench is used for verification. The injected inputs to the testbench are randomized with constraints, such that the design should produce accurate output. To unify the verification language, there is a dedicated methodology commonly known as Universal Verification Methodology (UVM); by this, the chapter is extended to experience the readers also through the coverage-based formal verification. For continuous functional verification, an intelligent regression model is also developed with the help of ML and scripting. With this repeated injection of various test cases is possible in

[1]J.B. Institute of Engineering & Technology, Hyderabad, India
[2]Department of Applied Electronics, Gulbarga University, Kalaburgi, Karnataka, India
[3]Department of Electronics & Telecommunication Engineering, Fr. C. Rodrigues Institute of Technology, Navi, Mumbai, India
[4]Mobiveil Technologies India Pvt. Ltd, Chennai, India
[5]Amrita School of Engineering, India

order to verify the functionality. Thus, with the adoption of the presented verification environment and distinctive approach, one can affirm that the design is ready to be deployed over the targeted semiconductor chips. As the verification is an unignorable procedure, this can be used to classify the algorithms developed in ML for data clustering, data encoding and its accurate analysis. More importantly, this chapter allows us to understand an intelligent verification model for testing the design with regression run with the corresponding set-up and the pass/failure analysis steps. This structure may result in a significant reduction of the simulation time for a VLSI verification engineer.

3.1   Introduction

With rapid growth in techniques and procedures involved in the development of microelectronic devices for the diversified applications in the market, there have also been a great research and design methodologies to come up with the end product of a desired functionality through an electronic device. Within this life cycle of the product being brought up to market end, there is a prominent stage where any electronic device is embedded with a specific processor to perform a task based on external inputs or feedbacks acquired from the real-time sensors. These small and tiny houses of transistors capable of performing such huge and complex tasks are designed and verified by thousands of engineers in such a way that as many instructions fed to a chip in a single run are counter-measured, analysed, get clarity over the bugs available in the design and plan for the verification management approaches to verify the logic design before it is brought in the world in the form of a chip. As designing the hardware's digital logic is a task prior of verifying the design, verification is also as important as the design is done carefully with respect to form factors of a chip like power, timing, area, latencies, etc. Thus to exercise these form factors in an exhaustive way without manually giving the inputs to cover the max combinations, we have several approaches in the verification stage to judge the functionality. As specified, this chapter will take you through the taxonomy of the basic verification methodology/plan for an RTL engineer comprising the study of SystemVerilog and UVM models.

Once the furnishing of hardware description over RTL is completed, there are few factors which is considered to be prominent before transiting the big code to verification tams. These factors include timing, area and power [1]. FPGA selected for the project has its own device factor's consumption estimation viewed by Electronic Design Automations (EDAs). This chapter is just focusing over the basic procedural steps to follow over an RTL code to verify its robust, exhaustive and regressive-based logic performance. This brings an aim of a front-end engineer as to have an idea over verification structures followed in various organisations. Verification yields two types of dividends having formal verification and dynamic verification [2]. The major bridging gap between these two verifications is inclusion of assertions and test cases during the verification environment build-up. As to confirm the behaviour of the design to meet the given specification, the verification run is particularly known to be as the functional verification which is indeed actually before generation of netlists and constraining the design. Once the design is synthesized and layout is arranged over the fabric which brings up the long chain of routes for fabric connectivity, in short, this gives an additional delay in logic performance; verifying these complex designs needs a very fast method so as to communicate the design with the test cases or reference models written in high-level languages such as C/C++, systemC, python, etc. In this context, the following pages will help you understand how these high-level languages help an interpreter actually to communicate the UVM/SystemVerilog-based environment talks to exchange the data seamlessly. Hopefully, we believe the readers of this chapter have a basic idea on how libraries of OVM, UVM and SystemVerilog work with respect to the latest release versions of these specific libraries. By this, it is to be brought in the context that this chapter shows how an explicitly built library maintained in the cloud repositories is also helpful in bringing up the complex test cases using high-level languages. In this high-level languages being brought up in the verification environment, the following section will allow you to understand Direct Programming Interface (DPI) used to merge the verification language and high-level language for verification purposes. Also to experiment a new methodology for the generation of randomness in seeding the input to a testbench environment, we are introducing an ML-based concept built over Python libraries so as to talk to the low-level modules in the presence of DPI-based approach. Though the SystemVerilog/UVM library has the package of generating random seeds for verifying an RTL behaviour, this basic theoretical information related to cluster of data seeding may help a verification environment to drastically identify the cluster gained at the output to be the desired values. For this, there are few ML algorithms helping to maintain the juncture between the Python language and the low-level verification languages. This helps in exercising the design regressively and exhausting the logic functionality by seeding a maximum number of combinations applying at the design under test (DUT). Apart from the usage of Python language, this chapter takes you through a basic methodology for bringing up the automation of verifying a design with the help of tool command language (Tcl) scripts for the ease of understanding the actual epitome of the verification from basic methodology to the add-ons of languages to speed up complex RTL design verification (DV) in a single run.

This in turn helps an organisation to meet up their end tasks earlier than they have actually scheduled for target meet. The basic and most common verification environment followed by engineers can be seen in Figure 3.1. Here we have internal elements performing transactions at higher level of language abstraction done by the interprocess communications modules such as mailboxes, semaphores and events. Here we will be concentrating over how we can choose a way to build an interface using DPI standards so as to exchange the function/tasks calling from the program written in other language, as in Python for the generation of thousands of seeds. Usually a verification environment consists of monitor, driver, virtual interfaces, scoreboard to compare values, bus functional model (BFM), generator and a whole environment to run all the functionalities in the class-based house modules.

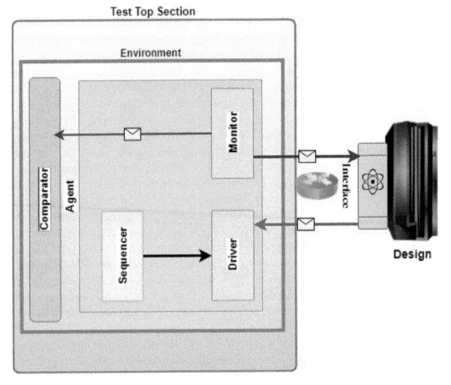

Figure 3.1   Verification environment root block structure

The above diagram portrays the major elements a verification environment structure has; in the context it shows the actual UVM-based verification environment built with the class-based modules extracted from object-oriented programming packages. Coming to its major functionality, it is done with the help of monitor and driver the agent class is consisting of, they help to maintain the interprocess communication to exchange the information or the seeds to be more technical in verification anomaly. Though we have a randomization facility to generate thousands of seeds in a random sequence to be fed as inputs to the actual RTL logic under tests, we have to make sure these are being exchanged with the outer languages with a proper interfacing mechanism. This mainly has broader views over transaction-level information exchanging. For this, the industry has been giving us the vast facilities to use the randomness method to generate and then exchange with the low-level languages like Verilog, VHDL, etc.

3.2   Literature study

Electronic circuits have a significant problem in terms of power usage. One strategy to cope with this problem is to think about it early in the design phase so that it can be addressed. Investigate alternative design options. Typically, a design flow begins with a high-level description of a whole system, requiring to produce precise model techniques for power modelling are available, employed, allowing for the establishment of a power relationship as well as other metrics. It is also necessary to take into account techniques for characterization of power that is both efficient and effective. This chapter's purpose is to give a summary of the registration transfer level first. Using power modelling and estimating approaches at the transistor level for FPGAs and ASICs are two types of devices. The second goal is to propose a classification of all techniques in accordance with a set of criteria [1]. For embedded systems, model-based system engineering is frequently used to streamline the design and development process with verification. It enables, in particular, the modelling of system design at a higher level of abstraction. As a result, to generate RTL code automatically, a model transformation process is carried out. To accomplish this, simulation is used for verification. The suggested meta-model, in particular, is built on various UVM concepts such as the scoreboard, monitor, agent and driver, among others, to allow simultaneous modelling of test benches and system design. The proposed meta-applicability model is demonstrated using a memory model case study [2]. UVM is used in this chapter to provide a verification platform that can swiftly verify the DUT. The test platform expertly employs UVM components and a flexible configuration scheme, demonstrating the UVM's many benefits. This verification platform is unique as it does not rely on UVM's reference model verification component. This verification platform is appropriate for modules that do not have algorithm models, such as high-speed to low-speed interfaces, interrupt handling modules, and so on. The interrupt handling module realizes the full and overflow of ring first input first output (FIFO), and the bus meets the protocol criteria, according to the results of the verification. Moreover, the coverage rate satisfies the verification requirements. Chip verification is becoming increasingly crucial in the chip research and development process, as it is a critical component of assuring the smooth tapeout of semiconductors [3]. Because of the high demand for system-level designs, the electronics semiconductor sector has seen remarkable expansion throughout the years [4]. High-performance computers, controls, telecommunications, image and video processing, consumer electronics and other applications rely heavily on system-level designs. RTL represents a synchronous digital circuit in terms of stream of data between hardware registers and the logical operative units performed on these signals in digital integrated circuit (IC) design. Each signal is presented to be a high-dimensional point in the toggle-pattern matrix, which is built from value change dumps (VCD) from a training set [5]. Few amounts of signals are automatically selected by clustering signals with comparable switching actions, and then the design-specific but workload-independent activity-based power model is built using regression on cycle-accurate power traces acquired from standard CAD tools. An FPGA is a logic device that may be modified by a client after manufacturing to conduct anything from simple logic gate functionalities to complicated systems on-chip or even AI systems. Scientific papers on Reference [6] they have found over 70 000 documents in the two major scientific databases to date. ScientoPy is utilised to do a scientometric analysis of the top FPGA applications, encompassing papers relevant to FPGAs from 1992 to 2018. Few among the top 150 applications were categorized as follows: digital control, communication interfaces, networking, computer security, cryptographic approaches, ML, digital signal processing, image and video processing, big data, computer algorithms and other applications. DV technologies are impacted by advancements in electronic system design. The Internet-of-Things and Cyber-Physical Systems paradigms presume devices that were immersed in physical surroundings, have limited resources, and must provide security, privacy, dependability, performance and low-power features [7]. In addition, a preliminary method to multidimensional verification using ML techniques was assessed. The constrained-random stimulus has become widespread as a technique of stimulating a design's functioning and ensuring it completely satisfies expectations as ICs have become increasingly complicated. In theory, random stimuli permit all conceivable combinations to be exercised given enough time, but in fact, a completely random technique will struggle to train all possible combinations in a timely manner with very complicated designs. As a result, steering the DV environment to generate difficult-to-hit combinations is frequently required. The resulting constrained-random technique is effective, but it frequently requires substantial human guidance to effectively exercise the design in the DV context. This method produces better-than-random results in a highly automated manner, allowing DV to meet its complete design coverage goals in a shorter time frame and with minimum resources [8]. In Reference [9], the goal of metric-driven verification is discussed as well as its significance in the current verification technique. It is proposed that the regression testing technique be included in the verification environment itself, due to known restrictions. The data gathered from the verification metrics can be utilized to fine-tune the simulation's testing operations. This method enables dynamic manipulation of the regression testing framework and may result in significant simulation time savings. The test segments were introduced in the presented solution. They can be launched at any moment in the simulation that is connected to the internal state of the DUT (checkpoint). Many new protocols are gaining traction and are now commonly utilized in the business. The AMBA Advanced Extensible Interface Protocol, developed by ARM processors, includes features that were not available in the preceding Advanced High-Performance Protocol. The practical results of several of the protocol's properties are shown in this document. It should be mentioned that verifying such protocols is a time-consuming and arduous operation. A verification IP already has the essential testbench-generating processes and may be readily combined with other tools [10]. Verifying a design basically needs well-prepared strategies allowing many vendors to rely over a strict verification plan for the whole system [11]. Many of the negative consequences of the process, voltage and temperature changes can be mitigated by bundled-data designs. They described an open-source CAD pipeline for synthesizing block design (BD) from RTL specifications using commercial tools and Perl and Tcl scripts. Edge is a flow that was created with the help of an open-source CPU called Plasma and Qualcomm Technologies, Inc. industrial design [12]. There has been a lot of research into reconfigurable technology. The application of FPGA as a developing reconfigurable platform for a controller solution was the subject of this review. It is an embedded system that allows for a great deal of freedom in the development of sophisticated ICs. The review's three goals are as follows: To begin, it looks into the contributions of FPGA-based controllers rather than ASIC-based controllers. Second, to demonstrate the influence and success criteria from past studies to improve controllers in terms of performance (response time, complexity, flexibility and cost design). Third, to determine the optimum way for combining these criteria to significantly increase the controller performance. To improve factor design, the majority of studies rely on four important criteria: efficiency of tuning and optimization methods, robust implementation technology to reduce cost with more flexible design, type of technology to reduce complexity and minimize design area and the ability of the controller to be used with different order systems which could greatly improve controller responses [13]. Today's technology has advanced to the point that a system may be put on a single chip, a concept known as system on chip (SoC). It entails microcontrollers and a variety of peripheral devices, each of which has its intellectual property (IP) called IP cores. Various protocols such as RS232, RS422 and UART are used to create serial communication between these IP cores. They execute point-to-point communication, which necessitates extensive wiring and multiplexing of all bus connections to transmit data to IP Cores. The benefit of I²C protocol is that it has a low wiring data transfer rate, which may be increased by using ultrafast mode. The ultrafast data transfer mode is a one-way data transfer mode. They use the system Verilog and UVM in the tool SimVision to verify the design of an I²C protocol between a master and a slave in this study [14]. The design of a 3-wire SPI protocol chip for ASICs and field-programmable gate arrays is presented in this study (FPGA). It is the first study to implement the SPI protocol using VLSI and FPGA technologies for testing and verification. The functions of the SPI protocol have been successfully tested using an oscilloscope. With only four pads, this study develops superior VLSI architecture (including system clock in ASIC design) with cheap cost and minimal complexity [15]. Hardware and software are designed and verified separately in a typical verification environment. The frequency of processors is no longer growing due to Moore's law's extinction. Moore's law is no longer valid, and time-to-market concerns are driving a new wave of technology that tightly integrates hardware and software. This is to improve computing performance. Furthermore, data in domains such as Data Analytics must be processed in real-time and with minimal latency. For applications that demand real-time and low-latency data processing, Solarflare's Application On-load Engine is a platform that combines an FPGA processing engine and low-latency server. Co-verification is not supported by the UVM, which instead relies on the DPI for co-simulation. Software emulation is done concurrently with hardware verification in co-verification when software is emulated separately on an Instruction Set Simulator [16].

Due to the enormous number of IPs in the system that needs to communicate, Network on Chip (NoC) has evolved as an interconnection option for modern digital systems, particularly SoC. Various systems and routers have been implemented, necessitating the creation of a reusable verification environment for testing single routers as well as entire networks. They offered a reusable testing environment for NoC platforms based on the UVM, which tests and certifies both routers and networks in a way that can be easily modified to match different routers and networks. Performance factors such as injection rate, throughput and latency were also evaluated by the environment [17]. Despite decades of effort, DV is still a costly and time-consuming part of the electronic system development process. With the introduction of SoC architectures, verification has evolved into a multi-platform, multi-tool, multi-technology process that spans the whole life cycle. This paper presented an instructional overview of current verification practice in the context of modern SoC DV, current industry trends and significant research problems [18]. In contrast to other Hardware Verification Languages (HVLs) such as Specman E, interactive debug is not a native component of SystemVerilog simulations. We propose an interactive debug library for UVM written in the SystemVerilog Direct Programming Interface in this work (SV-DPI). At its most basic level, this allows for high-level interactive debugging during simulation execution. This library offers the following features: 1) writing or reading a register using the UVM register abstraction layer; 2) generating, randomising, initialising and starting a UVM sequence on any sequencer; and 3) calling a user-specified SV function or task using the interactive debug prompt. They were also shown a debugging and regression approach that outlined the best practices for speeding up debugging and reducing regression run time. According to preliminary findings, employing an interactive debug library lowered debug turnaround time and regression run time dramatically. The UVM debug library is an open-source project that can be found on GitHub [19]. UVM stands for Universal Verification Methodology, which is a standardized approach to testing IC designs to achieve Coverage-Driven Verification (CDV). To signal progress in the DV, it combines automatic test generation, self-checking testbenches and coverage measurements. The CDV follows a different pattern than typical directed-testing methods. With the CDV, a testbench developer begins with a structured plan by defining the verification goals. Coverage monitors, which have been introduced to the simulation environment, are used to track progress. The non-exercised functionality can be detected this way. Furthermore, the additional scoreboards reveal unfavourable DUT behaviour. Three recent ASIC and FPGA projects that have successfully incorporated the new workflow have been developed: the CLICpix2 65 nm CMOS hybrid pixel readout ASIC design; C3PD 180 nm HV-CMOS active sensor ASIC design and the CLICpix chip's FPGA-based DAQ system [20]. The methodology aids us in improving the SoC's performance and lowering its costs. The most difficult task in the entire SoC is verification. Chips with multi-million gate designs have a higher level of complexity. In this study, the complexity issue in SoC was handled using an advanced technique called advanced verification methodology. The verification task's overall design effort is estimated to be almost 70%. The verification methodology utilized here is primarily aimed at maximising reusability for various design IP configurations in the SoC. The SoC's time to market is shortened thanks to its advanced reusable test bench development. The development of a test bench for advanced verification of the SoC [21]. The SystemVerilog UVM aims to boost verification efficiency by allowing teams to exchange tests and test benches across projects and divisions. One of the most crucial steps in the ASIC/VLSI design process is verification which takes up a lot of time and effort in the design flow cycle to ensure that the design is bug-free. As a result, a powerful and reusable verification approach is in high demand. UVM is based on various methodologies such as verification methodology manual (VMM), open verification methodology (OVM) and e reuse methodology (eRM). It can be used to verify designs written in a variety of languages, including Verilog, VHDL and System Verilog. UVM allows for a reusable verification environment, which saves time during the verification cycle [22]. Software models are used as a golden reference model for the algorithm after it has been finalize. They described a unified and modular modelling framework for image signal processing algorithms that can be used for a variety of applications, including ISP algorithm development, reference for hardware implementation, reference for firmware implementation and bit-true certification. The functional verification framework of image signal processors utilising software reference models is based on the UVM. IP-XACT-based solutions for the automatic production of functional verification environment files and model map files are also well described [23]. Technical publications frequently make subjective or unfounded assertions regarding today's functional verification process, such as verification consumes 70% of a project's overall work. Despite this, there are few trustworthy industry studies that quantify the functional verification process in terms of verification technology uptake, effort and efficacy. To overcome this knowledge gap, a recent global, double-blind functional verification study covering all electronic industry market categories was conducted. This is the largest independent functional verification research ever undertaken to our knowledge [24]. FPGA technology has progressed significantly. Some advancement may be in terms of previously available resources, while others may be in terms of overcoming traditional limitations or improving efficiency. The transition in focus to soft core/embedded processors has resulted in the transformation of FPGA from just hardware to a powerful System-on-Chip. IP cores and design tools have also progressed, with software developers providing improved support. The emergence of new FPGA capabilities on various industrial applications is examined in three primary areas: digital real-time applications, sophisticated control approaches and electronic instrumentation, with a focus on mechatronics, robotics and power electronics [25]. Because of its great efficiency and low power consumption, FPGA has become popular in new big data architectures and systems, allowing researchers to install enormous accelerators on a single chip. In this work, they propose the software defined accelerator (SODA) technology, which is a software-defined FPGA-based accelerator that aids in the reconstruction and re-organization of acceleration engines based on the needs of various computation applications. This SODA is made up of several layers. Large and complicated applications are decomposed into coarse-grained single-purpose RTL code libraries that perform specialised tasks in out-of-order hardware [26]. According to Moore's law, hundreds of gates are being added to the SoC architecture as technology shrinks. Meanwhile, getting a product to market is growing more complicated. Due to the rising complexity of SoC, verification has become more difficult. Because current methods are unable to handle the efficiency of growing design sizes, there is a need for innovation [27]. With the advent of multi-core computers, parallelizing performance-critical applications of many types has become a difficulty. Parallel computation aids in the division of big and difficult jobs into smaller units, each of which is handled by a different processor. This aids in improving performance and completing difficult jobs. A customizable parallel device known as a FPGA remains a minor area of study in parallel computing. The FPGA was discussed in this research study as a technique for improving parallel applications by functioning as a co-processor rather than conventional CPUs. The parallel architecture of an FPGA allows complex operations to be moved from the CPU and into specially designed logic inside the FPGA, resulting in excellent performance at a low cost. FPGAs are useful as development tools and are more cost-effective for computing applications. As a result, for a surging number of higher volume applications, FPGAs have shown to be a better option to traditional CPUs [28]. The overall development process becomes increasingly critical and demanding as the design complexity of SoC verification grows. UVM is a standard solution to SoC design complexity, even though there are still unsolved issues. The future of SoC verification technique is discussed by specialists from business and academia in this publication [29]. Ultra-High Frequency (UHF) radio frequency identification (RFID) is a fast-growing technology that uses RF signals to automatically identify things. RFID is currently being used for a variety of applications, including vehicle tracking and security, as well as asset and equipment tracking. Due to the module-reuse strategy and low-power techniques used in the digital baseband, the RFID tag's power consumption is minimized. For verification, an intelligent and adaptable testbench architecture based on UVM is developed. To improve efficiency and provide autonomous stimuli, complete algorithms for pathfinding (CAP) based on state transition graph are employed [30]. SoC verification is one of the popular trends in VLSI right now. Verification takes up most of the time. As a result, it was necessary to create a usable and efficient verification environment. UVM is a SoC functional verification methodology. UVM explains how to verify an IP and set up a productive verification environment. To distinguish between UVM-based and traditional verification, research was conducted [31]. The major reason for functional verification on hardware is to discover issues in the designers' design specifications and to evaluate the design functioning. The design is then tweaked as needed to achieve the intended functionality of the DUT. There are a variety of verification strategies that make the process more user-friendly. SystemVerilog is a huge and complex programming language. UVM is a powerful and versatile class library that has evolved over time [32]. UVM includes powerful SystemVerilog capabilities. It includes a reference verification mechanism in addition to a robust base class library. It was investigated whether the addition of certain SystemVerilog features aided in the evolution of UVM. The combination of UVM and SystemVerilog has been found to provide users with a comprehensive toolbox that can be used to solve a variety of challenges in the functional verification domain of hardware designs [33]. The Ninth Haifa Verification Conference HVC 2013 [34] organized by IBM Research was to advance the state-of-the-art and profession in verification and testing. A forum of industry experts, academic practitioners and researchers gathered here to share their work, exchange ideas and explore future testing and verification prospects for hardware, software and complex hybrid systems. One of the current difficulties in the pre-silicon validation area is the lack of a single framework for all pre-silicon valida-tion efforts, including security validation. As a result, multiple validation tool teams are having trouble communicating. As each team works to improve a specific tool for the project they serve, the project's geography shifts to keep up with the product development life cycle, tool updates and addressing specific tool adjustments, all of which must be communicated among several teams [35]. UVM is a verification approach for the IP and SoC. This is based on the SystemVerilog HVL and allows verification components to be reused. In complex systems, SoC verification is diffi-cult because it involves a lot of effort to validate numerous IP interface and on-chip inter-IP interaction. The reusability of IP verification environment is a desired but difficult approach [36]. The degree of complexity for component and system design for functional verification increases as the design and sophistication of Multiprocessor SoC designs grow to meet minimal power, speed, performance and functionalities. The objective of verification is to guarantee that the designed system is operating in accordance with the specified requirements. In this study, a flexible verification environment is introduced that adapts to the associated NoC framework [37]. Many obstacles were encountered in prior verification approaches, including reusability, maintenance, bug identification, and so on. The introduction of SystemVerilog UVM overcomes these obstacles. At the SoC level, where each IP is a black box and regarded as a golden block, IP level verification is an important factor. In this research, a set of reconfigurable image signal processing IPs is combined to meet the needs of a variety of advanced video processing SoCs [38]. Verification activities have begun to dominate the design effort as systems get more complicated. More efficient verification languages and tools have been devised to cope with rising com-plexity and enhance productivity at the ESL (Electronic System Level). UVM is a methodology for RTL and ESL verification that includes a complementary library. SVM with extensive TLM support based on System C was introduced in this chap-ter, and it was compared to UVM-related features [39]. The software drivers are produced only once the hardware is available. This reliance can result in a prolonged design cycle. It is not always easy to specify driver development and hardware/software interface models. A technique to formalize hardware/software interface requirements where concurrency is required is presented in this work, and this approach is proven using a practical scenario and elaboration of use [40]. This chap-ter provides an overview of programmable hardware trends in the semiconductor industry. FPGAs have become synonymous with development and reprogrammable computing. This chapter focuses on many new industry developments as well as FPGA, with the goal of being informative. The reasons for the emergence of differ-ent technologies, their benefits and drawbacks, and why FPGA is the dominating choice when it comes to programmable logic are all explored here. There is also debate about whether these technologies will continue to exist [41]. Building a test-bench to verify a hardware design is referred to as a software challenge. The basic elements of a design, namely registers, linkages between them, and the computation required to adjust their values, are all included in the RTL. The procedure for creat-ing an RTL design is similar to programming. In the software world, testbenches survive. Data structures and algorithms make up the testbench. Even though most of their creation and operation is software, they are hardware-aware because it is their role to regulate, adapt to and evaluate the hardware [42]. There is a desire to compare FPGAs and ASICs in terms of space, power consumption and performance. The scientific evidence characterizing the gap between FPGAs and ASICs are presented in this work. When compared to an identical ASIC, it was discovered that the FPGA takes up more space, performs slower, and consumes more power. It was eventually verified that using hard multipliers and dedicated memory blocks can save a significant amount of space and power while only having a modest influence on the latency between FPGAs and ASICs [43]. The industry's need for complicated and efficient high-performance controllers prompted rapid development of VLSI technology and EDA methodologies. EDA tools are used to generate, simulate and test a design without committing to hardware, allowing complicated systems and concepts to be quickly evaluated. Because of the increasing difficulty of control algorithms and chip density, efficient design methodologies are required [44]. DV has surged in popularity in the electronics industry. It began with the shift in verification requirements from ICs to SoCs and bigger systems, which was amplified by the rise in embedded processor utilization. Then it went on to expand the quantity and range of verification approaches and languages available. Finally, books containing instructions and advice on verification methodologies, languages, and tools, as well as how to combine all of them into a unified verification approach and process, have become more widely available [45]. As ASIC designs get more complicated, the complexity of the ecosystems in which they were implemented rises exponentially. There has been no parallel robust procedure in place for verification environments like an ASIC design's HDL may be subdivided into intelligible but small components whose behaviour can be grasped in a reasonable amount of time. Any verification environment established or generated for these design sub-blocks, whether written in HDL or any of the different verification or scripting languages now accessible, remains extremely complex. The goal of the team was to combine C++, Tcl and Perl into a unified, highly intelligent and usable ASIC verification environment [46–67].

3.3   Verification management approach: Case Study 1

The forthcoming [64] industrial revolution has the greatest man-made theories yet to be proven in actual practical scenarios, though the intention of the technology is to reduce the manpower and make use of the so-called computers at a greatest extent. When we make a note of the technology called "computer," we tend to aim towards the development of both hardware as well as software productions and yet here we are relating to one such field of computers where the core of its operations is embedded over a single fabric with the lightest and more and more thinner technology nodes developing by huge multinational companies. This in turn again gives an end user to reduce the man power and yet depend over the software so as to develop/demonstrate/simulate/calibrate an actual hardware which has to be brought up from the idea created to the end market for the consumers. ML is one such end where computers are used at its full potential which is again to study the computer algorithms with the help of the usage of huge amount of data nodes. Data nodes is a term referring to bunch of information pointing to one subject and these subjects may differ from point to point. To access these nodes or to identify the information in a very minute period of timescale, we need faster developed algorithms, as fast as it could also be utilised to judge a qubit (quantum bit) in the quantum computing. Having this phenomenal facility of ML, this chapter possesses the strategy to implement the randomization technique with the help of xorshift128 algorithm which is a part of ML. Internal to this, we have to keenly observe the network topology of the data redundancy and node accessibility, and this stage is well known to be the neural networks.

3.3.1 The pseudo random number generator in a verification environment

Basically machine learning is mainly used to identify the sequence of data being generated and let the perfect output with respect to the clusters collected and examined; this has a numerous stages of repeated processes in a neural network terminology. Deep learning is also one such ML task where huge amount of information is collected and passed throughout several algorithms to extract the exact output. Pseudo random number generator (PRNG) way of addressing the seeds towards the test/verification environment could yield us as most of the 95% of accuracy are from the processed end results.

Coming toward the xorshift128 algorithm, it is one such specific task or operation implemented pretty straightforward. Basically it has four internal variables suppose w, x, y and z representing the seed simultaneously. Instead of just hardcoding, we have special packages for the generation of these seeds. Each time the generator function has been called, this will shift the variables from y to x, z to y and w to z. Here in this context the variables are representing the actual binary values to be seeded or randomized at instance. The new value generated at w is now again executed by bit manipulations like left/right shits and XORing to the past values of w, x, y and z. From this we can observe that to generate one output suppose o_1, we need just two of the variables. No doubt that the other variables are also utilised in the further stages of the randomization, but at this instance, it is to be noted that for just one output variable we need lesser amount of input variables. As this PRNG algorithm is used in this context just to generate random amount of bit patterns, it is also important to note that this algorithm is cryptographically not highly secured. Now to implement this algorithm digitally is possible by introducing Linear Feedback Shift register (LFSR), but the delay has to be maintained as equal to the class-based modules as the transactions are being taken up to the higher level languages and it is undesirable to miss any sort of combination generated by LFSR modules in digital significance for verifying a specific design. As it has been mentioned about the timing, this parameter is not that closely observed during functional verification stage also it has to be made sure that high-level language is independent of time-consuming constructs and task specifications.

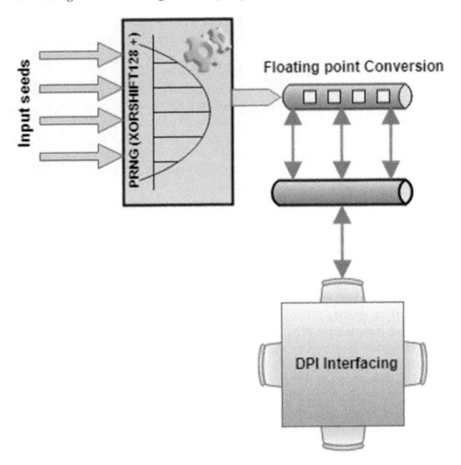

Figure 3.2   DPI linkage with actual scenario (PRNG and floating point conversion module)

In a statistical sense, xorshift algorithm generates a random number only when it has the status of the present state but it is purely unknown to a user. But the sequence it has generated by an ordinary pseudorandom generator often allows one to determine the internal state of the algorithm/generator. This in turn observing the fair long enough generated sequence allows a user to predict the future sequences in most of the cases. In this chapter, we have taken xorshift128 algorithm which consists of $2^{128}-1$ period and passes all the possible combinations on a huge stream of bits for a burst transfers. In a single task, this algorithm allows a user to generate a sequence of multiple random numbers. As in Figure 3.2 after generating a random number, we can see that this is followed by the single precision floating point converter which helps the digital logic to determine the signed and unsigned integers to follow the complex algorithms written in RTL.

Multilayer perceptions are the most prominent units in ML algorithms which are unifyingly known as neurons which combined with thousands of such units and technically

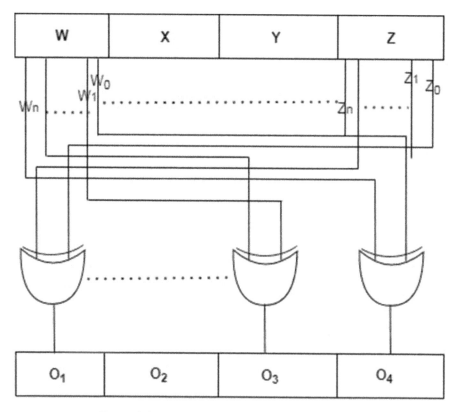

Figure 3.3   Internal structure of xorshift network

known to be a neural network. From Figure 3.3 as we are able to vision, the internal structure of the xorshift algorithm having four input seeds with the range 'n' is shifted multiple times with the other seed bits and is exported to form a new set of output seeds for the random bit generation.

3.3.2   Implementation of PRNG in higher abstraction language and usage of DPI

It makes sense now that the xorshift algorithms used to drive the PRNG algorithm use the sequence of internal states/patterns of bit streams to generate the future sequence. Now as this chapter is portraying the eccentric way of utilising these higher level languages in the RTL verification environment, it is also important to know how DPIs actually work and finally what are the essential elements to initialize our PRNG algorithm into the Python-based script so as to seed the input for the verification environment of a specific RTL logic. The reason to choose the bit length for xorshift as 128 bits is because as per Figure 3.3 we have four outputs which are 32-bit wide each.

Now as verification of a digitally described logics with the help of standard RTL languages seldom requires a need to communicate with the higher abstraction languages such as C, C++, systemC, Python, etc., this task is not done at ease just be instantiating the mutual variables and classes. During this special operation, there are several layers of abstraction where a system has to undergo several handshaking sort of mechanism which allows Python to be communicating with SystemVerilog. The first and the foremost layer which is way too important to acquire the languages written to communicate is the end user layer; this layer is responsible for initiating the transaction between SystemVerilog and other code, for instance, Python. This can be done by using specific function "*call_client()*" using system address and serial of port of the server. Followed by we have the connection layer which acts as the actual media between SystemVerilog and Python language. This can also be well known as the bridging layer between two different languages and this task is performed in the client-server mode. In this layer, there are several handshaking mechanisms to be followed where the end user and the actual server are having the mutual TCP/IP address to identify the socket for communication. The third one is the client layer which acts as the agent between the end user layer and the server layer. In this layer, a connection/transaction is initiated within this. With this, the end user (client) and the server are connected using the DPI-C. Basically to call the functions from C library into SystemVerilog, we have DPI-C. This makes sure that the data exchanged at both the ends are interpreted up to mark and are exactly the same. Thus to import the function, we have a straightforward keyword "*import DPI-C*" which can be written in SystemVerilog codes to extend the functions usage like test_bit, transform_bit, etc. Now to import the DPI features into C program as this forms a basic layer in between end user (client) and server knowingly DPI-C, we have a package in C language too where the keywords are prescribed as "*#include svdpi.h.*" These things are well maintained in the client layer, apart from this connection errors and data incoherency are also well prompted in this layer as in Figure 3.4. Finally, we have the server layer which is the actual oasis for the new

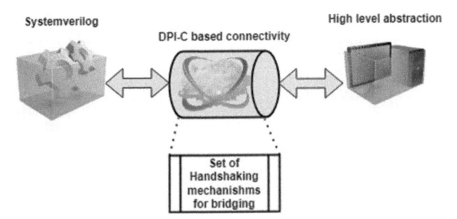

Figure 3.4   Block view of DPI and different languages on either side

language which needs to talk to our SystemVerilog code. Basically, this layer is also responsible for providing a clean response to a client from time to time. Here, the message is well decoded and received from the end user and generates the information to be reverted back to the client (end user). With this one successful transaction with client, the server is now responsible to close the connection indicating that the information has been successfully exchanged between the connection layer and vice versa. Usage of DPI directly in Python can be done by calling *"pythonbind11"* package bit; this has a disadvantage of not cohesively performing actions with the communication layers in between the client and server, making it hard to debug the code and its functionality.

Bridging of crucial high-level abstraction and low-level described languages needs a strong and precise interpreter in terms of computer science theory, as the mutual compilation feedbacks are necessary so as to spawn the exact output from the interfacing components used.

3.4   Verification management approach: Case Study 2

Tcl is a dynamic programming language that is powerful and simple to learn. It is suited for various applications, including online and desktop applications, networking, administration, testing, and so on. Tcl is an open-source and business-friendly language that is truly cross-platform, readily deployed and highly flexible. As one of the most complex SoC, FPGA and ASIC development flow steps, verification requires the development of novel methodologies. The following is an overview of Tcl compared to SystemVerilog and VHDL. Tcl is not the same as HDL or HVL! It is a general-purpose scripting language. Tcl is used for various practical purposes like scripting, DSL (domain-specific language) generation, testing and verification. Tcl is widely used throughout the industry as an embedded EDA and CAD language – it is utilized for automation, testing, configuring, "glue" languages and nearly every programming duty necessary in verification. It is preferable to work closely with synthesis/compile tools simulators, which provides significant benefits. But what do we know about it? Tcl expertise is not as widespread as C knowledge.

What are the critical differences between general-purpose Tcl, SystemVerilog and VHDL for verification? Tcl, unlike HDLs, operates outside of the simulator via the interpreter included with the EDA tool. It manages the simulator by interpreting scripts based on predefined commands – without the need for compilation. Console and GUI mode can control the simulator at several levels. But, most importantly, it is feasible to install a simulator inside and maintain a DUT or a DUT with a testing environment (UVM or another) in the same way.

Built-in vendor support:

- Mentor Modelsim/Questa – Tcl-based – over 350 well-documented commands in the "Command Reference Manual" and complete internals control is possible most of the time.
- Synopsys VCS – embedded Tcl – complete UCLI and DVE control
- Cadence Incisive – just one quote from the website: "For Electronic Design Automation (EDA) and Computer-Aided Design (CAD) applications, Tcl has become the de facto standard embedded command language."

UVM support, command extension to C/C++code and configurations, whereas Tcl is a powerful and versatile tool ideal for various situations and standard verification methods. The inbuilt Tcl interpreter in the simulator provides full language support for verifying clear DUT, expanding current test benches and working with varied settings.

The benefits of using Tcl for verification

1. It is possible to "edit, execute, stop and restart" Tcl scripts without recompiling or exiting the simulator.
2. Because of the nature of Tcl, it is far more expressive and prolific than SystemVerilog.
3. DSL support from scratch.
4. Flexible creation of any data structures
5. Automation and enhancements for simple static analysis
6. The most straightforward method for interacting with external simulator EDA/CAD tools.
7. An easy way to communicate with something written in another language.
8. There is no need for anything additional because Tcl is already included in EDA tools.

Due to language limitations, once a testbench is created in SystemVerilog, the user has little influence over the test scenario during simulation. Users are currently limited to using a different seed or poking/forcing signals within the simulation environment during simulation run time.

Consider the following situation: A user has a lengthy simulation that takes hours to complete. A testbench checker flags an error halfway through the simulation. If the user has to alter the stimulus to troubleshoot the problem, they must update the SV code, recompile the testbench and wait for a long time to identify the error again. The interactive debug library allows users to experiment with different debug circumstances without restarting the simulation. They can query the device status via register reads, try new device configurations via register writes, adjust the stimulus generated by the testbench by performing a new UVM sequence with a higher priority or invoke any testbench functions to assist in the identification of the problem.

They can test dozens of scenarios and find the bug in minutes rather than hours. The significant reduction in debug turnaround time increases productivity by isolating the bug rather than waiting for the simulation to compile/run.

```
SV_code
```

```
import uvm_debug_pkg ::*;
...
uvm_debug_utiluvn_debug - uvm_debug_util :: get ();
uvm_debu.prompt(1);
```

```
      Tcl commands
Ncsim> call debug_prompt
Debug prompt (help for all commands)
1000ns:debug>
```

The debug prompt helps experiment with different test scenarios in real time. If the same set of debug instructions is used repeatedly, loading a command file saves time on typing. The command and descriptions are given in Table 3.1.

On the other hand, the debug prompt lacks any built-in programming features and can only execute one command after another consecutively. To put it another way, the debug prompt is not a Turing complete language in and of itself. Fortunately, the simulator already includes a full-featured programming environment in the shape of the Tcl prompt.

The UVM debug library produces a Tcl wrapper function that calls the debug prompt, passes in and executes one debug command, and returns to the Tcl prompt with the debug command's return value.

Please remember that the Tcl script integration is currently in its early stages. Everything is executed in a single thread by the Tcl prompt.

It would be interesting to observe how well the UVM debug library performs when several threads call numerous debug instructions simultaneously.

Table 3.1   Command basis approaches

Command	Description
Help [command]	Displays the help message. With no argument, it lists all the available commands; otherwise it displays the help message of the command specified
Continue	Exits the debug prompt and continue the simulation
pause	Pauses the simulation and switch to the simulator's Tcl prompt
Run < runtime >	Runs the simulator for the specified time and go back to the debug prompt
History [list] |clear |save< file >	Lists all the previous command inputted by the user; clear the history; save the history to a command file
Repeat #	Repeats the specified line in the command history
Read < file >	Reads a command file
Save_checkpoint [-path< path >]< snapshot name>	Saves a check point snapshot

3.5   Challenges and research direction

We address the new challenges and directions that big data and AI pose in education research, policymaking and industry. Big Data and AI applications in education have made tremendous strides in recent years. This exemplifies a new trend in cutting-edge educational research.

3.5.1   Challenges in intelligent systems

Research in intelligent systems faces numerous challenges, many of which relate to computationally representing a dynamic physical world.

Inject the faults/errors: One of the most difficult challenges is determining how to inject the faults/errors.

For external faults, the stimuli delivered by the testbench to the DUT must be adjusted. Internal flaws require errors to be introduced into the DUT, but the design should not be altered.

Code coverage: Coverage is the most significant parameter of the verification process, and it is meticulously recorded during each test run in the traditional manner. Coverage collecting adds a substantial amount of time to the simulation time. It is sufficient to collect coverage for simply a subset of modules. The coverage level for the remaining modules may be correctly predicted using Deep Neural Networks.

Grouping of Test cases: ML techniques (which offer a means of implementing AI) can be effectively utilised to classify the causes of test failures. It is also feasible to group failing tests based on the reason for failure, although the results on that problem did not match the expected outcome.

Uncertainty: Physical sensors/effectors deliver limited, noisy, and erroneous data/action. As a result, any actions taken by the system may be wrong, both due to noise in the sensors and to restrictions in performing those actions.

Dynamic world: The physical world is constantly changing, necessitating judgments made on short time scales to account for environmental changes.

Time-consuming computation: Finding the best path to a goal necessitates a lengthy search through a massive state space, which is computationally expensive. The disadvantage of devoting excessive time to computing is that the world may change in the interim, rendering the computed strategy obsolete.

Mapping: A significant amount of information is lost during the transition from the 3D world to the 2D world. Changes in perspective, lighting, and scale; background clutter or motion; and grouping things with intra-/inter-class variations are all issues for computer vision.

In hardware verification, AI is applied. The specific language feature enables verification engineers to dynamically load coverage reports from prior runs into a test (to make the verification environment behave in accordance with coverage level %). Which e-language structures could adequately fulfil the necessity for giving relevant data to ML algorithms? Typically, the tests in a verification environment are grouped into one or more regressions and performed several times until the verification metrics are met. The current study is crucial in incorporating AI concepts into the IC verification process. ML in verification can be utilised in a variety of ways, including producing code for driving the full range of stimuli required to get a verified circuit into all of its functional states, assessing test results, fixing coverage gaps, and so on. However, a significant difficulty is determining which portions of the verification environment can best address automation objectives and which verification methodologies are most suited for giving data to automatic code generators. Some characteristics of e-language are mentioned in this chapter as welcome bridges between hardware verification and AI. Standard UVM is currently implemented in SystemVerilog. However, several other languages, such as MATLAB/Simulink®, VHDL and SystemC, are used for electronic system design. When selecting a language that is best suited for a specific application, it is advisable to always use the same verification approach and testbench library, as with C-based implementations.

3.6   Conclusion

Verification environment itself is a vast terra firma where thousands of verification plans and strategies meet the design specifications functionality and its pertained output is well scrutinised by coverage reports and design meeting the planned verification reports. So does the industry is on the verge of utilising many plans to meet the time to market strategy for faster consumer needs. In this chapter, a couple of separate methods have been brought where one can effectively utilise the trending ML algorithms with the help of high-level programming languages like Python for instance, to speed up the interfacing junction and to receive the data in a surplus amount with fraction of amount of time. This chapter has taken you through just the ideology for implementing the verification plan in a brisk through manner with the help of DPI. UVM architecture is well reserved for its root of ahead-plans to be maintained over different DUTs, so is the SystemVerilog's huge applicable concepts and language syntaxes act as a point of source for understanding UVM and making it conjoin with the methodologies described in the above sections making a drastic linkage in between high-processing algorithm with large data cluster identification and its randomisation conceptuality.

References

[1] Nasser Y., Lorandel J., Prevotet J.-C., Helard M. 'RTL to transistor level power modeling and estimation techniques for FPGA and ASIC: a survey'. *IEEE Transactions on Computer-Aided Design of Integrated Circuits and Systems.* 2021, vol. 40(3) 479–93.

[2] Anwar M.W., Qamar S., Azam F., Butt W.H., Rashid M. 'Bridging the gap between design and verification of embedded systems in model based system engineering'. *A Meta-model for Modeling Universal Verification Methodology (UVM) Test Benches'. ICCMS*; 2020. pp. 26–8.

[3] Zhou S., Geng S., Peng X., *et al.* 'The design of UVM verification platform based on data comparison'. *Proceedings of the 4th International Conference*

on *Electronic Information Technology and Computer Engineering (EITCE 2020)*; Xiamen China, 6–8 Nov; 2020. pp. 1080–5.

[4]   Singh D., Chandel R. 'Register-Transfer-level design for application-specific integrated circuits'. *Nanoscale VLSI*. 2020.

[5]   Kim D., Zhao J., Bachrach J., Asanović K. 'Simmani: runtime power modeling for arbitrary RTL with automatic signal selection'. *52nd Annual IEEE/ACM International Symposium on Microarchitecture (MICRO '52)*; New York; 2019. pp. 1050–62.

[6]   Ruiz-Rosero J., Ramirez-Gonzalez G., Khanna R. 'Field programmable gate array applications—a scientometric review'. *Computation*. 2019, vol. 7(4), p. 63.

[7]   Lai X., Balakrishnan A., Lange T., *et al*. 'Understanding multidimensional verification: where functional meets non-functional'. *Microprocessors and Microsystems*. 2019, vol. 71,102867.

[8]   Hughes W., Srinivasan S., Suvarna R., Kulkarni M. 'Optimizing design verification using machine learning: doing better than random'. *ArXiv*. 2019,arXiv:1909.13168v1.

[9]   Cieplucha M. 'Metric-Driven verification methodology with regression management'. *Journal of Electronic Testing*. 2019, vol. 35(1), pp. 101–10.

[10] Bera R., Sarkar S., Singh O., Saikia H. (eds.) *Advances in communication, devices and networking*. Vol. 537. Singapore: Springer; 2018. Available from https://link.springer.com/book/10.1007/978-981-13-3450-4

[11] Mehta A.B. 'ASIC/soc functional design verification' in *ASIC/soc functional design verification A comprehensive guide to technologies and methodologies*. Springer Nature Switzerland: Springer Publications; 2018.

[12] Zhang Y., Cheng H., Chen D., *et al*. 'Challenges in building an open-source flow from RTL to bundled-data design'. *24th IEEE International Symposium on Asynchronous Circuits and Systems (ASYNC)*; Vienna, Austria, 13–16 May; 2018. pp. 26–7.

[13] Alkhafaji F.S.M., Hasan W.Z.W., Isa M.M., Sulaiman N. 'Robotic controller: ASIC versus FPGA—a review'. *Journal of Computational and Theoretical Nanoscience*. 2018, vol. 15(25), pp. 1–25.

[14] Satapathy S., Bhateja V., Das S. (eds.). *'High Level Verification of I2C Protocol Using System Verilog and UVM'. Smart Computing and Informatics. Smart Innovation, Systems and Technologies*. 78. Singapore: Springer; 2018.

[15] Tuan M.-C., Chen S.-L., Lai Y.-K., Chen C.-C. 'A 3-wires SPI protocol CHIP design with application-specific integrated circuit (ASIC) and FPGA verification'. Proceedings of the 3rd World Congress on Electrical Engineering and Computer Systems and Science (EECSS'17); Rome, Italy; 2017.

[16] Birla S., Sharma S., Shukla N.K. 'UVM-powered hardware/software co-verification'. *Journal of Information and Optimization Sciences*. 2017, vol. 38(6), pp. 945–52.

[17] Eissa A.S., Ibrahem M.A., Elmohr M.A. 'A reusable verification environment for NoC platforms using UVM'. IEEE EUROCON 2017 -17th International Conference on Smart Technologies; Ohrid, Macedonia, 6–8 Jul; 2017.

[18] Chen W., Ray S., Bhadra J., Abadir M., Wang L.-C. 'Challenges and trends in modern SOC design verification'. *IEEE Design & Test*. 2017, vol. 34(5), pp. 7–22.

[19] Chan H. 'UVM interactive debug library: shortening the debug turnaround time'. DVCON 2017; San Jose; 2017.

[20] Fiergolski A., on behalf of the CLICdp collaboration. 'Simulation environment based on the universal verification methodology'. *Topical Workshop on Electronics for Particle Physic*; Karlsruhe, Germany; 2016.

[21] Renuka G., Ushashree V., Chandrasekhar Reddy P. 'Functional verification of complex SOC by advanced verification methodology'. *International Journal of VLSI System Design and Communication Systems*. 2016, vol. 4(12), pp. 1308–12.

[22] Pankaj S.V., Kureshi D.A.K. 'UVM architecture for verification'. *International Journal of Electronics and Communication Engineering & Technology*. 2016, vol. 7(3), pp. 29–37.

[23] Jain A., Gupta R. 'Unified and modular modeling and functional verification framework of real-time image signal processors'. *VLSI Design*. 2016, vol. 2016 1–14.

[24] Foster H.D. 'Trends in functional verification: a 2014 industry study'. *52nd ACM/EDAC/IEEE Design Automation Conference (DAC)*; San Francisco, CA, IEEE, 2015. pp. 1–6.

[25] Rodríguez-Andina J.J., Valdés-Peña M.D., Moure M.J. 'Advanced features and industrial applications of FPGAs—a review'. *IEEE Transactions on Industrial Informatics*. 2015, vol. 11(4), pp. 853–64.

[26] Wang C., Li X., Zhou X. 'SODA: software defined FPGA based accelerators for big data'. *Design, Automation & Test in Europe Conference & Exhibition (DATE)*; IEEE, 2015. pp. 884–87.

[27] Oddone R., Chen L. 'Challenges and novel solutions for soc verification'. *ECS Transactions*. 2014, vol. 60(1), pp. 1191–5.

[28] Opeyemi M.A., Justice Emuoyefarche E.O. 'Field programmable gate array (FPGA): a tool for improving parallel computations'. *International Journal of Scientific & Engineering Research*. 2014, vol. 5(2), pp. 2229–5518.

[29] Drechsler R. 'Panel: future soc verification methodology: UVM evolution or revolution?'. *Design, Automation & Test in Europe Conference & Exhibition (DATE)*; IEEE, 2014. pp. 1–5.

[30] Li Q., Xie Z., Su J., Wang X. 'UVM-based intelligent verification method for UHF RFID tag'. *IEEE International Conference on Electron Devices and Solid-State Circuits*; Chengdu, China, 18–20 Jun; 2014. pp. 1–2.

[31] Salah K. 'A UVM-based smart functional verification platform: concepts, pros, cons, and opportunities'. *9th International Design and Test Symposium*; Algeries, Algeria, 16–18 Dec; 2014.

[32] Raghuvanshi S., Singh V. 'Review on universal verification methodology (UVM) concepts for functional verification'. *International Journal of Electrical, Electronics and Data Communication*. 2014, vol. 2(3), pp. 101–07.

[33] Bromley J. 'If system verilog is so good, why do we need the UVM? sharing responsibilities between libraries and the core language'. *Proceedings of the 2013 Forum on specification and Design Languages (FDL)*; Paris, France, 24–26 Sep; 2013.

[34] Valeria Bertacco Axel Legay 'Hardware and software: verification and testing'. *9th International Haifa Verification Conference*; Haifa, Israel, Springer Cham, 2013. pp. 5–7.

[35] Kannavara R. 'Towards a unified framework for pre-silicon validation'. *Proceedings of the 4th International Conference on Information, Intelligence, Systems and Applications*; Piraeus, Greece, IEEE, 2013. pp. 321–26.

[36] Zhaohui H., Pierres A., Shiqing H, *et al.* 'Practical and efficient SOC verification flow by reusing IP testcase and testbench'. *2012 International SoC Design Conference (ISOCC)*; Jeju, Korea (South), IEEE, 2012. pp. 175–78.

[37] Lim Z.N., Loh S.H., Lee S.W., Yap V.V., Ng M.S., Tang C.M. 'A reconfigurable and scalable verification environment for noc design'. *Conference on New Media Studies (CoNMedia)*; Tangerang, Indonesia, IEEE, 2013. pp. 1–4.

[38] Jain A., Bonanno G., Gupta D.H., Goyal A. 'Generic system verilog universal verification methodology based reusable verification environment for efficient verification of image signal processing IPS/SOCS'. *International Journal of VLSI Design & Communication Systems*. 2012, vol. 3(6), pp. 13–25.

[39] Oliveira M.F.S., Kuznik C., Mueller W., *et al.* 'The system verification methodology for advanced TLM verification'. *Proceedings of the Eighth IEEE/ACM/IFIP International Conference on Hardware/Software Codesign and System Synthesis (CODES+ISSS)*; Tampere Finland, 7–12 Oct; 2012.

[40] Li J., Xie F., Ball T., Levin V., McGarvey C. 'Formalizing hardware/software interface specifications'. *26th IEEE/ACM International Conference on Automated Software Engineering (ASE 2011)*; Lawrence, KS, IEEE, 2011. pp. 143–52.

[41] Ahmed S., Sassatelli G., Torres L., Rouge L. 'Survey of new trends in industry for programmable hardware: FPGAs, MPPAs, MPSoCs, structured ASICs, eFPGAs and new wave of innovation in FPGAs'. *Proceedings of the 20th International Conference on Field Programmable Logic and Applications*; Milano, Italy, 2 Sep; 2010.

[42] Glasser M. *Open verification methodology cookbook, springer-verlag new york 2009, ISBN: 978-1-4899-8513-2*; 2009.

[43] Kuon I., Rose J. 'Measuring the gap between FPGAs and ASICs'. *IEEE Transactions on Computer-Aided Design of Integrated Circuits and Systems*. 2007, vol. 26(2), pp. 203–15.

[44] Monmasson E., Cirstea M.N. 'FPGA design methodology for industrial control systems—a review'. *IEEE Transactions on Industrial Electronics*. 2007, vol. 54(4), pp. 1824–42.

[45] Singh L., Drucker L., Khan N. *Advanced verification techniques: a systemC based approach for successful tapeout*. Academic Publisher Kluwer; 2004.

[46] McKinney M.D. 'Integrating Perl, Tcl and C++ into simulation-based ASIC verification environments'. *Sixth IEEE International High-Level Design Validation and Test Workshop*; Monterey, CA, 9 Nov; 2001. pp. 19–24.

[47] Haidar M., Kumar S. 'Smart healthcare system for biomedical and health care applications using aadhaar and blockchain'. *5th International Conference on Information Systems and Computer Networks, ISCON 2021, 2021*; GLA Mathura, 22–23 Oct 2021; 2022. pp. 1–5.

[48] Kumar S., Cengiz K., Vimal S., Suresh A, *et al.* 'Energy efficient resource migration based load balance mechanism for high traffic applications iot'. *Wireless Personal Communications, 1-14*. 2021, vol. 10(3).

[49] Kumar S., Ranjan P., Radhakrishnan R., Tripathy M.R. 'Energy efficient multichannel MAC protocol for high traffic applications in heterogeneous wireless sensor networks'. *Recent Advances in Electrical & Electronic Engineering.* 2017, vol. 10(3), pp. 223–32.

[50] Kumar S., Ranjan P., Ramaswami R., Tripathy M.R. 'Resource efficient clustering and next hop knowledge based routing in multiple heterogeneous wireless sensor networks'. *International Journal of Grid and High Performance Computing.* 2017, vol. 9(2), pp. 1–20.

[51] Punhani A., Faujdar N., Kumar S. 'Design and evaluation of cubic torus network-on-chip architecture'. *International Journal of Innovative Technology and Exploring Engineering (IJITEE), 1672-1676.* 2019, vol. 8(6).

[52] Dubey G., Kumar S., Kumar S., Navaney P. 'Extended opinion lexicon and ML-based sentiment analysis of tweets: a novel approach towards accurate classifier'. *International Journal of Computational Vision and Robotics.* 2020, vol. 10(6), pp. 505–21.

[53] Kumar S., Ranjan P., Radhakrishnan R., Tripathy M.R. 'Energy aware distributed protocol for heterogeneous wireless sensor network'. *International Journal of Control and Automation.* 2015, vol. 8(10), pp. 421–30.

[54] Singh P., Bansal A., Kamal A.E., Kumar S., Marla D.. (eds.) 'Road surface quality monitoring using machine learning algorithm' in Reddy A.N.R., Favorskaya M.N., Satapathy S.C. (eds.). *Intelligent Manufacturing and Energy Sustainability. Smart Innovation, Systems and Technologies.* 265. Singapore: Springer; 2022.

[55] Sharma A., Awasthi Y., Kumar S. 'The role of blockchain, AI and iot for smart road traffic management system'. *IEEE India Council International Subsections Conference, INDISCON*; Visakhapatnam, India, IEEE, 2020. pp. 289–96.

[56] Kumar S., Ranjan P., Singh P., Tripathy M.R. 'Design and implementation of fault tolerance technique for internet of things (iot)'. *12th International Conference on Computational Intelligence and Communication Networks (CICN)*; Bhimtal, India, IEEE, 2020. pp. 154–59.

[57] Singh P., Bansal A., Kumar S. 'Performance analysis of various information platforms for recognizing the quality of indian roads'. *10th International Conference on Cloud Computing, Data Science and Engineering*; Noida, India, IEEE, 2020. pp. 63–76.

[58]   Reghu S., Kumar S. 'Development of robust infrastructure in networking to survive a disaster'. *4th International Conference on Information Systems and Computer Networks, ISCON*; Mathura, India, IEEE, 2019. pp. 250–55.

[59]   Kumar S., Ranjan P., Ramaswami R., Tripathy M.R. 'An NS3 implementation of physical layer based on 802.11 for utility maximization of WSN'. *International Conference on Computational Intelligence and Communication Networks, CICN*; IEEE, 2015. pp. 79–84.

[60]   Kumar S., Ranjan P., Ramaswami R., Tripathy M.R. 'A utility maximization approach to MAC layer channel access and forwarding'. *Progress in Electromagnetics Research Symposium, Publisher: The Electromagnetics Academy, PIERS 2015, 6-9 July 2015, Prague, Czech Republic.*; 2015. pp. 2363–67.

[61]   Kumar S., Ranjan P., Ramaswami R., Tripathy M.R. 'EMEEDP: enhanced multi-hop energy efficient distributed protocol for heterogeneous wireless sensor network'. *5th International Conference on Communication Systems and Network Technologies (CSNT)*; Gwalior, India, IEEE, 2015. pp. 194–200.

[62]   Kumar S., Ranjan P., Ramaswami R. 'Energy optimization in distributed localized wireless sensor networks'. *Proceedings of the International Conference on Issues and Challenges Intelligent Computing Technique (ICICT)*; Ghaziabad, India, IEEE, 2014.

[63]   Sudhakaran S., Kumar S., Ranjan P., Tripathy M.R. 'Blockchain-based transparent and secure decentralized algorithm'. *International Conference on Intelligent Computing and Smart Communication 2019. Algorithms for Intelligent Systems*; Singapore: Springer; 2020.

[64]   Kumar S., Trivedi M.C., Ranjan P., Punhani A. *Evolution of Software-Defined Networking Foundations for IoT and 5G Mobile Networks*. 10. Hershey, PA: IGI Publisher; 2020. p. 350.

[65]   Sampathkumar A., Rastogi R., Arukonda S., Shankar A., Kautish S., Sivaram M. 'An efficient hybrid methodology for detection of cancer-causing gene using CSC for micro array data'. *Journal of Ambient Intelligence and Humanized Computing*. 2020, vol. 11(11), pp. 4743–51.

[66]   Nie X., Fan T., Wang B., Li Z., Shankar A., Manickam A. 'Big data analytics and IoT in operation safety management in under water management'. *Computer Communications*. 2020, vol. 154, pp. 188–96.

[67]   Shankar A., Jaisankar N., Khan M.S., Patan R., Balamurugan B. 'Hybrid model for security-aware cluster head selection in wireless sensor networks'. *IET Wireless Sensor Systems*. 2019, vol. 9(2) 68–76.

Chapter 4

Evaluation of machine learning algorithms on academic big dataset by using feature selection techniques

Mukesh Kumar[1], Amar Jeet Singh[1], Bhisham Sharma[2], and Korhan Cengiz[3]

Identifying the most accurate methods for forecasting students' academic achievement is the focus of this research. Globally, all educational institutions are concerned about student attrition. The goal of all educational institutions is to increase the student's retention and graduation rates and this is only possible if at-risk students are identified early. Due to inherent classifier constraints and the incorporation of fewer student features, most commonly used prediction models are inefficient and incur. Different data mining algorithms like classification, clustering, regression, and association rule mining are used to uncover hidden patterns and relevant information in student performance big datasets in academics. Naïve Bayes, random forest, decision tree, multilayer perceptron (MLP), decision table (DT), JRip, and logistic regression (LR) are some of the data mining techniques that can be applied. A student's academic performance big dataset comprises many features, none of which are relevant or play a significant role in the mining process. So, features with a variance close to 0 are removed from the student's academic performance big dataset because they have no impact on the mining process. To determine the influence of various attributes on the class level, various feature selection (FS) techniques such as the correlation attribute evaluator (CAE), information gain attribute evaluator (IGAE), and gain ratio attribute evaluator (GRAE) are utilized. In this study, authors have investigated the performance of various data mining algorithms on the big dataset, as well as the effectiveness of various FS techniques. In conclusion, each classification algorithm that is built with some FS methods improves the performance of the classification algorithms in their overall predictive performance.

[1]Department of Computer Science, Himachal Pradesh University, Summer-Hill Shimla-5, Himachal Pradesh, India
[2]Chitkara University School of Engineering and Technology, Chitkara University, Himachal Pradesh, India
[3]Department of Electrical-Electronics Engineering, Trakya University, 22030 Edirne, Turkey

4.1   Introduction

Today, universities are in a very competitive and complicated situation. There has been a lot of progress in technology and IT equipment, which has made it easier to store a lot of data in educational databases. If these data are not analyzed, it is just a lot of data. These data can be used with tools, methods, and techniques that help us look at it. We can look for patterns and hidden information. Data mining is a way to look for patterns and relationships in data that can help people make better decisions. People from different fields work together in this area. It combines techniques from statistics and artificial intelligence with those from neural networks, database systems, and machine learning.

Data mining offers a variety of methods for analyzing data. A human's ability to assess and extract the most important information from student databases is currently limited by the sheer volume of data available. It is the extraction of nontrivial, unknown, and potentially relevant information from a huge database through the process of knowledge discovery. A user's needs are taken into consideration when data mining is employed in knowledge discovery. A linguistic term for describing a subset of data is referred to as a "pattern definition." Data mining has a wide range of applications. Financial institutions employ it to uncover hidden correlations among various financial indicators, which they then use to spot potentially fraudulent activity. It is able to identify both fraudulent and legitimate behavior by analyzing previous data and turning it into valuable and accurate information [1]. By using data mining in healthcare, it is possible to identify correlations between disease and treatment success. It also aids health-care insurance providers in detecting fraud. This software is often used to find money laundering, drug trafficking, and other crimes. Customer demographic features and predicted behavior are two frequent uses of data mining in the telecommunications industry to boost profitability as well as reduce customer turnover. Based on the findings of data mining, marketing campaigns and pricing strategies can be developed. Data mining techniques are used in sales and marketing to uncover previously unnoticed patterns in past customer purchases. In market basket analysis, the results of data mining can be utilized to determine client purchasing habits and behavior patterns. Future trends and customer purchasing habits can be predicted using these data. When it comes to predicting how many customers will leave, the banking industry relies a lot on data mining. The increasing use of technology in educational systems has resulted in an enormous amount of data being made available to educators. A substantial amount of important information may be gleaned via educational data mining (EDM), which helps to provide a more accurate picture of learners and their learning processes. This software analyzes educational data and helps students overcome educational problems using data mining techniques. Similarly, to other data mining techniques' extraction processes, EDM extracts information from educational data that are engaging, interpretable, valuable, and innovative for the learner or teacher. EDM, on the other hand, is primarily geared toward the development of methods that make use of data that are unique to educational systems. After that, such strategies are used to increase understanding of educational phenomena and pupils, as well as the environments in which they learn [2]. Data and theory can help improve the quality of teaching and learning in schools by developing new computational methods that combine data and theory.

When it comes to the practical use of EDM, users can extract knowledge from student data. There are numerous applications for this knowledge, including the validation and evaluation of educational systems, the improvement of teaching and learning processes, and the establishment of the groundwork for a more effective learning process, among other things. Comparable concepts have been used successfully, particularly in commercial data, in many datasets, like online shopping carts, to boost sales profitability. Because data mining techniques have been proven successful in commercial data, they are being used more widely in a variety of fields. Notably, data mining has been applied to educational data in order to achieve research objectives such as improving the learning process and guiding students' learning, as well as gaining a more comprehensive understanding of educational phenomena. The situation is changing, however, as more people become interested in the application of data mining in the educational environment. Even though EDM has made less progress than other industries in this area, things are getting better.

Nowadays, universities operate in a very difficult and competitive atmosphere. It's becoming more and more common for educational databases to contain vast volumes of information, yet these data are useless if they are not analyzed further. It's possible to analyze these data using data mining tools, methods, techniques, and procedures. To determine the influence of various attributes on the class level, various FS techniques such as the CAE, IGAE, and GRAE are utilized. A crucial stage in the development of any country, and indeed in the development of our entire planet, is the acquisition of education. Consequently, data pertaining to the education sector is thoroughly analyzed in order to extract some useful information from it that will aid in the further development of students in the future. Consequently, data mining and machine learning are of paramount relevance for this purpose because there are numerous ways available to aid in the discovery of relevant information inside a large database of this nature [3].

Classification, clustering, and association rule mining are just a few of the data mining techniques that can be utilized to find the information that's been concealed in a database. Machine learning, together with data mining, is one of the most efficient and successful methodologies for forecasting performance in the disciplines of data analytics and information retrieval, respectively. It is used to forecast performance by constructing models and algorithms, similar to how data mining is used. Machine learning is used to learn and act in ways that are similar to those of human beings. Machine learning algorithms are often classified by either learning style or similarity in form or function, for example, classification, regression, decision tree, clustering, and deep learning algorithms, to name a few examples. A large number of attributes exist in the real-world database, and none of these attributes are necessary for predicting the pattern in a dataset to be found there. As a result, we must delete some features from the database in order to speed up the mining process and produce more accurate results. As a result, we have data mining techniques that may be used to remove certain attributes from a database for this purpose. FS is an important approach in the success of the data mining process since it allows us to select the helpful or relevant qualities in the dataset that are being used for the analysis [4].

In this study, a comparison of alternative FS approaches is made, as well as an examination of the impact of the strategies on classification algorithms. Any country's development depends on its educational system. So, take it seriously from the outset. They have their own systems and evaluators. Today's education includes online education, Massive Open Online Courses (MOOC) courses, intelligent tutorials, web-based education, project-based learning, seminars, and workshops [5]. But none of these systems work unless they are accurately evaluated. So, to make any school system successful, a clear evaluation mechanism is needed. Every educational institution creates a lot of data about each registered student, and if that data are not correctly analyzed, all resources are lost. It includes student acceptance, family info, and academic results. Every educational institution assesses their students [6]. In modern education, many tools are utilized to measure a student's academic achievement. Data mining is one of the greatest sophisticated computer tools used to monitor student progress. Currently, data mining is applied in almost every field where data are used. Data mining has several key applications in retail, marketing, banking, telecommunications, hospitality, hospital, and production management. This entire company uses data mining to increase sales and future growth. With the help of a built-in algorithm, it analyzes any organization's historical data to uncover hidden information [7]. So, we may say that data mining techniques can extract hidden information from any organization's data warehouse.

4.1.1   EDM

In Montreal, EDM hosted its first international research conference, which took place in 2008. Founded in 2011, the International Educational Data Mining Society is dedicated to advancing EDM. Since then, disciplines such as data mining, machine learning, pattern recognition, psychometrics, artificial intelligence, information visualization, and computational modeling have increased in popularity. EDM's ultimate goal is to improve education and to make decision-making processes more transparent [8]. Data that are made during teaching and learning can be used to find new information, correlations, and patterns in very large datasets.

Data mining has a wide range of applications. Customer behavior data may be used to improve customer loyalty, and it can also be used to uncover hidden correlations between various financial indicators in order to spot potentially illegal activity. It collects and analyzes past data in order to detect both fraudulent and nonfraudulent behavior. Data mining in healthcare makes discovering the connections between diseases and therapies easier [9]. Fraud detection is made easier for health-care insurers as well. It is used by law enforcement authorities to investigate money laundering, narcotics trafficking, and other criminal activities. Customer demographic features and predicted behavior are two frequent uses of data mining in the telecommunications industry to boost profitability as well as reduce customer turnover. Based on the findings of data mining, marketing campaigns and pricing strategies can be developed. Using data mining tools, companies can uncover previously unnoticed trends in customer purchase behavior [10]. Data mining results are used to discover customers' purchasing habits by analyzing market baskets and analyzing the combinations of products they purchase together. Additionally, it's used to make educated guesses about upcoming fashion and consumer trends. A significant amount of data mining is used in the banking business when projecting how many clients will quit. The amount of data produced and saved in many educational institutions has grown to the point that it is impossible to analyze it manually any longer. A new subject, EDM, has emerged as a result of the analysis of educational data.

4.1.2 EDM process

The EDM procedure is divided into four distinct stages. There are two stages to solving a data mining challenge: problem definition and problem translation. Along with the primary research topics, the project's goals and objectives are developed during this stage. It takes the most time to prepare and acquire data in the second phase. It can account for up to 80% of the total time spent on the investigation. In data mining, the quality of the data is a crucial issue. Source data must be discovered, cleansed, and formatted according to predetermined specifications in this step [11]. Ultimately, the parameters are set to their greatest potential values and various modeling techniques are applied. During the final stage of data mining, known as deployment, the results are organized and presented graphically and in reports. Because data mining is a recursive process, you must remember that it does not end when a specific solution is applied. It only has to be incorporated into a brand-new data mining workflow. To properly analyze the database, some important and frequently used data mining techniques are applied to get hidden information. Some of the major advantages of data mining process are mentioned below:

1. Data mining is used to discover patterns, forecast trends, and find relations, thus enabling the companies to decode the true potential of their precious data. The game-changing insights derived from data mining process enable the organizations to make informed business decisions, devise effective strategies, and gain a competitive advantage in the industry.
2. Organizations can learn in detail about the factors affecting and impacting market demographics. Alongside, they can uncover new business prospects, tap untouched markets that might extend beyond geographical boundaries, and expand the horizons.
3. They can understand the consumer better, know their preferences, age, spending habits, social media behavior, which product is preferred the most, etc., and offer them customized services accordingly. This consequently leads to increased loyalty and lesser churned out rate.

Data mining is described as the procedure of extracting hidden information from any larger raw dataset. It means with one or more software; the data patterns can be examined in huge data. It has applications in many areas, like science and research.

As a data mining application, companies can adapt more about their clients and can execute more efficient schemes for a number of business functions to leverage the resources in a more optimized and perceptive manner. This assists the companies to get closer to the goals and make better results.

It involves efficient data compilation, warehousing, and computer processing. To segment the data and to estimate the possibility of future events, it utilizes composite mathematical algorithms. It is also termed as knowledge discovery in databases (KDD). The main features of data mining are automatic pattern predictions based on trends, behavior analysis. The focus is given to huge datasets and databases, for discovering and documenting the fact groups based on clustering that are not known previously.

The algorithms of data mining are the step-by-step definition of the process utilized to bring meaning to the set of information. Some of them are quite simple and need little to comprehend and execute and some are very composite and need significant learning and an attempt to implement. The algorithms could be of several forms that depend on the data to be undertaken and the outcome to attain. In this section, numbers of data mining algorithms are defined with its types.

4.1.3   Methods and techniques

In the field of EDM, a diverse range of approaches and procedures are used. As a general rule, categorization and classification are the most often encountered applications. Among the most widely used methodologies are neural networks, decision trees, regression, and cluster analysis, to name a few examples.

Classification algorithms: In general, classification is a data mining technique that classifies data into target categories or classes based on the frequency with which they exist in a collection of information. With the help of this tool, analyzing and forecasting results become much easier. Classification must be done on each instance in order to achieve accurate prediction of the target class for each case in the dataset as a whole. The classifier training algorithm makes use of preclassified examples in order to identify the set of parameters that must be considered for classification [12]. This technique, which is frequently used in the educational sector, is used to classify students according to certain characteristics such as their age and gender, their grades and other academic achievements, their motivation and behavior, as well as their demographic and geographic characteristics.

Clustering algorithms: Clustering analysis is a technique for generating new clusters from datasets that have already been established. During the data preprocessing step, it is beneficial to identify homogeneous groups that can be used as input into subsequent models. A cluster analysis can be used to analyze and contrast different types of things such as students, courses, instructors, and other similar entities, among others. In the field of prediction, the practice of making calculated assumptions about future events on the basis of evidence that has been thoroughly investigated is defined [13]. It is possible to forecast the relationship between one or more independent variables and one or more dependent variables using the regression method. When conducting research, it is critical to distinguish between independent variables and response variables as much as possible. A wide range of applications, including business planning, financial forecasting, time series prediction, and trend analysis, can be made using this technique. Predictive analytics is used in the educational business to produce predictions regarding students' academic performance [14]. Examples include enrollment forecasts, final grade predictions, dropout predictions, and other similar predictions.

Association rule mining algorithm: Analyzing the likelihood of elements in a collection being associated is a data mining approach known as "association." The rules that control the relationships between things that occur in close proximity to one another are known as "association rules." Most of the time, when it comes to the analysis of sales transactions, association rules are applied. In addition to sales promotions and direct marketing, catalog design, cross-sell marketing, and recognizing company trends are also possible applications for this type of finding [15]. This method, which is regulated by a set of rules, can be used to start new courses or to start new educational institutions.

There are a lot of benefits and uses for EDM that will be talked about in more detail below. Recent years have seen the publication of a number of research papers and studies that look at how data mining can be used in educational settings. It is planned to go into deeper detail on some of these eventually. There are a lot of ways EDM can be used. For example, it can be used to help make decisions about which courses students should take. It can also be used to make better predictions about how students will do.

K-nearest neighbor (KNN): KNN is a nonparametric approach for classifying data points based on their proximity and correlation with other accessible data. This technique makes the assumption that similar data points can be located in close proximity to one another. As a result, it attempts to determine the distance between data points, typically using Euclidean distance, and then assigns a category based on the most frequent or average category.

Neural networks: Often used in conjunction with deep learning algorithms, neural networks process training data by simulating the interconnectedness of the human brain via layers of nodes. Each node is composed of several components: inputs, weights, a bias (or threshold), and an output. If the output value exceeds a predefined threshold, the node "fires," or activates, transmitting data to the network's next layer. Neural networks acquire this mapping function by supervised learning, changing according to the loss function via the gradient descent process. When the cost function is close to or equal to zero, we can be confident that the model will produce the correct answer.

In the rest of the chapter, the Materials and Methods section discusses the data preprocessing section on the selected datasets. The proposed algorithm and its implementation are presented in Section 4. The Results and Discussion section includes the result and discussion of this study. Finally, the Conclusion section concludes the article, and future scope directions are highlighted.

4.1.4   Application areas of data mining

Data mining is frequently employed in a wide variety of fields. There are numerous commercial data mining systems available today, but this field faces numerous problems. Modern businesses cannot exist in a data lacuna. They must evolve and adapt to technological advancements and emerging digital trends in order to stay ahead of the competition. As a result, organizations now place a premium on remaining current with all advancements in the field of data science and analytics. Data mining is one of these data science processes. It entails the analysis of already created datasets in order to glean new and relevant information. By segmenting massive datasets, recognizing trends, and forecasting outcomes, complicated data mining algorithms enable businesses to make sense of raw data. Data mining techniques are frequently used by business intelligence and data analytic teams to aid in the extraction of knowledge specific to their organization and industry. Several data mining applications include the following.

Data mining in healthcare: The application of data mining in the health-care field has resulted in some outstanding outcomes. With the use of data mining, it is possible to analyze and discover some of the health-care practices that serve to ensure quality while also assisting in cost reduction.

Sales and marketing: Companies acquire a vast quantity of data about their customers and prospects. By observing consumer demographics and online user activity, organizations may use data to optimize their marketing campaigns, improving segmentation, cross-sell offers, and customer loyalty programs, generating higher return on investment (ROI) on marketing efforts. Predictive analytics can also allow teams to set expectations with their stakeholders, offering yield projections from any increases or cutbacks in marketing investment.

Data mining in fraud detection: The procedures employed to detect fraudulent activities proved to be time-consuming. Detecting fraud has gotten simpler as a result of the emergence of data mining techniques. With the use of data mining, it has become easier to spot trends in data and to take steps to protect the privacy of users' information.

Data mining in customer segmentation: It assists in the segmentation of customers into groups so that products and services can be tailored to meet their specific demands.

Operational optimization: Using data mining techniques, process mining reduces operational expenses, allowing firms to run more effectively. A corporate leader's decision-making process has been improved by this method, which identifies costly obstacles.

Data mining in banking and finance: With the advent of broad computerization in the sector of banking, it has become easier to do data analysis and interpretation. When it comes to company information, it may be utilized to determine the relationship between information about the firm and the prices that are prominent in the market.

Data mining in multimedia: It is one of the most recent ways that is catching on because of the increasing capacity to extract important data with high accuracy.

In this process, data are extracted from several types of multimedia sources, such as audio, text and hypertext, video and still images, and the data are turned into a numerical representation that may be shown in a variety of forms, such as HTML. This method can be used for a variety of tasks, such as grouping and classification, performing similarity checks, and identifying relationships.

Data mining in distributed architecture: It is becoming increasingly popular because it allows for the mining of large amounts of information that is kept in multiple locations within a firm or across multiple companies. In order to collect data from many sources and deliver appropriate insights and reports based on it, highly sophisticated algorithms are used.

Data mining in education: The application of data mining in the realm of education has resulted in the development of what is known as EDM. It aids in the prediction of students' learning tendencies by providing them with data. It also aids in the analysis of learning outcomes and the formulation of decisions based on the information gained. According to the education data mining community, it is a new discipline that focuses on developing techniques to investigate unique data types from the educational environment and using them to better understand students and learn from them.

It is becoming increasingly popular to use data mining technologies in the subject of education, as seen by the tremendous increase in interest. Development approaches for discovering information from data obtained from the educational environment are part of this growing topic, which is now under investigation. This technique differs from standard data mining techniques in that it explicitly employs many degrees of meaningful hierarchy in educational data, as opposed to traditional data mining techniques. EDM is concerned with the collecting, archiving, and analysis of data that are connected to student learning and evaluation in a formal setting. It is common for researchers conducting EDM studies to use approaches that have been pulled from a variety of sources, such as psychometrics, machine learning, data mining, educational statistics, information visualization, and computer modeling. An interactive loop is created by the implementation of data mining in educational systems, which includes the phases of formation, testing, and improvement. The knowledge that has been discovered should be entered into the system's cycle, and the guide should support and boost overall learning. The system is used to transform data into knowledge and to filter the knowledge obtained through mining in order to aid in decision-making processes.

4.2 Literature survey

To complete this study on predicting academic performance of the students using different data mining techniques, we came across different research and review papers. During literature study on this topic, we found that a most of the researcher of EDM communities are trying to develop a system which effectively and efficiently predict the academic performance of the students. Although a lot of data mining algorithms are development in the past like classification algorithms that effectively predict the class level of any datapoint in the data. Most of the researcher in the literature considered different aspects of student attributes in consideration while collecting data for the dataset. We have different categories of student's attributes like academic, personal, family, social and institutional, and all these attributes contribute in the development of predictive models for academic performance prediction [16]. EDM is becoming more popular nowadays as a result of the proliferation of electronic resources, the use of online educational tools, and the Internet. Numerous studies are being conducted to improve educational materials and technologies. By leveraging EDM techniques to forecast or analyze student performance and to assist students who are receiving less than satisfactory grades, an artificial neural network classifier model was created that can benefit both students and teachers in discovering knowledge from the massive amount of data available in the educational sector.

Sentiment analysis was used to better understand students' learning styles and study plans in order to improve instruction [17]. After removing behavioral information from students, a model was suggested using data mining approaches that achieved a 22.1% high accuracy after removing behavioral features. Additionally, it was discovered that applying ensemble methods resulted in a 25.8% improvement in accuracy. The academic dataset contained 473 cases, and the Bayesian classifier achieved a 70% accuracy rate. To characterize student dropouts, the Naïve Bayes' classifier, artificial neural network (ANN), KNN, and J48 were employed. KNN and decision trees with 10-fold cross-validation achieved 87% and 79.7% accuracy, respectively. By building a hyperplane, support-vector machines (SVMs) distinguish classes in high-dimensional space [18]. On health-related data, data mining techniques such as LR and multi-classifiers achieved amazing results. Decision trees employ optimal ways to identify or reach a specific aim in the real world. Combining this principle with the ability to accelerate the training process explains their extensive use in EDM. On a dataset of 15,150 instances, a decision tree was utilized to predict whether courses pass or fail; 85.92% accuracy was achieved [19]. Another most important algorithms are there in Data mining that help to increase the accuracy level of any data mining classification algorithms. We have FS techniques like filter and wrapper method that help to reduce the different attributes of any dataset that are not very helpful in making prediction on any class. So, in literature, we came across many FS techniques like CAE (CorrelationAttributeEval), IGAE (informationGainAttributeEval), and GRAE (GainRatioAttributeEval) with Ranker as search method and are mostly used in literature [20].

During literature review we focus our review toward two main features: first is to check that which attributes of the student mostly affect the academic performance of the students and second which classification algorithms are mostly used by researcher to predict the result or performance of the student in academics. The last and most important point is to check the importance of FS in the prediction of the academic result. And in most of the research, we found that FS improves the performance of any prediction model. According to Hung *et al.*, classification algorithms like SVM, RF, and neural networks can all be used to identify at-risk students. The new method was better than other methods at both accuracy and sensitivity in tests on two different datasets: one from a school and the other from a university [21]. The

K-means algorithm was used to study the challenge of detecting the amount of student participation in a similar way. Furthermore, using the a priori association rules method, the authors were able to construct a set of rulers that were associated with student involvement and academic success. Researchers discovered that students' levels of involvement and academic performance in an e-learning environment have a favorable relationship, according to the results of their experiments.

According to Helal *et al.*, students' socio-demographic characteristics as well as their university admission basis and attendance type can be taken into account when predicting their performance. Rule- and tree-based algorithms were shown to be the most interpretable by the authors' experiments, making them the most suitable for educational settings [22]. Zupanc and Bosnic added semantic coherence and consistency characteristics to an existing automated essay evaluation system. The authors demonstrated that their proposed approach gave superior semantic feedback to the writer through experimentation. Aside from that, the accuracy of its grading was superior to that of other cutting-edge automated essay evaluation systems. Two layers of machine learning were proposed by Xu *et al.* to track and predict student performance in degree programs. According to their simulations, the proposed strategy outperformed benchmark strategies [23]. In this paper, the author compared the accuracy, F-measure, and true positive rate of 11 machine learning models. For the measures listed above, they found that the decision tree method outperformed alternative classifiers. The number of scholars working in EDM has skyrocketed in the last several years.

It is possible to employ EDM in a wide range of applications, including user grouping and student performance prediction [24]. In order to better comprehend students, teachers, and their many attributes, academics are developing new statistical methodologies and machine learning algorithms. Data analysis to improve student and teacher performance is nothing new. As a result of recent developments in educational institutions, such as the increase in computing facilities and the introduction of web-based learning, researchers are developing new ways for analyzing educational data. The information can be obtained via admissions, registration, library management, syllabus, and course management systems. It is possible to forecast student performance based on data, and this study employs four machine learning methods to accomplish so: the decision tree, the random forest classifier, gradient boosting classifier, and extreme gradient boosting classifier, among others. In order to forecast student performance, researchers use a variety of categorization techniques [25].

The author of this paper also used decision tree techniques, neural networks, and linear discriminant analysis to identify students who were at risk of failing the course and divide them into three categories: low-, intermediate-, and high-risk students [26]. Using classification techniques, it was possible to develop a profile of students who were most likely to fail or succeed in their studies. In order to forecast students' achievement, the author looked at socio-demographic and educational data from the pupils. Researchers used the Chi-square Automatic Interaction Detector decision tree technique to construct a predictive model that can identify students who are struggling to acquire new material [27]. Use of the Naive Bayes (NB) classification by Pandey allowed him to accurately identify bright kids from those who were more mediocre. Based on their previous results, their program was able to accurately forecast students' final grades.

A comparative study was undertaken in 2012 in order to estimate the student's performance. Study participants were asked to choose from among several decision-tree algorithms to see which one best predicted students' grade [28]. After testing a number of different classifiers, they came to the conclusion that a classifier's precision and accuracy should be taken into consideration when deciding which one should be used. They found that the Classification and Regression Tree algorithm (CART) algorithm, which was made to look like the decision tree algorithm, was the best. Five machine learning categorization models are tested by Sekeroglu *et al.* to see which one best predicts student achievement in higher education. According to the researchers' findings, data preprocessing procedures boost prediction accuracy [29].

So, after review, we selected an academic dataset from the University of California Irvine (UCI) repository and tried to implement the selected classification algorithms on that. Now, in our next step, FS algorithms are also used on the selected dataset and select the top 10 attributes for our implementation with all the classification algorithms [30]. Romero and Ventura highlighted the following applications for EDM: student modeling, performance prediction, data visualization, social network analysis, feedback to help managers, planning and scheduling, grouping students, and identification of undesirable behaviors. To identify kids who are at risk of failing their first year of education, Pal employed the categorization technique to analyze data from prior years' student dropout statistics [31]. Decision tree approaches were employed in conjunction with information on the student's previous education, family income, and parents' education to forecast the list of students that required further attention in order to lower the drop-out rate. The results of this study show that the machine learning model can use current student dropout data to build a good prediction model [32]. A deeper knowledge of student behavior and learning styles is essential for academic institutions to effectively manage current study programs and educational practices.

Data mining techniques and models can be used as decision-support tools in education by reviewing datasets and establishing the significance of the influence of specific variables, resulting in more successful research and an overall improvement in educational quality [33]. As a result of EDM, colleges can do a better job of allocating resources to their students. Different data mining algorithms such as decision tree, link analysis, and decision forest were utilized to investigate the preferences of students for courses, as well as their completion rates and professions of enrollment [34]. It was discovered through this study that there is a relationship between course category and enrollment professions, and it was also discovered that data mining is important for curriculum development and marketing in the sphere of higher education These findings may be utilized as a guideline for marketing and curriculum development efforts in the future.

4.3   Materials and methods

4.3.1   Dataset description

Students from two Portuguese secondary schools were studied for this dataset. Students' demographic, social, and school-related information were gathered through school reports and questionnaires. There is a math (mat) dataset and a Portuguese language performance (pl) dataset (por). G3 is strongly linked to G2 and G1 objective attributes. Graduation is divided into three periods: G1, G2, and G3, with the latter two representing the first and second semesters, respectively. Predicting the outcome of G3 on its own is more difficult, but it is also more advantageous.

4.3.2 Classification algorithms

Classification is a data mining technique for sorting and classifying items in a collection. Each instance of data must be classified in order to accurately forecast its place in the target class. A categorization model, for example, might be used to divide loan applicants into three groups based on their credit risk: low, medium, and high. The following are a few of the classification techniques that have been chosen for use:

Naïve Bayes' algorithm: The Bayes' theorem can be used to solve classification issues using the Naïve Bayes' technique, a supervised learning process. In order to develop machine learning models that are accurate in a range of situations, this classifier offers a simple and effective classification technique [35]. It is possible to use the Naïve Bayesian classifier to categorize datasets and to classify datasets using Bayes' theorem and the assumption that the predictors are independent. It is simple to build a Naïve Bayesian model since it does not require complicated iterative parameter estimations. For huge datasets in particular, it is a success. Classifiers that are more complicated are often outperformed by the Naïve Bayesian classifier because of its simplicity. Since it routinely beats more complicated categorization algorithms in a wide range of situations, it has become an increasingly popular tool. In order to arrive at the posterior probability, $P(c|x)$, we can use the Bayes' theorem to combine the prior probabilities: $P(x)$ and $P(x|c)$. Based on Naïve Bayes' classification, a classifier (c) is decided by a predictor (x) value that has no bearing on the other predictors' values. The scientific literature refers to this as class conditional independence.

Random forest algorithm: Random forests (also known as random decision forests) are an ensemble learning technique for classification and regression problems that involves training a large number of decision trees in a distributed form. Random forests are useful for classifying problems because they produce the classification that was selected by the majority of trees in the forest during classification. It is possible to find this well-known machine learning method in many different configurations as part of the supervised learning strategy. For both classification and regression issues in machine learning, machine learning can be used [36]. When it comes to solving complicated problems, it uses the notion of ensemble learning, which is the act of merging multiple classifiers into one model. For the purpose of increasing the projected accuracy of a dataset, the Random Forest classifier "combines a large number of decision trees on different subsets of that dataset and takes an average." With the random forest, instead of relying on a single decision tree, it takes into account the projections from each tree and predicts the final outcome based on a majority of votes. When a forest contains an excessive number of trees, overfitting might become an issue. Trees are more accurate and less likely to appear in a forest with a large number of trees. Using a random forest to predict the class of a dataset improves the likelihood that certain trees will predict the correct output while other trees will not. All the trees, however, properly predict the correct outcome when taken together. In order for the classifier to be able to accurately predict outcomes rather than make educated guesses, the dataset's feature variable must have a few real values. The correlation between the forecasts of each tree must be extremely low.

Decision tree algorithm: In statistics, data mining, and machine learning, the decision tree algorithm, also known as induction of decision trees, is a predictive modeling tool. From the observed qualities of an object's goal value, it employs a decision tree [37]. Supervised learning approaches such as decision tree can be used to address classification and regression problems; however, it is more typically used to tackle classification difficulties. Each leaf node in a tree-structured classifier represents a classification result, with internal nodes relating to dataset features and branching corresponding to rule sets. In a decision tree, the decision node and the leaf node are two of the nodes that make up the tree's branches. Instead of making decisions, decision nodes have several branches, but leaf nodes only report the results of those decisions. Decisions and tests are based on the dataset's characteristics. Graphic representations of all conceivable outcomes are used in this strategy. This is why the term "decision tree" was coined: it expands outward in a tree-like form from the root node. The CART method, which stands for Classification and Regression Tree algorithm, is used to create a tree for the purpose of classification and regression. According to the answer, the tree is divided into subtrees in a decision tree, which is a sort of decision tree (yes or no).

MLP algorithm: The MLP differs from a linear perceptron in that it has multiple layers and does not activate in a linear fashion. It has the capability of separating data that are not linearly separable, among other things. MLPs are feedforward artificial neural networks that generate outputs from a collection of inputs. A directed graph combines the input and output layers of an MLP's input nodes together to form a single unit known as a directed graph unit. Backpropagation is used by MLP to train the network and improve its performance. MLP is a deep learning method that uses machine learning [38]. Given that it is a neural network connected to several layers in a directed graph, the signal flow through the nodes of an MLP is restricted to one direction only. There are no linear activation functions in this system; instead, all nodes, with the exception of the input nodes, have non-linear activation functions as their activation functions. An approach known as backpropagation is used by MLPs to learn from their mistakes. MLP is classified as a deep learning technique since it makes use of multiple layers of neurons. MLP is frequently utilized in research in computational neuroscience and parallel distributed processing. It is also commonly used for supervised learning tasks, which is why it is so popular. Speech and image recognition, as well as machine translation, are just a few of the many applications available today.

DT algorithm: DTs are scheduled rule logic entries that are table-formatted and contain conditions (represented by the row and column names) and actions (represented by the intersection points of the table's conditional cases). DTs are used to organize and schedule rule logic entries. DTs are particularly useful when dealing with business rules that have a number of different conditions to consider. A decision tree or a switch-case statement in a programming language can also represent the information in a DT. A DT, sometimes referred to as a cause–effect table, is an effective tool for determining the relationships between various inputs and their associated outputs. The DT is derived from a logical diagramming approach known as cause–effect graphing, which is why the term "cause-effect table" was coined. Developing tests are made considerably easier by using DTs. Using this tool, testers can investigate the consequences of diverse inputs and other software states on business rules that must be correctly implemented in software [39]. When it comes to developing and testing complicated business rules, it gives a consistent approach. Developers will be able to do a better job with the help of this tool. Complex business rules necessitate the use of an organized approach to preparing requirements. Complex logic is another use for it.

JRip algorithm: It is represented by this class as the implementation of a propositional rule learner. This method, which is an optimized variant of the IREP, was devised by William W. Cohen. It is named after him. It performs repeated incremental pruning in order to reduce the number of errors (RIPPER). With its bottom-up approach to rule identification and learning, JRip classifies instances in the training data into groups and then discovers the set of rules that apply to all members of each group. Techniques such as cross-validation and having a specific quantity of words are employed in order to avoid overfitting the model.

Linear regression algorithm: Using LR, the odds ratio may be calculated even when there are many explanatory variables present. A binomial distribution rather than a linear distribution is used as the response variable in this method, which is very similar to multiple linear regression. Observed occurrence odds ratios are used to determine the outcome of the experiment. Linear regression, a fundamental statistical regression approach, can be used to do predictive analysis and explain the link between continuous variables in a calm and straightforward way [40]. Linear regression is a statistical approach that develops linear relationships between independent and dependent variables in accordance with its name. As a result, linear regression is the name given to this technique. Simplified linear regression refers to linear regression with only one input variable when there are no other variables in the dataset. The term "multiple linear regression" refers to the fact that the equation contains many different input variables. The output of this model is a slanted straight line that depicts the relationship between the two variables under consideration.

4.3.3 FS algorithms

Methods for reducing the number of variables used in a model's prediction of a target variable are known as FS. One way to think about an algorithm for selecting new feature subsets is to think of it as an amalgamation of a search approach and an evaluation measure. In order to identify the algorithm with the lowest error rate, we may simply test all potential subsets of characteristics and see which one works best. By reducing redundant and superfluous data, FS is a simple but effective solution to this problem [41]. A better knowledge of the model or data can be gained by eliminating the irrelevant data, which increases accuracy and decreases computing time. As a fundamental machine learning technique, FS helps focus the use of variables on those that are most useful and efficient for a given machine learning system.

Correlation attribute evaluator: The correlation attribute is used to compare and contrast the attributes in respect to the target class, which is defined as follows: Pearson's correlation approach is used to determine the degree of correlation between each attribute and the target class attribute in each attribute. It takes nominal properties into account on a value basis, with each value acting as an indicator. The educational dataset is evaluated using a combination of this attribute evaluator and the search ranking method, which is applied in conjunction with each other [42]. A correlation coefficient (Pearson's correlation coefficient) between an attribute and a class is used to determine the value of the attribute. Nominal attributes are analyzed value by value, with each value serving as a signal of the next value in the analysis. When determining the overall correlation for a nominal attribute, a weighted average is utilized (Figure 4.1).

Information gain attribute evaluator: The for-attribute's information gain is equal to the difference between the training set's a priori Shannon entropy and the conditional entropy. If the outcome attribute can be categorized individually for each of the attribute values, mutual information is equal to the total entropy [43]. A reduction in entropy or surprise can be quantified by dividing a dataset according to the value of a random variable. In this situation, a smaller entropy group or group of samples and consequently less surprise are implied by a bigger information gain. Information is a statistic for measuring how shocking an event is in terms of the number of bits it contains. According to the probability of an event, incidents that are less likely to occur are better documented than those that are more likely [44]. In statistics, the probability distribution of a random variable is referred to as its entropy, and it is a measure of the amount of information it contains. An equal probability distribution, in

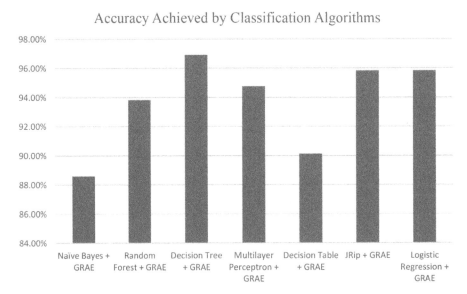

Figure 4.1   Graphical representation of accuracy level of classification algorithms

contrast to a skewed distribution, contains more information because all events have the same probability.

Gain ratio attribute evaluator: This method activates an evaluator for the gain ratio attribute and determines the value of an individual attribute by calculating the gain ratio of the class that contains the attribute. This method returns the evalua- tor's capabilities and allows an attribute evaluator to perform any additional post- processing on the given attribute collection [45].

4.3.4   *Data preprocessing phase*

Algorithm-1 illustrates the main methods for filling in missing data and resolving the problem of an imbalanced dataset, referred to as defects elimination utilizing the mean and median processes and resolving the imbalance problem. To begin developing the process model, this work performs data preprocessing at the lowest level. For data pre- processing, a proposed algorithm is presented that addresses the dataset's missing value and imbalance issues.

Algorithm 1:

Start here:

   # Handling Missing Value by Mean():

   1: Replace_Missing_Value_Mean(dataset)

   2: return dataset ['f1','f2','f3', ...,'fn']. replace ('0', mean())

   # Handling Missing Value by Median():

   3: Replace_Missing_Value_Median(dataset)

   4: return dataset ['f4','f5', ... ,'fn']. replace ('0', median())

   5: Train_Test_Data_Split(diabetes)

   # Handling imbalance problem by Oversampling:

   6: dataset_minority_oversampled(dataset)

   7: retrun resample(1, replace = True, n_samples = majority_class_instance)

   8: dataset = pd.concat([0, dataset_minority_oversampled])

   # Handling imbalance problem by Undersampling:

   9: dataset_majority_undersampled(dataset)

   10: retrun resample (1, replace = True, n_samples = minority_class_instance)

   11: dataset = pd.concat([0, dataset_ majority_undersampled])

End here.

The targeted output class has a range of 0–20, and there are 21 clusters in the ini- tial configuration. In terms of the classification task, this is an unreasonable solution

Table 4.1   New class level assigned to the dataset

Range of initial class given in the dataset	New cluster number assigned to the class level
Grade between 16 and 20	Class A
Grade between 14 and 15	Class B
Grade between 12 and 13	Class C
Grade between 10 and 11	Class D
Grade less or equal to 9	Class F

because it makes the classification process incredibly difficult, especially given the limited number of instances provided. In the given dataset, G1, G2, and G3 and the grade obtained by different students and for better results we find the final grade of the student by finding the average of all grades and create a new attribute named "Total Grade." As a result, I've assigned a group of clusters to a few class levels denoted by the letters A, B, C, D, and F in Table 4.1.

4.4   Implementation of the proposed algorithms

To identify the best classifiers that accurately generalized the data, we implemented various classification algorithms on a dataset of student academic performance. We chose different parameters for the algorithms that effectively analyze the dataset and increase their generalization accuracy [46]. Please keep in mind that all implemented classification algorithms undergo a 10-fold cross-validation to determine their correctness.

4.4.1   Model construction for the standard classifier

Numerous classification techniques were chosen and used to the dataset of student performance. We implement the following classification algorithms: Naïve Bayes, random forest, J48, MLP, DT, JRip, and LR. The table below summarizes the implementation results of various categorization algorithms using ten cross-validation (*k*-fold cross-validation) approaches. As our dataset is a balanced dataset with nearly equal distribution of data across five distinct classifications. According to Table 4.2, decision tree classification method had the greatest accuracy of 96.76% when compared to other classification algorithms such as Naïve Bayes, random forest, DT, MLP, JRip, and LR. As shown, the MLP method achieves the lowest accuracy of 84.59%. Random forest and JRip algorithms also obtained an acceptable level of accuracy, at 92.14% and 96.14%, respectively. To implement these algorithms, all of the dataset's attributes (up to 32) are considered. Other performance metrics such as mean absolute error (MAE), precision, recall, receiver operating curve (ROC) area, and F-measure are also considered in this table. As our dataset contains no outliers, we will use accuracy as our primary parameter for evaluating our classifier's effectiveness [47–57].

Table 4.2   Accuracy achieved by classification algorithm with all features of dataset

Classification algorithm	Accuracy (%)	MAE	Precision	Recall
Naïve Bayes + *k*-fold cross-validation	86.59	0.063	0.870	0.866
Random forest + *k*-fold cross-validation	92.14	0.118	0.924	0.921
Decision tree + *k*-fold cross-validation	96.76	0.017	0.968	0.968
MLP + *k*-fold cross-validation	84.59	0.078	0.846	0.846
DT + *k*-fold cross-validation	90.13	0.146	0.909	0.901
JRip + *k*-fold cross-validation	96.14	0.024	0.962	0.961
LR + *k*-fold cross-validation	87.51	0.049	0.877	0.875

When it comes to classifying datasets, accuracy is defined as the total number of correctly predicted items split into the total number of predictions generated by the algorithm. Graphical representation of *k*-fold cross-validation (classification algorithms with 10 cross-validation) implementation is shown in the figure below. According to the graph, when compared to other algorithms, the decision tree classification algorithm performs remarkably well.

The accuracy of a classification algorithm is defined as the ratio of correct predictions to total predictions generated by the algorithm for a particular dataset. Thus, accuracy as a performance metric for an algorithm is inadequate for issues involving imbalanced categorization [58–65]. The primary difficulty with the imbalance classification problem is that the overwhelming number of examples from the majority class will trump the minority class's examples. Which means that even the most unskilled models can get accuracy scores of up to 100%, depending on the severity of the class imbalance.

4.4.2   Implementation after attribute selection using ranker method

In this section, we will use the ranker search method to find the best attribute from the student's performance dataset that has the greatest effect on the classification algorithm's prediction accuracy. We attempted three alternative attribute evaluator methods with ranker search: CorrelationAttributeEval, InfoGainAttributeEval, and GainRatioAttributeEval. Following the implementation of the attribute evaluator algorithm, we picked ten distinct attributes that had the most influence on our prediction outcome. Table 4.3 illustrates the outcome of the complete procedure when applied to the student dataset. The first ten selected attributes from each technique are used to evaluate students' academic achievement and are determined to be the most predictive.

To identify the best classifiers that more accurately generalize the data, we apply various classification algorithms to a student performance dataset, selecting the parameters of the algorithms that most effectively analyze the data and enhance their generalization accuracy. Naïve Bayes, random forest, J48, MLP, DT, JRip, and LR are all implemented classification methods. Please keep in mind that all implemented classification algorithms undergo a 10-fold cross-validation to determine the algorithms accuracy when different parameter selections are used.

Implementation of classification algorithm after CAE FS: Classification, grouping, and regression algorithms all utilize a training dataset to establish weight factors that may be applied to previously unseen data for predictive purposes. Prior to executing a data mining technique, it is required to narrow down the training dataset to the most relevant attributes. Dimensionality reduction is the process of modifying a dataset in order to extract only the characteristics required for training. Due to its simplicity and computational efficiency, dimension reduction is critical since it minimizes overfitting. Thus, dimensionality reduction is critical throughout the data preprocessing phase. A correlation-based FS method selects attributes based on the usefulness of individual features for predicting the class label, as well as the degree of connection between them. We avoid strongly linked and irrelevant features. The CAE determines an attribute's value in a dataset by calculating the correlation between the attribute and the class attribute. Nominal qualities are assessed individually, with each value acting as a signal. A weighted average is used to generate an overall correlation for a nominal characteristic. We picked the top ten attributes with a threshold value larger than one using the aforementioned attribute evaluator CAE in conjunction with the ranker search strategy.

The following table summarizes the results of the implementation of several classification algorithms using CAE and the test option as k-fold cross-validation approaches. As shown in Table 4.4, the combination (LR + CAE + k-fold cross-validation) achieved the greatest accuracy of 97.84% when compared to other classification algorithms such as Naïve Bayes, random forest, decision tree, MLP, DT, and JRip. As can be seen, the MLP technique improves accuracy to 97.68%, which is significantly higher than the accuracy obtained without utilizing the FS approach. The remainder of the algorithms are also accurate to an acceptable level. Only the top 15 attributes of the dataset are considered when implementing these methods. Other performance metrics such as MAE, precision, and recall value are also considered in this table. As our dataset contains no outliers, we will use accuracy as our primary parameter for evaluating our classifier's effectiveness.

Table 4.3   Attribute selection with the help of ranker search method

Attribute evaluator	Attribute in decreasing order of their rank method
CorrelationAttributeEval (CAE)	31,32,33,15,21,1,7,8,14,27,13,4,28,3,30,2,22,11,16,9,19,25,24,5,29,26,20,18,23,17,12,10,6
InfoGainAttributeEval (IGAE)	32,33,31,15,21,1,9,7,14,11,28,27,3,10,4,16,12,22,2,20,19,18,5,23,17,6,29,26,30,24,8,25,13
GainRatioAttributeEval (GRAE)	32,33,31,15,21,1,3,7,14,16,28,27,4,9,11,12,22,18,10,2,20,19,5,23,17,6,25,30,26,13,24,29,8

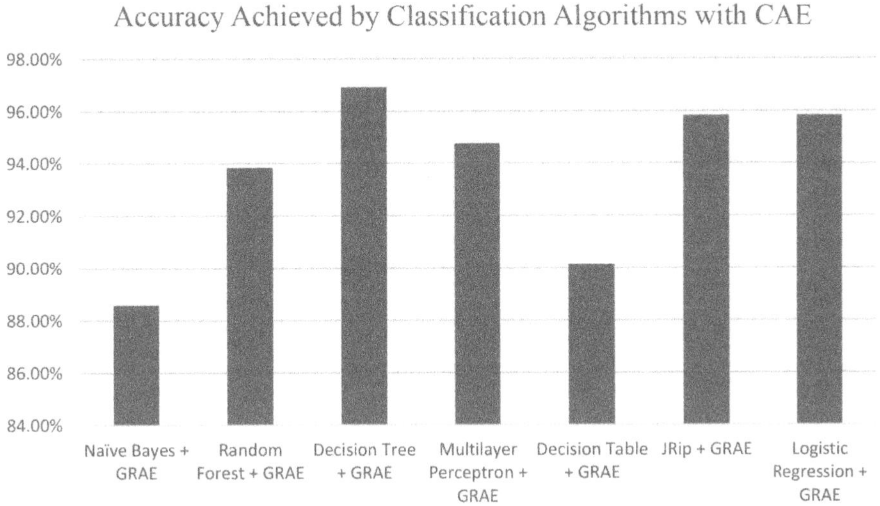

Accuracy Achieved by Classification Algorithms with CAE

Figure 4.2 *Graphical representation of accuracy level of classification algorithms with CAE*

Below Figure 4.2, is a graphical illustration of the implementation of the classification algorithms discussed previously using CAE and cross-validation (*k*-fold cross-validation) as testing methods? The graph clearly demonstrates that the LR algorithm outperforms all other algorithms considered. However, as illustrated in Figure 4.1, practically all classification systems obtain a prediction accuracy of greater than 90%.

Implementation of classification algorithm after IGAE FS: The strategy for selecting terms with the highest information gain scores is called information gain FS. Information gain quantifies the amount of information about a class prediction that is accessible in bits if all that is available is the presence of a feature and its associated class distribution. It determines the value of a characteristic by examining its correlation to the class. Nominal qualities are analyzed value by value, with each value acting as an indicator. A weighted average is used to determine the overall

Table 4.4 *Accuracy achieved by classification algorithm with CAE*

Classification algorithm	Accuracy (%)	MAE	Precision	Recall
Naïve Bayes + CAE + *k*-fold cross-validation	87.51	0.058	0.878	0.875
Random forest + CAE + *k*-fold cross-validation	95.83	0.061	0.959	0.958
Decision tree + CAE + *k*-fold cross-validation	96.91	0.0169	0.969	0.969
MLP + CAE + *k*-fold cross-validation	97.68	0.0172	0.977	0.977
DT + CAE + *k*-fold cross-validation	90.13	0.146	0.909	0.901
JRip+ CAE + *k*-fold cross-validation	95.53	0.0252	0.956	0.955
LR + CAE + *k*-fold cross-validation	97.84	0.0087	0.979	0.978

Table 4.5   Accuracy achieved by classification algorithm with IGAE

Classification algorithm	Accuracy (%)	MAE	Precision	Recall
Naïve Bayes + IGAE + *k*-fold cross-validation	87.98	0.0569	0.884	0.880
Random forest + IGAE + *k*-fold cross-validation	94.60	0.0782	0.947	0.946
Decision tree + IGAE + *k*-fold cross-validation	96.91	0.017	0.969	0.969
MLP + IGAE + *k*-fold cross-validation	95.37	0.032	0.954	0.954
DT+ IGAE + *k*-fold cross-validation	90.13	0.146	0.909	0.901
JRip+ IGAE + *k*-fold cross-validation	95.99	0.0239	0.960	0.960
LR + IGAE + *k*-fold cross-validation	94.60	0.0232	0.946	0.946

correlation of a nominal property. It determines the value of an attribute by calculating the information gained relative to the class.

The following Table 4.5 summarizes the results of implementing various classification algorithms using the IGAE as the FS algorithm and *k*-fold cross-validation as the test option method. According to Table 4.5, the (decision tree+ IGAE + *k*-fold cross-validation) achieved the highest accuracy of 96.91% when compared to other classification algorithms. As we can see, the MLP algorithm improves accuracy to 95.37%, which is significantly higher than the accuracy achieved without using the FS method. The remainder of the algorithms are also accurate to an acceptable level. Only the top 15 attributes of the dataset are considered when implementing these methods.

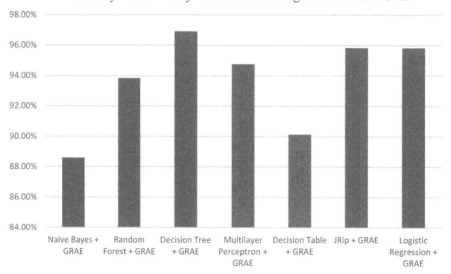

Figure 4.3   Graphical representation of accuracy level of classification algorithms with IGAE

Table 4.6   Accuracy achieved by classification algorithm with GRAE

Classification algorithm	Accuracy (%)	MAE	Precision	Recall
Naïve Bayes + GRAE + *k*-fold cross-validation	88.59	0.0565	0.889	0.886
Random forest + GRAE + *k*-fold cross-validation	93.83	0.074	0.939	0.938
Decision tree+ GRAE + *k*-fold cross-validation	96.91	0.017	0.969	0.969
MLP + GRAE + *k*-fold cross-validation	94.76	0.0283	0.948	0.948
DT+ GRAE + *k*-fold cross-validation	90.13	0.146	0.909	0.901
JRip+ GRAE + *k*-fold cross-validation	95.83	0.0232	0.959	0.958
LR + GRAE + *k*-fold cross-validation	95.83	0.017	0.959	0.958

Figure 4.3 illustrates the implementation of the above-mentioned classification algorithms using IGAE+ *k*-fold cross-validation. The graph demonstrates unequivocally that the decision tree classification algorithm outperforms all other techniques considered. However, as illustrated in Figure 4.1, practically all classification methods obtained greater than 87% prediction accuracy.

Implementation of classification algorithm after GRAE FS: The gain ratio is a change in the information gain that has the effect of lowering bias. Gain ratio is taken into account when selecting a characteristic since it takes into account the number and size of branches. This method compensates for the information gain by taking into account the intrinsic information contained within a split. The entropy of a given instance's distribution into branches is known as intrinsic information. As the amount of intrinsic information rises, the value of an attribute decreases as a result.

It determines the value of an attribute by calculating the gain ratio relative to the class. The following table summarizes the outcomes of implementing several classification algorithms using the GRAE as the FS algorithm and *k*-fold cross-validation as the test option method. According to Table 4.6, the decision tree+ GRAE + *k*-fold cross-validation achieved the greatest accuracy of 96.91 %, when compared to other classification algorithms. As can be seen, the MLP technique improves accuracy to 94.76%, which is significantly higher than the accuracy obtained without utilizing the FS approach. The remainder of the algorithms are also accurate to an acceptable level. Only the top 15 attributes of the dataset are considered when implementing these methods.

Below Figure 4.4. is a graphical representation of the above-mentioned classification algorithms implemented using the GRAE+ *k*-fold cross-validation approach. The graph clearly demonstrates that the decision tree+ GRAE + *k*-fold cross-validation technique outperforms all other algorithms considered. However, as illustrated in Figure 4.1, practically all classification algorithms obtain a prediction accuracy of greater than 88%.

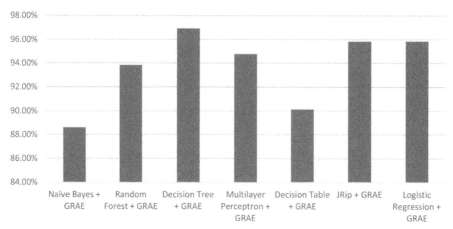

Figure 4.4   Graphical representation of accuracy level of classification algorithms with GRAE

4.5   Result analysis and discussion

A comparative examination of all of the implemented classification algorithms is presented in Figure 4.5. To begin, we evaluate the prediction accuracy of classification algorithms with FS (CAE, IGAF, and GRAF) approaches, using *k*-fold cross-validation as a testing method.

As seen in the following table, we can analyze each method separately:

Naïve Bayes' classification algorithm: *k*-fold cross-validation was used to test three alternative FS strategies. Naïve Bayes + GRAE + *k*-fold cross-validation performed incredibly well on the given dataset and achieved the maximum accuracy of 88.59% in our observations. According to Table 4.7, the classification algorithm that did not use FS method had the lowest accuracy of all FS methods (CAE, IGAE, and GRAE). With the FS algorithm, the Naïve Bayes' algorithm gains a maximum improvement of more than 2%.

Random forest classification algorithm: Random forest + CAE + *k*-fold cross-validation worked remarkably well on the supplied dataset, with a maximum accuracy of 95.83%. According to Table 4.7, the classification algorithm without employing FS method had the lowest accuracy of all FS methods (CAE, IGAE, and GRAE).

Decision tree classification algorithm: Decision tree+ CAE + *k*-fold cross-validation worked remarkably well on the supplied dataset, with a maximum accuracy of 96.91%. According to Table 4.7, the classification algorithm without employing FS method had the lowest accuracy of all FS methods (CAE, IGAE, and GRAE).

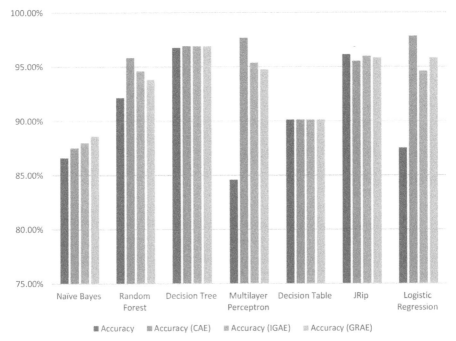

Figure 4.5   Graphical representation of classification algorithm with accuracy using CAE, IGAE, and GRAE

MLP classification algorithm: MLP + CAE + *k*-fold cross-validation performed remarkably well compared to other combinations on the given dataset, achieving maximum accuracy of up to 97.68% (see Table 4.7). According to the table, the classification algorithm based on FS achieved the highest accuracy. The FS approach provides a maximum improvement of more than 13% over MLP.

Table 4.7   Classification algorithm with accuracy using CAE, IGAE, and GRAE

Classification algorithms	Accuracy (%)	Accuracy (CAE) (%)	Accuracy (IGAE) (%)	Accuracy (GRAE) (%)
Naïve Bayes	86.59	87.51	87.98	88.59
Random forest	92.14	95.83	94.60	93.83
Decision tree	96.76	96.91	96.91	96.91
MLP	84.59	97.68	95.37	94.76
DT	90.13	90.13	90.13	90.13
JRip	96.14	95.53	95.99	95.83
LR	87.51	97.84	94.60	95.83

DT classification algorithm From Table 4.7, it is clear that DT classification algorithm without using FS method (CAE, IGAE, GRAE) achieved the same accuracy as with all features of the dataset.

JRip classification algorithm: When using a FS technique, the JRip algorithm's prediction accuracy is slightly reduced.

LR classification algorithm: LR + CAE + k-fold cross-validation performed remarkably well compared to other combinations on the supplied dataset, achieving the maximum accuracy of 97.84% (Table 4.7). According to the table, the classification algorithm without employing FS method had the lowest accuracy of all FS methods (CAE, IGAE, and GRAE). With the FS algorithm, the highest improvement LR algorithm gains is more than 10%.

4.6   Conclusion

If we want to have a better knowledge of the algorithms, we need to conduct a thorough evaluation of algorithms using multiple performance metrics. Performance criteria such as accuracy, MAE, precision and recall, among others, are taken into account when developing the model. Different metrics are used to evaluate the predictability, goodness, and error measurement of various algorithms before a final decision is made on a particular method. Since each problem has its own unique collection of qualities and characteristics, it is hard to anticipate in advance which performance metrics are better for certain challenges, according to the literature review. Since this is the case, multiple measurements should be taken in order to improve the algorithm's performance. Different data mining techniques and FS procedures were evaluated on the dataset in question, with positive results. Each FS strategy that is used to build a classification algorithm enhances overall implementation performance, according to our findings.

References

[1]   Wang X., Mei X., Huang Q., Han Z., Huang C. 'Fine-grained learning performance prediction via adaptive sparse self-attention networks'. *Information Sciences*. 2021, vol. 545(2), pp. 223–40.

[2]   Romero C., Ventura S. 'Educational data mining and learning analytics: an updated survey'. *WIREs Data Mining and Knowledge Discovery*. 2020, vol. 10(3), pp. 25–37.

[3]   Iatrellis O., Savvas Ilias K.., Fitsilis P., Gerogiannis V.C. 'A two-phase machine learning approach for predicting student outcomes'. *Education and Information Technologies*. 2021, vol. 26(1), pp. 69–88.

[4]   Romero C., Ventura S. 'Educational data mining: a review of the state of the art'. *IEEE Transactions on Systems, Man, and Cybernetics, Part C*. 2010, vol. 40(6), pp. 601–18.

[5]   Jauhari F., Supianto A.A. 'Building student's performance decision tree classifier using boosting algorithm'. *Indonesian Journal of Electrical Engineering and Computer Science*. 2019, vol. 14(3), pp. 1298–304.

[6] Hamoud A.K., Hashim A.S., Awadh W.A. 'Predicting student performance in higher education institutions using decision tree analysis'. *International Journal of Interactive Multimedia and Artificial Intelligence*. 2018, vol. 5(2), pp. 26–31.

[7] Slater S., Joksimović S., Kovanovic V., Baker R.S., Gasevic D. 'Tools for educational data mining'. *Journal of Educational and Behavioral Statistics*. 2017, vol. 42(1), pp. 85–106.

[8] Sokkhey P., Okazaki T. 'Hybrid machine learning algorithms for predicting academic performance'. *International Journal of Advanced Computer Science and Applications*. 2020, vol. 11(1), pp. 32–41.

[9] Saa A.A., Al-Emran M., Shaalan K. 'Mining student information system records to predict students' academic performance'. *The International Conference on Advanced Machine Learning Technologies and Applications (AMLTA2019)*; Springer, Cham, Cairo, Egypt, 28–30 Mar; 2019. pp. 229–39.

[10] Yadav A., Alexander V., Mehta S. 'Case-based instruction in undergraduate engineering: does student confidence predict learning'. *The International Journal of Engineering Education*. 2019, vol. 35(1), pp. 25–34.

[11] Ruiz S., Urretavizcaya M., Rodríguez C., Fernández-Castro I. 'Predicting students' outcomes from emotional response in the classroom and attendance'. *Interactive Learning Environments*. 2020, vol. 28(1), pp. 107–29.

[12] Raga R.C., Raga J.D. 'Early prediction of student performance in blended learning courses using deep neural networks'. *2019 International Symposium on Educational Technology (ISET)*; Hradec Kralove, Czech Republic, 2–4 Jul; 2019. pp. 39–43.

[13] Kuzilek J., Vaclavek J., Zdrahal Z., Fuglik V. 'Analysing student VLE behaviour intensity and performance'. *European Conference on Technology Enhanced Learning*; Springer, Cham, Delft, The Netherlands, 16–19 Sep; 2019. pp. 587–90.

[14] Sokkhey P., Okazaki T. 'Comparative study of prediction models on high school student performance in mathematics'. *34th International Technical Conference on Circuits/Systems, Computers and Communications (ITC-CSCC)*; IEEE, JeJu, Korea (South), 23–26 Jun; 2019. pp. 1–4.

[15] Sharma A., Yadav D.P., Garg H., Kumar M., Sharma B., Koundal D. 'Bone cancer detection using feature extraction based machine learning model'. *Computational and Mathematical Methods in Medicine*. 2021, vol. 2021, pp. 1–13.

[16] Kumar M., Bajaj K., Sharma B., Narang S. 'A comparative performance assessment of optimized multilevel ensemble learning model with existing classifier models'. *Big Data*. 2021

[17] Moubayed A., Injadat M., Shami A., Lutfiyya H. 'Student engagement level in an e-learning environment: clustering using k-means'. *American Journal of Distance Education*. 2020, vol. 34(2), pp. 137–56.

[18] Moubayed A., Injadat M., Shami A., Lutfiyya H. 'Relationship between student engagement and performance in e-learning environment using association

rules'. IEEE World Engineering Education Conference (EDUNINE); Buenos Aires, Argentina, 11–14 Mar; 2018.

[19]   Yadav S.K., Pal S. 'Data mining: a prediction for performance improvement of engineering students using classification'. *Journal WCSIT*. 2012, vol. 2(2), pp. 51–6.

[20]   Ramesh V., Parkavi P., Ramar K. 'Predicting student performance: a statistical and data mining approach'. *International Journal of Computer Applications*. 2013, vol. 63(8), pp. 35–9.

[21]   Hung J.-L., Shelton B.E., Yang J., Du X. 'Improving predictive modeling for at-risk student identification: a multistage approach'. *IEEE Transactions on Learning Technologies*. 2019, vol. 12(2), pp. 148–57.

[22]   Helal S., Li J., Liu L., *et al.* 'Predicting academic performance by considering student heterogeneity'. *Knowledge-Based Systems*. 2018, vol. 161, pp. 134–46.

[23]   Xu J., Moon K.H., van der Schaar M. 'A machine learning approach for tracking and predicting student performance in degree programs'. *IEEE Journal of Selected Topics in Signal Processing*. 2017, vol. 11(5), pp. 742–53.

[24]   Sekeroglu B., Dimililer K., Tuncal K. 'Student performance prediction and classification using machine learning algorithms'. *2019 8th International Conference on Educational and Information Technology, ICEIT 2019, Association for Computing Machinery*; Cambridge, 2–4 Mar; 2019. pp. 7–11.

[25]   Prabha S.L., Mohamed Shanavas A.R. 'Educational data mining applications'. *Operations Research and Applications: An International Journal*. 2014, vol. 1(1), pp. 23–9.

[26]   Baker R., Yacef K. 'The state of educational data mining in 2009: a review and future visions'. *Journal of Educational Data Mining*. 2009, vol. 1(1), pp. 3–17.

[27]   Romero C., Ventura S. 'Educational data mining: a review of the state of the art'. *IEEE Transactions on Systems, Man, and Cybernetics, Part C*. 2010, vol. 40(6), pp. 601–18.

[28]   Silva C., Fonseca J. 'Educational data mining: a literature review'. *Advances in Intelligent Systems and Computing*. 2016, vol. 520, pp. 87–94.

[29]   Ahmed A.B.E.D., Elaraby I.S. 'Data mining: a prediction for student's performance using classification method'. *World Journal of Computer Application and Technology*. 2014, vol. 2(2), pp. 43–7.

[30]   Baradwaj B.K., Pal S. 'Mining educational data to analyze student's performance'. *International Journal of Advanced Computer Science and Applications*. 2011, vol. 2(6), pp. 63–9.

[31]   Archana S., Elangovan K.D. 'Survey of classification techniques in data mining'. *International Journal of Computer Science and Mobile Applications*. 2009, vol. 2(2), pp. 65–71.

[32]   Khan I., Al Sadiri A., Ahmad A.R., Jabeur N. 'Tracking student performance in introductory programming by means of machine learning'. *4th MEC International Conference on Big Data and Smart City (ICBDSC)*; Muscat, Oman, 15–16 Jan; 2019. pp. 1–6.

[33] Al-Razgan M., Al-Khalifa A.S., Al-Khalifa H.S. 'Educational data mining: a systematic review of the published literature 2006-2013'. *Proceedings of the First International Conference on Advanced Data and Information Engineering (DaEng-2013)*; Singapore: Springer; 2014. pp. 711–19.

[34] Bhardwaj B.K., Pal S. 'Data mining: a prediction for performance improvement using classification'. *Computer Science Information Retrieval*. 2012, vol. 9(4), pp. 136–40.

[35] Baker R.S., Yacef K. 'The state of educational data mining in 2009: a review and future visions'. *Journal of Educational Data Mining*. 2009, vol. 1(1), pp. 3–17.

[36] Romero C., Ventura S. 'Educational data mining: a review of the state of the art'. *IEEE Transactions on Systems, Man, and Cybernetics, Part C*. 2010, vol. 40(6), pp. 601–18.

[37] Silva C., Fonseca J. 'Educational data mining: a literature review'. *Europe and MENA Cooperation Advances in Information and Communication Technologies*. Cham: Springer; 2017. pp. 87–94.

[38] Tsai C.-F., Tsai C.-T., Hung C.-S., Hwang P.-S. 'Data mining techniques for identifying students at risk of failing a computer proficiency test required for graduation'. *Australasian Journal of Educational Technology*. 2011, vol. 27(3), pp. 481–98.

[39] Li J., Li P., Niu W. 'Artificial intelligence applications in upper gastrointestinal cancers'. *The Lancet. Oncology*. 2020, vol. 21(1).

[40] Ma W., Adesope O.O., Nesbit J.C., Liu Q. 'Intelligent tutoring systems and learning outcomes: a meta-analysis'. *Journal of Educational Psychology*. 2014, vol. 106(4), pp. 901–18.

[41] Macfadyen L.P., Dawson S., Pardo A., Gasevic D. 'Embracing big data in complex educational systems: the learning analytics imperative and the policy challenge'. *Research & Practice in Assessment*. 2014, vol. 9, pp. 17–28.

[42] Mussack D., Flemming R., Schrater P., Cardoso-Leite P. 'Towards discovering problem similarity through deep learning: combining problem features and user behaviour'. *Proceedings of the 12th International Conference on Educational Data Mining (EDM 2019)*; Educational Data Mining Forum, 2019. pp. 615–18.

[43] Pu Y., Wu W., Jiang T. 'ATC framework: A fully automatic cognitive tracing model for student and educational contents'. *Proceedings of 12th International Conference on Educational Data Mining*; Educational Data Mining, 2019. pp. 635–38.

[44] Lahoura V., Singh H., Aggarwal A., *et al*. 'Cloud computing-based framework for breast cancer diagnosis using extreme learning machine'. *Diagnostics*. 2021, vol. 11(2), p. 241.

[45] Koundal D., Sharma B. 'Challenges and future directions in neutrosophic set-based medical image analysis' in *Neutrosophic set in medical image analysis*. Academic Press; 2019. pp. 313–43.

[46]   Singh K., Sharma B., Singh J., *et al.* 'Local statistics-based speckle reducing bilateral filter for medical ultrasound images'. *Mobile Networks and Applications*. 2020, vol. 25(6), pp. 2367–89.

[47]   Lahoura V., Singh H., Aggarwal A., *et al.* 'Cloud computing-based framework for breast cancer diagnosis using extreme learning machine'. *Diagnostics*. 2021, vol. 11(2), p. 241.

[48]   Haidar M., Kumar S. 'Smart healthcare system for biomedical and health care applications using aadhaar and blockchain'. *5th International Conference on Information Systems and Computer Networks, ISCON 2021*; Mathura, IEEE, 2022. pp. 1–5.

[49]   Kumar S., Cengiz K., Vimal S., Suresh A. 'Energy efficient resource migration based load balance mechanism for high traffic applications IoT'. *Wireless Personal Communications*. 2021, vol. 10(3), pp. 1–14.

[50]   Kumar S., Ranjan P., Radhakrishnan R., Tripathy M.R. 'Energy efficient multichannel MAC protocol for high traffic applications in heterogeneous wireless sensor networks'. *Recent Advances in Electrical & Electronic Engineering*. 2017, vol. 10(3), pp. 223–32.

[51]   Kumar S., Ranjan P., Ramaswami R., Tripathy M.R. 'Resource efficient clustering and next hop knowledge based routing in multiple heterogeneous wireless sensor networks'. *International Journal of Grid and High Performance Computing*. 2017, vol. 9(2), pp. 1–20.

[52]   Punhani A., Faujdar N., Kumar S. 'Design and evaluation of cubic torus Network-on-Chip architecture'. *International Journal of Innovative Technology and Exploring Engineering (IJITEE)*. 2019, vol. 8(6), pp. 1672–6.

[53]   Dubey G., Kumar S., Kumar S., Navaney P. 'Extended opinion lexicon and ML-based Sentiment analysis of tweets: a novel approach towards accurate classifier'. *International Journal of Computational Vision and Robotics*. 2020, vol. 10(6), pp. 505–21.

[54]   Kumar S., Ranjan P., Radhakrishnan R., Tripathy M.R. 'Energy aware distributed protocol for heterogeneous wireless sensor network'. *International Journal of Control and Automation*. 2015, vol. 8(10), pp. 421–30.

[55]   Singh P., Bansal A., Kamal A.E., Kumar S. 'Road surface quality monitoring using machine learning algorithm' in Reddy A.N.R., Marla D., Favorskaya M.N., Satapathy S.C. (eds.). *Intelligent Manufacturing and Energy Sustainability. Smart Innovation, Systems and Technologies*. 265. Singapore: Springer; 2022.

[56]   Sharma A., Awasthi Y., Kumar S. 'The role of blockchain, AI and iot for smart road traffic management system'. *IEEE India Council International Subsections Conference (INDISCON)*; Visakhapatnam, India, IEEE, 2020. pp. 289–96.

[57]   Kumar S., Ranjan P., Singh P., Tripathy M.R. 'Design and implementation of fault tolerance technique for internet of things (iot)'. *12th International Conference on Computational Intelligence and Communication Networks (CICN)*; Bhimtal, India, IEEE, 2020. pp. 154–59.

[58] Singh P., Bansal A., Kumar S. 'Performance analysis of various information platforms for recognizing the quality of indian roads'. *10th International Conference on Cloud Computing, Data Science & Engineering (Confluence)*; Noida, India, IEEE, 2020. pp. 63–76.

[59] Reghu S., Kumar S. 'Development of robust infrastructure in networking to survive a disaster'. *4th International Conference on Information Systems and Computer Networks (ISCON)*; Mathura, India, IEEE, 2019. pp. 250–55.

[60] Kumar S., Ranjan P., Ramaswami R., Tripathy M.R. 'An NS3 implementation of physical layer based on 802.11 for utility maximization of WSN'. *International Conference on Computational Intelligence and Communication Networks (CICN)*; Jabalpur, India, IEEE, 2016. pp. 79–84.

[61] Kumar S., Ranjan P., Ramaswami R., Tripathy M.R. 'A utility maximization approach to MAC layer channel access and forwarding'. *Progress in Electromagnetics Research Symposium*; Prague, Czech Republic, The Electromagnetics Academy, 2015. pp. 2363–67.

[62] Kumar S., Ranjan P., Ramaswami R., Tripathy M.R. 'EMEEDP: enhanced multi-hop energy efficient distributed protocol for heterogeneous wireless sensor network'. *Fifth International Conference on Communication Systems and Network Technologies*; Gwalior, India, IEEE, 2015. pp. 194–200.

[63] Kumar S., Ranjan P., Ramaswami R. 'Energy optimization in distributed localized wireless sensor networks'. 2014 International Conference on Issues and Challenges in Intelligent Computing Techniques (ICICT), Publisher: IEEE; Ghaziabad, India, 7–8 Feb; 2014.

[64] Sudhakaran S., Kumar S., Ranjan P., Tripathy M.R. 'Blockchain-based transparent and secure decentralized algorithm'. *International Conference on Intelligent Computing and Smart Communication 2019. Algorithms for Intelligent Systems*; THDC-Institute of Hydropower Engineering and Technology, Tehri, India, Singapore: Springer, 2020. pp. 327–36.

[65] Kumar S. *Evolution of software-defined networking foundations for iot and 5G mobile networks*. Hershey, PA: IGI Publisher; 2020. p. 350.

Chapter 5

Accurate management and progression of Big Data Analysis

Tanmay Sinha[1], Narsepalli Pradyumna[1], and K B Sowmya[1]

Statistical investigations are concerned with circumstances including arranging, information assortment, association of data, and scrutiny of compiled data, conversion, and exposure in a clear and chosen procedure. To do so, research techniques can be distinguished in two different ways: conclusion overviews and statistical surveying. In assessments of public sentiment, the primary objective is to assemble data about deciding subjects dependent on close-to-home meetings. Statistical surveying is directed through the market investigation of a specific item. Descriptive statistics are responsible for collection, association, depiction of information, estimation, and translation of coefficients, whereas inductive or inferential statistics, also known as the proportion of vulnerability or techniques that rely on likelihood hypothesis, are responsible for investigation and understanding of information related to an edge of vulnerability. In statistics, we look at how to use tables and charts. The tables organise and classify the data, while the graphics convey the information in a clear and easy manner, aiding in goal attainment.

5.1 Introduction

In today's world, most things are digital in nature. Every nine out of ten works are done digitally from buying vegetables to booking shows and so on. Our every digital transaction needs to be stored for safety reasons and for customer satisfaction and their preferences. So, a digital era indicates an enormous amount of data to be stored and processed. Therefore, we can also say that this is an era of data.

First of all, we will start with the definition of data which is a combination of the amount, pictures, or characters on which tasks are executed by a personal computer that can be renounced and passed on in the form of electrical signals and subsequently taped on attractive, optical, or mechanical account media. Big Data is also a kind of data having immense dimensions. Big Data is a term, which depicts

[1]Department of Electronics and Communication Engineering, Bengaluru, India

an array of information having enormous volume but increasing exponentially with increasing time. In a nutshell, this information is so enormous along with the complexity that no other traditional data the executive's device can cache or process in a fruitful manner. Let it be whether to increase customer friendliness or ease of deduction by the officials, we need to process and store data. This process is called Big Data Analysis.

In every place, whether service-oriented or not, data need to be stored. There are several important fields such as e-commerce, finance, education, healthcare, banking, social networking, purchase at department/grocery stores, and so on. Day-by-day, the exposure to such tremendous data is becoming increasingly common and one can achieve insights for supporting high-quality business choices and can form more experienced and customised higher quality services. For gathering data as per the requirement, MapReduce program is used enormously. To operate such Big Data and to attain greater performance, proper scheduling is essential. This scheduling is basically a job-giving technique to available resources in a way so that starvation can be reduced to a large extent and resources that are abundant can be utilised to a maximum. Enormous information is a term generally used for the processes that are unconventional and discoveries that are assumed to accumulate, compose, process, and arrange experiences from data sets that are extremely big. Presently, there will be discussion and gathering of extensive information at the crucial level that will specify the normal ideas which one may spill over in mind during investigation of the subject. Furthermore, we will ponder upon the procedures and advancements, which are employed right now in this process.

For the storage of huge quantity of information to reveal hidden patterns, correlations, and other insights, Big Data is used extensively. At present, analysis of data and decoding with immediate responses is possible, which is an attempt that is slower in rate and has less efficiency with more conventional business intelligence solutions. Big Data Analytics help organisations utilise their information and new opportunities are identified with usage of the same. A huge amount of information in a database can be compiled using Big Data, and retrieval of data and information from that database is also easy.

5.1.1   Examples of Big Data

As we have discussed, in the present data era, we have enormous data from various sources that need to be processed for proper usage and storage. Some of the examples of Big Data are as follows:

- Social Media

1. According to a measurement, social media can store more than 500 terabytes of information, which are new and cached into the databases of Facebook. This information is later created in the form of photographs along with video transfers, message trades, and also enables putting remarks, and so on.

2. Enables sending 500 million tweets
3. Enables sending 294 billion emails
4. Creation of 4 petabytes of data on Facebook
5. Creation of 4 terabytes of data using each connected car
6. Enables sending 65 billion messages on WhatsApp

- Enable almost 5 billion searches
- Stock markets in India generate about 1 terabyte of data every day.
- All our daily usage apps/websites have Big Data as we can easily say that companies like Amazon and Uber and banking apps and websites, etc., have more than a million customers; data regarding each and every product they are selling along with their sellers and data regarding various functionalities like shipment tracking, etc.
- We can consider various other applications like a self-driving car, UAVs, monitoring systems, anomaly detection, and many others, as depicted in Figure 5.1.

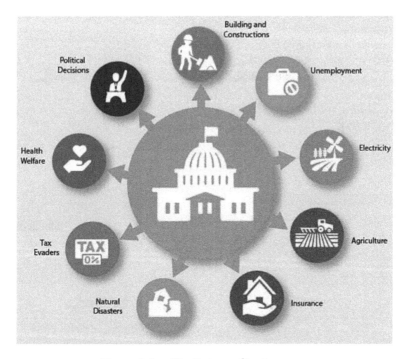

Figure 5.1   Big Data application areas

5.2   Big Data Analysis

Big Data is never accessed without proper processing since it makes the usage of data very difficult. Processing steps are used for identifying hidden patterns, market trends, and consumer preferences for the benefit of organisational decision-making.

The first step for Big Data Analysis is collecting the data but the raw data we collect from our sources may it be some websites or apps or any other platforms are unusable. We need to process and convert the enormous data set into meaningful data, which can be used by the organisation. This step is called Data Mining. This step is also called Knowledge Discovery in Databases. In this step, we derive crude but essential information from the data set. There are various methods for doing this like k-nearest neighbors (KNN), clustering, regression, association rules, sequential patterns, etc.

The second step is the actual analysis of processed data depending upon the need. We can use various machine learning algorithms and select the one/more data columns for solving the problem.

This combination of steps is called Big Data Analytics, i.e., Data collection – Raw data, Data mining – Mined data, and Data analysis.

Mined data can be classified as follows (see Figure 5.2):

- statistics
- machine learning
- visualisation
- information science
- database technology
- other disciplines

5.2.1   Life cycle of Big Data

The history of Big Data lies around the late nineteenth century. The first data overload came into picture in 1881 while calculating the census of 1880. To solve all the problems faced, Hollerith Tabulating Machine was developed which cut the processing

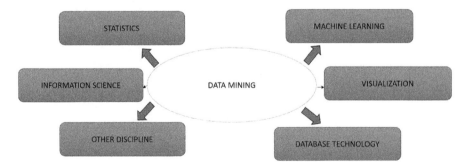

Figure 5.2   Uses of mined data

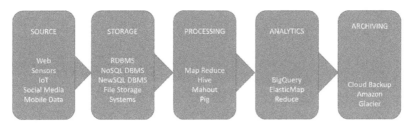

Figure 5.3   Different stages of Big Data Analysis

of data from 10 years labour work to 1 year. Following that, a German-Austrian Engineer Fritz Pfleumer developed a magnetic data storage on tape in 1928. This magnetic data storage was believed to store digital data. Another notable moment in the history of Big Data came into picture in 1948 where Shannon's information theory was evolved which laid the very basic functional block of today's information infrastructure. In 1970, Edgar F. Codd from IBM gave 'relational database' which explained how the information in the large databases can be accessed without identifying the source or the structural framework. In 2001, the main characteristics of Big Data, i.e., three Vs were presented in the paper by Doug Laney thereby paving the basic framing of Big Data further ahead. In the same year, software-as-a-service was also shared with the public. After developing these many foundation blocks in the direction of Big Data, there was a need for an open source software utility, which would act as a framework for such data. So, Hadoop was developed in 2005. Before 2007, no name was given to such humongous data. In a Wired Article: 'The End of Theory: The Data Deluge Makes the Scientific Method Obsolete', this humongous data were given a name, i.e., Big Data. The stage so obtained in 2007 was the beginning of the era of Big Data Computing. In 2017, IBM study analysed that around 2.5 quintillion of data are created every day and around 90% of the total world's data is created in just 2 years. This is one of the most remarkable works done in the field of Big Data.

From different sources such as web, sensors, Internet of things (IoT), social media, mobile data, etc., Big Data is collected and then it is stored in different database systems such as RDBMS, File Storage System, etc. [1–10].

After the storage process, different processing techniques are applied and the large data sets stored are processed; processing techniques include MapReduce, Mahout, etc. After processing, analysis of data is done and finally it is archived with Cloud Backup or Amazon Glacier.

This whole process is shown in Figure 5.3.

5.2.2   Classification of the Big Data

Broadly, classification of the Big Data can be done in three major domains, as shown in Figure 5.4.

- Structured

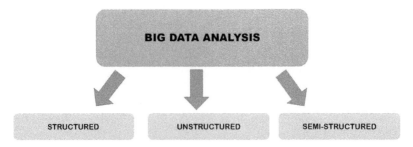

Figure 5.4   Classification for a Big Data Analysis

Organised information can be coined as a group of information, which can be set aside, directed, and handled as a properly fixed arrangement. With the passage of time, the software engineering abilities have progressed to a greater height and has led to processed formation which enables working with such required pieces of information (in this, configuration is more noticeable than time) and later on enables drawing a valid reason out of it. Besides, several issues have been developed due to procurement of an enormously large size of information having immense degree, which has led to shortening of common places due the fierceness of different zettabytes, which has led to large sizes of data [11–17].

• Unstructured

Basically, if any data whose form or structure is quite problematic to under-stand, such data or information can be termed as unstructured statistics. Despite the size being greater than any other data, there are quite a lot of problems or issues represented from this unstructured data as a way of preparing for figuring out a proper result out of the same. Coming to case studies, one of the most typical instances of unstructured data on record is assumed to be heterogeneous data delivery, which involves a combination of confidential and important content records, collection of snap shots and recordings, and few more data in the similar fashion. Nowadays, there is high abundance of data, which is readily available at the same moment with the institutions or the owners, or it can be said that the required basic data are available with the owners at any moment of time but the only difficulty is that they do not have the rough idea to get the required result or an incentive from that collective data keeping into consideration that the statistics available is in original or crude form or it can be said an unstructured organisation of the data [18–20].

• Semi-structured

Coming to semi-structured data, it includes both forms of statistics. So semi-structured can be designed as an organised or structured data structure but it cannot be said that it is structured to a great extent. Taking an instance of desk definition in DBMS, it can be said that semi-structure-based data is not at all structured data.

Basically, semi-structured data can be defined or said to be information, which is transcripted in an XML document.

5.2.3   Working of Big Data Analysis

Here in Figure 5.5, a typical flowchart has been given on how Big Data Analysis performs its job. It includes collection, processing, cleaning, and analysis of huge data sets which may help organisations to use their Big Data. We will see each process one by one.

a.   Collection of data: In this, data from various sources are collected. Data may be structured or unstructured and may vary from cloud to mobile applications.

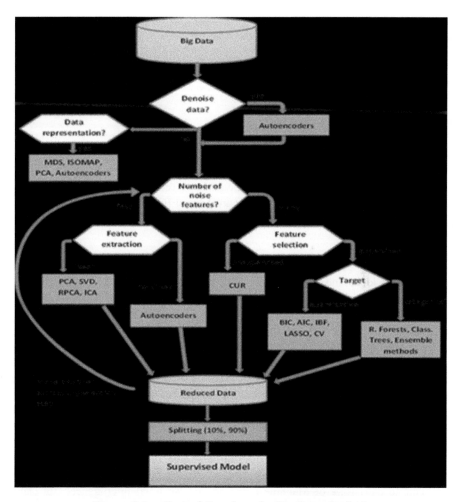

Figure 5.5   Typical flowchart for Big Data Analysis

These data will be stored in data warehouses from where it can be accessed with greater ease. Unstructured data may be stored in a data lake.

b. Processing of data: After the data are stored, the next step is to undergo analysis and then organise such that accuracy can be maintained. For processing the data, there are two ways which can be followed while doing, viz., batch processing and stream processing.

c. Cleaning of data: After processing of data, it is needed to enhance the quality of data and get more accurate results. If this cleaning of data is done properly, any duplicated data or irrelevant data will be eliminated.

d. Analysis of data: After cleaning of irrelevant data, we are left with the actual data needed. But still, conversion of those data sets into usable data might take time. For such purposes, we have few data analysis tools which may be followed to analyse the data more efficiently. Some of the data analysis tools are listed below:

i) Data mining
ii) Predictive analysis
ii) Deep learning
Implementation of Big Data Analytics can be understood from Figure 5.6.

5.2.4   Common flaws that undermine Big Data Analysis

- The size of the sample may not reflect the target population or process.
- All the data collected with time may not reflect the current scenario due to which efficiency of applying analytics to the situation reduces. There are many problems for proper management and progression of Big Data Analysis [21–24].

5.2.5   Advantages of Big Data Analysis

- Creative ideas and solutions can be derived from Big Data. Such creativity leads to better understanding of what the customer wants and targeting them more efficiently. Such data may be helpful for business purposes. Although it has the advantage of storing huge amounts of data within it and targeting customers more efficiently, there is one more advantage of such Big Data is that it helps in creating more growth opportunities. This may also lead to development of few new business areas [25–30].
- In the case of science and research, Big Data has led to great developments. Data science, one of the most trending topics nowadays, is possible only due to breakthroughs in the Big Data field since the more the data, the more accurate the prediction with proper algorithms.
- Real-time predictions, monitoring, and flaw detection are possible due to Big Data Analysis.
- Due to the nature of Machine Learning and Artificial Intelligence, Big Data Analytics is becoming an essential entity in the field.

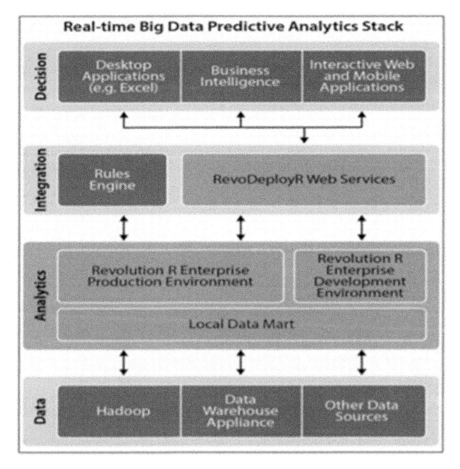

Figure 5.6   Big Data Analysis implementation layer

5.3.   Processing techniques

In processing Big Data, three major characteristics are taken into consideration. Those characteristics are volume of the data, velocity of the processing of the data, and wide variety of the data.

5.3.1   Traditional method

An example for traditional parallel and distributed processing involves huge data, e.g., top Spotify songs from 2010 to 2019 – by year. This data set can be found in Kaggle.com; in this data set, let us take a task like identifying the most liked music genre [31–34].

For completing this task using the traditional method:

1. Step 1: The whole data are split into small blocks and stored in different systems.
2. Step 2: Find the highest recurring genre for each part stored on the corresponding machine.
3. Step 3: Results are taken from each machine to produce the final output.

Some of the problems discovered in traditional methods are as follows:

1. **Critical path problem**: The path may get extremely long for some applications due to dividing data without proper management. The time which it takes to finish the task without delaying the next milestone or the actual completion date. Therefore, if there are any delays, the entire work will be delayed.
2. **Reliability problem:** In case of any hardware or software problem, the data will not be available which reduces its reliability. The management of this type of problem is a challenge.
3. **Splitting data issue:** The way to divide the data among systems and the place where to and how is something a problem; we need to find an efficient way to split the data to have no burden on any device.
4. **Single system may fail:** There should be a way for fault tolerance. For example, if one system is unable to produce the output for the final calculation, it should still be able to produce results depending on the other outputs.
5. **Accumulation of result:** We need a mechanism to accumulate the results produced by each machine to produce the final output.

Due to the above problems, a programmer needs to take the design issues into consideration while coding the application. To counter the problems that are present in traditional methods, we have generated an innovative way, i.e., MapReduce. It helps to take care of individually when using traditional approaches while processing large amounts of data in parallel.

MapReduce framework can be used by programmers to create complex applications with parallel computations without taking system issues into consideration.

5.3.2   MapReduce

MapReduce is a programming environment that allows for distributed and parallel processing of large data sets in a distributed environment.

As in its name, this framework is bi-staged:

1. Mapping
2. Reducing

It follows the same order as in its name: The first being comparison and the next being editor phase.

So the first is the task of comparing and creating key-value pairs based on count. This is the intermediate output of the process. This output is then entered into the editor.

The editor gets a pair of key values from several map jobs. The adjuster then consolidates these intermediate data sets (the intermediate key-value pair) into a smaller set of motors or key-value pairs, which is the final result.

As just mentioning the way cannot explain the process, let us take an example. Let us take one of the most popular examples: word count.

In this type, we will take a text file with many words in it. Let us assume that the content of the text file be as below:

Car, Bike, Cycle, Cycle, Bike, Car, Bike, Car, Bike, Cycle

The whole process can be divided into five steps

1. **Splitting the data**
2. **Mapping the data**
3. **Shuffling the data**
4. **Reducing the data**
5. **Final result**

Step 1: Splitting

Breaking the input into many chunks of data is done in this step. In this example, let us take the number of chunks to be three for ease of understanding.

Step 2: Mapping

Tokenise each mapper word and assign each token or word a hard-coded value (1). The reason for setting the hard-coded value to one is because we consider each word to be unique and appear once. This creates a list of key-value pairs, and the key is a single unit. Words and values are one. Therefore, in the first row (Car, Bike, Cycle), there are three key-value pairs – Car(1), Bike(1), Cycle(1). This process is repeated at all the nodes.

Step 3: Shuffling

The sorting and shuffling partition process is executed and all the same keyed ordered pairs are sent to each corresponding reducer. After this phase, each reducer has a list of values and a unique key corresponding to each value.

Step 4: Reducing

Now the reducer counts the values that exist in its list of values. As shown in the figure, reducer gets a list of values that are [1, 1, 1] for key Car. It then counts the number of 1 second in the list and returns the final output as – Car, 3.

Step 5: Final output

All output pairs are then collected and written to the output file. The process is pictorially shown in Figure 5.7.

5.3.3   *Advantages of MapReduce*

1. **Parallel processing**
2. **Data locality**

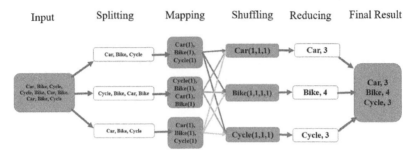

Figure 5.7   Word count overview

Parallel processing

MapReduce divides the job into multiple nodes, each node processing part of the job at the same time. As such, MapReduce is based on the divide-and-conquer paradigm and is useful for processing data at different nodes. Processing data in parallel at multiple nodes instead at a single node as conventional methods suggest significantly reduces the time it takes to process the data. It can also be called distributed processing as processing is distributed among different systems.

Data locality

In the case of data locality, the transfer of data from distinct data nodes to a single node, which is the processing unit for various processes does not happen at all. The nodes which are the processing units are further shared with the data nodes so as to make sure that the processing is going to take place at data nodes only when the case of MapReduce is taken into account.

Assuming the case of traditional systems, the data are first brought near to a processing device to process the same. But if the data become too large to be processed, sharing the same to processing nodes becomes problematic and thus causes problems, which are listed below:

- Poor cost-to-network performance ratio. It is costly to share data between nodes and it degrades the network performance.
- Processing the data at a single node causes a lot of delay.
- Processing nodes may overload and fail.

At present, MapReduce is one of the solutions, which is utilised to tackle the problem stated above by involving or deploying the units of processing into the data considered.

Thus, it can be observed in Figure 5.8 that the considered data are further shared among numerous nodes wherein each node is performing the processing step, which means processing some amount of data there itself.

Coming to the benefits associated with the same, few of them are listed below:

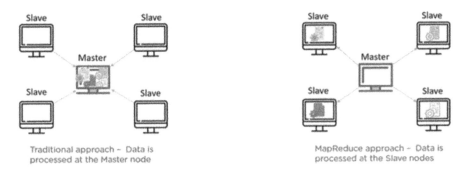

Figure 5.8   MapReduce approach for processing and data locality

1. Moving the processor to the data is very cost effective.
2. Reduced processing time.
3. Removes overburdening of any node.

5.4   Cyber crime

The first thing to be understood is cybercrime. Cybercrime can be explained as a virtual weapon to do illegal work relating to online stuff. This online stuff includes committing fraudism and child trafficking in unseen videos. In the present world, cybercrime has grown quite rapidly, which has a significant impact on the gross business and the economy worldwide. Digital hoodlums who are using the complex assault are growing each day in a progressive manner, and the hostile techniques utilised by them have become inadequate with respect to the development that is going on in the fields of knowledge and insights associated with it. Taking Big Data into account, it is doing a huge transformation in the perspective, which leans towards the developments that has been done or is going on in dangers relating to cybercrime. Coming to private or confidential data, each individual person possesses a unique identification card. This card encloses each and every detail of that individual starting from name and date of birth to the fingerprints. As a result, all the information of an individual can be accessed by anyone. This information can be accessed by the expert hackers and the information might be hacked. The mechanical discovery that has been done in the field of Big Data has made it feasible and accountable to handle huge data that are expanded and unstructured. Those kinds of data include secured military operation, stockpilation, accumulation, and handling the characterised scope in a progressive manner. This examination of Big Data empowers the privileged arrangements done for the information and the knowledge of the risk to be known, keeping aside the malevolent or the suspicious exercises performed by the potentially distorted or the monstrous informational indices. Current advancements in the direction of Big Data flash the mechanical control for concise reactions additionally to acknowledge or justify the cybercrime dangers. One of the examples is upsetting obviously distinguished malware assaults.

There are many branches which deal with this problem of cybercrime. Few of them are listed here:

- Usage of Big Data in forensics
- Taking the control over phishing and pharming using Big Data Analytics
- Usage of the architectures of the Big Data for security purposes especially cybersecurity
- Accounting Big Data with respect to criminal usage of IoT
- Cryptography and humongous data
- Privacy preserving retrieval, transmission, processing, and analysis of huge data
- Data-intensive detection and prevention of online identity theft
- Access control of huge data
- Big Data Analytics for online social network threats
- Analysis of the malware and botnets by using Big Data
- Involving the techniques of the Big Data in the detection of the intrusion
- Using data mining and machine learning in anti-cybercrime
- Development of formal models and ontologies for taking into account online criminal behaviour
- Criminal abuse of huge data technologies and resources
- Steganography analysis and covert/subliminal channels
- Usage of Big Data in Denial of service (DoS)/distributed denial of service (DDoS) Défense
- Adversary-resilient Big Data technologies
- Standardisation advances in Big Data for cybersecurity

5.4.1   Different strategies in Big Data to help in various circumstances

Due to the rapid development in data science, it is difficult to sort apparatus and strategies systematically. Few of them are reviewed here.

MapReduce Basically, this can be stated as a design which is used for huge tasks parallely that can be performed efficiently. The efficiency of such a structure depends on the deployment of the internal correlation in the data sets considered. Normally, such a case is not accounted for when digital evidence is the central point involved, rather a part of the file classified which looks similar to a task suits efficiently when portrayed in the programming environment of MapReduce. When they take different tasks into consideration, one of the most common among them in the field of forensics is swapping of the parts of the file that is coming from the whole file system picture or from unallocated space to file types, which are predefined. These definite file types include algorithms involved in machine learning classification such as logistic regression, k-means clustering, support vector machines (SVM), and so on. These algorithms can be attached to the MapReduce paradigm if the individual involved in the analysis of the document tries to mold all the possibilities of the correlations among individual parts. A more consolidated approach in the same direction can be merging the classification algorithms with a decision tree. Such integration approach yields a higher accuracy with respect to individual approach.

Decision trees and random forests These methods are generally brought to give productive results in the case of extortion detection software. Here, the main target is to identify the factual expectations or the predictions in the huge data set. For such cases, situation odd exchanges or irregular pursuing conduct can be used depending on the application and the usage.

Audio forensics Independent learning strategies under the overall meaning of 'blind signal separation' give agreeable results in separating two superimposed speakers or a sound from background noise in sound forensics. Among likely plans, they rely upon numerical support to track down the base-connected signs.

Image forensics Grouping techniques are helpful in picture legal sciences additionally to audit enormous arrangements of hundreds or thousands of picture records as in to recognise dubious pictures from the rest.

Neural networks For complex example acknowledgment in network legal sciences, neural networks are appropriate. This is fundamentally a helpful approach where the progressive depictions of the document framework are utilised to prepare the network to distinguish typical conduct of an application. Following the occasion, the framework can be used subsequently to outline an execution course of events on a legitimate picture of a record framework. Such neural networks are additionally used to recognise network traffic yet do not yield significant degrees of exactness.

Another strategy is utilised, e.g., natural language processing procedures including Bayesian classifiers and independent calculations for gathering like k-means, which is effective for origin confirmation or characterisation of huge groups of unstructured texts, messages in explicit.

5.4.2 *Big Data Analytics and cybercrime*

Big Data Analytics is really helpful in tackling the issues related to cybercrime as it is mainly developed for holding large volumes of data. It is much more than just handling the data organisations and the reason why it is like that is because of the well-organised data algorithms that form data analysis structures. Also it is capable of identifying the variety of cybercrime either it is hacking or an online fraud and this is done with the help of pattern recognition technology which identifies the similarities by studying the data attack surroundings. Besides just tackling the issue, Big Data Analytics has such a nice framework that it can predict the crime before it occurs as it has the capability of reading data and drawing conclusions from it. But this case it works well if artificial intelligence and machine learning are incorporated into the same platform. This ability to alarm the organisations before the attack of crime is boon for it as it may help in protecting the confidential data and develop much better network guards. Stepwise representation is shown in Figure 5.9.

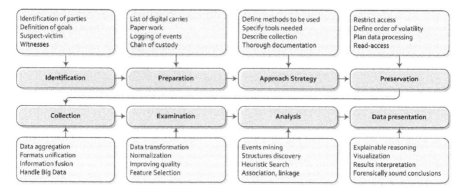

Figure 5.9   Big Data Analytics in cybersecurity

5.4.3   Security issues associated with Big Data

As we all know that Big Data is visualised in four dimensions, i.e., Volume, Variety, Velocity, and Veracity. Different mining algorithms and high-performance computing devices come into picture, and with the usage of such devices and algorithms, analysis can be performed with negligible time or consumption of least time. Keeping in mind all the advantages associated with Big Data, there are some high-level security issues relating to Big Data which is mentioned below:

a.   real-time analysis of data,
b.   confidential mannered storage of transaction logs and data linked with it,
c.   control access linked at granular level, and
d.   data provenance.

 For the analysis of humongous data, it is not compulsory to evaluate the same at a very high speed (approximately 30 00 00 000 m/s) rather it is important to store data securely. These security methodologies involve encryption and decryption of the data and these measures should be an integral part of the analysis because there are quite a lot of unethical experts who can extract the data without notifying anyone. Thus, there is a high requirement of giving an insight into Big Data Analysts about the problems or threats related to privacy of the data prevailing currently and proper involvement of such analysts is also expected for the development of much better tools to protect and prevent such threats or issues.

5.4.4   Big Data Analytics in digital forensics

Basically, digital forensics comes under forensic science whose focus is on identification, acquisition, processing, and analysis followed by formation of the report of the digital data stored. While Big Data is taken into consideration, there are few points which act as a challenge in the case of digital forensics. Considering the identification step, identifying the critical evidence out of humongous data available collectively seems impossible. Out of lakhs of data, there is a high probability that only 10% of the data obtained is useful from a forensic point of view. Traditionally, the data stayed in complete control of the forensic organisation itself but with the use of Big Data, for all data processing, forensic experts have to depend on the organisations to collect the data which simply increases the duration of analysis and find the facts among them. In many case studies, it is found that for just collecting and preserving the data, more than 24 hours are required. There are various characteristics of the data, viz., volume, intensity, etc., which do not match with the available methods in the present. So, examining and analysing such data in such a programming paradigm becomes challenging. Keeping in mind all the challenges faced in organising the data, special search and data mining techniques should be employed to make it more efficient. After organisation, the last step involved in digital forensics is presentation where the experts have to present the analysis or the findings done from the evidence in the court. Using traditional computers to present the analysis is easy compared to Big Data where the data is complex and providing the analysis of such data becomes tedious for the jury to understand and evaluate. Collectively, each step faces different challenges while using Big Data.

Thus, to face such challenges, a theoretical model of using Hadoop Distributed File system (HDFS) and cloud-based computing model is proposed. Hadoop or Apache Hadoop is basically an open source software that utilises the network of many computers to solve Big Data problems or huge data problems. To solve such Big Data problems, it uses the MapReduce framework, which is already explained. Coming to Hadoop Distributed File system, it is a file system component that is developed in such a way that it can store huge data sets effectively and efficiently and provides high bandwidth across the cluster for performing different applications of the end user.

Apart from HDFS, cloud-based computing models should be deployed in the case where Big Data is considered as such data contain terabytes of information. This architecture might prove to be cost effective and scalable.

5.5   Real-time edge analytics for Big Data in IoT

We all know that our tendencies are shifting from manual to autonomous devices. These devices are connected in a way thereby creating a chain of appliances transferring/sharing data and other resources. These are called IoT where the connection will be due to the internet/intranet/cloud. But if we keep all the processing in a single processor then the load will be huge as well as the response will be slower. For example, if we take an autonomous car then due to development in internet-based gadgets, e.g., traffic sensors, disseminated camcorders, and associated apparatuses, a surge of information is being created, which is handled utilising edge-registering assets. The image of a vehicle in front of it or the traffic signals should be processed faster to avoid the dangers of the road, and if we depend on cloud, e.g., then the appliance should first transfer the data to the cloud where it will process the whole information and send its reply in the form of a command to the respective functional unit. This will take a lot of time compared to the case where we can give the data required only for the command to the command unit. This can be achieved by Edge Analytics. In this we process the data from the input at the source itself thereby reducing the information transfer to the command unit thereby reducing the response time.

The ascent of Big Data acquires uncommon new advantages and opens a few application areas. The significant undertakings can misuse the IoT-created information and surmise the business esteem by performing information investigation. In particular, a few applications would require continuous edge examination to rapidly discover helpful relationships, client inclinations, shrouded designs, and other significant data that can help associations and chiefs to take increasingly educated business activities. These difficulties speak to a few open doors for analysts in the area to research various bearings including data combination, AI, and explanatory instruments structure.

The study of IoT-produced data is very important to meet the demands and satisfy the consumers. The conventional investigation methods will not be suitable due to the enormous data about various details like limits for various tasks like registrations, timeframes for various tasks, etc. The IoT-created Big Data has novel

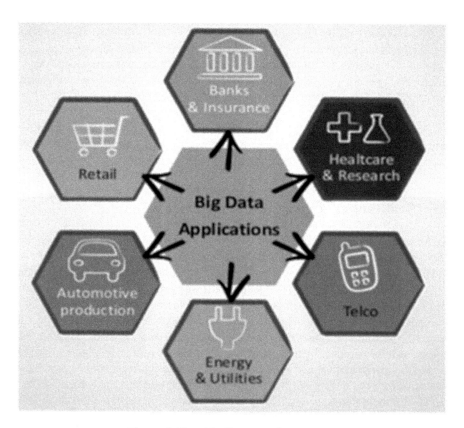

Figure 5.10   Big Data in edge systems

qualities, e.g., discontinuous clamour age, exceptionally unstructured, and dynamic nature. These qualities make it difficult for constant investigation. The authorities must take the issue of locally accessible and appropriate computational assets to overcome the difficulty in continuously handling and examining the collected data. The desire to improve the data handling has opened doors for interdisciplinary research and innovation, e.g., Machine learning, AI, pattern recognition.

Big Data Analytics has a wide range of applications. Some of the major applications of Big Data Analytics can be understood from the following web chart in Figure 5.10.

In banks and insurance companies, Big Data is very much helpful as it connects the organisation directly to the repository of customer financial data. Due to its capability to store large volumes of data securely, it has been proven really helpful for the healthcare and research industries. Prior to this, all the historical data and other important reports of patients, number of surgeries done per day in a hospital, etc., were kept in handmade records in the record room where chances of losing the record were quite high. With the advancement of Big Data, this problem has been resolved to a great extent. In the case of retail industries, the connection between users and large- and medium-sized industries has been developed with the advancement of Big Data. In the present scenario, social media is the link for all this and this social media has grown with the development of Big Data.

Therefore, Big Data has a wide range of applications in the present scenario and it is very helpful for accurate management of data.

5.6   Conclusion

With the knowledge of Big Data, we can minimise the effort for product enhancement, and accumulation of new data can help in increasing user friendliness using our understanding in logical programming. Logical programming has made the entire information examination simpler. Establishing patterns reduces the time to break down the enormous data in a cost-effective pattern. They speak to a real jump forward and an away from to acknowledge huge gains regarding proficiency, efficiency, income, and gainfulness. Big Data Analysis is very important for proper functioning in this digital era since everything is digital in nature. We need to be careful about our data leakages and while notifying our personal data. With the help and cooperation of both business and innovation experts, the age of Big Data will reach greater heights. Besides all this, Big Data Analytics is really helpful for medium and large organisations to connect with users all over the world through social media.

Transcript from one of the most alluring speakers on the Big Data circuit, Google's Avinash Kaushik, from his introduction at [12], 'A Big Data Imperative: Driving Big Action':

'I really don't generally think about the guarantee of information except if they can convey on that guarantee that accompanies the information'.

References

[1]   HongJu X., Fei W., FenMei W., XiuZhen W. 'Some key problems of data management in army data engineering based on big data'. *IEEE 2nd International Conference on Big Data Analysis (ICBDA)*; Beijing, China, IEEE, 2017. pp. 149–52.

[2]   Sagiroglu S., Sinanc D. 'Big data: a review'. *International Conference on Collaboration Technologies and Systems (CTS)*; San Diego, CA, IEEE, 2013. pp. 42–47.

[3]   Shalaginov A., Johnsen J.W., Franke K. 'Cyber-crime investigations in the era of big data'. *IEEE International Conference on Big Data (Big Data)*; Boston, MA, IEEE, 2017. pp. 3672–76.

[4]   Jo J., Joo I., Lee K. 'Constructing national geospatial big data platform: current status and future direction'. *IEEE 5th World Forum on Internet of Things (WF-IoT)*; Limerick, Ireland, IEEE, 2019. pp. 979–82.

[5]   Lee C.K.M., Yeung C.L., Cheng M.N. 'Research on iot based cyber physical system for industrial big data analytics'. *IEEE International Conference on Industrial Engineering and Engineering Management (IEEM)*; Singapore, IEEE, 2015. pp. 1855–59.

[6]   Mazumdar S., Wang J. 'Big data and cyber security: a visual analytics perspective' in Parkinson S., Crampton A., Hill R. (eds.). *Guide to Vulnerability Analysis for Computer Networks and Systems. Computer Communications and Networks*. Cham: Springer; 2018.

[7]   Terzi D.S., Terzi R., Sagiroglu S. 'Big data analytics for network anomaly detection from netflow data'. *International Conference on Computer Science and Engineering (UBMK)*; Antalya, Turkey, IEEE, 2017. pp. 592–97.

[8]   Azvine B., Jones A.. (eds.) 'Meeting the future challenges in cyber security' in Dastbaz M., Cochrane P. (eds.). *Industry 4.0 and Engineering for a Sustainable Future*. Cham: Springer; 2019.

[9]   Priyadarshini S.B.B., BhusanBagjadab A., Mishra B.K. 'The role of IoT and big data in modern technological arena: a comprehensive study' in Balas V., Solanki V., Kumar R., Khari M. (eds.). *Internet of Things and Big Data Analytics for Smart Generation. Intelligent Systems Reference Library*. 154. Cham: Springer; 2019.

[10]   Puthal D., Ranjan R., Nepal S., Chen J. 'IoT and Big Data: An Architecture with Data Flow and Security Issues' in Longo A. (ed.). *Cloud Infrastructures, Services, and IoT Systems for Smart Cities. IISSC 2017, CN4IoT 2017*. 189. Springer, Cham; 2018.

[11]   Praveena M.D.A., Bharathi B. 'A survey paper on Big Data analytics'. *International Conference on Information Communication and Embedded Systems (ICICES), Publisher: IEEE*; Chennai, India; 2017. pp. 1–9 pp..

[12]   Singh S., Singh N. 'Big Data analytics'. *2012 International Conference on Communication, Information & Computing Technology (ICCICT)*; 2012. pp. 1–4.

[13] Jayasingh B.B., Patra M.R., Mahesh D.B. 'Security issues and challenges of big data analytics and visualization'. *2nd International Conference on Contemporary Computing and Informatics (IC3I)*; Greater Noida, India, 14–17 Dec; 2016. pp. 204–8.

[14] Gupta B., Kumar A., Dwivedi R.K. 'Big data and its applications– a review'. *2018 International Conference on Advances in Computing, Communication Control and Networking (ICACCCN)*; Greater Noida, India, IEEE, 2018. pp. 146–49.

[15] Haidar M., Kumar S. 'Smart healthcare system for biomedical and health care applications using aadhaar and blockchain'. *5th International Conference on Information Systems and Computer Networks (ISCON)*; Mathura, India, 22-23 Oct 2021; 2022. pp. 1–5.

[16] Kumar S., Cengiz K., Vimal S., Suresh A. 'Energy efficient resource migration based load balance mechanism for high traffic applications IoT'. *Wireless Personal Communications*. 2021, vol. 10(3), pp. 1–14.

[17] Kumar S., Ranjan P., Radhakrishnan R., Tripathy M.R. 'Energy efficient multichannel MAC protocol for high traffic applications in heterogeneous wireless sensor networks'. *Recent Advances in Electrical & Electronic Engineering*. 2017, vol. 10(3), pp. 223–32.

[18] Kumar S., Ranjan P., Ramaswami R., Tripathy M.R. 'Resource efficient clustering and next hop knowledge based routing in multiple heterogeneous wireless sensor networks'. *International Journal of Grid and High Performance Computing*. 2017, vol. 9(2), pp. 1–20.

[19] Punhani A., Faujdar N., Kumar S. 'Design and evaluation of cubic torus Network-on-Chip architecture'. *International Journal of Innovative Technology and Exploring Engineering (IJITEE)*. 2019, vol. 8(6), pp. 1672–6.

[20] Dubey G., Kumar S., Kumar S., Navaney P. 'Extended opinion lexicon and ML-based sentiment analysis of tweets: a novel approach towards accurate classifier'. *International Journal of Computational Vision and Robotics*. 2020, vol. 10(6), pp. 505–21.

[21] Kumar S., Ranjan P., Radhakrishnan R., Tripathy M.R. 'Energy aware distributed protocol for heterogeneous wireless sensor network'. *International Journal of Control and Automation*. 2015, vol. 8(10), pp. 421–30.

[22] Singh P., Bansal A., Kamal A.E., Kumar S. 'Road Surface Quality Monitoring Using Machine Learning Algorithm' in Reddy A.N.R., Marla D., Favorskaya M.N., Satapathy S.C. (eds.). *Intelligent Manufacturing and Energy Sustainability. Smart Innovation, Systems and Technologies*. 265. Singapore: Springer; 2022.

[23] Sharma A., Awasthi Y., Kumar S. 'The role of blockchain, AI and IoT for smart road traffic management system'. *Proceedings of the IEEE India Council International Subsections Conference (INDISCON)*; Visakhapatnam, India, 3-4 Oct; 2020. pp. 289–96.

[24] Kumar S., Ranjan P., Singh P., Tripathy M.R. 'Design and implementation of fault tolerance technique for internet of things (iot)'. *12th International*

Conference on Computational Intelligence and Communication Networks *(CICN)*; Bhimtal, India, IEEE, 2020. pp. 154–59.

[25] Singh P., Bansal A., Kumar S. 'Performance analysis of various information platforms for recognizing the quality of indian roads'. *Proceedings of the Confluence 2020 - 10th International Conference on Cloud Computing, Data Science and Engineering*; Noida, India, IEEE, 2020. pp. 63–76.

[26] Singh P., Bansal A., Kumar S. 'Performance analysis of various information platforms for recognizing the quality of indian roads'. *Proceedings of the Confluence 2020-10th International Conference on Cloud Computing Data Science and Engineering*; Noida, India, IEEE, 2020. pp. 63–76.

[27] Reghu S., Kumar S. 'Development of robust infrastructure in networking to survive a disaster'. *IEEE*; Mathura, India, 2019. pp. 250–55.

[28] Kumar S., Ranjan P., Ramaswami R., Tripathy M.R. 'An NS3 implementation of physical layer based on 802.11 for utility maximization of WSN'. *Proceedings of the International Conference on Computational Intelligence and Communication Networks*; Jabalpur, India, IEEE, 2016. pp. 79–84.

[29] Kumar S., Ranjan P., Ramaswami R., Tripathy M.R. 'Progress in electromagnetics research Symposium'. *A Utility Maximization Approach to MAC Layer Channel Access and Forwarding.* 2015, vol. 2015, pp. 2363–7.

[30] Kumar S., Ranjan P., Ramaswami R., Tripathy M.R. 'EMEEDP: enhanced multi-hop energy efficient distributed protocol for heterogeneous wireless sensor network'. *Proceedings of the 5th International Conference on Communication Systems and Network Technologies CSNT*; Gwalior, India, IEEE, 2015. pp. 194–200.

[31] Kumar S., Ranjan P., Ramaswami R. 'Energy optimization in distributed localized wireless sensor networks'. Proceedings of the International Conference on Issues and Challenges Intelligent Computing Technique (ICICT); Ghaziabad, India, 7-8 Feb; 2014.

[32] Sudhakaran S., Kumar S., Ranjan P. 'Blockchain-Based Transparent and Secure Decentralized Algorithm'. *International Conference on Intelligent Computing and Smart Communication 2019. Algorithms for Intelligent Systems*; Singapore: Springer; 2020.

[33] Kumar S., Trivedi M.C., Ranjan P. *Evolution of Software-Defined Networking Foundations for IoT and 5G Mobile Networks.* Hershey, PA: IGI Publisher; 2020. p. 350.

[34] Chauhan R., Kumar S. 'Packet loss prediction using artificial intelligence unified with big data analytics, internet of things and cloud computing technologies'. *5th International Conference on Information Systems and Computer Networks (ISCON)*; Mathura, India, IEEE, 2021. pp. 1–6.

Chapter 6

Cram on data recovery and backup cloud computing techniques

Dharanyadevi P[1], Julie Therese M[2], Senthilnayaki B[3], Devi A[4], and Venkatalakshmi K[5]

The present digital world technology is evolving at a rapid pace. To store, manage and protect the digital information, it is necessary to back up and recover the data with utmost efficiency. As a solution, cloud computing that offers customers a wide range of services can be used. Storage-as-a-Service (SaaS) is one of the cloud platform's services, in which a large volume of digital data is maintained in the cloud database. Enterprise's most sensitive data are stored in the cloud, ensuring that it is secure and accessible at all times and from all locations. At times, information may become unavailable due to natural disasters such as windstorms, rainfall, earthquakes, or any technical fault and accidental deletion. To ensure data security and availability under such circumstances, it is vital to have a good understanding of the data backup and recovery strategies. This chapter examines a variety of cloud computing backup and recovery techniques.

6.1 Introduction

Cloud computing is an idea of affording on-demand network access to a communal pool of configurable computing resources (e.g., network, servers, applications, services and storage) that may be swiftly supplied and released with no service provider

[1]Department of Computer Science and Engineering, Puducherry Technological University, Puducherry, India
[2]Department of Electronics and Communication Engineering, Sri Manakula Vinayagar Engineering College, Puducherry, India
[3]Department of Information Science and Technology, College of Engineering, Anna University, Chennai, India
[4]Department of Electronics and Communication Engineering, IFET College of Engineering, Villupuram, India
[5]Electronics and Communication Engineering, University College of Engineering Tindivanam, Tindivanam, India

or administrative effort contact. The cloud computing affords the computing services via the Internet in order to afford more elastic resources. The major advantage of using cloud services is that we have to pay only for the services we use, which helps to run the organization efficiently in terms of economical scale [1].

6.1.1 Origin of cloud

- "Cloud computing" has its origin in the untimely days of the Internet, when we drew the network as a cloud [1].
- "First cloud around networking (TCP/IP abstraction), which was hidden from us by the cloud"—Kevin Marks, Google.
- A second cloud has formed around the documents (WWW data abstraction).
- The cloud abstracts the complexities of servers, data, apps, and assorted platforms from the infrastructure (—Jeff Bezos, Amazon CEO).

6.1.2 Sole features of cloud computing

- Shared and extensible responsibility
- Outsourcing data and applications
- Virtualization and hypervisors
- Multi-tenancy
- Service-level agreements
- Compliance and regulations
- Heterogeneity

Cloud computing has been hailed as the definitive and far-reaching solution to IT companies' growing storage expenses. Cloud computing has emerged as one of the most popular strategies for delivering IT services. Clouds have arisen as a computing infrastructure that enables the dynamically scalable, virtualized supply of computing resources as a utility. IT behemoths including Amazon, Google, IBM and Microsoft have all launched cloud computing initiatives. Because of the financial benefits, data outsourcing to cloud storage servers is becoming more popular among businesses and customers.

6.1.3 Advantages of cloud computing

- Easy implementation
- Accessibility
- No hardware required
- Efficient recovery
- Flexible for growth
- Cost per head

Table 6.1   Types of storage

Parameters	Hot storage	Cold storage	Warm storage
Characteristic	Very fast access	Fast access	Medium speed access
Application	Data storage	Cloud services	Remote server
Examples	Hard drives, flash drives and SSDs	Cloud drives, Google cloud storage and Amazon Web Services (AWS)	Cheaper and larger spinning drives

6.1.4   Disadvantages of cloud computing

- Bandwidth issues
- No redundancy
- No longer in control

Storage devices created primarily for cloud-based provisioning are represented by the cloud storage device mechanism. In order to enable the pay-per-use method, cloud storage devices are frequently equipped to provide fixed-increment capacity allotment. The security, integrity and secrecy of cloud storage are the major concerns. Many larger organizations use cloud storage to enfold their information. Cloud storage is mostly used for backing up user's data. Due to a large backup of stored data, cloud storage struggles with several issues such as efficiency, storage and security problems. The three types of storages are hot storage, warm storage and cold storage. The differences between the three storages are illustrated in Table 6.1.

Approximately 2.5 quintillions of information are produced every day, as per the survey conducted by Vouchercloud. In 2013, the data traffic is 28 875 GB/s according to the survey, which then rose to 50 000 GB/s by 2018 [2]. In the cloud storage environment, the greatest obstacle is to handle larger data and sustain an enhanced information generation rate. However, in different language, we can say that the cloud offers services that can be classified into three groups such as Infrastructure as a service (IaaS), Platform as a service and Software as a service.

Cloud computing is now being used as a backup resource for storing data [1, 3]. A service-oriented business model is used in cloud computing. Data backup is very essential because of the high chances of hardware failure, software errors or human mistakes, which lead to the loss of confidential information. Because of the greater risk for failures or theft, backup of data is more essential than ever for devices like desktop computers, laptops and mobile phones.

Smartphones are generally more widely used as computing devices, so a great deal of data is stored on those devices [4]. These reasons make it more important to store data in the cloud and hence avoid failures or security threats on the devices. Due to the rapid technical development, smart devices make data recovery more difficult to recover the saved data from the cloud; henceforth, mobile devices face challenges in backup and retrieval of data in a cloud environment.

Data recovery is the process of restoring the lost data due to data exploitation or deletion unknowingly, or the data not being accessible due to technical reasons. The restoration process is done from the system where the information was already backed up.

The types of data that you certainly should be backing up may include:

1. Any files: word documents and excel spreadsheets are common examples of information-carrying files that must be backed up. The document may also be emailed to a mailbox or uploaded to a cloud service, allowing it to be accessed at any time and from any place.
2. Any important entries made during the day should be secured and copied. Emails, calendar entries, browsing data, contacts, social media records and some unnoticed applications are some of the entries.
3. The media files such as photographs, images, audio and video. Media files are usually much bigger, necessitating a different approach while storing in the cloud.

Here are a few significantly relevant backup technique recommendations: First and foremost, any backup containing confidential information should be encrypted. Second, copies can be stored both in offline and online locations. Third, always double-check the backups to ensure that the data can be recovered at ease.

Restore data contained in deleted or corrupted files in full or in part. If file deletion is not exceeded (or the disc is not formatted after deletion), the area enclosed by the deleted file will be retrievable via popular software. In case of corrupted files (or stored on damaged media), customized software and specialized technology are needed for the recovery of damaged files. This chapter addresses the study of quantitative analysis on data recovery and backup techniques. The cloud storage is equal to data and cloud computing is equal to processes.

The chapter is organized as follows: Section 6.2 addresses the various recovery and backup techniques, and Section 6.3 discusses a thorough overview of the survey on different data recovery and backup technologies used in the cloud as well as their benefits and drawbacks. Section 6.4 addresses the chapter's conclusion and it is backed by references.

6.2 Classification of data recovery and backup

6.2.1 Recovery

The data recovery services are offered to collect data by recovery techniques. Different companies offer different strategies. The data recovery techniques used in the following devices are:

Hard Drive Recovery: A significant number of data recovery services happen due to hard disc failures. Due to the advanced technology, hard drives are grow larger, and more data retrieval is needed than ever, as users or customers are concerned about losing their data.

Optical Recovery: Optical media are an optical device that writes or reads data, e.g., CDs and DVDs. Many complications can lead to a failure of optical media: the CD or DVD can be scratched; the CD or DVD player can destroy the media.

Removable Recovery: These removable storage devices have a high chance to erase the data than the other media platforms already discussed; hence, they are less incurred.

RAID Recovery: It is really difficult to have Redundant Array of Inexpensive Devices (RAID) systems because of the extreme skills required to build, manage and maintain. Fault and configuration problems are more likely to occur. If RAID is not backed up correctly, business failure or severe loss can be incurred.

Tape Recovery: Tape is used mostly for backup successive storage media; it uses huge backup space. Experts having distinctive technologies and software tools use tape as a recovery device.

Digital Recovery: Cameras, handheld storage devices and flash media are included in the digital media. Since they are cheaper, a growing market for many goods has been created for recovery. Data recovery organizations have introduced suitable solutions for digital data loss.

6.2.2   Backup

Laxmi *et al.* explained that cloud backup is a kind of service used by the cloud to create, edit, maintain and re-establish enterprise cloud resources and infrastructure [5]. This is achieved through the internet remotely. Both online backup and remote backup can be called as cloud backup. In cloud computing, the online backup via the internet can be used anywhere at any time [6]. Online backup can be used without paying much importance to technical/physical management that includes HSDR (High-Speed Data Rate Transfer), PCS (Parity Cloud Service), ERGOT (Efficient Routing Grounded on Taxonomy) and Linux Box.

Advantages

- It delivers high performance through parallel use.
- The PCS is very quick and easy to use. Further versatile for data retrieval based on the parity retrieval service.

Disadvantages

- *High access to the Internet:* To retrieve the data, it requires fast Internet speed. The users cannot access the files in case of network problems.
- *Data are held on the server of third parties:* Though backup of the main server to an external server seems to be a good idea, it can also be a disadvantage. If something goes wrong with the external server, users lose the data.
- *Determine the bandwidth grant:* While some service providers allow unrestricted bandwidth, many other providers provide a restricted allowance and can charge an extra fee when users exceed their allocation.

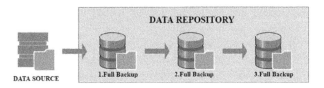

Figure 6.1   Full backup strategy

The three major categories of backup services are full backup, differential backup and incremental backup. The definitions of three types of backup techniques are as follows:

Full backup: A complete backup or full backup is shown in Figure 6.1. The full backup is the most essential and primary kind of backup process. This category of backup copies all details into a different media package. The benefits of full backup are it can be carried out after each operation and a complete copy of all data will be available within a single medium.

Differential backup: The strategy used in differential backup is shown in Figure 6.2. It copies all modified results from the last backup. However, every time it is executed, it continues to copy all changed data and it takes additional space and time to complete the previous complete backup.

Incremental Backup: It is a gradual backup process that could only duplicate customer data that has changed since the last backup. The benefit of an incremental backup is that it duplicates only a few records and hence consumes less time and space. By this way, this operation is faster and requires less memory necessary for backup savings; this process is shown in Figure 6.3.

6.3   Study on data recovery and backup cloud computing techniques

6.3.1   Backup of real-time data and recovery using cloud computing

Karishma *et al.* proposed backup of real-time data and recovery using cloud computing. The author explained that the data backup and recovery are essential to manage the data expeditiously. The author has proposed Seed Block Algorithm (SBA). The SBA is an efficient technique for data recovery. First and foremost, the SBA algorithm is proposed to decrease the recovery time. In addition, the algorithm performs two tasks during the recovery phase [7]. In the first task, users can collect data from

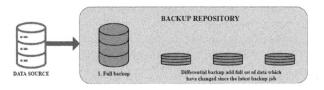

Figure 6.2   Differential backup strategy

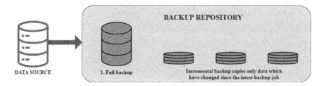

Figure 6.3   Incremental backup strategy

remote locations without the network connection. Second, if the cloud storage gets debased, which leads to loss of data, the user can recover the data easily. It also focuses on the data security stored on the remote server. The working mechanism of the SBA technique is as follows:

- As shown in Figure 6.4, the remote data recovery server, main cloud and the number of consumers are the components of the SBA.
- The first step is to establish random numbers for each client in the central cloud as a unique user ID.
- The second step is to create a seed block value for a user. For this, exclusively-OR (XOR) operation is executed between the user ID and the random number when the user is trying to access the main cloud so that the user ID is being recorded in the cloud.
- When the user in the main cloud generates a new file, the seed block value of that client is stored in the remote data backup server.
- The folder of the user remains XORed with the seed block value of the same user in the cloud server.
- The resulted XORed file gets stored in the remote data backup server as a file.
- If unlucky, the file which is in the main cloud gets corrupted or deleted, the user can access his/her file by doing an XOR operation between the file and the seed block value of that respective user.

The technologies used in SBA techniques are as follows:

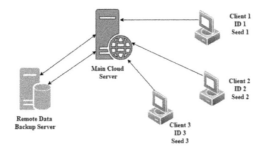

Figure 6.4   Real-time data backup and recovery

- *High-security distribution and rake technology (HS-DRT):* HS-DRT technology is used in devices like tablets and smartphones. But its implementation cost is high and has less redundancy.
- *Parity cloud services:* This technique provides reliability and privacy. Additionally, the cost of implementation is low.
- *Efficient routing grounded on taxonomy (ERGOT):* This technique also provides privacy. But it is more complex to implement and takes more time to recover the data.
- *Linux box:* The Linux box is a computer running a version of LINUX, simple and easy to implement. Yet it requires more bandwidth.
- *Cold/Hot backup strategy:* This technique helps only during failures. At the same time, the cost of implementation increases as the size of data increases.

Advantages
- SBA takes less time to perform the recovery operation.
- It provides data integrity and security.
- It also ensures reliability of data.
- The implementation of this algorithm is easy and also a cost-efficient method.
- When the main cloud could not provide the requested data to the user, it aids in recovering the lost data from the remote location.

Disadvantages
- The cost of implementation increases as the size of data increases.
- SBA takes more time to recover the data.

6.3.2   Data recovery and security in cloud

Jayachander *et al.* explained that cloud computing is very popular because of the rapid number of services given to an individual user and the organization as a whole [8]. Data recovery is the main concept of cloud computing. Using data recovery tools, the one who has the access to infrastructure can recover the files even if it was deleted from the cloud. So data recovery can lead to security issues. The author has introduced rename method. The rename method is used to meet the security concern, it is used to protect information and it works by renaming all files. It changes the file format; if the file is in JPEG then the file format is changed to mp3 by the rename module. This does not delete the original file, but without understanding the actual data format, prediction of the original data is impossible. Many who have access to infrastructure cannot retrieve the content without understanding it. Without fear of recovery, data can be removed in the cloud [9].

Advantages

- PhotoRec application is used to recover the data even if the data were removed from the memory location.
- Using memory analysis software, the deleted data from the cloud can be retrieved after deletion from the cloud.
- If the confidential records about users are erased by mistake, they can be recovered.
- Rename module gives high protection to the user's information.
- Rename changes the format of the original data type so data cannot be predicted or hacked by anyone.
- The information contained in the data remains understandable unless the exact type of data is known; as the original data format is difficult to know, data cannot be retrieved.

Disadvantages

- Security problems are created with data recovery tools.
- Cloud servers recover the private data of users even if they delete the data from the cloud.
- Reconstructing the user's data results in compromise of privacy.

6.3.3   Amoeba: An autonomous backup and recovery solid-state drives for ransomware attack defense

Donghyun *et al.* explained that ransomware is a type of malicious software that prevents users from using their devices and other computing resources unless they pay a ransom. Because ransomware can cause rapid economic loss, an efficient technique of ransomware mitigation is imperative [6]. Existing methods for detecting and avoiding ransomware rely on recognizing known ransomware behaviors. In the existing methods, the flash guard and SSD (Solid-State Drives) — Insider is used for data backup. In this chapter, Amoeba is proposed to solve the problem of ransomware affecting the SSD backup and retrieval process. Amoeba instinctively executes ransomware intrusion detection, alerting the entire system, data backup and retrieval within the SSD.

In the proposed method, for all page write activity, Amoeba measures the probability of ransomware attacks. In the Ransomware Attack Risk Indicator (RARI) hardware module, the Direct Memory Access (DMA) controller is expanded to include a NAND flash inside the SSD. The RARI module calculates all page's risks and is used to decide whether the page is to be backed up.

Ransomware Risk Calculation: Intensity, similarity and entropy of Amoeba's RARI are used to identify possible ransomware attack risk indicators. By counting the number of written requests, the intensity of the attack can easily be measured. This is supported by Flash Translation Layer (FTL) firmware which is introduced at a low price. The DMA controller gets access to new and old data to measure similarities between the data. Therefore, it must issue the NAND flash memory with an extra page, which is read, to store older data. Fresh information, old information from the flash memory and the re-assembly of the controller are read from the main memory. Amoeba uses a powerful classifier of ransomware that shows entropy, similarity and strength. The RARI value is produced by standardizing the three indicators using the new methodology named MinMaxScaler and carrying out the logistics categorization. The following equation can be used to formulate the RARI value:

$$\rho = \frac{1}{1+^{-\zeta}}, \zeta = \alpha * SIM + \beta * ENT + \gamma * INT + \delta \tag{6.1}$$

Here in (6.1), the result of linear equations is given by ζ; the mean entropy, similarity and write intensity are given by SIM,ENT, INT; the mean weights are α, β, γ and δ stands for bias.

Backup and Recovery: To incorporate the recovery and backup function, Amoeba utilizes the Out-Of-Band (OOB) section of a page. The page's OOB segment includes the RARI value and Backup Page Number. The backup technique initially tests whether the write request follows the read-after-write pattern for every overwrite request. Subsequently, it verifies if the present valid page RARI value is greater than the threshold value specified. Amoeba would consider it as a written request of ransomware attack if both the requirements are met. If one of them is not met, it is considered as a regular write request.

Advantages
- For quick ransomware detection, amoeba inserts special RARI computing equipment in the DMA module.
- It autonomously backs ups and restores the computer.
- RARI is an implementer using TFL at a low cost.

Disadvantages
- The detection of ransomware attacks and the management of backup data from any device have limited efficiency.
- Consequently, low-level backup pages, which have a low likelihood of being infected with ransomware, are invalidated by the SSD, when the backup state page space becomes too large. It limits the backup page size by stabilizing the SSD's performance.

6.3.4 A cloud-based automatic recovery and backup system for video compression

Megha *et al.* explained that cloud computing provides data recovery and backup efficiently. It is the technique of storing the data or services in a remote place where one can gain access to it from anywhere and at any time [10]. Compression techniques are an integral part in cloud computing, as it decreases the bandwidth required for storing and accessing information from the cloud. Loading data takes place via both local backup as well as cloud backup. In the local backup, compression takes place for the video files with the help of FFMPEG (Fast Forward MPEG (Motion Picture Experts Group)) [11]. The cloud backup takes place in Microsoft one drive, where the graphs of compressed and uncompressed files are examined for reduced bandwidth. And the user alone can access the data from the cloud at any time from anywhere across the world. Thus, two backups are carried out which will help in the protection of data along with compression techniques for reduced bandwidth. The core objective of the chapter is to provide two backups and video compression in the cloud.

The existing system of Dropbox storage does not have a recovery methodology. If the data are lost in the local system, it will automatically get lost from the Dropbox. Secondly, to store heavy files like audio and video files into the Dropbox, lots of internet data are needed. This makes it difficult to back up and recover data for a user. Hence moving to cloud-based recovery and backup which uses a Dropbox system with automatic recovery is vital. The video files would get compressed in the background and stored in the cloud. The background entities involved in the proposed system are as follows:

- *Skydrive API's Library:* It is provided by the Microsoft cloud services for storing a large amount of data. It is also called as OneDrive or SkyNet.
- *FFMPEG:* It is a multi-media framework used for the compression of video and audio files.
- *Cloud Storage as a Service:* It is nothing but providing storage of huge amount of data as a service in the cloud.
- *File System Tracker:* It is a web-based program for monitoring and transferring items.

To communicate with the cloud from the system, .NET is an efficient language for the browser. Three methods must automatically carry out simultaneously in the local storage as well as cloud storage. They are automatic backup, recovery system and video compression. The system performs pre-backup check daily.

Advantages
- Cloud-based recovery and backup uses a Dropbox system with automatic recovery. It helps in recovering data from the cloud storage even though the data have been deleted from the local storage. This is called as dual backup.
- The system also provides video compression with the help of libx264 encoder at the back group automatically before backing them up into the cloud storage.
- The system also provides high reliability of user data.

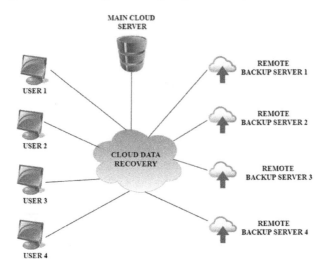

Figure 6.5   Three modules of EGA

6.3.5   *Efficient and reliable data recovery techniques in cloud computing*

Praveen *et al.* described that cloud computing provides various computing services for global communication; one such service is SaaS [12]. Sensitive and essential data are stored in the cloud in a remote site and can be accessed from anywhere at any time. And if there is a failure or disaster, these data should be kept secure. For this, data backup and recovery methods should be used to preserve the level of security [13].

Many methods exist for recovering data from the cloud, but most of them are inefficient and unreliable. A system with three modules has been proposed and it is named as an Enriched Genetic Algorithm (EGA) to meet efficiency and reliability in the data recovery process. The modules are user module, remote backup server and main cloud server, as shown in Figure 6.5. Data are stored in both main cloud server and remote server to meet efficiency, and to provide reliability, more backup servers are used [14–17].

The procedure followed in EGA is as follows:

- User uploads file to the main cloud server and the number of backup cloud servers.
- Hash code H1 of the file is generated and it is stored in the database.
- The number of copies of replicas is selected for storage.
- The size of the file is calculated.
- For downloading the files, the user has to select the file and download it. If it is not in the main cloud, then it should be recovered from the backup storage.
- For recovering file, hash function H2 is generated.
- If both hash functions H1 and H2 are equal, then the original file is recovered.

Advantages
- If the data are lost in the main server, it can be recovered from the cloud server.
- Provides reliability by creating a number of backup servers.
- Multi-server system increases the data availability.
- Hashing function like MD5 is generated to provide integrity.
- Uploaded either in two-block or four-block server.
- Four-block server provides flexibility, i.e., lost files can be recovered from any backup servers.

Disadvantages
- Requires more storage space.
- Four-block server takes more upload and recovery time than two-block servers.
- A replica of the same file is created N times.

6.3.6   Cost-efficient remote backup services for enterprise cloud

Yu *et al.* explained that the backup process creates large transmission overheads and potential faults as a result of long-distance and expensive network communication. The author proposes Neptune, a well-organized remote communication service, as a solution to this issue. Neptune sends enormous information dynamically between long-haul data centers. The cost-effective filtration structure makes it easier. The Neptune filtration is seen as ignoring consistency and compacting data similarity as clouds are composed of duplicate information. In this chapter, the data filtration uses two main techniques: chunk-level de-duplication and delta compression. The objective of these two techniques is to avoid the transmission of redundant data.

The de-duplication scheme divides the files into a large number of chunks. Each of which is individually recognized by a hash signature and is known as a fingerprint. Duplicate chunks must be ignored when examining their fingerprints. In addition, delta compression compresses the same regions by calculating the variations between them. Exploiting and exploring the features of redundancy increase the efficiency of remote backups [18, 19]. In a rational environment for an effective web redundancy exclusion scheme, the Neptune is feasible. It also increases the use of network resources availability.

Data Filtration: As already mentioned, there are two categories of data filtration:

1. Chunk level de-duplication
2. Data compression

The de-duplication is a vital part of a modern backup that separates data packets into variable-length chunks and afterward substitutes duplicate chunks for their pre-stored samples with pointers. A de-duplication method can recognize each chunk via its hash code, i.e. fingerprint. However, in reality, due to various lengths of chunks, the de-duplication method handles data on a bigger entity known as a container. A container is fixed in size and is commonly used as reading and writing units. To secure the location of the network traffic, Neptune adds the chunks into the containers. Neptune often utilizes the container as a pre-fetching device. The Least Recently Used (LRU) algorithm is used to remove the preserved cached in a container.

The second one is a rapid and more powerful design delta compressor. It exploits file correlations and can generate compressed files drastically in a smaller size. To enhance network transmission, therefore, it takes considerably smaller bits to transmit; just the difference (or delta) between two data is required. A compressor that allows two inputs is used in delta compression, where one input is the destination file that has to be compressed and the second is a source file used for reference. The creator of the delta compressor identifies and replicates the discrepancies between both the destination and the source files. The delta and source data are used to produce an accurate replica of the destination from the compressor.

Delta Compression and Recovery: It is suggested that a delta-based decompression scheme can calculate the distinction between several identical files besides the original one to provide an economical and effective recovery solution. The users can artificially pick the base file or automatically by Neptune, which uses well-known and powerful clustering algorithms. Neptune requires only maintaining the deltas from other de-duplicated files and the base file. The delta-based architecture will reduce consumption of device resources dramatically and enable data recovery functionalities. Neptune stores all the base files even if they are chosen for retrieval by another user in order to promote the data retrieval during data recovery. Neptune performs delta decoding procedures by computing the database files and the deltas when customers want to retrieve information.

Advantages
- The most important idea of the chapter is to detect similarities, delta chains along with compression and restoration, and to evaluate performance using industrial datasets in the modern world.
- It provides remote backups at a low cost.
- It does not allow additional calculation on the deltas which reduces the latency.
- Neptune often uses shortcut delta chains to help quick data recovery.

Disadvantage
- Time consumption is high.
- Due to the complexity of the procedures, financial inefficiency is likely to occur.

6.3.7   DR-cloud: Multi-cloud-based disaster recovery service

Yu *et al.* explained Cloud Disaster Recovery (CDR). CDR is a technology that allows remote computers to be recovered and backed up in a cloud-based milieu.

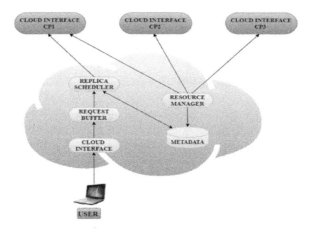

Figure 6.6   Disaster recovery in multi-cloud environment

CDR is predominantly an IaaS approach that backs up and designates the data in Remote Off-site Cloud Server database. IT systems are being used by an increasing number of providers, and some of them are financial and non-financial services. Many significant businesses and government services use the process of disaster management to protect key data and to reduce downtime triggered by disaster device defects [19–33].

The different types of methods used in CDR are regular backup or persistent information synchronization and preparation for a standby network in geographically isolated areas [34–37]. Figure 6.6 shows the disaster recovery in the multi-cloud environment.

Advantages
- Using multiple clouds not only allows picking the most cost-effective options but it also allows choosing the best cloud services to fulfill specific business needs.
- Adopting a multi-cloud strategy can also enable businesses to avoid vendor lock-in decreasing their dependency on a single cloud supporter.
- Using the retrieval of multi-cloud catastrophes, one can duplicate their resources to a secondary cloud provider in some other location.
- Respective cloud provider's Disaster Recovery (DR) services are planned to deal with numerous cloud suppliers.

Disadvantages
- If the system is not managed correctly, the costs of the use of this system may increase and the business agility will be affected.
- A secured approach and a multi-cloud approach are the crucial areas to be handled effectively.

Table 6.2   Data recovery and backup cloud computing techniques

Title	Techniques	Pros	Cons
Backing up of real-time data and recovery using cloud computing	Seed block algorithm	• It takes less time to perform the recovery. • It ensures reliability.	• The cost of implementation increases as the size of data increases. • SBA takes more time to recover the data.
Data recovery and security in the cloud	Rename method	The data can be recovered even it is removed from the memory locations.	Security and privacy problems are created.
An autonomous backup and recovery SSD for ransomware attack defense	Amoeba	• Autonomous computer backup and restoration. • Negligible at cost.	It limits the space of the backup sites.
A cloud-based automatic recovery and backup system with video compression	It uses a Dropbox system with automatic recovery	• Provides better bandwidth. • Also provides high reliability of data.	• Security is less. • Time consumption is high.
Efficient and reliable data recovery technique in cloud computing	EGA	• Multi-server system increases the data availability. • Provide reliability by creating more number of backup servers.	• Requires more storage space. • Replicas of the same file are created N times.
Cost-efficient remote backup servers for enterprise clouds	Neptune	• Cost-effective remote backups. • Reduces the amount of computation time it takes for the intermediate deltas.	• Time consumption is high. • Due to the complexity of the procedures, the financial inefficiency is likely to occur.
DR-Cloud: Multi-cloud-based disaster recovery	DR-Model cloud	• Allows replication of resources to a different geographic region using a second cloud provider.	This methodology is made more difficult due to complicated security services and a multi-cloud approach.

- The major problem in multi-cloud is handling, reliability, consistency, and high accessibility with most service providers.
- In situations where data recovery is not handled effectively, financial inefficiency is likely to occur.

Table 6.2 illustrates the data recovery and backup and cloud computing techniques. The table explains the techniques, advantages and disadvantages,

6.4 Conclusion

The cloud provides an advancement of using internet in different ways. It boosts many new technologies on the internet. Cloud is basically computing as a service. All the services are used by a broad range of cloud service consumer with different classes of devices. Cloud works on pay-as-you-go, where you pay only for the resource used. The major use of the cloud is for data storage, data centers for a backup or availability purpose. The data have to travel a long distance and pass through many different networks before reaching the data centers. This chapter addresses the various data backup and recovery techniques used in cloud computing with its advantages and disadvantages. The backup techniques focus on efficiency, reliability, implementation costs and minimum complexity. The best way to save the data is backing them up in online, i.e., cloud storage. The system may face many ransomware attacks or disasters; it is possible to access data from the cloud by maintaining its privacy. This chapter also discusses various recovery techniques that help the users in case of no data backup availability.

References

[1] Dharanyadevi P., Venkatalakshmi K. 'Proficient selection of gateway and base station by adroit algorithm in cloud-VMesh network'. *International Journal of Communication Systems*. 2016, vol. 30(6).

[2] Dihuni. *Every Day Big Data Statistics - 2.5 Quintillion Bytes of Data Created Daily. Dihuni* [online]. 2020. Available from https://www.dihuni.com/2020/04/10/every-day-big-data-statistics-2-5-quintillion-bytes-of-data-created-daily/ [Accessed 9 Jun 2021].

[3] Kumar M., Sujatha P., Dharanyadevi P. 'A detailed study with novel approach for Extenuating DDoS in cloud computing'. *Mitigating EDoS in Cloud Computing Using In-Cloud Scrubber Service. LAP LAMBERT Academic Publishing*. 2012.

[4] Levitin G., Xing L., Dai Y. 'Optimal Backup Distribution in 1-out-of- ${N}$ Cold Standby Systems'. *IEEE transactions on systems, man, and cybernetics. Systems*. 2015, vol. 45(4), pp. 636–46.

[5] Therese M.J., Dharanyadevi P., Harshithaa K. 'Integrating IoT and cloud computing for wireless sensor network applications'. *Cloud and IoT-Based Vehicular Ad Hoc Networks*. 2021, pp. 125–43.

[6]   Min D., Park D., Ahn J., *et al.* 'Amoeba: an autonomous backup and recovery SSD for Ransomware attack defense'. *IEEE Computer Architecture Letters.* 2018, vol. 17(2), pp. 245–8.

[7]   Monisha S., Venkateshkumar D.S. 'Cloud computing in data backup and data recovery'. *International Journal of Trend in Scientific Research and Development.* 2018, vol. 2(6), pp. 865–7.

[8]   Dharanyadevi P., Therese M.J., Venkatalakshmi K. 'Internet of things-based service discovery for the 5G-VANET milieu'. *'Cloud and IoT–Based Vehicular Ad Hoc Networks', Publisher: Wiley.* 2021, pp. 31–45.

[9]   Surbiryala J., Rong C. 'Data recovery and security in cloud'. *9th International Conference on Information, Intelligence, Systems and Applications (IISA), Akynthos, Greece*; IEEE, 2018.

[10]   Therese M.J., Devi A., Kumar T. A. 'Interfacing FOG and cloud computing for IOT applications'. *Recent Developments In Computing, Electronics and Mechanical Sciences.* 2020.

[11]   Raigonda M.A., Raigonda M.R., Raigonda M.R. 'A cloud based automatic recovery and backup system with video compression'. *International Journal Of Engineering And Computer Science.* 2016, vol. 5(9).

[12]   Therese M.J., Ezhilarasi C., Harshitha K., Jayasri A. 'Secured data partition and transmission to cloud through FOG computing for IOT application'. *IJAST.* 2020, vol. 29(11), pp. 921–31.

[13]   Kumar S., Ranjan P., Ramaswami R. 'EMEEDP: enhanced multi-hop energy efficient distributed protocol for heterogeneous wireless sensor network'. *Proceedings of the 5th International Conference on Communication Systems and Network Technologies, CSNT 2015*; Gwalior, India, 4-6 Apr 2015; 2015–194–200

[14]   Kumar S., Ranjan P., Ramaswami R. 'Energy optimization in distributed localized wireless sensor networks'. *Proceedings of the International Conference on Issues and Challenges Intelligent Computing Technique (ICICT)*; Ghaziabad, India, IEEE, 2014.

[15]   Chauhan R., Kumar S. 'Packet loss prediction using artificial intelligence unified with big data analytics, internet of things and cloud computing technologies'. *5th International Conference on Information Systems and Computer Networks (ISCON)*; Mathura, India, 2021. pp. 1–6.

[16]   Sudhakaran S., Kumar S., Ranjan P., Tripathy M.R. 'Blockchain-based transparent and secure decentralized algorithm'. *International Conference on Intelligent Computing and Smart Communication 2019. Algorithms for Intelligent Systems*; Singapore: Springer. THDC-Institute of Hydropower Engineering and Technology, Tehri, India, 2020.

[17]   Kumar S., Trivedi M.C., Ranjan P. *Evolution of Software-Defined Networking Foundations for IoT and 5g Mobile Networks.* Hershey, PA: IGI Publisher; 2020. p. 350.

[18]   Devi A., Julie Therese M., Premalatha G. 'Cloud computing based intelligent bank locker system'. *Journal of Physics: Conference Series.* 2021, vol. 1717(1), p. 012020.

[19]   Kumar S., Ranjan P., Radhakrishnan R., Tripathy M.R. 'Energy efficient multichannel MAC protocol for high traffic applications in heterogeneous wireless sensor networks'. *Recent Advances in Electrical & Electronic Engineering.* 2017, vol. 10(3), pp. 223–32.

[20]   Ali S.A., Affan M., Alam M. 'A study of efficient energy management techniques for cloud computing environment'. *9th International Conference on Cloud Computing, Data Science & Engineering (Confluence)*; 2019.

[21]   Hua Y., Liu X., Feng D. 'Cost-efficient remote backup services for enterprise clouds'. *IEEE Transactions on Industrial Informatics.* 2016, vol. 12(5), pp. 1650–7.

[22]   Yu Gu., Dongsheng Wang., Chuanyi Liu. 'DR-cloud: multi-cloud based disaster recovery service'. *Tsinghua Science and Technology.* 2014, vol. 19(1), pp. 13–23.

[23]   Chakraborty B., Chowdhury Y. 'Disaster recovery: background'. *Introducing Disaster Recovery with Microsoft Azure.* 2020, pp. 1–41.

[24]   Kumar S., Ranjan P., Ramaswami R., Tripathy M.R. 'Resource efficient clustering and next hop knowledge based routing in multiple heterogeneous wireless sensor networks'. *International Journal of Grid and High Performance Computing.* 2017, vol. 9(2), pp. 1–20.

[25]   Kumar S., Cengiz K., Vimal S., Suresh A. 'Energy efficient resource migration based load balance mechanism for high traffic applications IoT'. *Wireless Personal Communications.* 2021, vol. 10(3).

[26]   Haidar M., Kumar S. Smart healthcare system for biomedical and health care applications using aadhaar and blockchain. *5th International Conference on Information Systems and Computer Networks (ISCON)*; Mathura, India, 22-23 Oct 2021; 2022. pp. 1–5.

[27]   Punhani A., Faujdar N., Kumar S. 'Design and evaluation of cubic Torus network-on-chip architecture'. *International Journal of Innovative Technology and Exploring Engineering.* 2019, vol. 8(6), pp. 2278–3075.

[28]   Dubey G., Kumar S., Kumar S., Navaney P. 'Extended opinion lexicon and ML-based sentiment analysis of tweets: a novel approach towards accurate classifier'. *International Journal of Computational Vision and Robotics.* 2020, vol. 10(6), pp. 505–21.

[29]   Kumar S., Ranjan P., Radhakrishnan R., Tripathy M.R. 'Energy aware distributed protocol for heterogeneous wireless sensor network'. *International Journal of Control and Automation.* 2015, vol. 8(10), pp. 421–30.

[30]   Singh P., Bansal A., Kamal A.E., Kumar S. 'Road surface quality monitoring using machine learning algorithm' in Reddy A.N.R., Marla D., Favorskaya M.N., Satapathy S.C. (eds.). *Intelligent Manufacturing and Energy Sustainability. Smart Innovation, Systems and Technologies.* 265. Singapore: Springer; 2022.

[31]   Kumar S., Ranjan P., Ramaswami R., Tripathy M.R. 'A utility maximization approach to MAC layer channel access and forwarding'. *Progress in Electromagnetics Research Symposium*, Jan; 2015. pp. 2363–7.

[32]   Kumar S., Ranjan P., Ramaswami R., Tripathy M.R. 'An NS3 implementation of physical layer based on 802.11 for utility maximization of WSN'. *Proceedings of the International Conference on Computational Intelligence and Communication Networks, CICN 2015*; 2016. pp. 79–84.

[33]   Reghu S., Kumar S. 'Development of robust infrastructure in networking to survive a disaster'. *4th International Conference on Information Systems and Computer Networks, ISCON 2019*; 2019. pp. 250–5.

[34]   Singh P., Bansal A., Kumar S. 'Performance analysis of various information platforms for recognizing the quality of Indian roads'. *Proceedings of the Confluence 2020-10th International Conference on Cloud Computing, Data Science and Engineering*; 2020. pp. 63–76.

[35]   Sharma A., Awasthi Y., Kumar S. 'The role of blockchain, AI and IoT for smart road traffic management system'. *Proceedings of the IEEE India Council International Subsections Conference*; INDISCON 2020; 2020. pp. 289–96.

[36]   Kumar S., Ranjan P., Singh P., Tripathy M.R. 'Design and implementation of fault tolerance technique for Internet of things (IoT)'. *Proceedings of the 12th International Conference on Computational Intelligence and Communication Networks, CICN 2020*; 2020. pp. 154–9.

[37]   Chauhan R., Kumar S. 'Packet loss prediction using artificial intelligence unified with big data analytics, Internet of things and cloud computing technologies'. *5th International Conference on Information Systems and Computer Networks*; 2021. pp. 01–6.

Chapter 7

An adaptive software-defined networking (SDN) for load balancing in cloud computing

Swati Lipsa[1], Ranjan Kumar Dash[1], and Korhan Cengiz[2]

The Internet of Things can be perceived as a collection of millions of devices that are connected among each other and with the internet as a connectivity backbone to acquire and share real-time data for providing intelligent services. The tremendous rise in the number of devices requires an adequate network infrastructure to remotely deal with data orchestration. To overcome this issue, a new approach of infrastructure sharing over the cloud among service providers has transpired, with the goal of lowering excessive infrastructure deployment costs. The software-defined networking (SDN) is a networking architecture that enables network operators and users to monitor and manage the network devices remotely and more flexibly by using software that runs on external servers. As SDN and cloud integration improves reliability, scalability, and manageability, this chapter combines cloud infrastructure with SDN. Although SDN-based cloud networks have numerous advantages as mentioned above, there still exist certain challenges that draw the attention of researchers like energy efficiency, security, load balancing, and so on. The work carried out in this chapter is an attempt to address one of the challenging tasks, namely the load balancing, by developing a new multiple-controller load-balancing strategy. The proposed strategy effectively balances the load even if one or more super controllers fail. Furthermore, results are simulated and compared under different operational environments, both with and without the Modified Bully algorithm. The comparison results ensure that the introduced technique exhibits better performance with metrics such as packet loss, packet transmission ratio, and throughput.

7.1   Introduction

"The Internet of Things (IoT) is a network of physical objects (or 'things') equipped with sensors, software, as well as other technologies that facilitate interaction and

[1]Department of IT, Odisha University of Technology and Research, India
[2]College of IT, University of Fujairah, UAE

exchange of information between devices and systems via the internet" [1]. This means the Internet of Things (IoT) is a network that comprises internet-enabled smart devices that can gather, transmit, and process data from their application environments using embedded devices like sensors, CPUs, and different types of communication hardware. IoT devices can be connected to an IoT gateway to exchange the acquired sensor data from various devices. The sensor data can then be processed locally or routed to the cloud for further analysis. The data collected by these devices can be translated into valuable information such as finding patterns, providing suggestions, helping in decision-making, and identifying potential problems that may arise without the need for human intervention in the majority of the cases. In this manner, an IoT application interacts with smart devices that automate processes to meet certain requirements. The application domain ranges from the medical and healthcare sector to smart home, industrial automation, smart cities, smart grids, transportation and logistics, retail, and so on. This paves the way for advanced services aimed at raising the standard of living.

The IoT is perceived as a key frontier that has the ability to improve nearly all aspects of our life. It enables humans to live and work smartly and achieve control over their daily activities to a large extent. Many businesses have started to use this technology because it gives firms a real-time glimpse of how their systems operate, providing insights into anything from machine performance to logistics operations and supply chain management. This technology comes with numerous benefits, some of which include: the capability to monitor and manage activities, saving money, time, and resources by automating processes, allowing analytical decisions to be made more quickly and precisely, improving the Quality of Service (QoS), and enhancing customer experience. The IoT still has a lot of unexplored opportunities. This technology may attain its full potential if all devices are able to interact with one another, independent of brand or company.

As the number of devices appears to be escalating by leaps and bounds, and there is an enormous amount of data being generated, the traditional network infrastructure is struggling to catch up with this new digital era. The traditional network infrastructure fails to effectively manage the network resources, especially during peak hours. Traditional networking supports the old-fashioned approach of networking strategy that uses fixed and dedicated hardware devices like routers and switches to monitor network traffic. Traditional networks are becoming more sophisticated as more protocols are used to increase reliability and network speeds. The absence of open and standard interfaces hinders interoperability. Network devices are limited in their ability to evolve since they are built on proprietary hardware and software and are static. The traditional networks were well adapted to static traffic patterns and featured a plethora of protocols tailored to particular tasks. Due to the complexity of traditional network components making modifications to networks to accommodate flexible traffic patterns has grown extremely difficult.

Traditional networks have a high management overhead. In traditional networking infrastructures, businesses are frequently tied to a specific vendor, without any standard procedures for configuring devices across network providers. It is becoming increasingly challenging for network administrators to manage various network devices and interfaces from various vendors. A network upgrade necessitates alterations to the configuration of numerous devices. Furthermore, networks must expand to accommodate hundreds or thousands of new devices with varying performance and service requirements. When it comes to configuring the network system, the network provider faces significant challenges in making modifications to the network system, as individual devices must be manually programmed for any change in the network infrastructure. Another issue is the degradation of scalability as well because networks are congested and cannot be rapidly reconfigured to serve critical traffic. The conventional method of network management is being rendered outdated by the increasingly large amounts of data traffic, complicated network design, and growing expectations to enhance the performance of the network. The inability to fulfill these demands is a big drawback of traditional networks. These limitations make it difficult for IoT devices to communicate in a versatile and reliable manner [2].

In the light of the aforementioned issues, Software-Defined Networking (SDN) is perceived to be a technology enabler for delivering adequate solutions [3]. It has emerged as a modern and promising model for migrating from existing traditional networks and facilitates users with more programmability and easier resource management. It is a networking architecture in which the control plane (network's control functions) and data plane (packet forwarding) are decoupled and the network controller is centralized. This architecture varies from conventional networks that regulate network traffic through specialized hardware devices such as switches and routers. SDN allows the use of software to establish and manage a virtual network, as well as traditional hardware.

There are numerous motivating reasons underlying the development of SDN. Some of them include: lead to faster provisioning and administration of network resources, has the potential to simplify statically designed networks, the network can be overviewed conveniently from a single place, offers cost-effective operation as administrative cost decreases and server utilization increases, adheres to open standards, and is compatible with network hardware from any manufacturer. The objective of SDN is to enable network administrators and enterprises to respond quickly to changing business requirements. SDN can be updated swiftly and in bulk, without reconfiguring each device manually. Since this architecture optimizes the network operations and can be programmed through software, they are more versatile, agile, and scalable as well as fit well with cloud architecture. As a result, SDN has become an important component of a cloud-based framework [4]. The advantages of integrating SDN with cloud computing include operational cost reduction, security, reduced downtime, cloud abstraction, etc. These capabilities of SDN-enabled cloud computing make this an ideal choice for effectively managing the dynamic nature of IoT.

Despite its diverse capabilities and unique characteristics, SDN introduces new challenges for network engineers and service providers emphasizing on energy efficiency, performance, security, load balancing, and virtualization [5]. To make the maximum utilization of an SDN-based cloud network, the system must balance the load among multiple devices in the network, and our work concentrates on harnessing the benefits of a balanced SDN network.

The rest of this chapter has been organized as follows: Section 7.2 delves into related studies on load balancing with SDN controllers. Section 7.3 describes the basic background related to SDN architecture in a subtle way. Section 7.4 specifically discusses the taxonomy of load balancing in SDN. Section 7.5 provides an insight into the implementation of our proposed algorithms. An illustration of the proposed algorithm is given in Section 7.6. The proposed mechanism's performance is discussed and the outcomes are analyzed in Section 7.7. The summary of the work as well as future research potential is presented in Section 7.8.

7.2 Related works

The work carried out in [6] introduces a distributed architecture-based load-balancing technique for SDN controllers called a dynamic and adaptive algorithm, which is demonstrated by implementing a prototype system based on floodlight. The OpenFlow switch and controller packages [7] are used to create an SDN-based cloud computing platform that enables certain functions such as energy conservation, load balancing, etc. To resolve the issue of managing elephant flows in data center networks, an SDN-based load-balancing (SBLB) strategy for elephants [8] is addressed in this chapter that adapts multiple routing paths to distribute the load in response to changing load conditions. The paper [9] presents OpenFlow Round-Robin (RR) and OpenFlow Least-Connections algorithms to overcome the limitations of conventional load-balancing algorithms. It is found that the OpenFlow Least-Connections algorithm performs better as compared to the OpenFlow RR algorithm in balancing the load and has a shorter response time. A middlebox based on the Clos network and SDN is developed [10] to improve bandwidth usage while ensuring QoS for data centers. The authors in [11] present a technique based on employing an appropriate configuration for the SDN controller operating parameters in order to minimize the SDN controller computational load by modifying the activity of the control functions with little influence on the efficiency of the functions. An architecture facilitating software-defined clouds is formulated in [5] that emphasizes on mobile, web, and enterprise cloud applications, and the same is evaluated for two use cases, namely, QoS-aware bandwidth allocation and bandwidth-aware energy-efficient VM (Virtual Machine) placement.

The dependence on a single controller can lead to scalability issues, so Sufiev and Haddad [12] have proposed a multi-controller architecture as a solution that enables dynamic load balancing and reduces the interdependence between Super Controller and Regular Controller. The load-balancing technique developed in Reference [13] is based on multiple distributed controllers. Furthermore, the experiment was done using floodlight and exhibits that this technique can dynamically balance each controller's load while minimizing load-balancing time. The paper [14] presents an Ant Colony Optimization (LLBACO) for link load-balancing approach that can balance network link traffic, increase QoS, and reduce network overhead. The work carried out in Reference [15] introduces an SDN-enhanced Inter cloud Manager (S-ICM) to assign network flows in the crowded cloud network. The comparison of S-ICM with existing works RR allocation and honeybee foraging algorithm (HFA) reveals that S-ICM outperforms HFA and RR in terms of mitigating system saturation. Kanagavelu and Aung [16] implement an SBLB framework with a load-aware policy that is employed using an OpenFlow switch and a controller. This approach distributes the load across the servers and can be used in lieu of commercial load balancers.

The paper [17] outlines and categorizes load-balancing strategies in SDN networks, as well as their benefits and limitations. The Nio technology [18] is employed in place of the cluster method for developing a method for controller-to-controller communication in multiple SDN controller architectures that effectively balances the load between these (or the) multiple controllers. Greedy-based Service Orientation Algorithm and SA (Simulated Annealing)-based Service Orientation algorithm have been introduced in Reference [19] to minimize the data transmission time of IoT devices and balance the load among various Service Functions (SF) by forwarding fixed packets to the SF having the lowest load. A taxonomy is created in Reference [20] to represent distinct features of SDN cloud computing that gives an in-depth description of each component, with an emphasis on data center power management, traffic monitoring, network function virtualization, and security. To enhance resource utilization and reduce user response time, an SBLB service for cloud-based servers is described in Reference [21]. A load adjustment approach is used in Reference [22] to accomplish load balancing among multiple controllers by applying the said approach to each controller.

This study [23] explores the load-balancing mechanisms implemented in the SDN, classifying them into two types: deterministic and nondeterministic. The performance of centralized and distributed controllers is compared in Reference [24] based on three algorithms, viz. random, RR, and weighted RR algorithm. The results suggest that distributed controllers outperform centralized controllers in certain parameters such as single point of failure, scalability, and response time, with the weighted RR algorithm being the best among the three algorithms focused in this chapter. The significance of load balancing on network performance metrics [25] is visualized using three types of controllers, namely, hub-like controller, spanning tree protocol-based controller, and a load-balancing-based controller. The comparison aspects of formerly used controllers reveal that the network's links are less congested, which improves the overall performance of the network. The proposed service orchestration and data aggregation methodology [26] collects data packets and organizes data as services to minimize data redundancy and service response time. The work in [27] adds to the discussion by categorizing current evolving load-balancing approaches in SDN as traditional and artificial intelligence-based techniques to improve QoS. A hierarchical edge-cloud SDN controller system model is built in [28] to optimize network scalability and scale down computation delay in SDN networks under QoS criteria even while dealing with a large-scale network.

From this cumulative study, we can have a view that the implementation of SDN in a cloud computing environment is significantly essential in deploying networks that are customizable and manageable. The network controller in SDN is centralized and facilitates automated network management. The controller acts as the gateway between the user and the server. Due to the dense traffic inside the network, issues of bottlenecks may arise at gateways. Hence, the load of such networks discussed earlier needs to be distributed evenly to avoid congestion. While some studies concentrated on static load balancing, some on dynamic load balancing, and others on diverse multipath routing algorithms to control traffic, they all had one thing in common: they were all about traffic management. There are also shreds of evidence of developments that have integrated both load balancing and routing to resolve the bottleneck at gateways.

But looking into the load-balancing techniques in the previously explained algorithms, they can be termed as practically insufficient to deliver a substantial amount of efficiency even while working in the multi-controller distributed SDN architecture. In a distributed architecture, multiple controllers can be arranged either in a flat or hierarchical manner. The controllers arranged in a hierarchical fashion typically consist of a controller on top level that acts as the super controller and manages the load among local controllers. However, the possibilities of a single point of failure cannot be ruled out as there is only a single super controller in the hierarchy. The existing studies pertaining to multiple controllers do not discuss the way of finding an alternative in case of a super controller failure as mentioned earlier. Our proposed algorithm promises to cater to the needs of an effective load-balancing mechanism by finding a replacement strategy in case of a super controller failure in a hierarchically distributed SDN architecture. This will prove to be an algorithm for niche categories in the area of load balancing.

7.3   Architecture overview of SDN

A SDN architecture [29] specifies how a networking and computing infrastructure can be designed using a combination of open and software-based applications. SDN eliminates the need for a tight coupling between network configuration and traffic engineering from the underlying hardware infrastructure, enabling systematic and consistent network control through open application programming interfaces (APIs). This architecture is categorized into three distinct layers [30], as follows:

1.   Infrastructure layer: networking devices that monitor the network's routing and data processing capabilities are orchestrated in this layer. These devices can be a collection of switches and routers in a data center responsible for handling packets according to the rules set by a controller. This layer deals with gathering various network parameters like the flow of traffic, topology, network utilization, etc., and sends them to the control layer. This layer acts as the physical layer over which network virtualization is established using the control layer.
2.   Control layer: this layer is perceived as the brain of SDN. The SDN controller serves as a bridge between the application and infrastructure layer. This layer owes its intelligence to the centralized SDN controller software that controls network infrastructure. The controller accepts the application layer's requirements

and conveys them to the networking devices. It also sends back the information fetched from networking devices to the application layer.

3. Application layer: services and applications running in this layer describe the behavior of a network. These applications are programs that employ APIs to communicate their desired network requirements and behavior to the SDN controller. Furthermore, these applications can provide the network's abstract view by obtaining information from the controller for appropriate decision-making. There are numerous types of applications that can be developed like network configuration and management, intrusion detection systems, traffic monitoring and control, business policies, etc. In the real world, these applications offer a range of end-to-end solutions for corporate and data center networks.

The APIs act as the control point for all network components. The APIs in the SDN framework are known as southbound and northbound interfaces that represent the communication between controllers, network devices, and applications. A southbound interface enables a network component, i.e., controllers to interact with lower-level components, i.e., switches and routers. OpenFlow is a southbound API used by the administrators to add, amend, and delete entries in the internal flow table of network switches and routers allowing the network to accommodate real-time traffic demands. On the contrary, a northbound interface facilitates communication between higher-level components, i.e., it is the connection between the controller and the application. The end-user application conveys its requisites to the network, such as data, storage space, bandwidth, and so on, and the network replies to the application with the appropriate resource based on the resource availability.

Despite the fact that a controller utilizes just one-third of the OpenFlow protocol, it is very vital. A controller manages and regulates all of the switches and routers, creates a virtualized network, and forwards the incoming packets. Taking into consideration the significance of controller in the SDN framework and the variegation of architectures and deployments in the business and research fields, there is a demand to evaluate and benchmark all of these options with respect to numerous performance indicators. When the traffic increases due to the increase in dynamic arrival of incoming packets, the potentiality of a single controller to provide service for the overwhelming traffic decreases in terms of processing power, bandwidth limits, and memory. This leads to the network relying on a single SDN controller facing a catastrophic bottleneck making it the point of failure [31]. Due to this limitation, the SDN network is susceptible to face issues related to packet loss, scalability, load balancing, reliability, and performance degradation. Therefore, this situation necessitates the role of multiple controllers to address concerns pertaining to load balancing and performance improvement.

7.4   Load-balancing framework in SDN

Load balancing refers to the approach of distributing computational tasks among a set of resources. It is the technique of sharing network traffic across multiple servers. The

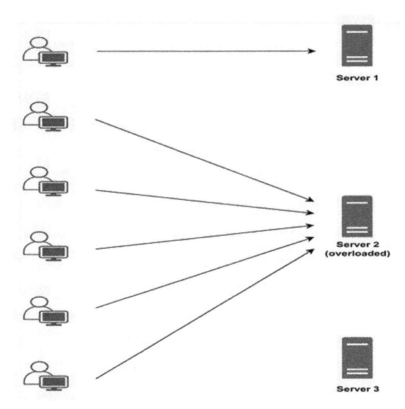

Figure 7.1   Network without load balancing

goal of load balancing is to deal with unexpected traffic surges, maximize throughput, reduce latency, reduce response time, speed up the performance, and evade the over-burden of any single resource. Figures 7.1 and 7.2 depict an overview of a network without and with load balancing, respectively.

7.4.1   Classification of SDN controller architectures

Load balancing in the SDN framework may be classified into various subcategories based on different viewpoints. This chapter classifies load balancing, as shown in Figure 7.3.

7.4.1.1   Distributed architecture

Distributed architecture deals with the dispersion of loads over the entire set of oper-ating nodes rather than relying completely on a single node. The controllers and switches both act as nodes and have many-to-many interactions among themselves. Here, every controller operates as a super controller, capable of making decisions based on the network it is operating. However, before an overloaded controller can decide to reroute incoming packets, it must first acquire load information from other

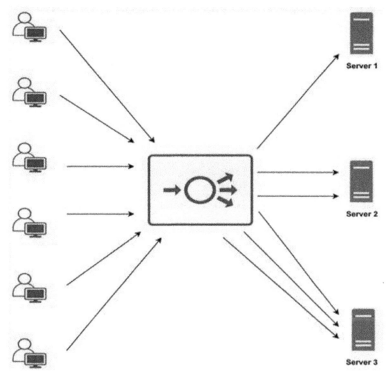

Figure 7.2   Network with load balancing

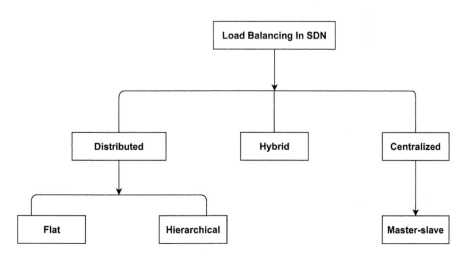

Figure 7.3   Taxonomy of load balancing in SDN

controllers. This load information is acquired on a real-time basis [32]. This approach promises to exhibit improved scalability over centralized architecture. There are two types of distributed control plane layouts, i.e., flat and hierarchical [11].

7.4.1.2 Hybrid architecture

Hybrid serves as an architecture where both distributed and centralized architecture coexist [33]. This architecture has the advantage of distributed processing and centralized control where the distributed processing part is borrowed from distributed architecture and the latter from the centralized architecture.

7.4.1.3 Centralized architecture

A specialized super controller is used in the centralized approach for gathering the loading statuses of all other controllers and coordinating traffic management. This specialized super controller acts as a coordinator that maintains the global controller load information table. When there is an uneven load distribution among controllers, the controller decides to balance the load using the load information table. However, when the super controller fails or becomes overloaded, the whole network comes down due to a single point of failure, just like when only one controller is employed [22].

7.5 Problem statement

7.5.1 Selection strategy of controller head

Considering the global perspective of traffic density in the control plane, the super controller incorporates a dispatcher strategy needed for controlling and monitoring the load distribution of flow signals among the local controllers. The super controller or controller head manages multiple local controller clusters, where each cluster represents a network that consists of local controllers associated with multiple number of switches and routers. Local controllers compute the routing path for the incoming stream of signal packets acquired from both the super controllers and the switches. Meanwhile, after computing the routing path, local controllers must communicate their own traffic conditions to their respective super controllers to ensure that the super controller preserves the real-time traffic flow information of all local controllers.

As the super controller deals with the traffic administration of all local controllers, a single super controller due to its limited capacity might cause an unpleasant delay during extreme traffic conditions. This reason brings forth the idea of having multiple super controllers to efficiently balance the heavy traffic load among all super controllers, i.e., if a controller fails abruptly, the system can be revived by migrating all of the failed controller's communication to other working controllers. These multiple super controllers coupled together must be utilized in a coordinated manner to provide load balancing. This coordinated fashion of controllers can be achieved using the Bully algorithm in this scenario. "In distributed computing, the Bully algorithm is a method for dynamically electing a coordinator or leader from a group of distributed computer processes. The process with the highest process ID number from among the non-failed processes is selected as the coordinator" [34,35,36,37,38,39,40,41,42].

There can be different strategies for the replacement of super controllers depending on the kind of applications and the number of super controllers that fail or become overwhelmed in certain instances of time. In case of failure of a single super controller, the same can be replaced by another super controller, whereas the failure of multiple super controllers can be handled by replacement of inactive super controllers by another set of multiple super controllers. We have applied the Modified Bully algorithm for efficient determination of such replacement strategies of super controllers in case of failures.

The Modified Bully algorithm treats super controllers in the same way that the Bully algorithm handles processes. A Modified Bully algorithm is a leader election algorithm that dynamically elects a coordinator or leader from a collection of passive super controllers. In this algorithm, weight is assigned to the passive super controller based on the hop distance between the passive and active super controller. The passive super controller with the highest assigned weight from among the available passive super controllers is selected as the candidate replacement for the failed super controller [43,44,45,46,47,48,49,50,51].

When a super controller becomes overloaded and fails, the system undertakes load balancing and redirects packet flows to another super controller with a lower load. As a result, the proposed SDN architecture's load management technique focuses on coordination among all super controllers.

Modified Bully algorithm entails the following steps:

1. Each passive super controller has been assigned a unique weight with respect to each active super controller.
2. Every active super controller knows the assigned weight to each of the passive super controllers.
3. The passive super controller that detects the failure of the active super controller initiates the election.
4. Several passive super controllers can initiate an election simultaneously, and the passive super controller with the highest assigned weight is elected as the new coordinator.

There are two types of super controllers, viz. active and passive. Each active super controller exhibits two states, i.e., ACTIVE and FAILED, whereas each passive super controller can take up two states, i.e., AVAILABLE and NOT_AVAILABLE.

Algorithm 1 Modified_Bully_Algorithm(S$_i$)

Input : S,N,W,C,m

>   *for each passive controller S$_j$ do*
>   *assign S$_j$(W) =[hop count distance from active super controller S$_i$]*
>   *end for*
>   *for each passive controller S$_j$ do*
>   *if S$_j$.state=NOT_AVAILABLE then*
>   *continue*
>   *end if*
> *ifS$_j$(W)>S$_i$(W) , for all passive controller S$_i$, where i≠j*
>   *send(S$_i$, S$_j$, 'ELECTION')*
>   *time=Wait()*
>   *if time<timeout and response(S$_j$) = 'OK' then*
>   *make S$_j$ as COORDINATOR*
>   *break*
>   *end if*
>   *end if*
>   *end for*
>   *return(S$_j$)*

The function *send(S$_i$,S$_j$,'ELECTION')* represents that *S$_i$* sends 'ELECTION' message to *S$_j$*. Similarly, *response(S$_j$)* represents the response from *S$_j$*.

7.5.2   Network setup

Let S be a set of super controllers and S_i be the ith super controller. Let N be the set of networks and N_j be the jth network, such that for S_iN_j represents that the jth network is managed by the ith super controller. A controller is active if it has at least one network to handle, otherwise, it is passive. An active controller possesses a flow table of the network under its control, whereas a passive controller maintains the flow table of all networks controlled by the active controller. Let W be the weight assigned to passive super controllers and W_k be the weight of kth super controller. Let W' be the weight assigned to active controllers such that $W' > W$. Let m be the number of packets to be processed by super controller S_i and C be the capacity of the super controller to process incoming packets such as $C(S_i)$ is the capacity of the ith super controller.

Algorithm 2 Load Balancing Algorithm

for each set of packets m do
$\qquad$ *if m < C(S$_i$) then*
$\qquad\qquad$ *process(S$_i$, m)*
$\qquad$ *else*
$\qquad\qquad$ *process(S$_i$, m-C(S$_i$))*
$\qquad\qquad$ *set S$_i$.state = FAILED//while no*
COORDINATOR
$\qquad\qquad\qquad$ *S$_j$=Modified_Bully_Algorithm(S$_i$)*
$\qquad\qquad\qquad$ *Make S$_j$ as COORDINATOR*
$\qquad\qquad\qquad$ *process(S$_j$, m-C(S$_i$))*
$\qquad$ *end if*
$\qquad$ *if S$_i$.state=ACTIVE*
$\qquad\qquad$ *send COORDINATOR message*
$\qquad\qquad$ *make S$_i$ as COORDINATOR*
$\qquad$ *end if*
$\qquad$ *end for*

The function *process(S$_i$, m)* represents that i[th] super controller processes *m* number of packets.

7.6 Illustration

The illustration of the above configuration (i.e Figure 7.4 and Figure 7.5) can be explained as follows.

For instance, the S consists of seven S_i, namely S_1, S_2, S_3, S_4, S_5, S_6, and S_7, where S_1, S_3, S_5, and S_7 are active and manage networks N_1, N_2, N_3, and N_4, respectively, as shown in Figure 7.6. The super controllers S_2, S_4, and S_6 are passive. Weights are assigned to the passive controllers (i.e. S_2, S_4, and S_6) on basis of the number of hops from the starting point. Assuming that S_1 is the starting point, S_1 is one hop away from S_2, so weight assigned for S_1 to $S_2 = 4$. Likewise, if only passive controllers are included, the weight assigned for S_1 to $S_6 = 3$ and S_1 to $S_4 = 2$. In a typical scenario, the following conditions might arise while working with such types of networking environments.

$\qquad$ i. S_1 *fail, S_2 available:*
Suppose S_4 tries to communicate with S_1 and receives no reply from S_1. So S_4 gets to know that S_1 has failed and starts the election for replacing

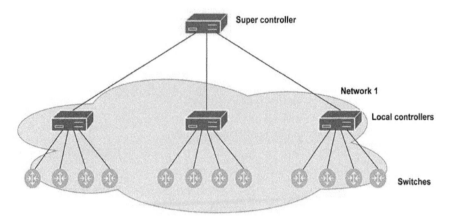

Figure 7.4   Network configuration of the super controller and local controller

S_1. To start with S_4 broadcasts ELECTION messages to passive super controllers assigned with higher weight than S_4, i.e., S_6, S_2, and S_1. Similarly, S_6 also broadcasts ELECTION messages to passive super controllers assigned with higher weight than S_6, i.e. S_2, and S_1, and S_2 being the passive super controller with the highest weight sends ELECTION messages only to S_1. Both S_6 and S_2 reply to S_4 with OK messages to confirm that they will participate in the election, whereas S_1 sends no reply owing to its failed state. Similarly, S_2 also replies to S_6 with an OK message to confirm that it will participate in the election and again S_1 sends no reply. As S_4 and S_6 have received OK messages from S_2 who is higher in weight from both of them, so now S_4 and S_6 are dropped from the election process and wait for COORDINATOR message as other passive super controllers with higher weight are actively participating in the election. As S_2 is the passive super controller with the highest weight and never receives an OK message from any other passive super controller, it is now elected as the replacement for the failed S_1 and S_2 sends out COORDINATOR messages to the rest of the passive super

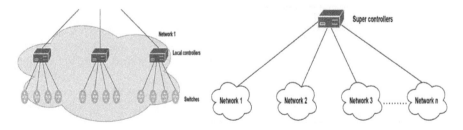

Figure 7.5   Super controller implementation framework

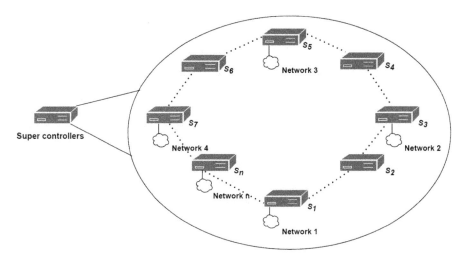

Figure 7.6   Illustration of super controller consisting of multiple super controllers

controllers, i.e., S_4 and S_6. It does not send a COORDINATOR message to S_1 as it is failed.

ii. S_1 fails, S_2 not available, and S_6 available:
If S_1 fails then S_2 is the most preferable replacement for S_1 because of its highest weight. But if S_2 is not available (i.e. failed or overloaded), then the same election process as described for the first condition will be initiated and S_6 being the next highest weight passive super controller after S_2 will be elected as the replacement for the failed S_1.

iii. S_1 fail, substitute selected and higher weighted S_1 revives or available:
In this condition, S_1 has failed and S_2 is selected as the replacement for the failed S_1 in the same procedure as discussed for the first condition. But whenever S_1 revives after S_2 is selected for the replacement, S_1 being the highest weighted super controller does not start an election rather it sends a COORDINATOR message to all passive super controllers including S_2, which implies it is available and can handle its own packet and S_2 is set free.

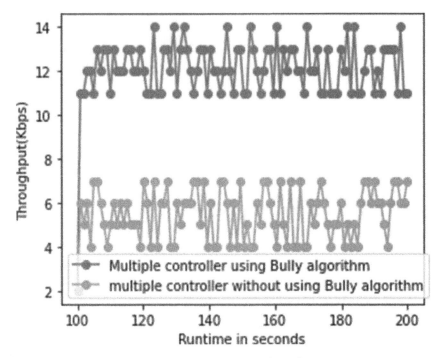

Figure 7.7   Runtime vs. throughput

7.7   Results and discussion

The simulation of the proposed model is performed by using the python programming language with the help of the POX tool. POX tool is an open-source platform for SDN controllers like OpenFlow. The super controllers as well as the switches are configured to operate over the virtual networks.

The following two criteria are taken into consideration for the simulation of the proposed model:

Case I: Allowing the super controller to transmit packets to the appropriate network without using the Modified Bully algorithm, even if one or more super controllers are down.

Case II: When a super controller fails, the Modified Bully algorithm is employed to find a replacement for it.

Both scenarios are compared to determine the performance in terms of various metrics such as throughput, packet transmission ratio (PTR), and packet loss (as shown in Figures 7.7–7.9,).

7.7.1   Comparison of throughput

The observations of the simulation of the two scenarios are recorded once one or more super controllers start failing (i.e. after 100 s of operation), the reason being

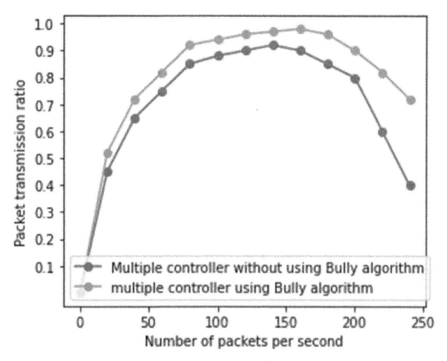

Figure 7.8   Number of packets per second vs. packet transmission ratio

they behave similarly in the absence of failure (Figure 7.7). This figure depicts the overall network throughput over runtime with a moderate number of packets per second. Both of the aforementioned situations have a nearly identical performance by fluctuating over two levels of throughput. However, implementation of the Modified Bully algorithm for load balancing results in a remarkable increase in overall system throughput compared to not using the Modified Bully algorithm, because the Modified Bully algorithm easily finds a replacement to combat super controller failure.

7.7.2   Comparison of PTR

The PTR is calculated using the following formula:

$$PTR = \frac{P_s}{P_T} \tag{7.1}$$

where P_S = number of packets processed successfully and P_T = total number of packets received.

By using (7.1), the PTR is evaluated for both cases, as shown in Figure 7.8. This figure indicates how the PTR of the total network increases when the number of packets received per second increases up to a certain value beyond which the PTR of the system shows a gradual decrease with further increase in the number of packets

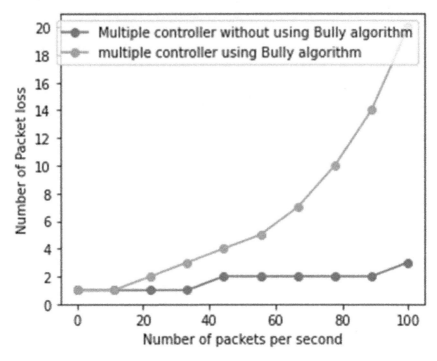

Figure 7.9   Number of packets per second vs. number of packet loss

received per second, due to increase number of packet loss. Here these values are termed as threshold values which are 0.92 at 120 packets/s and 0.98 at 175 packets/s for the two cases, respectively.

7.7.3   Comparison of number of packet loss

Figure 7.9 demonstrates the amount of packet loss as a percentage of the total number of packets generated per second. The increase in the number of packets increases the quantity of data to be transferred; this raises the likelihood of packet errors. It is observed that the loss of packets in our proposed algorithm is considerably less than the scenario where there is no implementation of the Modified Bully algorithm. The application of the Modified Bully algorithm will have a significant impact on reducing the amount of packet loss due to lesser congestion inside the network.

7.8   Conclusion

In spite of the features of SDN that emerge as a break-through technique for handling complicated networking operational difficulties, there are some possibilities of a computational resource-limited controller being overwhelmed by heavy traffic and then experiencing unexpected delays. A multi-controller architecture evolves as a solution to the issues faced by the single controller, but uneven load distribution in multi-controller deployment systems remains an inevitable concern. To avoid this unbalanced load congestion and escalate network performance, we have introduced a hierarchical multiple-controller load-balancing algorithm. Our proposed algorithm dynamically manages network flow by distributing the workload across multiple super controllers to optimize network resources. The result indicates that our approach enhances the network efficiency and flexibility, and boosts the overall network performance, by minimizing the overload and the delay between controllers. We aspire to analyze more parameters in the future and deploy this interface in a real testbed to demonstrate its efficacy in real-world scenarios.

References

[1] Aazam M., Khan I., Abdullah Alsaffar A., Huh E.-N. 'Cloud of things: Integrating Internet of things and cloud computing and the issues involved'. 11th International Bhurban Conference on Applied Sciences & Technology (IBCAST); Islamabad, Pakistan, 14-18 Jan; 2014.

[2] 'Traditional network infrastructure model and problems associated with it'. *Journal of Pluribus Networks*. 2012, vol. 14(2). Available from https://pluribusnetworks.com/blog/traditional-network-infrastructure-model-and-problems-associated-with-it/

[3] Ojo M., Adami D., Giordano S. 'A SDN-iot architecture with NFV implementation'. *IEEE Globecom Workshops (GC WKSHPS)*; Washington, DC, USA, IEEE, 4-8 Dec, 2016. pp. 1–6.

[4] Barros S. 'Applying software-defined networks to cloud computing'. 33rd Brazilian Symposium on Computer Networks and Distributed Systems; Vitória, ES, Brazil, 18-22 May; 2015.

[5] Buyya R., Calheiros R.N., Son J., Dastjerdi A.V., Yoon Y. 'Software-defined cloud computing: architectural elements and open challenges'. *International Conference on Advances in Computing, Communications and Informatics (ICACCI)*; Delhi, India, 24-27 Sep; 2014.

[6] Zhou Y., Zhu M., Xiao L., *et al.* 'A load balancing strategy of SDN controller based on distributed decision'. IEEE 13th International Conference on Trust, Security and Privacy in Computing and Communications; Beijing, China, 24-26 Sep; 2014.

[7] Yen T.-C., Su C.-S. 'An SDN-based cloud computing architecture and its mathematical model'. International Conference on Information Science, Electronics and Electrical Engineering; Sapporo, Japan, 26-28 Apr; 2014.

[8] Liu J., Li J., Shou G., Hu Y., Guo Z., Dai W. 'SDN based load balancing mechanism for elephant flow in data center networks'. International Symposium on Wireless Personal Multimedia Communications (WPMC); Sydney, NSW, 7-10 Sep; 2014.

[9] Zhang H., Guo X. 'SDN-based load balancing strategy for server cluster'. IEEE 3rd International Conference on Cloud Computing and Intelligence Systems; Shenzhen, 27-29 Nov; 2014.

[10] Tu R., Wang X., Zhao J., Yang Y., Shi L., Wolf T. 'Design of a load-balancing middlebox based on SDN for data centers'. IEEE Conference on Computer Communications Workshops (INFOCOM WKSHPS); Hong Kong, China, 26 Apr-1 May; 2015.

[11] Caba C., Soler J. 'Mitigating SDN controller performance bottlenecks'. 24th International Conference on Computer Communication and Networks (ICCCN); Las Vegas, NV, 3-6 Aug; 2015.

[12] Sufiev H., Haddad Y. 'A dynamic load balancing architecture for SDN'. IEEE International Conference on the Science of Electrical Engineering (ICSEE); Eilat, Israel, 16-18 Nov; 2016.

[13] Yu J., Wang Y., Pei K., Zhang S., Li J. 'A load balancing mechanism for multiple SDN controllers based on load informing strategy'. 18th Asia-Pacific Network Operations and Management Symposium (APNOMS). IEEE; Kanazawa, Japan, 5-7 Oct; 2016.

[14] Wang C., Zhang G., Xu H., Chen H. 'An ACO-based link load-balancing algorithm in SDN'. 7th International Conference on Cloud Computing and Big Data (CCBD); Macau, China, 16-18 Nov; 2016.

[15] Kang B., Choo H. 'An SDN-enhanced load-balancing technique in the cloud system'. *The Journal of Supercomputing*. 2018, vol. 74(11), pp. 5706–29.

[16] Kanagavelu R., Aung K. 'Software-defined load balancer in cloud data centers'. Proceedings of the 2nd International Conference on Communication and Information Processing; Singapore, 26-29 Nov; 2016.

[17] Li L., Xu Q. 'Load balancing researches in SDN: a survey'. 7th IEEE International Conference on Electronics Information and Emergency Communication (ICEIEC); Macau, China, 21-23 Jul; 2017.

[18] Benamrane F., Mamoun M.B., Benaini R, Ben Mamoun M., Redouane B. 'New method for controller-to-controller communication in distributed SDN architecture'. *International Journal of Communication Networks and Distributed Systems*. 2017, vol. 19(3), pp. 357–67.

[19] Chien W.-C., Lai C.-F., Cho H.-H., Chao H.-C. '*Journal of* Network and Computer Applications'. *A SDN-SFC-based service-oriented load balancing for the IoT applications*. 2018, vol. 114, pp. 88–97.

[20] Jungmin S., Buyya R. 'A taxonomy of software-defined networking (SDN)-enabled cloud computing'. *ACM Computing Surveys*. 2018, pp. 1–36.

[21] Abdelltif A.A., Ahmed E., Fong A.T., Gani A., Imran M. 'SDN-based load balancing service for cloud servers'. *IEEE Communications Magazine*. 2018, vol. 56(8), pp. 106–11.

[22] Wang K.-Y., Kao S.-J., Kao M.-T. 'An efficient load adjustment for balancing multiple controllers in reliable SDN systems'. *IEEE International Conference on Applied System Invention (ICASI), Chiba, Japan*; 2018.

[23] Neghabi A.A., Jafari Navimipour N., Hosseinzadeh M., Rezaee A. 'Load balancing mechanisms in the software defined networks: a systematic and comprehensive review of the literature'. *IEEE Access*. 2018, vol. 6, pp. 14159–78.

[24] Ahmed H., Ramalakshmi R. 'Performance analysis of centralized and distributed SDN controllers for load balancing application'. *2nd International Conference on Trends in Electronics and Informatics (ICOEI)*; Tirunelveli, India, 11-12 May; 2018.

[25] Chahlaoui F., El-Fenni M.R., Dahmouni H. 'Performance analysis of load balancing mechanisms in SDN networks'. Proceedings of the 2nd International Conference on Networking, Information Systems & Security; Rabat Morocco, 27-29 Mar; 2019.

[26] Liu Y., Zeng Z., Liu X., Zhu X., Bhuiyan M.Z.A, Alam Bhuiyan M.D. 'A novel load balancing and low response delay framework for edge-cloud network based on SDN'. *IEEE Internet of Things Journal*. 2019, vol. 7(7), pp. 5922–33.

[27] Belgaum M.R., Musa S., Alam M.M., Su'ud M.M. 'A systematic review of load balancing techniques in software-defined networking'. *IEEE Access*. 2020, vol. 8, pp. 98612–36.

[28] Lin F.P.-C., Tsai Z. 'Hierarchical edge-cloud SDN controller system with optimal adaptive resource allocation for load-balancing'. *IEEE Systems Journal*. 2019, pp. 265–76.

[29] Haleplidis E. 'Overview of RFC7426: SDN layers and architecture terminology'. *IEEE Softwareization*; IEEE, 2017.

[30] Rana D.S., Dhondiyal S.A., Chamoli S.K. 'Software defined networking (SDN) challenges, issues and solution'. *International Journal of Computer Sciences and Engineering*. 2019, vol. 7(1), pp. 884–9.

[31] Salman O., Elhajj I.H., Kayssi A., Chehab A. 'SDN controllers: A comparative study'. 18th Mediterranean Electrotechnical Conference (MELECON); Lemesos, Cyprus, 18-20 Apr; 2016.

[32] Ma Y.-W., Chen J.L., Tsai Y.H., Cheng K.H., Hung W.C. 'Load-balancing multiple controllers mechanism for software-defined networking'. *Wireless Personal Communications*. 94; 2017. pp. 3549–74.

[33] Amin R., Reisslein M., Shah N. 'Hybrid SDN networks: a survey of existing approaches'. *IEEE Communications Surveys & Tutorials*. 2018, vol. 20(4), pp. 3259–306.

[34] Haidar M., Kumar S. 'Smart healthcare system for biomedical and health care applications using aadhaar and blockchain'. *5th International Conference on Information Systems and Computer Networks (ISCON)*; Mathura, India, IEEE, 22-23 Oct 2021, 2022. pp. 1–5.

[35] Kumar S., Cengiz K., Vimal S., Suresh A. 'Energy efficient resource migration based load balance mechanism for high traffic applications IoT'. *Wireless Personal Communication*. 10; 2021. pp. 1–19.

[36] Kumar S., Ranjan P., Radhakrishnan R., Tripathy M.R. 'Energy efficient multichannel MAC protocol for high traffic applications in heterogeneous wireless sensor networks'. *Recent Advances in Electrical & Electronic Engineering*. 2017, vol. 10(3), pp. 223–32.

[37] Kumar S., Ranjan P., Ramaswami R., Tripathy M.R. 'Resource efficient clustering and next hop knowledge based routing in multiple heterogeneous wireless sensor networks'. *International Journal of Grid and High Performance Computing*. 2017, vol. 9(2), pp. 1–20.

[38] Punhani A., Faujdar N., Kumar S. 'Design and evaluation of cubic Torus Network-on-Chip architecture'. *International Journal of Innovative Technology and Exploring Engineering*. 2019, vol. 8(6), pp. 2278–3075.

[39] Dubey G., Kumar S., Kumar S., Navaney P. 'Extended opinion lexicon and ML-based sentiment analysis of tweets: a novel approach towards accurate classifier'. *International Journal of Computational Vision and Robotics*. 2020, vol. 10(6), pp. 505–21.

[40] Kumar S., Ranjan P., Radhakrishnan R., Tripathy M.R. 'Energy aware distributed protocol for heterogeneous wireless sensor network'. *International Journal of Control and Automation*. 2015, vol. 8(10), pp. 421–30.

[41] Singh P., Bansal A., Kamal A.E., Kumar S. 'Road surface quality monitoring using machine learning algorithm' in Reddy A.N.R., Marla D., Favorskaya M.N., Satapathy S.C. (eds.). *Intelligent manufacturing and energy sustainability. smart innovation, systems and technologies*. Vol. 265. Singapore: Springer; 2022.

[42] Sharma A., Awasthi Y., Kumar S. 'The role of blockchain, AI and IoT for smart road traffic management system'. *IEEE India Council International Subsections Conference (INDISCON)*; Visakhapatnam, India, 3-4 Oct; 2020. pp. 289–96.

[43] Kumar S., Ranjan P., Singh P., Tripathy M.R. 'Design and implementation of fault tolerance technique for internet of things (IoT)'. *Proceedings of the 12th International Conference on Computational Intelligence and Communication Networks (CICN)*; Bhimtal, India, 25-26 Sep; 2020. pp. 154–9.

[44] Singh P., Bansal A., Kumar S. 'Performance analysis of various information platforms for recognizing the quality of indian roads'. *Proceedings of the 10th Confluence of the International Conference on Cloud Computing, Data Science and Engineering*; Noida, India, IEEE, 29-31 Jan, 2020. pp. 63–76.

[45] Chauhan R., Kumar S. 'Packet loss prediction using artificial intelligence unified with big data analytics, internet of things and cloud computing technologies'. *5th International Conference on Information Systems and Computer Networks (ISCON)*; Mathura, India, 22-23 Oct; 2021. pp. 1–6.

[46] Reghu S., Kumar S. 'Development of robust infrastructure in networking to survive a disaster'. *4th International Conference on Information Systems and Computer Networks, ISCON*; Mathura, India, IEEE, 21-22 Nov, 2019. pp. 250–55.

[47] Kumar S., Ranjan P., Ramaswami R., Tripathy M.R. 'An NS3 implementation of physical layer based on 802.11 for utility maximization of WSN'. *2015 International Conference on Computational Intelligence and Communication Networks, CICN*; Jabalpur, India, IEEE, 12-14 Dec, 2016. pp. 79–84.

[48] Kumar S., Ranjan P., Ramaswami R., Tripathy M.R. 'A utility maximiza-
      tion approach to MAC layer channel access and forwarding'. *Progress in
      Electromagnetics Research Symposium*; Prague; 2015. pp. 2363–7.
[49] Kumar S., Ranjan P., Ramaswami R., Tripathy M.R. 'EMEEDP: enhanced
      multi-hop energy efficient distributed protocol for heterogeneous wireless
      sensor network'. *5th International Conference on Communication Systems
      and Network Technologies, CSNT*; Gwalior, India, IEEE, 4-6 Apr, 2015. pp.
      194–200.
[50] Kumar S., Ranjan P., Ramaswami R. 'Energy optimization in distrib-
      uted localized wireless sensor networks'. *Proceedings of the International
      Conference on Issues and Challenges Intelligent Computing Technique
      (ICICT)*; Ghaziabad, India, IEEE, 7-8 Feb, 2014.
[51] Sudhakaran S., Kumar S., Ranjan P., Tripathy M.R. 'Blockchain-based trans-
      parent and secure decentralized algorithm'. *International Conference on
      Intelligent Computing and Smart Communication 2019*; Singapore; 2020.

Chapter 8

Emerging security challenges in cloud computing: an insight

Gaurav Aggarwal[1], kavita Jhajharia[2], Dinesh Kumar Saini[2], and Mehak Khurana[3]

Cloud computing has been evolved as a new computing prototype with the aim of providing reliability, quality of service and cost-effective with no location barrier. More massive databases and applications are relocated to an immense centralized data center known as the cloud. Cloud computing has enormous benefits of no need to purchase physical space from a separate vendor instead of using the cloud, but these benefits have security threats. The resource virtualization, the data and the machine are physically absent in the cloud; the storage of data in the cloud causes security issues. An unauthorized person can penetrate through the cloud security and can cause data manipulation, data loss or theft might take place. This chapter has described cloud computing and various security issues and challenges that are present in different cloud models and cloud environment. It also gives an idea of different threat management techniques available to encounter security issues and challenges. The RSA algorithm implementation has been described in detail, and the Advance Encryption Standard policy, along with its implementation, has also been discussed. For better clarification, several reviews are conducted on the existing models.

8.1 Introduction

8.1.1 An introduction to cloud computing and its security

The unique term 'cloud' [1, 2] was taken from the diagrams of a computer network, where the diagram hides the critical complexity of infrastructure associated within a mesh of computer network. Cloud computing technology provides many services including software as a service (SaaS), platform as a service (PaaS) and infrastructure

[1]Department of Information Technology and Engineering, Amity University in Tashkent, Uzbekistan
[2]Scool of Computing and Information Technology, Manipal University Jaipur, Jaipur, India
[3]Department of Computer Science and Engineering, The NorthCap University, Gurugram, India

as a service (IaaS) that are the primary concern in cloud computing technology. The main aspects of cloud computing technology consist of sharing of resources, services on-demand, compatibility of connectivity with various devices, perfect accountability of services and complete access of network. The cloud reduces the investment cost and software license cost as well. The main concern remains with the cloud is the security of valuable data and its computing. The cloud storage services allow data owner to move valuable data from the local machine to remotely located cloud storages, which release cloud user's impediment for managing as well as maintaining their data at local devices. Cloud computing is a distributed architecture, and its objective is clear. It is dedicated to providing convenient data storage and quick computing through virtualizations of computing resources. It enhances the collaboration, scalability, flexibility to adapt rapidly changing new technology and provide overall cost reduction through efficient computing. Cloud computing continues to evolve in the new era of internet-based technology with reliable, ubiquitous and on-demand services. Cloud computing is a combination of service-oriented architecture [3], virtualization and advanced technologies with a strong dependency on internet-based applications. Google has introduced the MapReduce [2, 4] framework along with Apache's Hadoop Distributed File System (HDFS) [5], which is processing a large amount of shared data with less time using the internet-based applications.

In the present days, the enterprises are combining private and public cloud servers due to virtualization, and global storages of data and hence security for storage of data and computation stole the spotlight. The storage of containers at the server and moving them between multiple cloud environments need greater security in data at rest and as well as in moving stages. In the present era, uses of cloud have been increased at a larger scale.

There are online transactions, customer services, email accessing, online exams, banking services, e-governance, and so on. All these services are run on a cloud-based platform. So the security of those services requires enormous attention. Cloud computing is dependent on vulnerable internet. The involvement of heterogeneous architectures with different Cloud Service Providers (CSPs) raises more significant security threats (Figure 8.1). Moreover, CSPs store the user's data at different locations without knowing customers that also invite security issues. So, the security paradigm needs to be changed to a new dimension.

The so-called security concepts such as authorization, authentication and identification are no longer stand firm to prevent valuable data stored in the server of CSPs by a cloud user and its safe transaction within the network from possible threats. Several essential management techniques with encryption and decryption strategies are adapted to safeguard the user's data when it is stored in the cloud storage and on transmission in the network as well. The data are encoded before it is warehoused in cloud storage.

Numerous techniques are adopted to protect the data when it is traveling through the network's nodes. Despite undertaking so many precautions, security remains a big question.

Are the data safe? Are the security measures taken so far appropriate? Due to rapid changes in technology, security architectures also need further enhancement.

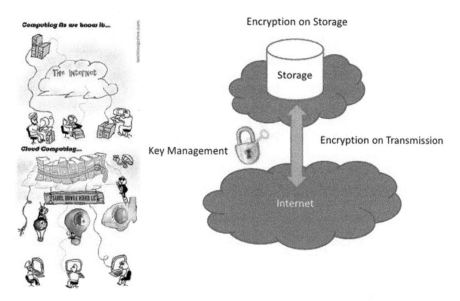

Figure 8.1   Encryption policy

It is well known that whenever the data are traveling in the insecure network, there is no such fool-proof technique which can assure complete security for user's data.

8.2   The security issues in different cloud models and threat management techniques

Before we move toward the details of data security and its transaction in the cloud environment, we need to know about the characteristics of cloud architecture. According to the definition of the National Institute of Standards and Technology (NIST) [6], a complete model of the cloud is built up with five most important features, in which three are the service models and four deployment models. Every cloud model has different security issues, which need to be addressed in detail.

8.2.1   Five most indispensable characteristics

A cloud model should always have the below-mentioned five essential characteristics [6, 7] for efficient acceptance of the cloud users.

1. Broad network access: The cloud model should have open standards for all Applications Running Interfaces (APIs). It should be able to function on all IP.HTTPs and REST protocols and resources should be available to users from anywhere with an internet connection.
2. Rapid elasticity: Cloud model should always be able to allocate the resources among the users dynamically. It should release the additional resources

dynamically to the users as and when needed. The cloud model should be fully automated.

3. Measured service: The cloud services are metered, like a utility, and the users only pay for services used by them. The most important is that the services can be canceled at any time by the users.
4. On-demand self-service: In the cloud model, users are abstracted from the implementation, and the service is based on time (real-time) delivery. The services are accessed through a self-service network interface.
5. Resource pooling: The requested resources are pooled from the common sources, which builds a scale of economies. Common infrastructure gains high efficiency and runs at greater network bandwidth.

8.2.2   *The security issues in cloud service model*

A cloud service model provides three types of services to the users as follows [2, 8]:

1. SaaS
2. PaaS
3. IaaS

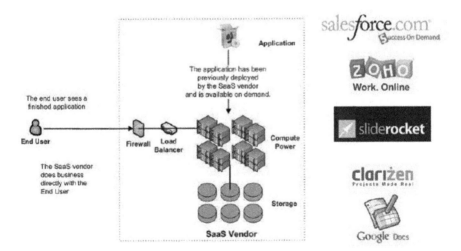

Figure 8.2   Software as a service model

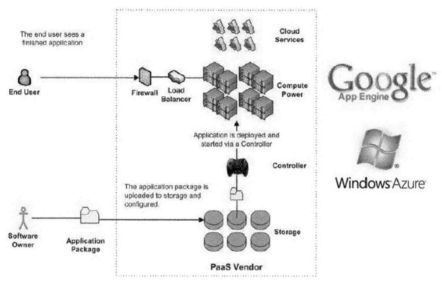

Figure 8.3   Platform as a service model

8.2.2.1 Security issues in software as a service model

In the security issues in software as a service (SaaS) model (Figure 8.2) , the CSP provides various applications running in cloud infrastructure, which are available as a service to the customer. The various applications are available and accessible to users through a web-based device like an email (web browser). In this service, required software, operating system and network are provided by SaaS vendors [9]. The SaaS users have no control over the data security because all managements are done by SaaS providers only. As the applications are provided through an open network, any flaws in web applications and attackers may violet the data security at any point of time. Traditional security protections are not strong enough in this scenario for the adequate protection of data from possible threats. The customers have their instances of applications which may be customized as per their needs.

Each customer gets different instances from the vendor and providers depend on multitenancy model which create significant security issues in the cloud environment. The backup from third party providers also raises many security issues like confidentiality, vulnerability, etc.

8.2.2.2   Security issues in PaaS model

In PaaS model (Figure 8.3), consumers are encouraged to deploy their software or acquired applications to the cloud platform provided by the vendors. Users are permitted to use various computer software languages, available libraries, other

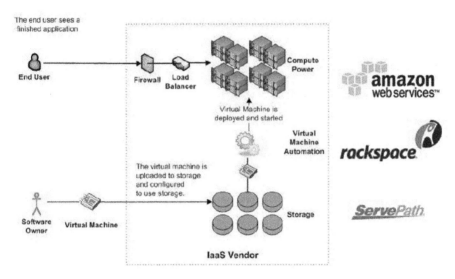

Figure 8.4   Infrastructure as a service model

services and tools offered by the service providers. The network servers, operating systems or storages are managed by the providers only. The security of PaaS services depends upon protected and dependable networking and a safe web browser. In a PaaS platform, there are two types of securities that are needed to be maintained by service providers. The first one is the security and safety of the PaaS stage itself, i.e., the runtime machine and another one is the security of the user's applications deployed on the PaaS platform. The PaaS owner generally uses third-party service components which are called as mashups [10, 11], a combination of many source elements into a single combined unit. Mashups are more prone to threats when they are not handled carefully on open networks.

8.2.2.3   Security issues in IaaS model

In IaaS (Figure 8.4), the consumers are capable of installing and running their software or applications and related operating systems for processing, storing, networking and other fundamental resources. The customers need not manage the cloud infrastructures but have the control to manage over their storage system, operating systems and installed applications. In the IaaS model, service providers offer a pool of resources like servers, storages and other infrastructures through virtualization. In virtualization systems, consumers are using the same machine for running different applications at a time, and they are also allowed to generate, duplicate, modify, share, gist and push back virtual machines. The complexity of interconnections among various virtual machines and user's applications leads to many security

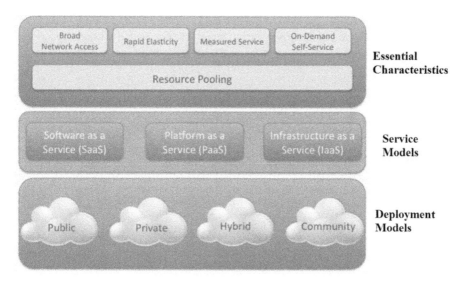

Figure 8.5   *The complete cloud model*

threats. Though Virtual Machine Monitor (VMM) [12, 13] software is used for the separation of virtual machines which are running simultaneously; flaws in VMM applications need to be sifted through because any single snag in VMMs can break down the whole systems.

8.2.3   Security issues in cloud deployment models

A cloud deployment model can have four different categories as follows:

1. Private cloud
2. Public cloud
3. Community cloud
4. Hybrid cloud

In these types of cloud models (Figure 8.5), the service providers provide the complete package of networking, data storage, platform and software infrastructures to the cloud users.

8.2.3.1   Security issues in private cloud

When cloud infrastructures are deployed for exclusive use for a single organization having manifold users, this is a business model where it is possessed, administered and operated by a single organization or a third party or may be managed by the collaboration of both. In the private cloud, resources and applications which are made available by the cloud providers are pooled together for sharing the resources by the cloud users. In view of security issues, though the private cloud is more secure than any other deployment model, the authenticity of the users is needed to be guaranteed carefully. Any unauthorized use may break the security wall and create a threat to the cloud. In a private cloud, CSPs need to maintain and resolve all security issues. The main advantage of the private cloud is that all resources are shared among the authorized private personnel and bound to internal use only.

8.2.3.2   Security issues in public cloud

When cloud infrastructures are set up for open use for the general public, it is handled and operated by some government or business organizations. It exists in the premises of cloud providers. In the public cloud, all the resources are common and shared among the customers dynamically, and a computing mechanism which is called pay-per-use utility is maintained. This type of cloud is less secure as the resources are shared among the public on-demand basis. It is vulnerable to malicious attacks by a third party. Robust authentication techniques are needed to ensure secure user data. Examples of such types of cloud are Microsoft Azure and Google App Engine.

8.2.3.3   Security issues in community cloud

Open Cirrus Cloud Computing Testbed, a collection of federal data centers across six sites stretching from North America to Asia, is a typical example of community cloud, which is when a cloud infrastructure is shared by numerous organizations in a community and is managed by a third party. Another example of community cloud is Facebook which is most popular nowadays. The community cloud model is less secure in comparison to other deployment models. There is no robust mechanism to separate users from each other in the cloud deployment. Account hijacking, stealing of information and privacy of data are affected in this type of model. So the security needs to be strengthened enough to safeguard user's data.

8.2.3.4   Security issues in hybrid cloud

It is a hybrid of private and public clouds, in which a private cloud is connected to one or more external services and functions as a single unit within a secure network. It has an open architecture that allows it to connect to other management or supervisory systems. Amazon Web Service is an example of a hybrid cloud (AWS). The security of data storage is provided through applications acting as a firewall, spam filter, etc. Because of the collaboration of different models, it is more prone to security threats. There may be issues like Service-Level Agreement (SLA) [14] among the cloud providers (SaaS, PaaS and IaaS providers) and cloud users. The service providers may blame each other for any shortcomings arise upon the security issues of the applications, servers or tools.

8.2.4   Security challenges in the cloud environment

The primary goal of cloud computing is to increase processing power such that millions of instructions can be executed each second (Figure 8.6). Cloud computing is made up of two parts: the user end and the cloud end. The user end includes

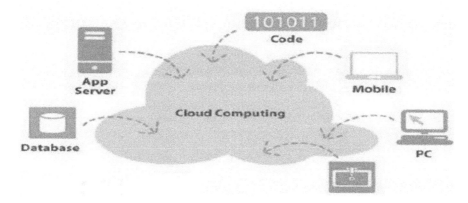

Figure 8.6   The cloud computing environment

the user's devices, such as a computer, laptop, mobile phone, or any other access device, as well as any application software that requires cloud services access. The cloud end consists of high-speed computing devices, servers and distributed database system which provide the required access to the clients and hence form a cloud environment.

The user end needs to connect his accessing devices like PC, laptop or mobile to the cloud to access his data stored in a server in the cloud through an interface software using the internet. The cloud being a distributed architecture, the user data are stored in CSP's server, and the place of the server is unidentified to the clients and the users.

The CSP's servers are managed by administrative groups to whom users need to depend upon for safeguarding data and maintaining its privacy. The administrative group members, who are trading with user's data, can be a threat to secrecy and privacy of user's data. A threat management policy ensures that the cloud should not be able to determine any evidence about the client's data. The followings are the security challenges which need immense attention.

8.2.4.1   Vulnerabilities

Applications like Gmail, Yahoo or Facebook are provided to users via an internet browser. Attackers are penetrating the client's computer or application by using the web browser. Customary security solutions are not sufficient to protect data from attacks. Consequently, advanced measures are required to be enforced. In the virtualization technique, varied instances running on the same corporeal machine need to be secluded. A VMM [15, 16] software is implemented to separate substantial resources from different virtual machines running simultaneously. There are vulnerabilities in Microsoft Virtual PCs or Microsoft Virtual Servers that can allow a casual visitor or third party to run malicious code on the host or another operating system. Two virtual machines using a covert channel can communicate with each other bypassing all the rules defined by the VMMs. Another cloud threat is called

Threat 11 [17]. In this, an attacker creates a negative Virtual Machine image containing malware or virus. Then the attackers publish it on the provider's storage area. The users then retrieve them and infect the whole cloud environment.

To counter this attack, **Mirage** [18], an image management system, was proposed, which focuses on the access control mechanism, image filtrations, derivation tracking system and warehouse maintenance services. VMs are to be root-locked, so that virtualized guest environment is not permitted to interface with the host systems.

8.2.4.2   Attack in networks

8.2.4.2.1   Sniffer attacks

Data in a network travel from one node to another as a packet. Capturing of these packets by intruders in a network is termed as sniffer attack. The data packets which are not encrypted may be accessed and modified by the unauthorized guests, and hence, vital data packets may lose its identity. A sniffer detection program through the Network Interface Card guarantees that the data linked to specific systems in the network are recorded so that its identity of data remains intact. Address Resolution Protocol (ARP) [19] is used to detect sniffing attacks, where it maps the IP address with the MAC address of the machine so that the data travel toward the designated machine only. Another method called Round Trip Time [19] is also used in a sniffing detection platform to detect a sniffing attack in networks. Here also attackers try to copy the MAC address and capture the data by using their own modified software.

8.2.4.2.2   Spoofing attack

When a malicious party launches attacks which target network hosts and steal data, it then spreads malware or bypasses access controls by imitating another user's device. Internet Protocol (IP) address spoofing, ARP spoofing, and Domain Name Server (DNS) server spoofing are all examples of typical spoofing attacks. To attack a network, attacker must link his MAC address and IP address of any actual existing user in the network. The attacker sends spoofed IP address. Here the data which is meant for the original user are sent to the attacker, and the attacker steals the information and modifies data; this type of data is also included in session hijacking and man-in-the-middle attacks.

A DNS associates an IP address to a domain name and vice versa. DNS resolves Uniform Resource Locators (URLs), email IDs and other readable domain names in their respective IP addresses. In this type of attack, the attackers modify the server to redirect the domain name to a different IP address and infect the data with malware. Spoofing attacks can be mitigated to some extent by utilizing packet filtering, spoofing detection software and cryptographic network protocols (TLS, SSH and HTTPs).

8.2.4.3   Reused IP address

This is a big security issue in terms of network security. Users migrate from one network to another network frequently. So the old user when migrated from the current network to another one, the old user's IP address is reconfigured to a new user. A cache log for IP addresses of the departing users in the DNS server [20] remains active for a specific time and the time lag or delay between the reassigned IP addresses and the cache log in DNS server creates a significant security issue. Hence, the attackers may use the cache log of the DNS and modify the DNS with malware which would violate the originality of the data of new users.

8.2.4.4   Relationship with the third party

The PaaS providers offer web services of different vendors along with their programming language. Cloud provider sometimes subcontracts a third party for data backup in order to recover data in case of adversity. So the use of multitenant architecture and flaw in either one may affect the other, and the interconnection complexities raise many security issues. There must be some mechanism or agreed-upon policies, i.e., SLA among the CSPs, subcontracted parties and cloud users to counteract those issues which can be a security threat for stored data.

8.2.5   *The threat management techniques*

8.2.5.1   Cryptography

Cryptography is meant as the nonfeasibility of breaking the encryption system and unable to compute the information about exchanged messages. The main aim of cryptography is to safeguard the data over an insecure communication channel. Several techniques are used in cryptography to encrypt and decrypt data. The different cryptographic techniques are discussed with their relative advantages and disadvantages in the following paragraphs.

8.2.5.1.1   The private key cryptography

Suppose party M needs to send a secret message m to party N which should not be intercepted by a third party. The **Private Key Encryption** [21] was the traditional solution to this problem. The two parties (M and N) meet together and decide to pass the message by agreeing upon a combination of data encryption and decryption algorithm 'E' and 'D' and some additional data 'S.' The additional information is kept secret between M and N. Now, the intruder may know the 'E' and 'D' algorithm but not aware of the secret key 'S.' When M wants to send a communication 'm' over an uncertain channel, M encrypts the plaintext message 'm' by computing the **cipher text c=E(S, m)** and sends c to N. After receiving c, N decrypts the c by **computing m=D(S, c)**. The intruder does not know S and hence unable to decrypt c to get the message m. This mechanism is useful for a small amount of data or message and if the data are handled by two users only. Now, in the present days, data are not handled by users alone. A significant amount of data needs to be shared among millions of different users. Hence a cryptographic key needs to be flexible enough to handle such big data. A cryptographic algorithm needs to be strong enough to protect the data. So the private essential encryption technique became obsolete in modern days.

8.2.5.1.2   The public key cryptography

The requirement of M and N to share a secret key 'S' in order to encrypt and decrypt the message 'm' was dropped by the development of the **Public Key Cryptography** [21]. In this method, the receiver N can publish authenticated information which is called Public Key. The receiver issues the Public Key to anyone who wants to send information, including the intruder party. There is an encryption algorithm containing a Public Key which whoever can recite can transmit an encrypted message to a person whom the sender did not meet personally. The receiver, by using his secret private key, can decrypt the sender's message at his convenience. A trapdoor function is included in the public key encryption algorithm. A trapdoor mathematical function is a single-side function which contains some trapdoor or secret data. The receiver alone can retrieve the information to decrypt the sender's encrypted message. Diffie and Hellman introduced it in 1976 in the seminal work.

Suppose, M needs to deliver a message m to N,

M needs to compute ξ (f, m)= f(m)= c and sends to N, where c is the encrypted message.

To decrypt c=f (m),

N needs to compute f^{-1} (c)= f^{-1} (f(m))= m. f is a trapdoor function.

The public key cryptography is suitable for multiuser systems. Though the public key encryption is more secured than the private key, in practical cases, the secret key needs to be transmitted over the communication channel. Hence, the discovery of the secret key by the adversary during transmission may cause a threat. One significant advantage of pubic key encryption is that it can facilitate the digital signatures for authentication, but sharing of secret keys requires trust on the opposition party that he should not compromise the secrecy of the secret key.

8.2.5.1.3   Data encryption standard with the fixed message

The Data Encryption Standard (DES) [21] is a symmetric block cipher which was discovered by the National Institute of Standard and Technology (NIST) (Figure 8.7). Suppose there is a fixed 64-bit message m that defines the function f(K)= DES_K (m) which takes a key K to 64-bit output f(K). This seems like a one-way function and uses a Feistel structure of 16 rounds.

The DES is nowadays considered to be insecure [22] because of a possible brute force attack in 2008 due to its small key length. The same is superseded by Advance Encryption Standard (AES) in recent days.

8.2.5.1.4   The Advance Encryption Standard

In AES [21], a substitution-permutation network is used. Its origin is Rijndael cipher. The Rijndael cipher uses a different key and block size. It does not use the Fiestel network, which is used in DES. The AES utilizes a fixed block and set size of 128 bits. A 128, 192 or 256 bits key size is used. The key size is any multiple of 32 bits with a minimum 128 and a maximum 256 bits. It conducts on a 4 × 4 column-major order matrix of bytes which is termed as the state.

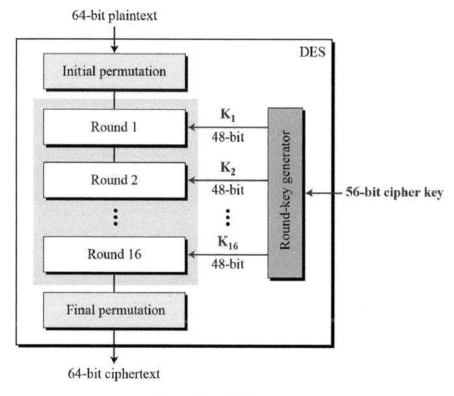

Figure 8.7   DES operation

For instances, suppose there are 16 bytes, starting from x0, x1, x2, x3 ... to x15. These bytes can be represented as the following:

$$\begin{bmatrix} x_0 & x_4 & x_8 & x_{12} \\ x_1 & x_5 & x_9 & x_{13} \\ x_2 & x_6 & x_{10} & x_{14} \\ x_3 & x_7 & x_{11} & x_{15} \end{bmatrix}$$

The key size identifies the number of replications of transformation rounds which translate the input message, i.e., the plaintext, in the final outcome, i.e., the cipher text. The AES operation can be illustrated as follows (Figure 8.8):

The key length decides the number of rounds that an AES operation should have. It performs ten sets for 128-bit keys, 12 sets for 192-bit keys and 14 sets for 256-bit keys.

Each set of AES again has four subprocesses (Figure 8.9):

1. SubBytes
2. ShiftRows

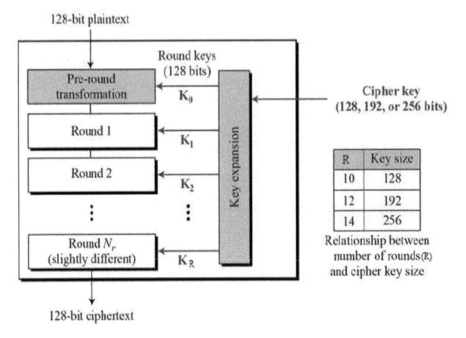

128-bit plaintext

128-bit ciphertext

Figure 8.8   AES operation

3. MixColumn
4. AddRounKey

The **biclique attack** is one kind of **Meet-In-The-Middle (MITM)** technique. It uses a biclique arrangement to expand the number of possible attack sequences by the MITM attack. In AES, the biclique attack is best known as single key attack. The attack has $2^{126.1}$ as computational complexity, and hence, it is known a theoretical attack that is based on security of the AES has not been cracked till now. Care must be taken for correct implementation of AES and acceptable key management policy.

8.2.5.2   The RSA algorithm

The **RSA algorithm** [22] is the public key encryptosystem used for encryption of message and secure data transfer in a network. In this cryptosystem, the key is public, i.e., open to all. The decryption key is kept private which is called the private key. The RSA is drawn from the initial letters of the surname **Ron Rivest**, **Adi Samir** and **Leonard Aldeman**, the inventors of the algorithm. The RSA is the most evident algorithm, and it can be applied to safeguard the data in the cloud [23].

The RSA algorithm comprises four primary phases, namely: (1) key generation, (2) key distribution, (3) encryption and (4) decryption.

The RSA algorithm deals with two keys, namely, the public and a private key. To encrypt a message, public key is used whereas to decrypt the message private

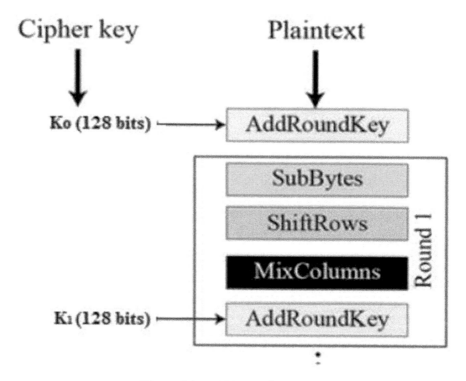

Figure 8.9   *AES round operation*

key is used. Here, we find three big positive integers *a, p* and *d* so that the integrated exponentiation for all *m*:

(m^a)^p mod d = m

Even knowing *a, d* or even *m*, it is very tough to find *p*.

Modular exponentiation: It is exponentiation calculated over a modulus. It is useful for public-key cryptography. It computes the residual when an integer *b* is put up to the eth power (the exponent), i.e., b^e is divided by appositive integer *m* (the modulus). The modular exponentiation c is calculated as $c \equiv b^e$ (mod *m*).

8.2.5.2.1   Key generation of RSA

The key generation is a crucial part of the RSA algorithm. To generate the key, two prime numbers are selected distinctly. The prime numbers are of same magnitude and selected randomly. Now compute n=p.q. For both the private key and public key n is used as modulus and its length is expressed in bits which are termed as key length. Calculate $\varphi(n)= \varphi(p). \varphi(q)=(p-1)(q-1)= n- (P+q-1)$. Find out e $\equiv d^{-1}$ (mod $\varphi(n)$). In simple terms, it can be stated that for a given d.e $\equiv 1$(mod $\varphi(n)$), take out the solution for e. With the length of e being short and small Hamming weight, more efficient encryption can be achieved.

Here, e and d are released as public key exponent and private key exponent, respectively. Public key is generated by merging the public exponent e and modulus n, similarly for private key generation, modulus n and private exponent d are merged.

8.2.5.2.2   The RSA key distribution

If Tom intends to convey a message to Jerry, Jerry needs to transmit public key (d, a) so that Tom can transmit the message via a reliable but may not a secure channel. Jerry does not share the private key.

8.2.5.2.3   Encryption

Suppose Tom wants to send message M to Jerry. First, Tom needs to turn the message M in integer m, in a manner $0 \leq m < d$ and gcd (m, d)=1 by utilizing a padding scheme which is a prearranged reversible protocol. Tom then calculates the cipher text c using Jerry's public key a corresponding to **c=m^a mod d**. Even for 500-bit numbers, this can be done efficiently using modular exponentiation. Tom then sends c to Jerry.

8.2.5.2.4   Decryption

After receiving the message, Jerry can now recover the message m with the private key exponent p by calculating $c^p = (m^a)$ $^P=m$ mod d. Jerry finds the original message M using m and reversing the padding scheme.

8.3   Review on existing proposed models

8.3.1   SeDaSC

Ali *et al.* [14] proposed a model on Secure Data Sharing on Cloud (SeDaSC) titled 'SeDaSC: Secure Data Sharing in Cloud.' In their model, the user file is encrypted by a single encryption key called the **master key**. After encryption of the file, the master key is then divided into two different key shares for every user. One key part is possessed by the user, which keeps away the intruder (insider threat) from the user data and another key part is retained from a reliable third-party body which is termed as **Cryptographic Server (CS)**. The master key is then deleted permanently. The key part alone cannot decrypt user data. It needs to generate the master key again with the help of the two key parts to decrypt the user's file. See Figure 8.10.

8.3.1.1   Working of the 'SeDaSC' model

There are three main entities in 'SeDaSC' model, namely: (a) users, (b) CS and (c) the cloud. In the primary phase, a user or data holder loads the data, list of users who are going to use the data and the parameters which are needed to generate an Access Control Lists (ACL) in the CS. The CS then being a reliable third party takes all the responsibilities of access control, key management, encryption and decryption of the data/file. The CS generates a master key and encrypts the data with the produced

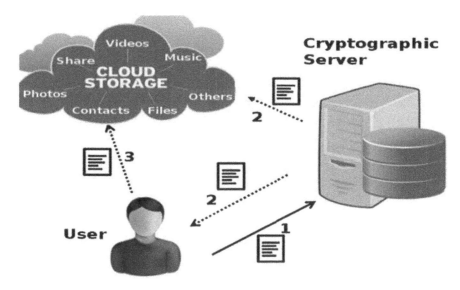

Figure 8.10   The basic idea of SeDaSC methodology

master key. To prevent the regeneration of the original master key, the master key is divided into two parts. Secure overwriting is used to delete the original master ley. One part is the CS retains the key along with the ACL list maintained by the CS and the other part is being sent to the users in the circle. The encrypted file is stored in the cloud by the CS on behalf of the users. A CSP maintains the cloud storage [24–32].

The user, when wants to retrieve the data, sends an access request to the CS. The CS, after receiving the request, downloads the required user's file and asks for the key part available with the user. After receiving the user key part, it authenticates and reconstructs the master key with the help of the user's key, and CS maintained portion of the key for that particular user. The user's file is then decrypted with the master key newly generated and sent back to the user who requested the data. If a new member joins with the existing group, the new user ID is added to the ACL, and two parts of the key are again generated. For the member who is leaving the group, his identification is deleted from the existing ACL. There is no possibility of accessing the data by the departing member, as he is having only the user part of the key [33–40]. The 'SedaSc' model also suggests that the frequent encryption/decryption is not required in the event of any change in the group membership.

The 'SeDaSC' model claims that the methodology can be utilized in mobile cloud computing in supplement to existing conventional cloud computing since the cryptographic server performs compute-intensive operation.

8.3.1.2   Discussions on SeDaSC model

Though the SeDaSC model seems to be muscular in terms of safety and privacy of data, it lacks in addressing so many issues. The model itself is a complex one. The computational burdens in this model make it unhealthy for handling millions of data and keeping user's data separate from other users in the network. The following issues need to have greater attention to upgrade the security issues for the data.

1.   The cryptographic server (CS) :
     1.   To maintain a CS in the cloud environment is a considerable task and two-step generation of user key will impose an intensive computation cost and an overburden increase in pay-per-use definitely would discourage the cloud users from storing their data.
     2.   The administrators of the CS may not be trustworthy. The tainted administrators may retain the user's portion of the key, and the data security and privacy may be violated.
     3.   A duplicate ACL list for the outgoing members of the group may exist in the server as a mirror image and can be used by the departing members as they are already holding the user portion key.
     4.   The CS may not receive a response due to unreachability/withdrawal/denial of service at any point in time, and then whole data will be lost. There is no mechanism to recover the data as the user alone cannot recover the data without the CS portion of the key. Moreover, the encryption and decryption of data are done by the CS only. So the users have no control over their data.
2.   The sharing of keys within a multitenant cloud environment is not recommended.
3.   The CSP needs to maintain user's records along with the CS records and an additional network link with the CS, which makes the cloud environment a critical mesh.

8.3.2   The 'SecCloud' protocol

Lifei, Haojin Jhu *et al.* [41] introduced a privacy cheating discouragement and secure computation auditing protocol which is named as 'SecCloud.' They claimed that the proposed 'SecCloud' is the first protocol that bridges between protected storage and protected computation auditing into the cloud. It achieves the privacy cheating discouragement through specified verifier signature, batch verification and probabilistic sampling techniques. They also tried to develop a 'practical secure-aware cloud computing experimental environment' which is named 'SecHDFS,' a test platform to employ 'SecCloud.'

8.3.2.1   The working of the 'SecCloud'

The model considers a general cloud computing model which is having several cloud servers S1 to S_N. The servers are in control of one or multiple CSPs. A mobile phone or a laptop (called as cloud users or CU) which is having lesser storage is connected to CSP to avail the resources (computation and storage) of the cloud. It is also assumed that there are verification agencies or VAs trusted by CUs and responsible for auditing the storages and computing of the CSPs. VAs are assumed to be having more powerful computing capability than CUs. See Figure 8.11.

Now, if any adversary $\mathcal{A}$ could corrupt a small group of cloud servers and affect these servers to introduce numerous cheating attacks as below:

a. Storage cheating attacks: when the adversary modifies the store data to negotiate data integrity or discloses the confidential data to purchase interest or both.
b. Computing cheating attack model: The attack can be for data computation security of the cloud. The attackers can leave the cloud with erroneous computing for the users, yet the data seem to be original.
c. Privacy cheating attack model: The attackers can reveal or leak the data to the public for business competition. If the data are not encrypted, i.e., plaintext data, the data can be sold out by the adversary.

To protect the valuable data from the attackers, the 'SecCloud' provides two concepts as follow:

a. Secure computation confidence (SCC): to specify the trust level of computation security
b. Secure storage confidence (SSC): to improve the confidence level of storage security

The SCC shall be defined as $|F'|/|F|$ and SSC is defined as $|X'|/|X|$,
where F is the total critical computation request, F' is the computation carried out precisely, X is the requested data set and X' is the honestly returned data set. If the values of SCC and SSC are both equal to 1, then the cloud computation and cloud storage are regarded as trusted. Otherwise, they are semitrusted.

Based on the above probability, the report suggests two definitions which would safeguard the cloud storage and calculation in the same way.

The protocol is able to achieve the following goals:

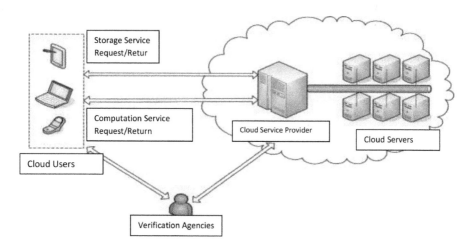

Figure 8.11   Cloud computing architecture in SecCloud protocol

a. Data storage security by the effective auditing of CU and VA.
b. Data computation security by VAs verification and auditing by CU and VA [42, 43].
c. Privacy cheating discouragement because of verification by a designated party and discouraging CSPs for revealing privacy of CUs data even if the attackers attack the servers.

8.3.2.2   Discussion on 'SecCloud' protocol

Before running the proposed protocol, there is a need for system set-up step by the System Initialization Operator (SIO) which generates the system parameters *params* and the master secret key 's.' There is another offline user registration step in which user needs to register to SIO, and after submitting the customer ID to SIO, the user receives system parameter *params* and a secret key.

The proposed protocol performs the following four steps:

a. The proposed protocol requests for a storage space to the CSPs and the CSP allocates a space by returning a space index *i* for the message to be stored.
b. The CUs need to sign each transmitted message block to enable the VAs for auditing.
c. CUs carry out data encapsulation for precomputing a session key by using the Bilinear Diffie-Hellman method. The CUs then send the data encrypted by the session key and corresponding signature pairs to the cloud for storage.

When the data are needed to be received, then the CSP decrypts the packet by using its session key to recover data signature pairs and check the signature for data authenticity by VAs using its secret key. The authority for checking the signatures is held by the CSP and VA only, and hence, it is claimed that the data are secured and protected.

Though the 'SecCloud' protocol claims to be robust and reliable, its shortcomings can be found as below:

a. The computing and transmission overhead is the primary concern here. The computing and transmission of encrypted data are very much involved and take much time which may cause time-out for access to the servers.
b. Here in this proposed model, we are again going to be dependent on a third party, i.e., Verification Auditors (which may reveal the valuable user's data and cause a threat. Verification auditors need to be persuaded that the cloud servers use the data on the exact location so that the cloud server's cheating behavior should not be detected.
c. In some cases, the users may face a denial of service due to the fact that verification auditors may become unresponsive due to connection loss with the users or servers.

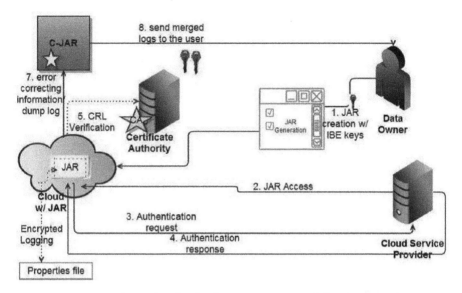

Figure 8.12   The cloud information accountability framework

8.3.3   Data accountability and auditing for secure cloud data storage

Prassanna *et al.* [44] and the team have evaluated the structure for data account-ability and reviewed cloud user data in the distributed cloud. They have proposed a mechanism that is technically monitoring any data access collected in the cloud with reviewing mechanism. The mechanism also suggests privacy – maintaining public auditing model for customer data that uses the cloud storage services in cloud computing.

8.3.3.1   Working of the 'data accountability and auditing' model

In cloud information processing (Figure 8.12), the model uses the principle of object-oriented technique. There is a component logger that is connected to the cloud cli-ents' data. The extraction is performed when the user data are retrieved from the remote server, and logging information is replicated with accessed data. The user's current processing of data and the component are accounted and kept a replica in the component log harmonizer. The second logger establishes the essential centralized element to enable the user to log in it.

The data user can come to know that whether the data are accessed by some-body else by the log harmonizer which keeps track of logging credentials of every data accessories.

The model again proposed a third-party auditing authority who is responsible for auditing the data accessibility. Vulnerability exists due to internal threats.

Here, it is noticed that most of the models are relying on a third party which is the leading cause of concern in the security issues of cloud computing. In this advanced era of technology, it is not advisable to rely on a third party.

8.4 Conclusion and future prospectives

The storage, virtualization as well as the various virtualization techniques and the network in use encompass a more significant security concern in a cloud computing environment. The security of user's data needs to be ensured at the highest level. Due to the complex architecture of the cloud, it is a big challenge to ensure the security of data at all levels in the cloud environment. Interconnections are complex among different architectures of CSPs. PaaS providers hire SaaS vendors for their service and also sometimes a third party for the backup of the user's data. The different providers must agree upon an SLA to secure the user's data. Users must be informed that what levels of standard securities are available with the CSPs and how their data are being stored.

This chapter discusses various security issues and challenges that are present in different cloud models and cloud environment. It gives a complete idea of other threat management techniques available to encounter security issues and challenges. Also, the chapter reviews the different proposed approaches published by various journals. The report explains an entirely different process (secure key transmission model) to enhance the security of the above issues and challenges, discussions and comparisons with the existing models.

References

[1] Cloud computing [online]. 2020Wikipedia. Available from https://en.wikipedia.org/w/index.php?title=Cloud_computing&oldid=987774983 [Accessed 9 Nov 2020].

[2] Buyya R., Pandey S., Vecchiola C. *Cloudbus Toolkit for Market-Oriented Cloud Computing.* Cloud Computing; Berlin, Heidelberg; 2009. pp. 24–44.

[3] IBM Software. 2020IBM [online]. Available from https://www.ibm.com/products/softwarehttps://www.ibm.com/products?types[0]=software [Accessed 9 Nov 2020].

[4] Ren Y., Tang W. 'A service integrity assurance framework for cloud computing based on MapReduce'. *IEEE 2nd International Conference on Cloud Computing and Intelligence Systems*; Hangzhou, China, 30 Oct-1 Nov; 2012. pp. 240–4.

[5] Karun A., Karat C. 'A review on hadoop—HDFS infrastructure extensions'. IEEE Conference on Information & Communication Technologies; Thuckalay, India, 11-12 Apr; 2013.

[6] Mell P., Grance T. The NIST definition of cloud computing. 800-145. National Institute of Standards and Technology, Gaithersburg, MD: NIST SP; 2011.

[7] Fernandes D.A.B., Soares L.F.B., Gomes J.V., Freire M.M., Inácio P.R.M. 'Security issues in cloud environments: a survey'. *International Journal of Information Security*. 2014, vol. 13(2), pp. 113–70.

[8] *Security guidance for critical areas of focus in cloud computing v4.0 [online]. cloud security alliance*. Available from https://cloudsecurityalliance. org/artifacts/security-guidance-v4/

[9] *Understanding-the-Cloud-Computing-Stack* [online]. Available from https://www.diversity.net.nz/wp-content/uploads/2011/03/Understanding-the-Cloud-Computing-Stack.pdf [Accessed 9 Nov 2020].

[10] *Cloud Security and Privacy* [online]. Available from https://www.oreilly.com/ library/view/cloud-security-and/9780596806453/ [Accessed 9 Nov 2020].

[11] Keene C. *What Is Platform as a Service (PaaS)* [online]?Available from http://www.keeneview.com/2009/03/what-is-platform-as-service-paas.html [Accessed 9 Nov 2020].

[12] Hashizume K., Rosado D.G., Fernández-Medina E., Fernandez E.B. 'An analysis of security issues for cloud computing'. *Journal of Internet Services and Applications*. 2013, vol. 4(1), p. 5.

[13] Jansen W.A. 'Cloud hooks: security and privacy issues in cloud computing'. *44th Hawaii International Conference on System Sciences, IEEE*; Kauai, HI, 2011. pp. 1–10.

[14] Ali M., Dhamotharan R., Khan E., *et al.* 'SeDaSC: secure data sharing in clouds'. *IEEE Systems Journal*. 2017, vol. 11(2), pp. 395–404.

[15] Zhang F., Chen H. 'Security-preserving live migration of virtual machines in the cloud'. *Journal of Network and Systems Management*. 2013, vol. 21(4), pp. 562–87.

[16] Subashini S., Kavitha V. 'A survey on security issues in service delivery models of cloud computing'. *Journal of Network and Computer Applications*. 2011, vol. 34(1), pp. 1–11.

[17] treacherous-12-top-threats [online]. Available from https://downloads.clou dsecurityalliance.org/assets/research/top-threats/treacherous-12-top-threats. pdf [Accessed 9 Nov 2020].

[18] Wei J., Zhang X., Ammons G., Bala V., Ning P. 'Managing security of virtual machine images in a cloud environment'. *CCSW '09: Proceedings of the 2009 ACM Workshop on Cloud Computing Security, ACM*; Chicago, IL, 2009. pp. 91–96.

[19] Ohlman B., Eriksson A., Rembarz R. 'What networking of information can do for cloud computing'. *18th IEEE International Workshops on Enabling Technologies: Infrastructures for Collaborative Enterprises, IEEE*; Groningen, Netherlands, 2009. pp. 78–83.

[20] Zhang L., Zhou Q. 'CCOA: cloud computing open architecture'. *2009 IEEE International Conference on Web Services, IEEE*; Los Angeles, CA, 2009. pp. 607–16.

[21] Goldwasser S., Bellare M. *Lecture notes on cryptography. introduction to modern cryptography [online]*. 2008. Available from https://cseweb.ucsd. edu/~mihir/papers/gb.pdf

[22]   Rivest R.L., Shamir A., Adleman L. *A method for obtaining digital signatures and public-key cryptosystems, communications of the ACM*. Vol. 21; 1978. pp. 120–26.

[23]   Wei J., Zhang X., Ammons G., Bala V., Ning P. 'Managing security of virtual machine images in a cloud environment, ACM 91-96'.2009, vol. 6(1).

[24]   Kumar S., Ranjan P., Ramaswami R., Tripathy M.R. 'EMEEDP: enhanced multi-hop energy efficient distributed protocol for heterogeneous wireless sensor network'. *Fifth International Conference on Communication Systems and Network Technologies (CSNT), IEEE*; Gwalior, India, 2015. pp. 194–200.

[25]   Kumar S., Ranjan P., Ramaswami R. 'Energy optimization in distributed localized wireless sensor networks'. International Conference on Issues and Challenges in Intelligent Computing Techniques (ICICT); Ghaziabad, India, 7-8 Feb; 2014.

[26]   Chauhan R., Kumar S. 'Packet loss prediction using artificial intelligence unified with big data analytics, internet of things and cloud computing technologies'. *5th International Conference on Information Systems and Computer Networks (ISCON), IEEE*; Mathura, India, 2021. pp. 1–6.

[27]   Sudhakaran S., Kumar S., Ranjan P., Tripathy M.R. 'Blockchain-based transparent and secure decentralized algorithm'. International Conference on Intelligent Computing and Smart Communication 2019. Algorithms for Intelligent Systems; Singapore: Springer; 2020.

[28]   Kumar S., Trivedi M.C., Ranjan P., Punhani A. *Evolution of Software-Defined Networking Foundations for IoT and 5G Mobile Networks*. Hershey, PA: IGI Publisher; 2020.

[29]   Kumar S., Ranjan P., Radhakrishnan R., Tripathy M.R. 'Energy efficient multichannel MAC protocol for high traffic applications in heterogeneous wireless sensor networks'. *Recent Advances in Electrical & Electronic Engineering*. 2017, vol. 10(3), pp. 223–32.

[30]   Kumar S., Ranjan P., Ramaswami R., Tripathy M.R. 'Resource efficient clustering and next hop knowledge based routing in multiple heterogeneous wireless sensor networks'. *International Journal of Grid and High Performance Computing*. 2017, vol. 9(2), pp. 1–20.

[31]   Kumar S., Cengiz K., Vimal S., Suresh A. 'Energy efficient resource migration based load balance mechanism for high traffic applications IoT'. *Wireless Personal Communications*. 2021, vol. 10(3).

[32]   Kumar S., Cengiz K., Trivedi C.M., *et al.* 'DEMO enterprise ontology with a stochastic approach based on partially observable Markov model for data aggregation and communication in intelligent sensor networks'. *Wireless Personal Communication*. 2022.

[33]   Punhani A., Faujdar N., Kumar S. 'Design and evaluation of cubic torus Network-on-Chip architecture'. *International Journal of Innovative Technology and Exploring Engineering*. 2019, vol. 8(6), pp. 2278–3075.

[34]   Dubey G., Kumar S., Kumar S., Navaney P. 'Extended opinion lexicon and ML-based sentiment analysis of tweets: a novel approach towards accurate

classifier'. *International Journal of Computational Vision and Robotics.* 2020, vol. 10(6), pp. 505–21.

[35] Kumar S., Ranjan P., Radhakrishnan R., Tripathy M.R. 'Energy aware distributed protocol for heterogeneous wireless sensor network'. *International Journal of Control and Automation.* 2015, vol. 8(10), pp. 421–30.

[36] Singh P., Bansal A., Kamal A.E., Kumar S.. (eds.) 'Road surface quality monitoring using machine learning algorithm' in Reddy A.N.R., Marla D., Favorskaya M.N., Satapathy S.C. (eds.). *Intelligent Manufacturing and Energy Sustainability. Smart Innovation, Systems and Technologies.* 265. Singapore: Springer; 2022.

[37] Kumar S., Ranjan P., Ramaswami R., Tripathy M.R. 'A utility maximization approach to MAC layer channel access and forwarding'. *Progress in Electromagnetics Research Symposium, Publisher: The Electromagnetics Academy*; Prague, Czech Republic, 2015. pp. 2363–67.

[38] Kumar S., Ranjan P., Ramaswami R., Tripathy M.R. 'An NS3 implementation of physical layer based on 802.11 for utility maximization of WSN'. *International Conference on Computational Intelligence and Communication Networks (CICN), IEEE*; Jabalpur, India, 2016. pp. 79–84.

[39] Reghu S., Kumar S. 'Development of robust infrastructure in networking to survive a disaster'. *4th International Conference on Information Systems and Computer Networks (ISCON), IEEE*; Mathura, India, 2019. pp. 250–55.

[40] Singh P., Bansal A., Kumar S. 'Performance analysis of various information platforms for recognizing the quality of indian roads'. *10th International Conference on Cloud Computing, Data Science & Engineering (Confluence), IEEE*; Noida, India, IEEE, 2020. pp. 63–76.

[41] Wei L., Zhu H., Cao Z., *et al.* 'Security and privacy for storage and computation in cloud computing'. *Information Sciences.* 2014, vol. 258(4), pp. 371–86.

[42] Kumar S., Ranjan P., Singh P., Tripathy M.R. 'Design and implementation of fault tolerance technique for Internet of Things (IoT)'. *2020 12th International Conference on Computational Intelligence and Communication Networks (CICN)*; Bhimtal, India, 25-26 Sep; 2020. pp. 154–9.

[43] Sharma A., Awasthi Y., Kumar S. 'The role of blockchain, AI and iot for smart road traffic management system'. *IEEE India Council International Subsections Conference (INDISCON), IEEE*; Visakhapatnam, India, 2020. pp. 289–96.

[44] Prassanna J., Punitha K., Neelanarayanan V. 'Towards an analysis of data accountability and auditing for secure cloud data storage'. *Procedia Computer Science, Elsevier.* 2015, vol. 50(4), pp. 543–50.

Chapter 9

Factors responsible and phases of speaker recognition system

Hunny[1] and Ayush Goyal[2]

The method of identifying a speaker based on his or her speech is known as automatic speaker recognition. Speaker/voice recognition is a biometric sensory device that recognizes people by their voices. Most speaker recognition systems nowadays are focused on spectral information, which means they use spectral information derived from speech signal segments of 10–30 ms in length. However, if the received speech signal contains some noise, the cepstral-based system's output suffers. The primary goal of the study is to see the various factors responsible for improved performance of the speaker recognition systems by modeling prosodic features, and phases of speaker recognition system. Furthermore, in the presence of background noise, the analysis focused on a text-independent speaker recognition system.

9.1 Study of related research

Many researchers have labored to develop various methods and algorithms for analyzing speech signals and simplifying speech and speaker recognition processes. In Reference [1], recent audiovisual (AV) fusion research is summarized. In References [2–6], a method is proposed to solve the issue of visual speech recognition.

The fusion of multiple biometric characteristics for identity authentication has shown strong benefits as compared to conventional systems based on unimodal biometric attributes. By combining visual speech and face information simultaneously, a new multimodal verification approach is explored in this study. Unlike face authentication, the proposed method uses visual speech lip movement features, which can reduce the risk of being duped by a fake face picture. To extract features of the face and visual expression, a Linearity Preserving Projection transform and a Projection Local Spatiotemporal Descriptor are used.

[1]KIET Group of Institutions, Delhi-NCR, Ghaziabad, India
[2]Department of Electrical Engineering and Computer Science, Texas A&M University – Kingsville, Kingsville, TX, USA

To combine the multisource biometric features, an Extreme Learning Machine-based fusion method is used in the corresponding score level to generate a fused score for the final verification. Experiments on the OuluVS database have shown that the proposed approach is capable of producing very good results.

Auxiliary loss multimodal GRU model [7] is divided into three sections:

- Feature extraction
- Data augmentation
- Fusion and recognition

Direction of arrival (DoA)-[8], TDoA or interaural time difference (ITD)-[9–12], ILD-[13–16], and HRTF-based processes are the most popular passive sound source localization methods.

A number of localization methods have been proposed for multiple signal estimation, covariance approximation, and signal parameter estimation using rotational invariance techniques [17]. Methods based on ILD, on the other hand, are often valid for a single dominant sound source [high signal-to-noise ratio (SNR)] in case of single dominant sound source [13–16], to name a few.

The minimum number of microphones available for ILD- or TDE-based methods is three [9–12] and [18–26]. Only HRTF-based techniques can be used to calculate the arrival angle. GCC with an ML estimator [20] is a widely used tool for TDE. Later References [18, 19, 21, 25, 27] suggested a slew of methods for developing GCC in the presence of noise.

For high accuracy robust speaker localization, a new PHAT-based approach known as steered response pattern-phase or power-phase transform was recently proposed [26]. The disadvantage of this method is that it takes longer to process than PHAT [22], as it necessitates the identification of a large number of user locations. References [13, 28, 29] used ILD to pinpoint the location of sound sources. While these studies used ILD-based methods to locate a source, Reference [30] used a pair of microphones to try 2D sound source localization using TDE- and ILD-based methods simultaneously. Reference [15] addresses a typical scenario of 3D localization with four or more sensors to boost source position accuracy. Sen and Nehorai recently used the Brown–Duda HRTF model to model multipath delays close to the sensor [23], and frequency-dependent head-shadow effects, in order to investigate 3D direction finding using auditory system of human with only two sensors [31].

In the last decade, several papers have attempted to use HRTF in combination with TDE to estimate elevation and azimuth angle of arrival [32]. Reference [33] concentrated on a straightforward beamforming technique. The Taylor series expansion [34] linearization solution has a high computational complexity, iterative processing, and needs a tolerable initial estimation of the location for convergence. Reference [9] suggested a method based on the assumption of a distant source. In the small error field, Reference [35] proposed a solution that can achieve the Cramer–Rao lower bound. When sensors are spread at random, the situation becomes more complicated. The intersection of a series of hyperbolic curves found by TDoA estimates using non-Euclidean geometry [36]. Reference [37] determines the emitter location in this case.

9.2 Phases of speaker recognition system

In the below-mentioned subsections, previous research work on recognition system of speaker is analyzed and addressed for each developmental phase.

9.2.1 Speaker database collection

This is where the development of a speaker recognition system starts. The development and evaluation of speaker recognition systems rely heavily on the basic speech database [38]. Changes in the field of speaker recognition could be influenced by the availability of speech databases.

When collecting speaker database for biometric speaker recognition, the most important factors to consider are session and channel variability, but other variables are also important to consider. Figure 9.1 depicts some of the most critical variables.

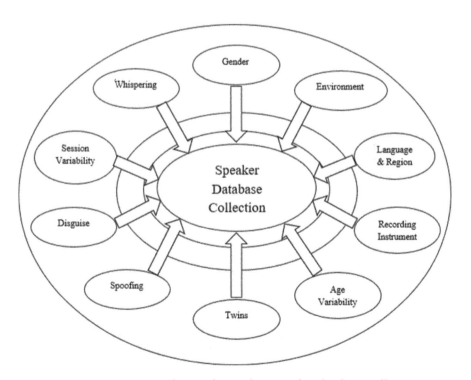

Figure 9.1   Various factors for a robust speaker database collection

9.2.1.1 Variability of session

Session variability applies to a phenomenon that causes differences between two recordings of the same speaker [39]. To put it another way, two different samples of speech recorded by the same person are unidentifiable by the computer [40].

Intersession variability is caused by a number of factors as follows.

9.2.1.1.1 Channel of transmission

It is a big part of why there is so much variation between sessions. This occurs due to differences in the transmission channels' characteristics. Despite the fact that speech signals obtained from voice transmitted over mobile phones (i.e., wireless channel) may differ from speech samples transmitted over landlines (i.e., wired channel), speech signals collected from voice transmitted over landlines (i.e., wired channel) may differ.

9.2.1.1.2 Characteristics of transducer

"Transducer" means a system that converts one signal into another. In the case of speech, a microphone is a transducer that transforms an audio signal into an electric signal. After that, the electrical signal is transformed into a speech sample, which is then saved. The type of microphone used has an effect on the speech sample's accuracy. The speaker recognition system cannot correctly identify the target speaker when different microphones are used in training and testing equipment [41].

9.2.1.1.3 Noise of environment

The amount of noise in different recording sessions can also vary, which may cause intersession variability. Due to number of things such as traffic, people talking near the recording site, and nearby industry, noise may be triggered [42].

9.2.1.1.4 Variability of intraspeaker

Same speaker's speech samples may have intersession variability because the acoustic characteristics of the speech sample are primarily dependent on the speaker's age, and psychological health, emotional state, and other factors. As a result, if there is a significant time delay between training samples and testing recordings, the features of the same speaker's voice can differ significantly. Intersession variability [43] must be compensated for reliable speaker recognition. Compensation methods such as feature mapping, feature warping, and others have been introduced [44, 45].

In contrast to biometric speaker recognition, there are a number of other aspects that must be discussed in forensic speaker recognition. The main causes of these problems are uncontrolled recording conditions and a lack of background speech data for comparison. To create a database for a forensic application, the developer must adhere to certain legal requirements. The law officials imposed some restrictions for the use of this content, one of which is that the final database cannot reveal a speaker's identity [15]. Real phone conversations from real police cases are included in the database. AHUMADA 3, a speech database recorded in Spain, is similar. Database Availability and Database Mismatch in the Sense of Forensics [46] are two major issues in FSR.

9.2.1.2   Gender

Biometric systems use sources like iris, palm-print, face, hand geometry, and voice, etc., to recognize individuals [47]. Along with above-mentioned characteristics, some ancillary knowledge about the user can be used to build a secure and user-friendly biometric device. Height, gender, age, and eye color of the individual person are examples of ancillary details. These are referred to as "Soft Biometric" characteristics. These characteristics may be continuous or discrete in nature. Gender is a discrete soft biometric characteristic. Despite the lack of distinctiveness in the use of soft biometric traits, gender can be used to filter [24] a broad biometric database [48]. Male and female speaker's voices vary greatly in the shape of some aspects of the speech signal, allowing them to separate out a huge amount of unnecessary data and a considerable amount of time is saved.

9.2.1.3   Environment

Researchers have recently become concerned about mismatch among training and testing environments. Speaker model synthesis [49], factor analysis [50], and feature mapping [51] are some of the techniques developed to address this problem. Parallel condition data are needed for accurate speaker recognition because features of the speech signal are influenced by surrounding conditions. Speech sample collected in the soundproof setting will have much better quality than the one recorded in a noisy classroom or library. A database with speech samples collected in various environments, such as a soundproof space, a noisy classroom, a library, an auditorium, and a market, should be created for this purpose.

9.2.1.4   Language and region

Speakers in a text-independent environment are not limited in what they may say for verification. This is an implicit verification while speaker is engaged in some activity, i.e., filing a complaint or conversing with a service representative. The majority of the speaker recognition scheme is bound to a single language [31]. India is a country with a large number of regional languages, making it a highly multilingual country. In addition, each region has its own influence on the language and its acoustic characteristics. In addition, different dialects of the same language are used in various parts of India. Pitch, energy, phenomes, and other acoustic characteristics of English spoken in North India differ from English spoken in South India. As a consequence, it is important to see how multiple languages, as well as a single language spoken in various areas, affect the system of speaker recognition [52, 53].

9.2.1.5   Instrument of recording

Speech samples may be recorded using a variety of instruments. The quality of the speech samples is influenced by the methods of recording. A digital voice recorder, laptop, cell phone, microphone, and long-distance phone call are some of the devices that can be used to build a quality database [54].

9.2.1.6   Age variability

The issue of aging and variations in speech quality is intertwined. Over time, the aging effect becomes more pronounced, and the standard of speech becomes more likely to deteriorate. Because of the aging effect, accuracy of any biometric system degrades over time [55, 56]. However, the impact of age variability on speaker recognition has received the attention of sporadic research. The problem of aging in a speaker recognition system can be solved by database updating at regular intervals.

A better, but more difficult, approach is to automatically adapt aging-related changes. The lack of a database is the most significant challenge in developing such a method. The public access to the longitudinal speaker database, which spans more than three years, is inaccessible. The key source of variability in the TCDSA (Trinity College Dublin Speaker Aging) database was ageing, but variance in speech quality was inevitable for such a long period of time. As a result, for a long-term and large-scale method, the database must contain data from different speakers at different times, or the database should be constantly updated in this manner.

9.2.1.7   Spoofing

Types of spoofing attacks are: (a) impersonation, (b) speech synthesis, (c) voice conversion, and (d) replay. Impersonation is when someone attempts to imitate another person who is a real speaker. The synthetization of the voice for the authentic speaker is done by using a speech synthesizer to spoof the verification process [57]. Conversion of voice is a method of spoofing the computer in which attacker's voice is automatically converted into the voice of a legitimate speaker using a conversion tool. The goal genuine speaker's prerecorded speech samples are replayed using a playing computer, which can be a cell phone, music player, or any other player. As a result, steps should be taken right from the start, during the compilation of speech databases, to prevent attacks of spoofing.

9.2.1.8   Whispering

The effect of deliberate speech behavior alteration on speaker recognition is studied, and a flaw in speaker recognition systems is presented. Whispered speech, a form of disguised speech created psychologically and/or physiologically, has recently piqued the interest of researchers [58]. Along with research into its acoustic characteristics, such as formant frequencies, corresponding bandwidth, and endpoint detection, researchers are also interested in its applications, such as reconstruction, speaker recognition, and so on. Whispered speech characteristics are:

i.   Since vocal cords do not vibrate, exhalation is the source of excitation.
ii.   SNR of whispered speech is low.
iii. When whispering, the enunciator's psychology is vulnerable [59].

9.2.1.9 Twins

Since 1990, the birth rate of twins has increased by an average of 3% each year, according to statistics [60]. Even though identical twins account for just 0.2 percent of the world's population, their numbers are comparable to the populations of countries such as Greece and Portugal. As a result, a biometric system capable of accurately distinguishing between identical twins that share the same genetic code is urgently needed [61]. The results showed that the voice and expression parameters of the twin pairs differ to varying degrees of similarity and dissimilarity.

9.2.1.10 Different speaking styles and situational mismatch

Unknown speech samples are captured from various sources, most of which are unknown to the speaker who utters them. As a result, the style of speaking can be similar to or completely different from that of the stored speech database [62].

A regular telephone conversation, something read by the speaker, or the speech in which the speaker is shouting over someone is all examples of the style. It is likely that the recorded speech contains the samples of two and more people (as in a meeting) or that someone is deliberately concealing to cause doubt. This may also be part of a police-suspect interview or a telephone information exchange [63].

9.2.1.11 Different stress levels and mental state of the speaker

Speech samples can result in an error if the speaker is in a different mental state at the time of two samples to be compared. For example, if one speech sample was taken when the speaker was in a normal mental state and another speech sample was taken when the speaker was ill mentally or in the influence of a sedative drug. The intraspeaker variability in both samples can be very high. Different levels of stress may also trigger this, regardless of whether the stress is physical, mental, or emotional [63].

9.2.1.12 Sparse background data

Due to legal issues with forensic database selection, the history database needed for the creation of speaker recognition model is scarce [64]. As a result, researchers have access to a limited amount of forensic data. No such data are available in the Indian context to our knowledge. A number of researchers have tried their hardest to compile databases with various samples approximate close to the practical data as possible, but not able to solve all of the above-mentioned issues.

Table 9.1 contains a list of few of the most well-known databases from all over the world. In India, some databases are also being created. The Chandigarh-based Center for Forensic Science Laboratory (CFSL) has created one database. To solve the issue of dialect variance and disguise as well as channel heterogeneity, they gathered a collection of ten different languages. One more database was created for a robust speaker recognition system that is not language-based. Captured samples in Hindi, Marathi, and Urdu to provide a diverse data for cross-lingual and multilingual speaker recognition as well as captured 180 Hindi, 200 Marathi, and 70

Table 9.1   Some available database for speaker recognition

S. no.	Name of database	Language used	Duration/ size	No. of speakers		−Type of data/ Text Used	EER	References
				M	F			
1	AHUMADA I, II, III	Spanish	–	150	250	Sentences/ Digits/ Words	0.5	[65]
2	ESTER- I, II	French	100 Hours	–	–	News, Debates, Tv Shows	1.1	[66]
3	ETAPE	French	30 Hours	–	–	News, Debates, Tv Shows	–	[67]
4	AUS-TALK	English	3,000 Hours	1,000		Story/ Sentences/ Digits/ Words	–	[68]
5	REPERE	French	60 Hours	–	–	News, Debates, Tv Shows	–	[69]
6	WHISPE	Spanish	5,000 words	5	5	Words	–	[70]
7	CIVIL-CORPUS	Spanish	20 Hours	28	32	Sentences/ Digits/ Words	–	[71]
8	NFI-FRITS	Dutch	4,188 Conversation	604		Conversations	12.1	[72]
9	FABIOLE	French	310 utterances	130		News, Debates, Tv Shows	2.5	[73]

Urdu speakers who record these samples by using various equipment for channel variability.

They also gathered databases for identical twins for the requirements of such information by forensic scientists. Another effort, using five separate networks in parallel, was made to build a database of 200 speakers in English and many Indian languages in the soundproof as well as noisy places. These databases are commonly used for biometric and forensic applications, and they still have some flaws. Many research issues, such as databases for crying and shouting voices, distance from the microphone, age variability, and spoofing, remain unsolved despite these efforts.

9.2.2   Feature extraction

The second step is to extract features from various speech signals. Speech has many characteristics, but a few characteristics are necessary to distinguishing various speakers.

Following are the optimal characteristics of the ideal function:

- It should be easily extracted from the speech signal.
- It should not be influenced by age variations.
- It should be used consistently and naturally in voice.

- It must be impossible to imitate or mimic.
- It should be robust for distortion and noise.

Multiple features must be used for speaker recognition, as all the above-mentioned characteristics are not fulfilled by a single feature. At the same time, the number of features considered for processing and recognition should be limited, as few techniques can handle high-dimensional data [11].

These characteristics have disadvantages as well, such as being less discriminative and easily mimicked. High-level functionality often necessitates a more complex framework. As a result, no function can be considered the best for recognition, and feature selection is a trade-off between robustness, discriminative property, and device implementation viability.

9.2.2.1 Short-term spectral features

Because of articulatory gestures, sound signals are extremely nonstationary. As a result, speech signal is broken into short frames for a pseudo-stationary signal. These short frames have a length of about 20–30 ms, and for extraction of spectral features, these frames can be considered stationary during this period. Glottal voice source causes a downward sloping spectrum, resulting in very low intensity at higher frequency range. Therefore, in order to raise the higher frequencies, these frequencies must be pre-emphasized [74].

The magnitude continuum is thought to be more significant and is usually retained for further processing on the basis of assumption that the phase spectrum contains only minor perceptual information. The "spectral envelop of the continuum" contains a vast information in speaker identification. The spectral envelop is a global form of DFT's magnitude spectrum. Lower frequencies receive more band-pass filters in order to reflect them with greater resolution [75].

Transformations are now used to reduce the dimensionality of sub-band energy values, which was previously used as features directly [76].

Multiple features used in combination, on the other hand, will lower the recognition error rate. In reality, any function from MFCC, LPCC, LSF, and PLP can be used depending on the application.

9.2.2.2 Voice source features

These characteristics bear speaker-specific data such as glottal pulse shape, fundamental frequency, and so on. The efficiency of the speech is determined by the parameters [77–90]. Close-phase covariance analysis can be done if the vocal folds are closed. Other methods have employed parameters such as residual phase, glottal flow model, cepstral coefficient, higher order statistics, and others. Voice source features are less reliant on phonetic content, while features of vocal tract are far more reliant on phonetic factors and, as a result, require extensive phonetic coverage, which necessitates a significant amount of data for training and testing. It is also noticeable that combining these two features will increase accuracy.

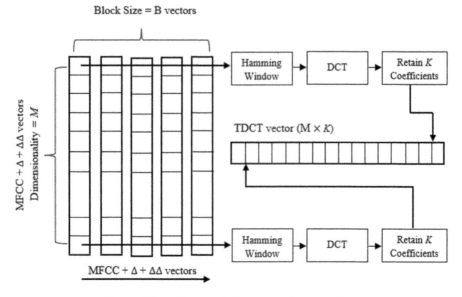

Figure 9.2   Temporal discrete cosine transform

9.2.2.3   Spectro-temporal features

Two spectro temporal details, i.e., formant transitions and energy modulation, may be used to extract a lot of speaker-specific detail. To provide temporal details to the functions, the delta (Δ) and double delta (Δ^2) coefficients, which are first- and second-order derivative estimates, can be used. The successive feature vector coefficient's time difference is used to calculate these coefficients and then combined with the original coefficients. If the number of original coefficients is n, then the total number of coefficients with Δ and (Δ^2) coefficients will be 3 n. For each frame, the process is repeated.

Figure 9.2 depicts the temporal discrete cosine transform process. Performance can be improved by integrating cepstral and temporal features instead of cepstral system alone, but the change was minor, and further study is needed before it can be used. Speaker recognition may also use modulation frequency as a feature. Details about the rate at which the speaker says words and some other stylistic attributes are included in the modulation frequency.

Speech intelligibility is measured using less than 20 Hz modulation frequencies. To achieve the highest efficiency with this function, a temporal window of 300 ms was used with less than 20 Hz modulation frequencies. Instead of spectrogram magnitudes, discrete cosine transform (DCT) can be applied to temporal trajectories for the reduction of dimensionality of the spectro-temporal features. DCT has an advantage over DFT in that it can minimize dimensionality while maintaining the relative phases of feature vectors, allowing phonetic- and speaker-specific information to be contained. Instead of using amplitude-based approaches, frequency modulation can be used to improve the unit. To separate speech signals into sub-band signals, band-pass filter bank can be used. Then, using dominant frequency components like frequency centroids, extraction of formant frequency features is done. Center and pole frequency difference in the sub-band can then be used as a frequency modulation-based function.

9.2.2.4   Prosodic features

Since prosody is such an important aspect of speech interpretation, it is critical to use prosodic features for the improvement of speech processing. In general, prosodic features are paired with other acoustic features for use in recognition systems; however, there are some drawbacks, such as the range of prosodic features, and therefore framework handling segmental features cannot accommodate these features. These features, which include pause length, syllable stress, speaking rate, pitch or tempo, intonation patterns, and energy distribution, are referred to as supra-segmental features.

Another issue is determining speaker differences through the processing of prosodic data, which can be instantaneous or long-term. Furthermore, the characteristics may be dependent on aspects that the speaker may alter deliberately. The fundamental frequency (F_0) is a prosodic function that is commonly used. Combination of F_0 (fundamental frequency) and spectral based features has proven to be the most efficient and reliable in noisy environments. Energy and length, in addition to F_0 related features, are much accurate than other prosodic features. F_0 is now explored in depth because it is the most critical prosodic function. F_0 includes both physiological and learned knowledge and these two information are essential for recognizing a speaker.

9.2.2.5   High-level features

Speakers can also be discriminated against based on the words they use often during a conversation. Doddington began doing research in this field in 2001 [78]. To discriminate against the speakers, an idiolect (a speaker's specific vocabulary) was used. The idea behind using high-level features is to turn utterances into the sequence of tokens and then distinguish various speakers based on the occurrence of a similar pattern of tokens. These tokens may be words, phonemes, or prosodic variations such as pitch or energy rises or falls. Figure 9.3 depicts the second and third phases, namely feature extraction and feature matching.

9.2.3   Feature mapping

Speaker identification/matching is the next, which is done after the features from speech signals have been extracted. The codebook model, statistic model, and template model are the most commonly used speaker recognition models.

Speakers can be identified using a variety of techniques. Major groups of these techniques:

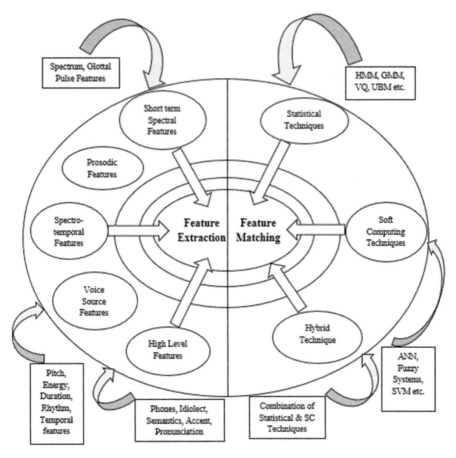

Figure 9.3   Second phase-feature extraction and final phase-feature matching

9.2.3.1   Statistical techniques

These techniques include HMM, GMM, UBM (Universal Background Model), and Vector Quantization (VQ), etc.

9.2.3.2   Soft-computing techniques

Soft-computing techniques are based on human mind's cognitive actions. Neural networks and fuzzy logic are two approaches that are developed by combining various methods for solving real-world problems.

9.2.3.3   Hybrid techniques

These techniques combine mathematical and soft computing techniques to take advantage of the benefits of both.

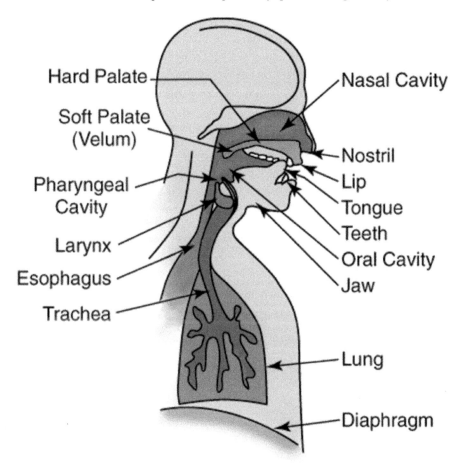

Figure 9.4 Human speech production system

9.3 Basics of speech signals

Speech signal is an input for each speech processing technique listed above. As a result, learning the fundamentals of speech signals is important. The basics of speech signals are presented here. First and foremost, in order to build good speech and speaker recognition systems, the human voice development and perception method and speech signal action must be understood.

9.3.1 Speech production system

Figure 9.4 depicts the speech production system. The diaphragm is displaced to produce sound, either to sniff into the lungs or to emit air. When air is expelled, it passes through the windpipe (trachea) and larynx, where vocal cord vibrations can have an effect. After that, the air travels into the pharyngeal cavity, oral cavity, and nasal cavity [91–99]. The final sound quality is now determined by the arrangement of articulators: velum (soft palate), tongue, lips, and mandible (jaw).

9.3.2 Speech perception

When compared to machines, humans hear speech sounds differently. Complex mathematical techniques are not used to analyze sound spectrum. The brain is very good at separating informative stimuli from distracting noises. These loud noises may come from variety of sources, such as large engine or a person speaking in French (if that person does not understand French language).

The human brain ignores almost all types of noise in order to retrieve important information. Another significant benefit of human speech recognition system is the capacity of humans to concentrate their attention on a single voice among many [100–103].

Using a phase mismatch of speech signals reaching the individual ear, the task of extracting one voice is accomplished. For people who can only listen with one ear, this intrusion is difficult to eliminate.

9.3.3 Speech signals

Density of medium affects speed at which speech is delivered. The amplitude of sound signal's air pressure variation and time is represented by the speech waveform.

This is similar to periodic signal and corresponds to articulated speech sounds such as vowels and voiced consonants such as "b," "w," and "z." Another form of speech sound is erratic which is aperiodic and appears to be caused by a random change in air pressure.

The hissing sounds in s' and sh', for example. These speech waveforms correspond to a pure tone and can be used to characterize more complex speech samples. Speech sounds are defined by a sinusoid. This pure form is very useful when discussing the properties of speech sounds.

9.3.4 Properties of the sinusoids

When plotted against time, sinusoid is simply a smooth up-down movement. A sinusoid can yield three different types of measurements, all of which together describe the waveform's shape. The measurements are broken down into subsections below.

9.3.4.1 Amplitude

Maximum movement of sinusoid above and below the zero-crossing relation is called amplitude. The amplitude of a speech signal represents its energy, and hence its loudness.

The calculation of amplitude can be done in a variety of ways. Amplitude calculation may be performed in a unit of pressure since it is related to degree of air pressure variation. It is usually expressed in decibels (dB), which is a logarithmic scale measurement for amplitude relative to normal signal. The dB scale is useful because it corresponds to how humans experience loudness.

9.3.4.2 Frequency

The number of cycles per second can be used to define frequency. An oscillation from zero-crossing reference to a peak, down to a peak below zero-crossing reference, and back to the zero-crossing reference is referred to as a loop.

The unit of frequency measurement is cycle/second. The time duration is the inverse of the frequency, or the amount of time it takes to complete a loop. Pitch of a speech sound is believed to change with difference in frequency (though the pitch is a more complex perceptual quantity).

9.3.4.3 Phase

Phase can be described as the location of sinusoid's starting point. Sinusoids that start at maxima have a phase of zero degrees, while those that start at minima have a phase of 180 degrees.

The phase is extremely difficult to interpret, but relative phase differences between two signals are much easier to detect. In fact, it is the foundation of human binaural hearing, as the human brain deduces the location of source of a speech sound based on phase differences heard in both the ears.

9.3.5 Windowing signals

Speech signals are studied over a brief period of time since signals can be considered stationary during this time period, requiring the speech signal to be separated into small chunks. As a result, before study, speech signals are windowed or cut out as a smaller section.

Signal is multiplied by a window function with an amplitude of one in area of interest and zero elsewhere, referred to as windowing. As a result, only the windowed signal is kept, while the rest is discarded. Rectangular window's disadvantage is abrupt shifts at the edges, as well as the distortion created by this in the signal to be analyzed.

A hamming window, which is relatively smooth window shape, is used to reduce distortion. It is beneficial to use hamming window, particularly when using frequency domain techniques. A rectangular window is useful for number of time-domain techniques. In order to calculate a broad signal, successive windows must be used.

9.3.6 Zero-crossing rate

The zero-crossing rate (ZCR) is the number of zero-crossings per second, or rate at which signal crosses midline in one second. This determines primary frequency of signals, i.e., frequency with greatest amplitude. When RMS and ZCR are combined, they can easily distinguish between voiced and unvoiced speech.

Unvoiced speech signals have a high zero-crossing rate, whereas voiced speech signals have a high RMS, so the properly weighted number of ZCR and RMS would be high for voiced signals and low for unvoiced signals.

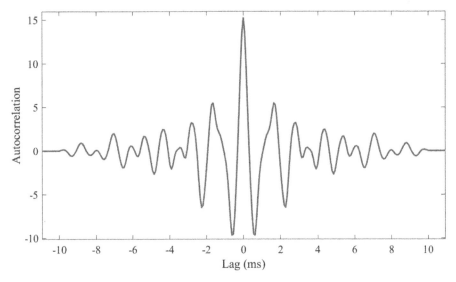

Figure 9.5   Autocorrelation of signal

9.3.7   Autocorrelation

Autocorrelation can be used to measure the pitch of voice. This approach is based on evaluating the relationship between speech signal and its delayed counterpart. When the delay is a pitch time, the phase of speech and its retarded variant will change, i.e., if one signal increases, another will rise as well, and vice versa.

When the delay is half the pitch time, there will be uncorrelated and out-of-phase signals, which means that if one signal rises, others drop, and vice versa. The autocorrelation curve shown in Figure 9.5 is obtained by plotting the degree of correlation versus lag between signal and delayed version of same signal.

A peak can be seen in plot at a point that relates to the lag of pitch duration. As a result, autocorrelation can be used to determine a sound's pitch.

9.4   Features of speech signals

The following characteristics of the speech signal are discussed:

- Physical features
- Perceptual features
- Signal features

9.4.1   Physical features

Following are some of these characteristics:

- Power
- Fundamental frequency
- Spectral features
- Duration of sound

9.4.1.1   Power

It is directly proportional to amplitude in speech signal and can be described as work done per second. The higher the power present in the signal, the louder the speech tone. Power calculation may also be used to determine presence of silence in a speech signal as well as the dynamic range.

Windowing the speech signal, squaring the sample, and obtaining mean afterward may be used to evaluate the strength in speech signal for short period of time.

The energy present in a specific frequency band may be used to detect the edges of speech signal. Applying a hard energy threshold to differentiate between frames with no signal and frames with low energy, such as the edges of fade, cannot work.

9.4.1.2   Fundamental frequency

The signals that are either periodic or pseudo-periodic which have a validated fundamental frequency, which is denoted by f_o. Periodic signals repeat themselves indefinitely with a period of τ, i.e., $(w(t+\tau) = w(t))$ and $f_o = \tau^{-1}$ for a maximum τ. The pseudo-periodic signal nearly repeats itself is represent by $(w(t+\tau) = w(t) + \varepsilon)$.

From one period to the next, the signal varies slightly, but still, $f_o = \tau^{-1}$ is valid, where ε corresponds to tolerance value. In this case, the signal is periodic if the calculated f_o is constant or roughly constant and true for the remaining signal. f_o is used to acquire the speech signal's edges.

The idea is that the significant variance in f_o is more likely to occur at the end of word rather than in the middle.

9.4.1.3   Spectral features

Of the many simple spectral features, bandwidth is one of most significant spectral features. Spectrum of different frequencies available in speech signals is named as bandwidth. To differentiate music from speech sounds, bandwidth (a spectral feature) is used.

9.4.1.4   Duration of sound

The period of sound is simply the length of time the sound lasts. This is used as a function of particular application based on multimedia database. If the unknown sound's duration appears to be similar to reference template, duration matching techniques may be used.

9.4.2   *Perceptual features*

The aim of extracting perceptual features from a speech signal is to determine which features humans use to distinguish between speech sounds.

The following are a few of them:

- Pitch
- Prosody

9.4.2.1   Pitch

Since pitch includes so much knowledge about speech signals, it tends to be a better perceptual function. It appears to be identical to a physical property known as frequency.

Frequency, on the other hand, is an absolute and numerical quantity, while pitch is a subjective and fluid quantity. It is perceptible; nevertheless, no human being can identify a particular pitch value.

9.4.2.2   Prosody

Prosody is a perceptual characteristic of speech that correlates to changes in pitch and phoneme duration, as well as significant pauses during a spoken word, which suggest deeper meaning.

It can also be used to emphasize a single word in a sentence. Prosody research for classification assumes that speech has already been understood and that prosody offers additional context. In the absence of understood voice, prosody may be used.

9.4.3   *Signal features*

Signal features are linked to speech sample's characteristics. In computer systems, a speech sample reflects the sound of speech.

These characteristics are statistical and quantitative in nature and are commonly related to how speech signals have been translated into information that computers can understand.

9.4.3.1   ZCR-related features

ZCR is a measurement of the number of zero-crossings per second. The spectral content of speech signals is determined by ZCR. The fundamental frequency (f_o) was determined using ZCR.

By first using filters to filter out high-frequency components that can degrade the measurement, a zero-crossing rate-based f_o detector can be created.

However, the cut-off frequencies of the filters must be chosen with care, as if they are not, the filters may delete f_o partially in order to remove as many high-frequency contents as possible.

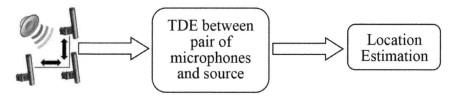

Figure 9.6 Stages of speaker localization

A ZCR-based f_o detector can be used to detect patterns in zero crossings and to hypothesize a measure of f_o-based patterns.

9.5 Localization of speaker

The method of calculating a person's position in room based on sound signal received by an array of microphones is known as speaker localization.

As shown in Figure 9.6, speaker localization can be done in two stages:

1. Calculate the TDE between each microphone pair and the source.
2. Estimated time delays and microphone distance information are used to determine the source's position.

Microphone arrays are arranged in a circular pattern in this method, but the issue is acoustic environment in which array is mounted. The microphones pick up not just the speech signals but also the reverberated signals as well as the ambient noise in this situation.

Meeting rooms with various types of sensors have recently become common. These are referred to as smart meeting spaces, and they use a microphone array to record multiperson meetings.

Additionally, the registered data can be used to automatically structure and index meetings.

9.6 Conclusion

On the basis of extensive literature review, we identified the various factors affecting the database of speech signal. Further study motivates us to explore the various techniques of feature extraction, and feature mapping techniques to identify the speaker have been explored based on the extracted features of speech signals.

References

[1] Alcazar V.J.L.L., Maulana A.N.M., Mortega II R.O., Samonte M.J.C. 'Speech-to-visual approach e-learning systems for the deaf'. *11th*

International Conference on Computer Science and Education, Nagoya, Japan; IEEE, 2017. pp. 239–43.

[2]   Chen S.-H., Wang J.-F., Chen M.-H, *et al*. 'A design of far-field speaker localization system using independent component analysis with subspace speech enhancement'. *11th IEEE International Symposium on Multimedia, 2009. ISM'09*; San Diego, CA, IEEE, Hyatt Regency Mission Bay Spa and Marina, 2009. pp. 558–61.

[3]   Duda R.O., Martens W.L. 'Range dependence of the response of a spherical head model'. *The Journal of the Acoustical Society of America*. 1998, vol. 104(5), pp. 3048–58.

[4]   Fang B.T. 'Simple solutions for hyperbolic and related position fixes'. *IEEE Transactions on Aerospace and Electronic Systems*. 1990, vol. 26(5), pp. 748–53.

[5]   Feng W., Guan N., Li Y., Zhang X., Luo Z. 'Audio visual speech recognition with multimodal recurrent neural networks'. *International Joint Conference on Neural Networks*; 2017. pp. 681–8.

[6]   Fernandez-Lopez A., Martinez O., Sukno F.M. 'Towards estimating the upper bound of visual-speech recognition: the visual lip-reading feasibility database'. *12th IEEE International Conference on Automatic Face and Gesture Recognition*; 2017. pp. 208–15.

[7]   Xenaki A., Gerstoft P. 'Grid-free compressive beamforming'. *The Journal of the Acoustical Society of America*. 2015, vol. 137(4), pp. 1923–35.

[8]   Richardson M.H., Formenti, D.L. J. 'Global curve fitting of frequency response measurements using the rational fraction polynomial method'. *Proceedings of the Third International Modal Analysis Conference, Publisher: Society for Experimental Mechanics*; 1985. pp. 390–97.

[9]   Hahn W.R. 'Optimum signal processing for passive sonar range and bearing estimation'. *The Journal of the Acoustical Society of America*. 1975, vol. 58(1), pp. 201–7.

[10] Lee H. 'A novel procedure for assessing the accuracy of hyperbolic multilateration systems'. *IEEE Transactions on Aerospace and Electronic Systems*. 1975, vol. AES-11(1), pp. 2–15.

[11] Schmidt R.O. 'A new approach to geometry of range difference location'. *IEEE Transactions on Aerospace and Electronic Systems*. 1972, vol. AES-8(6), pp. 821–35.

[12] Van Etten J. 'Navigation systems. fundamentals of low- and very-low-frequency hyperbolic techniques 192-212'. *Electrical Communication*. 1970, vol. 45(3).

[13] Birchfield S.T., Gangishetty R. 'Acoustic localization by interaural level difference'. *IEEE International Conference on Acoustics, Speech, and Signal Processing, Proceedings. (ICASSP'05), Vol. 4, IEEE, Philadelphia Convention Center*; Philadelphia, PA, 19–23 Mar; 2005. pp. iv–1109.

[14] Ho K.C., Sun M. 'An accurate algebraic closed form solution for energy-based source localization'. *IEEE Transactions on Audio, Speech and Language Processing*. 2007, vol. 15(8), pp. 2542–50.

[15] Ho K.C., Sun M. 'Passive source localization using time differences of arrival and gain ratios of arrival'. *IEEE Transactions on Signal Processing*. 2008, vol. 56(2), pp. 464–77.

[16] Julián P., Andreou A.G., Riddle L., Shamma S., Goldberg D.H., Cauwenberghs G. 'A comparative study of sound localization algorithms for energy aware sensor'. *IEEE*. 2004.

[17] Xu Z., Liu N., Sadler B.M. 'A simple closed form linear source localization algorithm'. *IEEE Military Communications Conference, MILCOM 2007*; IEEE, Gaylord Palms Resort and Convention Center, Orlando, FL, 29–31 Oct; 2007. pp. 1–7.

[18] Brandstein M.S., Silverman H.F. 'A practical methodology for speech source localization with microphone arrays'. *Computer Speech & Language*. 1997, vol. 11(2), pp. 91–126.

[19] Brandstein M.S., Adcock J.E., Silverman H.F. 'A closed-form location estimator for use with room environment microphone arrays'. *IEEE Transactions on Speech and Audio Processing*. 1997, vol. 5(1), pp. 45–50.

[20] Knapp C., Carter G. 'The generalized correlation method for estimation of time delay'. *IEEE Transactions on Acoustics, Speech, and Signal Processing*. 1976, vol. 24(4), pp. 320–7.

[21] Lleida E., Fernández J., Masgrau E. 'Robust continuous speech recognition system based on a microphone array'. *Proceedings of the 1998 IEEE International Conference on Acoustics, Speech and Signal Processing*; Vol. 1, IEEE, Washington State Convention and Trade Center, Seattle, WA, 12–15 May; 1998. pp. 241–4.

[22] Omologo M., Svaizer P. 'Acoustic event localization using a cross power-spectrum phase-based technique'. *IEEE International Conference on Acoustics, Speech, and Signal Processing, ICASSP-94*; Vol. 2, IEEE, Adelaide, South Australia, Australia, 19–22 Apr; 1994. pp. II–273.

[23] Razin S. 'Explicit (noniterative) Loran solution'. *Navigation*. 1967, vol. 14(3), pp. 265–9.

[24] Stéphenne A., Champagne B. 'Cepstral prefiltering for time delay estimation in reverberant environments'. *International Conference on Acoustics, Speech, and Signal Processing, ICASSP-95, Vol. 5, IEEE, ICASSP 1995*; Detroit, MI, 9–12 May; 1995. pp. 3055–8.

[25] Svaizer P., Matassoni M., Omologo M. 'Acoustic source location in a three-dimensional space using cross power spectrum phase'. *IEEE International Conference on Acoustics, Speech, and Signal Processing, ICASSP-97, Vol. 1, IEEE, ICASSP '97*; Munich, Germany, 21–24 Apr; 1997. pp. 231–4.

[26] Zhang C., Florêncio D., Zhang Z. 'Why does PHAT work well in low noise, reverberative environments?'. *IEEE International Conference on Acoustics, Speech and Signal Processing, ICASSP 2008, IEEE, ICASSP 2008*; Las Vegas, NV, 31 Mar, 4 Apr; 2008. pp. 2565–8.

[27] Wang H., Chu P. 'Voice source localization for automatic camera pointing system in videoconferencing'. *IEEE International Conference on Acoustics,*

Speech, and Signal Processing, ICASSP-97; Vol. 1, IEEE, Munich, Germany, 21–24 Apr 1997; 1997. pp. 187–90.

[28]   Sheng X., Hu Y-H. 'Maximum likelihood multiple-source localization using acoustic energy measurements with wireless sensor networks'. *IEEE Transactions on Signal Processing*. 2005, vol. 53(1), pp. 44–53.

[29]   Blatt D., Hero A.O. 'Energy-based sensor network source localization via projection onto convex sets'. *IEEE Transactions on Signal Processing*. 2006, vol. 54(9), pp. 3614–19.

[30]   Cui W., Cao Z., Wei J. 'Dual-microphone source location method in 2-d space'. *IEEE International Conference on Acoustics, Speech and Signal Processing, ICASSP 2006*; Vol. 4, IEEE, Toulouse Pierre Baudis Congress Center Toulouse, France, 14–19 May; 2006. pp. IV–IV.

[31]   Sen S., Nehorai A. 'Performance analysis of 3-D direction estimation based on head-related transfer function'. *IEEE Transactions on Audio, Speech, and Language Processing*. 2009, vol. 17(4), pp. 607–13.

[32]   Kulaib A., Al-Mualla M., Vernon D. '2D binaural sound localization for Urban search and rescue robotic'. *The 12th International Conference on Climbing and Walking Robots*; Istanbul, Turkey; 2009. pp. 9–11.

[33]   Carter G. 'Time delay estimation for passive sonar signal processing'. *IEEE Transactions on Acoustics, Speech, and Signal Processing*. 1981, vol. 29(3), pp. 463–70.

[34]   Foy W. 'Position-location solutions by Taylor-series estimation'. *IEEE Transactions on Aerospace and Electronic Systems*. 1976, vol. AES-12(2), pp. 187–94.

[35]   Abel J.S., Smith J.O. 'Source range and depth estimation from multipath range difference measurements'. *IEEE Transactions on Acoustics, Speech, and Signal Processing*. 1989, vol. 37(8), pp. 1157–65.

[36]   Eisenhart L.P. *A treatise on the differential geometry of curves and surfaces*. 26. Ginn, Paderborn dSPACE GmbH Rathenaustraße; 1909.

[37]   Sommerville D.M.Y. *The Elements of Non-Euclidean Geometry*. 288. North Chelmsford, MA: Dover Books on Mathematics Courier Corporation; 2012.

[38]   Haris B.C., Sinha R. 'Exploring sparse representation classification for speaker verification in realistic environment'. *Centenary Conference-Electrical Engineering*; Bangalore: Indian Institute of Science; 2011. pp. 1–4.

[39]   Ramos D., Gonzalez-Dominguez J., Gonzalez-Rodriguez J. 'High-performance session variability compensation in forensic automatic speaker recognition'. *The Journal of the Acoustical Society of America*. 2010, vol. 128(4),2378.

[40]   Kenny P., Boulianne G., Ouellet P., Dumouchel P. 'Speaker and session variability in GMM-based speaker verification'. *IEEE Transactions on Audio, Speech and Language Processing*. 2007, vol. 15(4), pp. 1448–60.

[41]   Vogt R.J., Baker B.J., Sridharan S. 'Modelling session variability in text independent speaker verification'. *Eurospeech/Inter-speech: Proceedings of*

the 9th European Conference on Speech Communication and Technology; 2005. pp. 3117–20.

[42] Vogt R., Sridharan S. 'Explicit modelling of session variability for speaker verification'. *Computer Speech & Language*. 2008, vol. 22(1), pp. 17–38.

[43] Benzeghiba M., De Mori R., Deroo O., *et al.* 'Automatic speech recognition and speech variability: a review'. *Speech Communication*. 2007, vol. 49(10-11), pp. 763–86.

[44] Pelecanos J., Sridharan S. 'Feature warping for robust speaker verification'. *Proceedings of 2001 A Speaker Odyssey: The Speaker Recognition Workshop. European Speech Communication Association*; ISCA, 2001. pp. 213–18.

[45] Reynolds D.A. 'Channel robust speaker verification via feature mapping'. *IEEE International Conference on Acoustics, Speech, and Signal Processing, (ICASSP'03)*; 2003. pp. II–53.

[46] Mignot R., Chardon G., Daudet L. 'Low frequency interpolation of room impulse responses using compressed sensing'. *IEEE/ACM Transactions on Audio, Speech, and Language Processing*. 2014, vol. 22(1), pp. 205–16.

[47] Ichinof M., Komatsuff N., Jian-Gangfff W., Yunffj Y.W. 'Speaker gender recognition using score level fusion by adaboost'. *11th International Conference on Control Automation Robotics & Vision*; 2010. pp. 648–53.

[48] Wayman J.L. 'Large-scale civilian biometric systems-issues and feasibility'. *Proceedings of Card Tech/Secur Tech ID*; 1997. p. 732.

[49] Teunen R., Shahshahani B., Heck L. 'A model-based transformational approach to robust speaker recognition'. *Sixth International Conference on Spoken Language Processing*; 2000.

[50] Yin S.-C., Rose R., Kenny P. 'A joint factor analysis approach to progressive model adaptation in text-independent speaker verification'. *IEEE Transactions on Audio, Speech and Language Processing*. 2007, vol. 15(7), pp. 1999–2010.

[51] Adami A.G., Mihaescu R., Reynolds D.A., Godfrey J.J. 'Modeling prosodic dynamics for speaker recognition'. *IEEE International Conference on Acoustics, Speech, and Signal Processing, Proceedings (ICASSP'03), Hong Kong, China*; 2003. pp. IV–788.

[52] Rao K.S., Maity S., Reddy V.R. 'Pitch synchronous and glottal closure based speech analysis for language recognition'. *International Journal of Speech Technology*. 2013, vol. 16(4), pp. 413–30.

[53] Bhattacharjee U., Sarmah K. 'A multilingual speech database for speaker recognition'. *IEEE International Conference on Signal Processing, Computing and Control, Publisher: IEEE, Solan, India*; 2012. pp. 1–5.

[54] Pradhan G., Prasanna S.M. 'Significance of speaker information in wideband speech'. *National Conference on Communications (NCC), Publisher: IEEE, Bangalore, India, DOI: 10.1109/NCC.2011.5734710*; 2011. pp. 1–5.

[55] Algazi V.R. 'Physical and filter pinna models based on anthropometry'. *Proceedings of 122nd Convention Audio Engineering Society, Presented at the 122nd Convention2007 May 5–8 Vienna, Austria*; 2007. pp. 718–37.

[56] Batteau D.W. 'The role of the Pinna in human localization'. *Proceedings of the Royal Society of London. Series B, Biological Sciences*. 1967, vol. 168(1011), pp. 158–80.

[57] Roffler S.K., Butler R.A. 'Factors that influence the localization of sound in the vertical plane'. *The Journal of the Acoustical Society of America*. 1968, vol. 43(6), pp. 1255–9.

[58] Oldfield S.R., Parker S.P. 'Acuity of sound localisation: a topography of auditory space. II. Pinna cues absent'. *Perception*. 1984, vol. 13(5), pp. 601–17.

[59] Chenghui G., Heming Z., Zhi T. 'Speaker identification of whispered speech with perceptible mood'. *Journal of Multimedia*. 2014, vol. 9(4), pp. 553–61.

[60] Martin J.A., Kung H.-C., Mathews T.J., *et al.* 'Annual summary of vital statistics: 2006'. *Pediatrics*. 2008, vol. 121(4), pp. 788–801.

[61] Hofman P.M., Van Riswick J.G., Van Opstal A.J. 'Relearning sound localization with new ears'. *Nature Neuroscience*. 1998, vol. 1(5), pp. 417–21.

[62] Brown C.P. Modeling the elevation characteristics of the head related impulse response. [Master's Theses and Graduate Research]. San Jose State University Scholar Works; 1996.

[63] Campbell J.P., Shen W., Campbell W.M., Schwartz R., Bonastre J.-F., Matrouf D. 'Forensic speaker recognition'. *IEEE Signal Processing Magazine*. 2009, vol. 26(2), pp. 95–103.

[64] Hwang S., Park Y., Park Y. 'Sound source localization using HRTF database'. *Proceedings of International Conference on Control, Automation, and Systems (ICCAS2005), KINTEX Gyeonggi-Do*; Korea (South), 2–5 June; 2005. pp. 751–5.

[65] Ortega-Garcia J., Gonzalez-Rodriguez J., Marrero-Aguiar V. 'AHUMADA: a large speech corpus in Spanish for speaker characterization and identification'. *Speech Communication*. 2000, vol. 31(2-3), pp. 255–64.

[66] Madden S.C., Galliano F., Jones A.P., Sauvage M. 'ISM properties in low-metallicity environments-I. mid-infrared spectra of dwarf galaxies'. *Astronomy & Astrophysics*. 2006, vol. 446(3), pp. 877–96.

[67] Gravier G., Adda G., Paulson N., Carré M., Giraudel A., Galibert O. 'The ETAPE corpus for the evaluation of speech-based TV content processing in the French language'. 2012.

[68] Dhall A., Goecke R., Joshi J., Wagner M., Gedeon T. 'Emotion recognition in the wild challenge'. *Proceedings of the 15th ACM on International Conference on Multimodal Interaction*; 2013. pp. 509–16.

[69] Galibert O., Kahn J. 'The first official repere evaluation'. *First Workshop on Speech, Language and Audio in Multimedia (SLAM 2013), 43-48*; 2013.

[70] Marković B., Jovičić S.T., Galić J., Grozdić Đ. 'Whispered speech database: design, processing and application'. *International Conference on Text, Speech and Dialogue*; Berlin, Heidelberg: Springer; 2013. pp. 591–8.

[71] Segundo E.S., Alves H., Trinidad M.F. 'Civil corpus: voice quality for speaker forensic comparison'. *Procedia - Social and Behavioral Sciences*. 2013, vol. 95(2), pp. 587–93.

[72] Vloed D.V., Bouten J., van Leeuwen D. 'NFI-FRITS: A forensic speaker recognition database and some first experiments'. *The Speaker and Language Recognition Workshop*; Joensuu, Finland, 16–19 Jun 2014; 2014.

[73] Ajili M., Bonastre J.F., Kahn J., Rossato S., Bernard G. 'Fabiole, a speech database for forensic speaker comparison'. *Proceedings of the Tenth International Conference on Language Resources and Evaluation (LREC'16)*; 2016. pp. 726–33.

[74] Harrington J., Cassidy S. *Techniques in Speech Acoustics*. Dordrecht: Kluwer Academic Publishers; 1999.

[75] Smith J., Abel J. 'Closed-form least-squares source location estimation from range-difference measurements'. *IEEE Transactions on Acoustics, Speech, and Signal Processing*. 1987, vol. 35(12), pp. 1661–9.

[76] Besacier L., Bonastre J.F., Fredouille C. 'Localization and selection of speaker-specific information with statistical modeling'. *Speech Communication*. 2000, vol. 31(2-3), pp. 89–106.

[77] Kinnunen T., Li H. 'An overview of text-independent speaker recognition: from features to supervectors'. *Speech Communication*. 2010, vol. 52(1), pp. 12–40.

[78] Doddington G. 'Speaker recognition based on idiolectal differences between speakers'. *Proceedings of Seventh European Conference on Speech Communication and Technology (Eurospeech 2001), Eurospeech 2001 - Scandinavia*; 2001. pp. 2521–24. Available from https://www.isca-speech.org/archive_v0/archive_papers/eurospeech_2001/e01_2521.pdf

[79] Haidar M., Kumar S. 'Smart healthcare system for biomedical and health care applications using aadhaar and blockchain'. Presented at 5th International Conference on Information Systems and Computer Networks, ISCON 2021, Publisher: IEEE; Mathura, India.

[80] Kumar S., Cengiz K., Vimal S., Suresh A., *et al.* 'Energy efficient resource migration based load balance mechanism for high traffic applications IoT'. *Wireless Personal Communications*. 2021, vol. 10(3).

[81] Kumar S., Ranjan P., Radhakrishnan R., Tripathy M.R. 'Energy efficient multichannel MAC protocol for high traffic applications in heterogeneous wireless sensor networks'. *Recent Advances in Electrical & Electronic Engineering*. 2017, vol. 10(3), pp. 223–32.

[82] Kumar S., Ranjan P., Ramaswami R., Tripathy M.R. 'Resource efficient clustering and next hop knowledge based routing in multiple heterogeneous wireless sensor networks'. *International Journal of Grid and High Performance Computing*. 2017, vol. 9(2), pp. 1–20.

[83] Punhani A., Faujdar N., Kumar S. 'Design and evaluation of cubic torus Network-on-Chip architecture'. *International Journal of Innovative Technology and Exploring Engineering (IJITEE)*. 2019, vol. 8(6).

[84] Dubey G., Kumar S., Kumar S., Navaney P. 'Extended opinion lexicon and ML-based sentiment analysis of tweets: a novel approach towards accurate classifier'. *International Journal of Computational Vision and Robotics*. 2020. vol. 10(6), pp. 505–21.

[85]   Kumar S., Ranjan P., Radhakrishnan R., Tripathy M.R. 'Energy aware distributed protocol for heterogeneous wireless sensor network'. *International Journal of Control and Automation*. 2015, vol. 8(10), pp. 421–30.

[86]   Singh P., Bansal A., Kamal A.E., Kumar S. 'Road surface quality monitoring using machine learning algorithm' in Reddy A.N.R., Marla D., Favorskaya M.N., Satapathy S.C. (eds.). *Intelligent Manufacturing and Energy Sustainability. Smart Innovation, Systems and Technologies*. 265. Singapore: Springer; 2022.

[87]   Sharma A., Awasthi Y., Kumar S. 'The role of blockchain, AI and iot for smart road traffic management system'. *Proceedings of the 2020 IEEE India Council International Subsections Conference, INDISCON 2020, Publisher: IEEE, Visakhapatnam, India*; 2020. pp. 289–96.

[88]   Kumar S., Ranjan P., Singh P., Tripathy M.R. 'Design and implementation of fault tolerance technique for internet of things (iot)'. *Proceedings of the 12th International Conference on Computational Intelligence and Communication Networks, CICN 2020, Publisher: IEEE, Bhimtal, India*; 2020. pp. 154–59.

[89]   Singh P., Bansal A., Kumar S. 'Performance analysis of various information platforms for recognizing the quality of indian roads'. *Proceedings of the Confluence 2020 - 10th International Conference on Cloud Computing, Data Science and Engineering, Publihser: IEEE, Noida India*; 2020. pp. 63–76.

[90]   Singh P., Bansal A., Kumar S. 'Performance analysis of various information platforms for recognizing the quality of indian roads'. *Proceedings of the Confluence 2020-10th International Conference on Cloud Computing, Data Science and Engineering, Publisher: IEEE, Noida, India*; 2020. pp. 63–76.

[91]   Reghu S., Kumar S. 'Development of robust infrastructure in networking to survive a disaster'. *4th International Conference on Information Systems and Computer Networks, ISCON 2019, Publisher: IEEE, Mathura, India*; 2019. pp. 250–55.

[92]   Kumar S., Ranjan P., Ramaswami R., Tripathy M.R. 'An NS3 implementation of physical layer based on 802.11 for utility maximization of WSN'. *Proceedings of the International Conference on Computational Intelligence and Communication Networks, CICN 2015, Publisher: IEEE, Jabalpur, India*; 2016. pp. 79–84.

[93]   Kumar S., Ranjan P., Ramaswami R., Tripathy M.R. 'A utility maximization approach to MAC layer channel access and forwarding'. *Progress in Electromagnetics Research Symposium, PIERS 2015, The Electromagnetics Academy, 6-9 July 2015, Prague, Czech Republic*; 2015. pp. 2363–67.

[94]   Kumar S., Ranjan P., Ramaswami R., Tripathy M.R. 'EMEEDP: enhanced multi-hop energy efficient distributed protocol for heterogeneous wireless sensor network'. *Proceedings of the 5th International Conference on Communication Systems and Network Technologies, CSNT 2015*; Gwalior, India, IEEE, 2015. pp. 194–200.

[95]   Kumar S., Ranjan P., Ramaswami R. 'Energy optimization in distributed localized wireless sensor networks'. *Proceedings of the International Conference on Issues and Challenges Intelligent Computing Technique (ICICT), IEEE*; Ghaziabad, India, 2014.

[96]   Sudhakaran S., Kumar S., Ranjan P., Tripathy M.R. 'Blockchain-based transparent and secure decentralized algorithm'. *International Conference on Intelligent Computing and Smart Communication 2019*. Algorithms for Intelligent Systems.; Singapore: Springer; 2020.

[97]   Kumar S., Trivedi M.C., Ranjan P., Punhani A. *Evolution of Software-Defined Networking Foundations for IoT and 5G Mobile Networks*. Hershey, PA: IGI Publisher; 2020. p. 350.

[98]   Sampathkumar A., Rastogi R., Arukonda S., Shankar A., Kautish S., Sivaram M. 'An efficient hybrid methodology for detection of cancer-causing gene using CSC for micro array data'. *Journal of Ambient Intelligence and Humanized Computing*. 2020, vol. 11(11), pp. 4743–51.

[99]   Nie X., Fan T., Wang B., Li Z., Shankar A., Manickam A. 'Big data analytics and IoT in operation safety management in under water management'. *Computer Communications*. 2020, vol. 154(1), pp. 188–96.

[100] Shankar A., Jaisankar N., Khan M.S., Patan R., Balamurugan B. 'Hybrid model for security-aware cluster head selection in wireless sensor networks'. *IET Wireless Sensor Systems*. 2019, vol. 9(2), pp. 68–76.

[101] Shankar A., Pandiaraja P., Sumathi K., Stephan T., Sharma P. 'Privacy preserving E-voting cloud system based on ID based encryption'. *Peer-to-Peer Networking and Applications*. 2021, vol. 14(4), pp. 2399–409.

[102] Kumar A., Abhishek K., Nerurkar P., Ghalib M.R., Shankar A., Cheng X. 'Secure smart contracts for cloud-based manufacturing using ethereum blockchain'. *Transactions on Emerging Telecommunications Technologies*. 2022, vol. 33(4), e4129.

[103] Chauhan R., Kumar S. 'Packet loss prediction using artificial intelligence unified with big data analytics, internet of things and cloud computing technologies'. *5th International Conference on Information Systems and Computer Networks (ISCON)*; 2021. pp. 1–6.

Chapter 10

IoT-based water quality assessment using fuzzy logic controller

A. Hendry[1], K. Ghousiya Begum[1], A. Hariharan[1], and K. J. Aravind[1]

Water is an essential resource that we use in our daily life. The standard of the water quality must be observed in real time to make sure that we obtain a secured and clean supply of water to our residential areas. A water quality-monitoring and decision-making system (WQMDMS) is implemented for this purpose based on Internet of Things (IoT) and fuzzy logic to decide the usage of water (drinking or tap water) in a common water tank system. The physical and chemical properties of data are obtained through continuous monitoring of sensors. The work describes in detail the design of a fuzzy logic controller (FLC) for a water quality measurement system, to determine the quality of water by decision-making, and accordingly, the usage of water is decided. The WQMDM system measures the physico-chemical characteristics of water like pH, turbidity, and temperature by the use of corresponding analog and digital sensors. The values of the parameters obtained are used to detect the presence of water contaminants and accordingly, the quality of water is determined. The measurements from the sensor are handled and processed by ESP32, and these refined values follow the rules determined by the fuzzy inference system (FIS). The output highlights the water quality that is categorized as very poor, poor, average, and good. The usage of the water will be determined by the results obtained using the FLC and as per the percentage of water quality, the water is decided as drinking water or tap water.

10.1 Introduction

To understand the quality of water, we should know the chemical, physical, and natural features of the water based on the norms of its operation. It is not easy to say that "water is good" or "water is bad." Water quality is generally determined in

[1]School of EEE, SASTRA Deemed University, Thirumalaisamudram, Thanjavur, Tamil Nadu, India

relation to the usage of water. ESP32 microcontrollers are used in IoT-based water quality monitoring systems. The sensing devices like pH, turbidity, and DS18B20 temperature sensors are interfaced with ESP32. The ESP32 receives the data from sensors and updates them in the cloud platform ThingSpeak with the help of the Internet via Wi-Fi. The live data from ThingSpeak will be fed into MATLAB® as the input for the fuzzy logic system.

Fuzzy logic is a computational approach to representing the vagueness or the uncertainty rather than mentioning the "good or bad" (the integer values 1 or 0) boolean sense on which ultra-modern computers are based. Fuzzy logic is an introductory control system that depends on the state of the input and affair depends on the rate of change of that state.

In the work done by Unnikrishna Menon *et al.* [1], a system is described for the quality assessment and monitoring of the river water based on wireless sensor networks (WSN) that support both remote and continuous monitoring of the quality levels of water in India. In their work, they used only a pH sensor and tested the different conditions of pH like lemon juice, rainwater, and drinking water. They used Zigbee technology to transmit the data from sensing devices to the cluster head.

Bokingkito and Caparida [2] proposed a water quality assessment system for finding out the decrease in aquaculture (fisheries) production. He and Zhang [3] presented a work based on wireless water monitoring networks and remote data centers and suggested using the CC2430 microprocessor as a core hardware platform. The WSN is constructed on the Zigbee communication module. The WSN scans the parameter and uses the GPRS DTU with the TCP/IP protocol to send the live readings to the Internet. Pande *et al.* [4] presented a manuscript to assess the quality of drinking water for housing society. The proposed system collects the parameters like temperature, turbidity, level, and pH to measure the quality of water samples. They suggested the use of ESP8266 Wemos d1 mini and Raspberry pi for simple, faster, efficient, real-time, monitoring of data. Sarwar *et al.* [5] presented a study on the designed fire detection and warning systems for buildings based on a fuzzy logic theory and carried out the simulation tasks in the MATLAB Fuzzy Logic toolbox. They used Arduino Uno R3 and fuzzy logic to predict only the true incidents of fire with the data obtained from temperature, humidity, and flame sensor. They proposed a control mechanism that can activate water showers when it detects fire. Lambrou *et al.* [6] worked on the design of monitoring water quality at consumer sites using the optical and electrochemical sensors installed in the pipelines. They proposed a system with a PIC32 MCU board that gathers water quality parameters from sensors and sends the data to the ARM platform and to the Internet that stores data and send email or message to the notification node through Zigbee. Using event detection algorithms, the alarms were activated to detect the water quality standards.

Faruq *et al.* [7] designed and implemented a cost-effective, simple water quality assessment system with calibrated sensors for measuring parameters like temperature, turbidity, and pH, which will be shown on the LCD monitor. They just detected the water quality without using IoT. Vigueras-Velázquez *et al.* [8] discussed a work to evaluate the freshwater quality in farming tanks to grow whitefish (Chirostoma estor water quality) and used sensors to measure dissolved oxygen (DO), pH,

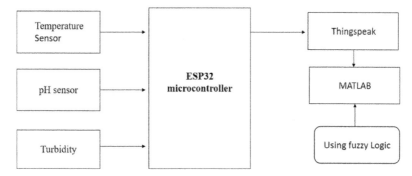

Figure 10.1   Working model

temperature, non-ionized ammonia, and total ammonia. The main aim is to maintain the ideal conditions for the sustained growth of fish. Better aquaculture water assessment was made probable by the implementation of weighted FIS. Pasika and Gandla [9] also proposed a smart water quality assessment system using Arduino mega with ultrasonic, pH, turbidity, temperature sensors, and Wi-Fi ESP8266 node MCU with the cloud platform. Baghavan and Saranya [10] proposed a sensor network with AI to identify the pollutants in water so that the water can be subjected to a purification process. Kothari *et al.* [11] developed a system to test the rainwater, tap water, well water, and purified RO water using sensors, viz., for measuring temperature, TDS, pH, and DO, along with Arduino mega2560 and GSM module. Chowdury *et al.* [12] also discussed how the WSN along with a microcontroller is used for processing and

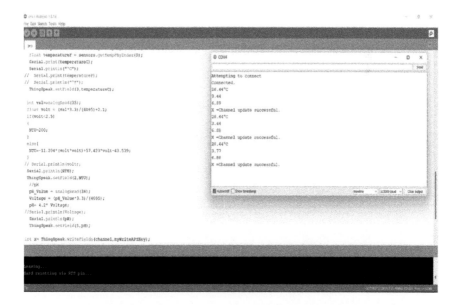

Figure 10.2   Arduino IDE and monitor window

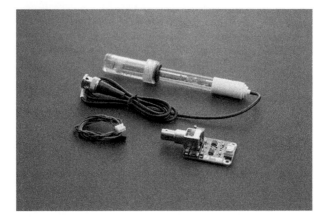

Figure 10.3   E-201C pH sensor

establishing the inter- and intra-node communication among sensors for pollutant monitoring of water for Bangladeshi populations. They were able to acquire the real-time data and were able to access using remote monitoring and IoT. The collected data were displayed on a PC through an expert system and DL neural network models, in comparison with the typical values that generate computerized alert messages if the obtained value is above the threshold limit [13–20].

Based on the motivation from the previous studies, the proposed system of monitoring the water quality and decision-making has been implemented in real time for consumer application using only ESP32 with pH, temperature, and turbidity sensors for processing and monitoring, and the fuzzy logic system is implemented for decision-making. It does not require any data centers as we are storing and displaying the measured water quality parameters in the cloud platform. This proposed system is economical and cost effective, and the prediction will be more accurate.

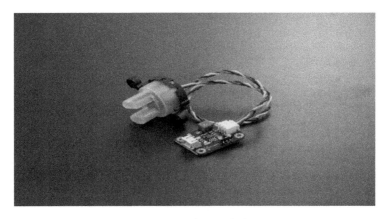

Figure 10.4   Analog turbidity sensor

Figure 10.5   DS18B20 temperature sensor

We can measure the water quality of water tank systems that are installed in multiple locations and also get the live data in the cloud system [21–36].

10.2   Experimental procedures

The proposed system incorporates an ESP32 microcontroller and sensors like E-201C for measuring pH value, analog turbidity sensor, and DS180B20 digital

Figure 10.6   ESP32 microcontroller

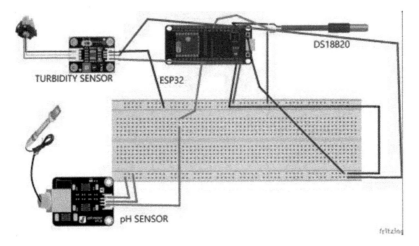

Figure 10.7   Hardware circuit design

sensor to sense the temperature of the water, as shown in Figure 10.1. The hardware is configured, and the C language program code is scripted in Arduino IDE to obtain the anticipated format of the sensor data. The sensor parameters, namely, temperature, turbidity, and pH values can be seen in Arduino serial monitor, as shown in Figure 10.2 which is sent to Thinspeak, and the respective data are obtained in MATLAB via Thing speak. In MATLAB, using fuzzy logic rules, the degree of quality, and clearness of the water are determined.

Sensors and microcontroller

pH sensor (E-201C): The pH of any solution is a quality metric that represents the acidity or basicity. The pH scale is a log scale of hydrogen ions in solution (range of 0–14 and a neutral point of 7). The values above seven determine a base or alkaline solution, and values below seven indicate an acidic solution. It operates on a 5-V power supply and is presented in Figure 10.2. Its response time is <1 min and internal resistance is less than or equal to 250 MΩ. For drinking, water pH should be between 6.5 and 8.5. The sensor needs to be calibrated where it will display the voltage and pH value.

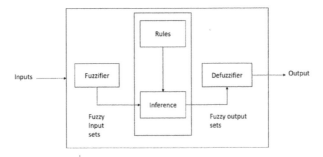

Figure 10.8   Fuzzy inference system

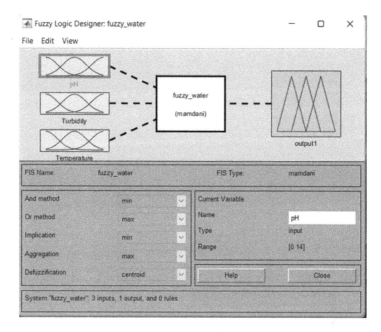

Figure 10.9   Fuzzy logic designer

Turbidity sensor: The turbidity sensor measures the opaqueness or cloudiness in the water. It measures the transmittance rate and scattering rate of visible light to identify suspended particles in water like clay, slit, microorganisms, and organic matter. The operating voltage and current are 5 V DC and 40 mA. The turbidity changes with the quantity of total suspended solids in water. It also gives an analog output of 0–4.5 V. For drinking water, the turbidity value should be between 0 and 5 NTU. The response time is <500 ms. The module size is 38.6 mm × 22.1 mm.

Temperature sensor (DS18B20): The temperature of the water specifies the hotness or coldness of the water. The DS18B20 temperature sensor whose usable temperature ranges from –55 to +125°C. This is a digital temperature sensor that provides an accurate reading. It utilizes one-wire interface and has 9–12-bit selectable resolution.

ESP32: The proposed system uses this microcontroller that is the brain of the proposed system. ESP32 is programmable hardware with 36 pins and designed to control the circuit logically and it can be programmed by using Arduino IDE. It has inbuilt Wi-Fi and Bluetooth. Its operating voltage ranges from 2.3 to 3.6 V, and its operating current is around 80 mA. It has a flash memory of 4 MB and SRAM memory of 512 kB. Its clock frequency ranges from 80 to 240 MHz and its data rate is 54 Mbps.

The components and sensors used are shown in Figures 10.2–10.6 .

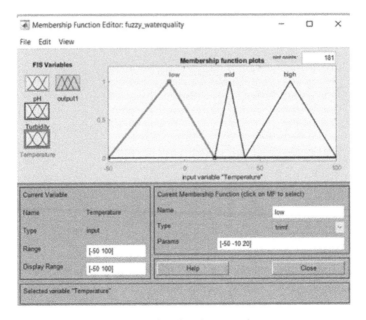

Figure 10.10   Membership function for temperature

10.3   Working

The suggested system adopts three sensing devices (temperature, pH, and turbidity), ESP32, and the ThingSpeak platform. Only one microcontroller with inbuilt Wi-Fi and Bluetooth module is used. Obtaining the input values from the sensors and determining the degree of membership level for each input value from sensors using fuzzy expressions are the first stage in utilizing fuzzy logic rules to evaluate the water condition (also known as membership function). The sensors (pH, turbidity, and DS18B20 temperature sensor) that are interfaced with the ESP32 microcontroller are processed using the program in Arduino IDE from which the sensor readings will be sent to ThingSpeak. The live readings from ThingSpeak will be fed into the FLC in MATLAB. Figure 10.7 shows the hardware circuit connections.

Fuzzy logic designer

Figure 10.8 depicts a block schematic of the proposed system that uses the fuzzy-based decision-making system. These steps of the proposed fuzzy logic decision-making system comprise (a) initialization of linguistic variables, membership functions, and construction of rules, (b) fuzzification where the crisp values of input data are converted to fuzzy values using membership functions, (c) evaluation of knowledge-based rules and combining the results of each rule, and (d) defuzzification where the output values are transformed to non-fuzzy values.

The hardware and software components like ESP32, the three sensors (temperature, pH, and turbidity), Matlab, and ThingSpeak make up the whole system. The

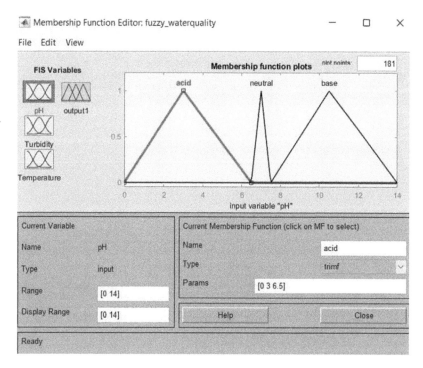

Figure 10.11   Membership function for pH

diagrammatic description of fuzzy logic is shown in Figure 10.8, which indicates the initial stage in applying fuzzy rules to identify the grade of membership functions of each input vector using FIS. After evaluating the water condition, the input values are allotted to the output vector, and the rules are constructed by defining the membership functions. The fuzzy input can contain up to three states from a linguistic standpoint. The specific rules allow the user in determining the conditions of input variables as low, mid, and high. The goal of this research is to create a fuzzy logic system that can classify water quality into four levels and show real-time data in ThingSpeak. The MATLAB-modeled fuzzy logic control system is shown in Figure 10.9. In this figure, the input variables are defined as temperature, pH, and turbidity. The FIS is implemented using the Mamdani method. Finally, the output variables are displayed as four levels of quality.

Membership function

Here, the crisp values are represented as fuzzy values with the help of membership functions. The fuzzification process adopted for every input and output parameter is discussed in the following.

Membership function of temperature

As shown in Figure 10.10, the three fuzzy (linguistic) variables for input temperature are used and shown as membership functions. They are labeled as low, medium, and high. The universe of discourse has units in the range of −50° to 100°.

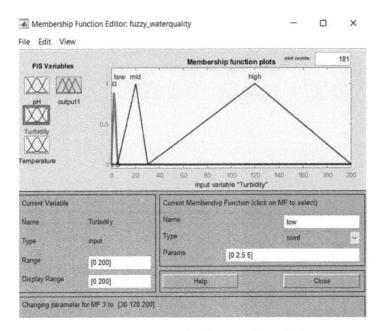

Figure 10.12   Member function for turbidity

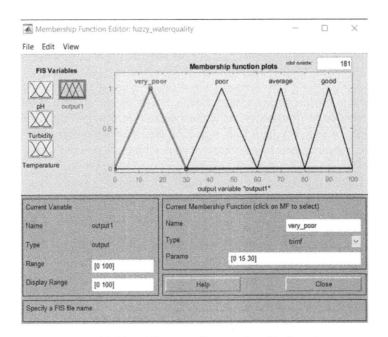

Figure 10.13   Water quality membership function

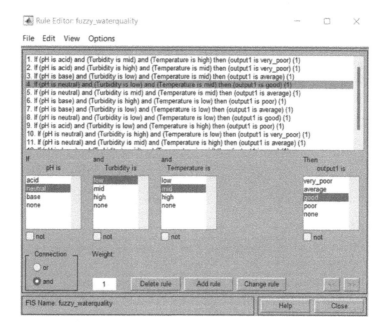

Figure 10.14   Fuzzy logic rule editor

The low has a range of –50° to 20°, the medium has a range of 20° to 40°, and the high has a range of 40°–100°. The triangular membership function is used.

Membership function of pH

Figure 10.11 displays three levels of pH, which are acid, neutral, and base. The unit of pH has a range of 0–14 pH. The acid has a range of 0–6.5 pH, the neutral has a range of 6.5–7.5 pH, and the base has a range of 7.5–14 pH.

Membership function of turbidity

Figure 10.12 shows three levels of turbidity as low, mid, and high. The unit of turbidity has a range of 0–200 NTU. The low has a range of 0–5 NTU, the medium has a range of 5–30 NTU, and the high has a range of 30–200 NTU.

Membership function of output water quality

The linguistic variables of the output are determined into four categories (very poor, poor, average, and good). The quality of water is determined by the range of variables as very poor from 0% to 30%, poor as 30% to 60%, average as 60% to 80%, and good as 80% to 100%, which are mentioned in Figure 10.13.

Fuzzy rule editor for water quality

Figure 10.14 represents the MATLAB rule editor, where rule sets for fuzzy water quality are implemented. The pH is represented by the first box, the turbidity variables are represented by the second box on the left, the temperature variables are represented by the third box on the right, these sides of the box indicate the input variables, and the level of water quality is represented by the right box.

The results of four different samples of water are displayed as rule viewer in Figures 10.15–10.18. The first three columns represent the pH, turbidity, and

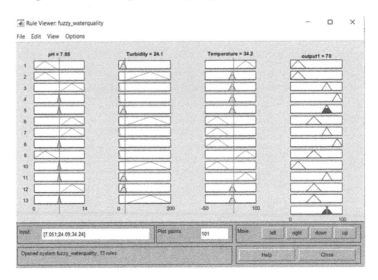

Figure 10.15   Rule viewer for water sample 1

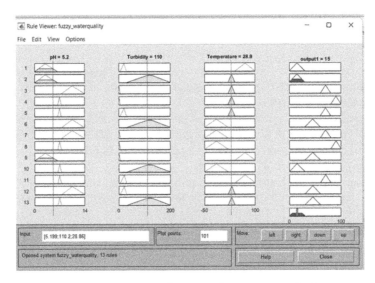

Figure 10.16   Rule viewer for water sample 2

temperature, and the last column indicates the water quality in percentage. Figure 10.15 displays the first water sample quality of percentage 70 as pH value is 7.05, turbidity value is 24.1 NTU, and the temperature is 34.2°C, which indicates that it can be used as tap water for cleaning and washing. The second water sample is taken whose pH is 5.2, turbidity value is 110 NTU, the temperature value is 28.9°C, and the water quality percentage is 15, as shown in Figure 10.16 and cannot be used as drinking water. The third water sample is taken whose pH is 6.85, turbidity value

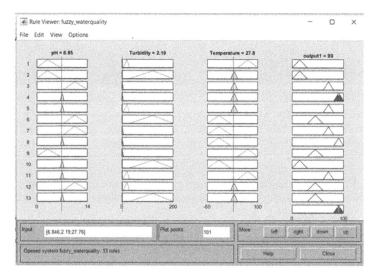

Figure 10.17   Rule viewer for water sample 3

is 2.19 NTU, the temperature value is 27.8°C, and the water quality percentage is 90, as shown in Figure 10.17. This implies that the quality of water is good and can be used as drinking water. The final water sample is taken whose pH is 8.18, turbidity value is 81 NTU, the temperature value is 46.5°C, and the water quality percentage is 50, as shown in Figure 10.18, which can be used for cleaning purposes. Figure 10.19 displays the surface viewer of the water quality decision-making system.

Defuzzification

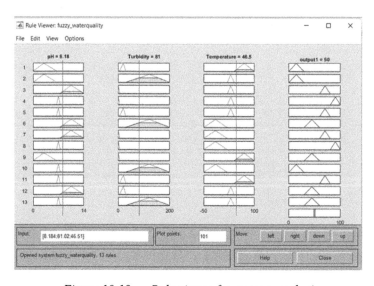

Figure 10.18   Rule viewer for water sample 4

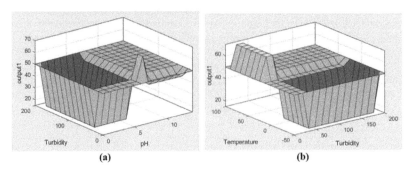

(a)   (b)

*Figure 10.19   Surface viewer for water quality decision-making system: (a)
pH, turbidity versus output and (b) turbidity, temperature versus
output*

The whole monitoring and decision-making of the water quality system are now complete as inference and defuzzification are built-in functions that are executed by MATLAB. Therefore, defuzzification is the final step in implementing the FLC where the output is expressed as if condition statements and stored in the knowledge-based system database. Here, fuzzification of the scalar values, application of rules, generation of fuzzy output, and conversion to scalar quantity take place. The commonly issued defuzzification methods are centroid and weighted average methods. The centroid method is used here as it provides accurate and efficient [5]. After the defuzzification process, the water quality percentage is displayed.

Figure 10.20 shows the hardware connections of the sensors (pH, turbidity, and DS18B20 temperature sensor) with the ESP32 microcontroller and interfaced with the Arduino IDE; from there, the sensor readings will be sent to ThingSpeak.

Table 10.1   Decision-making of water quality system

Sample	Parameter	Measured value	Water quality %	Decision
1	pH	7.104	70	Activate tap water motor
	Turbidity	15.12 NTU		
	Temperature	27.06°C		
2	pH	7.05	90	Activate drinking water motor
	Turbidity	3.4 NTU		
	Temperature	27.75 °C		
3	pH	6.871	50	Activate tap water motor
	Turbidity	200 NTU		
	Temperature	27.75 °C		

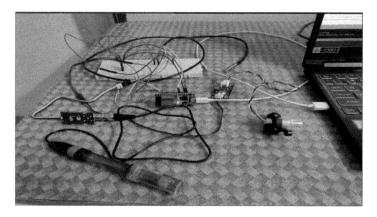

Figure 10.20   Hardware circuit

10.4   Results and discussions

Several trials were done to evaluate the proposed water monitoring system's performance. The system's performance is determined by the delicate nature of the water. The conducted trials listed below represent the precision of water quality. Several trials were conducted to evaluate the proposed water quality monitoring system's performance, as shown in Tables 10.1 and 10.2. Out of these trials, three trial instances are visually represented as trials with bad, average, and acceptable water quality, respectively. The water quality index is indicated in the trials below from 0% to 100% in terms of the rate of changes in pH, turbidity, and temperature.

ThingSpeak data

ThingSpeak is an open-source cloud-based platform for gathering, envisaging, and analyzing live data received from sensors. The ThingSpeak application is

Table 10.2   Table of FLC results

Water sample	pH	Turbidity NTU	Temperature ⁰ C	Water quality %	Quality level
1	6.8	3.4	28.8	90	Good
2	6.2	15	30	70	Average
3	7.1	15.3	27.5	70	Average
4	6.9	28	7.25	50	Poor
5	6.3	200	27	30	Very poor
6	7.2	2	31	90	Good
7	8	20	26	40	Poor
8	6	10	40	50	Poor
9	6.85	2.19	27.8	90	Good
10	8.18	81	46.5	50	Poor
11	5.2	110	28.9	15	Very poor

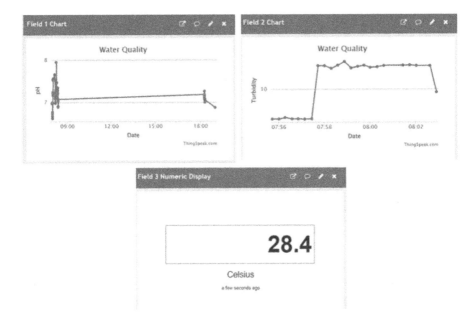

Figure 10.21   Sample 1 sensor readings in ThingSpeak

available as a MATLAB library function, and we use it to get real-time water metrics. The data from the sensors are displayed in the ThingSpeak interface as shown in Figures 10.21–10.23) which is then sent to the FLC, and the water quality is calculated and displayed for three different samples.

Results of MATLAB implementation

The water quality percentage of the three different samples determined using the FLC designed in MATLAB is displayed in Figures 10.24–10.26.

After the experiments, all the results were obtained, and the data are given in Tables 10.1 and 10.2. As you can see from the tables, the percentage of water quality is obtained, ranging from 15% to 90%, which explicates that the suggested system is working in accordance with the defined rules in the FLC.

10.5   Conclusion

In the proposed system, we have successfully constructed the hardware and software tools for WQMDMS using the ESP32 microcontroller, sensors like pH, turbidity, and DS18B20 temperature sensor, MATLAB-based fuzzy logic control, and ThingSpeak cloud platform. The circuit operates in error-free conditions and provides us with the expected output. Continuous data samples can be obtained using the present proposed system that will help us to determine the water quality more accurately. The proposed system is portable to determine the water quality tank systems across multiple areas. We can also determine the leakages in the pipeline by

Figure 10.22   Sample 2 sensor readings in ThingSpeak

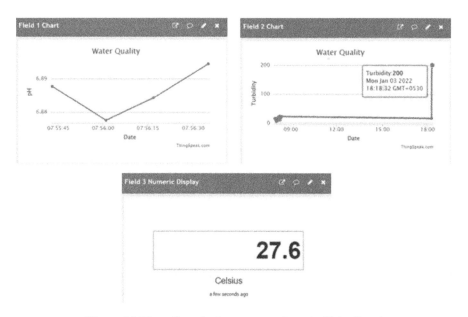

Figure 10.23   Sample 3 sensor readings in ThingSpeak

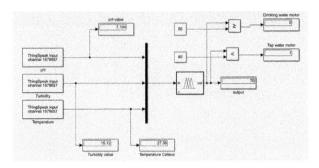

Figure 10.24   FLC result for sample 1

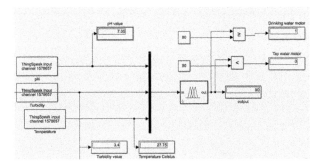

Figure 10.25   FLC result for sample 2

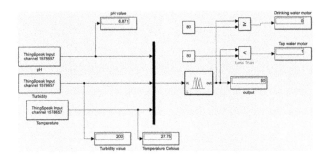

Figure 10.26   FLC result for sample 3

seeing the variation in water quality levels across the different locations. The future scope of the system is as follows:

- Controlling the motor system of the water tank to pump water
- To sense and process more water quality parameters
- To develop the water distribution system using pressure and flow sensor
- Getting alert notifications for the water quality levels through the mobile app
- To detect leakages in pipelines.

References

[1] Unnikrishna Menon K.A., Divya P., Ramesh M.V. 'Wireless sensor network for river water quality monitoring in india'. *Third International Conference on Computing, Communication and Networking Technologies (ICCCNT'12), IEEE*; Coimbatore, India, 2012. pp. 1–7.

[2] Bokingkito P.B., Caparida L.T. 'Using fuzzy logic for real - time water quality assessment monitoring system'. *Proceedings of the 2018 2nd International Conference on Automation, Control and Robots (ICACR 2018). Publisher: Association for Computing Machinery (ACM)*; Bangkok Thailand, 2018. pp. 21–25.

[3] He D., Zhang L.X. 'The water quality monitoring system based on WSN'. *2nd International Conference on Consumer Electronics, Communications and Networks (CECNet), IEEE*; Yichang, China, 2012. pp. 3661–64.

[4] Pand A.M., Warhade K.K., Komati R.D. 'Water quality monitoring system for water tanks of housing society'. *International Journal of Electronics Engineering Research*. 2017, vol. 9(7), pp. 1071–8.

[5] Sarwar B., Bajwa I., Ramzan S., Ramzan B., Kausar M. 'Design and application of fuzzy logic based fire monitoring and warning systems for smart buildings'. *Symmetry*. 2018, vol. 10(11),615.

[6] Lambrou T.P., Anastasiou C.C., Panayiotou C.G., Polycarpou M.M. 'A low-cost sensor network for real-time monitoring and contamination detection in drinking water distribution systems'. *IEEE Sensors Journal*. 2014, vol. 14(8), pp. 2765–72.

[7] Faruq M.O., Emu I.H., Haque M.N., Dey M., Das N.K., Dey M. 'Design and implementation of cost-effective water quality evaluation system'. *IEEE Region 10 Humanitarian Technology Conference (R10-HTC)*; Publisher: IEEE, Dhaka, Bangladesh, 2017. pp. 860–63.

[8] Vigueras-Velázquez M.E., Carbajal-Hernández J.J., Sánchez-Fernández L.P., Vázquez-Burgos J.L., Tello-Ballinas J.A. 'Weighted fuzzy inference system for water quality management of Chirostoma estor estor culture'. *Aquaculture Reports*. 2020, vol. 18, p. 100487.

[9] Pasika S., Gandla S.T. 'Smart water quality monitoring system with cost-effective using IoT'. *Heliyon*. 2020, vol. 6(7) e04096.

[10] Bhagavan N.V.S., Saranya P.L. 'Water pollutants monitoring based on internet of things' in *Inorganic pollutants in water*. Elsevier; 2020. pp. 371–97.

[11] Kothari N., Shreemali J., Chakrabarti P., Poddar S. 'Design and implementation of iot sensor based drinking water quality measurement system'. *Materials Today: Proceedings*. 2021, vol. 3, pp. 1–10.

[12] Chowdury M.S.U., Emran T.B., Ghosh S., *et al.* 'IoT based real-time river water quality monitoring system'. *Procedia Computer Science*. 2019, vol. 155(3), pp. 161–8.

[13] Kumar S., Cengiz K., Trivedi C.M., *et al.* 'DEMO enterprise ontology with a stochastic approach based on partially observable Markov model for data

aggregation and communication in intelligent sensor networks'. *Wireless Personal Communication.* 2022.

[14] Kumar V., Arablouei R., Cengiz K., Vimal S., Suresh A. 'Energy efficient resource migration based load balance mechanism for high traffic applications IoT'. *Wireless Personal Communications.* 2022, vol. 10(3), pp. 1623–44.

[15] Kumar S., Ranjan P., Radhakrishnan R., Tripathy M.R. 'Energy efficient multichannel MAC protocol for high traffic applications in heterogeneous wireless sensor networks'. *Recent Advances in Electrical & Electronic Engineering.* 2017, vol. 10(3), pp. 223–32.

[16] Kumar S., Ranjan P., Ramaswami R., Tripathy M.R. 'Resource efficient clustering and next hop knowledge based routing in multiple heterogeneous wireless sensor networks'. *International Journal of Grid and High Performance Computing.* 2017, vol. 9(2), pp. 1–20.

[17] Punhani A., Faujdar N., Kumar S. 'Design and evaluation of cubic torus network-on-chip architecture'. *International Journal of Innovative Technology and Exploring Engineering, Publisher: Blue Eyes Intelligence Engineering.* 2019, vol. 8(6), pp. 1672–76.

[18] Dubey G., Kumar S., Kumar S., Navaney P. 'Extended opinion lexicon and ML-based sentiment analysis of tweets: a novel approach towards accurate classifier'. *International Journal of Computational Vision and Robotics.* 2020, vol. 10(6), pp. 505–21.

[19] Kumar S., Ranjan P., Radhakrishnan R., Tripathy M.R. 'Energy aware distributed protocol for heterogeneous wireless sensor network'. *International Journal of Control and Automation.* 2015, vol. 8(10), pp. 421–30.

[20] Singh P., Bansal A., Kamal A.E., Kumar S. 'Road surface quality monitoring using machine learning algorithm' in Reddy A.N.R., Marla D., Favorskaya M.N., Satapathy S.C. (eds.). *Intelligent Manufacturing and Energy Sustainability. Smart Innovation, Systems and Technologies.* 265. Singapore: Springer; 2022.

[21] Sharma A., Awasthi Y., Kumar S. 'The role of blockchain, AI and iot for smart road traffic management system'. *IEEE India Council International Subsections Conference (INDISCON), IEEE*; Visakhapatnam, India, 2020. pp. 289–96.

[22] Kumar S., Ranjan P., Singh P., Tripathy M.R. 'Design and implementation of fault tolerance technique for internet of things (iot)'. *12th International Conference on Computational Intelligence and Communication Networks (CICN), IEEE*; Bhimtal, India, IEEE, 2020. pp. 154–59.

[23] Singh P., Bansal A., Kumar S. 'Performance analysis of various information platforms for recognizing the quality of Indian roads'. *10th International Conference on Cloud Computing, Data Science & Engineering (Confluence), IEEE*; Noida, India, 29–31 Jan; 2020. pp. 63–76.

[24] Reghu S., Kumar S. 'Development of robust infrastructure in networking to survive a disaster. *4th International Conference on Information Systems and Computer Networks, (ISCON)*; Mathura, India, 21–22 Nov; 2019. pp. 250–5.

[25] Kumar S., Ranjan P., Ramaswami R., Tripathy M.R. 'An NS3 implementation of physical layer based on 802.11 for utility maximization of WSN'. *2015 International Conference on Computational Intelligence and Communication Networks (CICN), IEEE*; Jabalpur, India, 2016. pp. 79–84.

[26] Kumar S., Ranjan P., Ramaswami R., Tripathy M.R. 'A utility maximization approach to MAC layer channel access and forwarding'. *Progress in Electromagnetics Research Symposium, Publisher: The Electromagnetics Academy*; Prague, Czech Republic, 2015. pp. 2363–67.

[27] Kumar S., Ranjan P., Ramaswami R., Tripathy M.R. 'EMEEDP: enhanced multi-hop energy efficient distributed protocol for heterogeneous wireless sensor network'. *Fifth International Conference on Communication Systems and Network Technologies, IEEE*; Gwalior, India, 2015. pp. 194–200.

[28] Kumar S., Ramaswami R., Rao A.L.N. 'Energy optimization in distributed localized wireless sensor networks'. *Proceedings of the International Conference on Issues and Challenges Intelligent Computing Technique (ICICT), IEEE*; Ghaziabad, India, 2014. pp. 350–55.

[29] Sudhakaran S., Kumar S., Ranjan P., Tripathy M.R. 'Blockchain-based transparent and secure decentralized algorithm'. *International Conference on Intelligent Computing and Smart Communication. Algorithms for Intelligent Systems, Springer*; THDC-IHET, 2020. pp. 327–36.

[30] Kumar S., Trivedi M.C., Ranjan P. *Evolution of Software-Defined Networking Foundations for IoT and 5G Mobile Networks*. Hershey, PA: IGI Publisher; 2020. p. 350.

[31] Sampathkumar A., Rastogi R., Arukonda S., Shankar A., Kautish S., Sivaram M. 'An efficient hybrid methodology for detection of cancer-causing gene using CSC for micro array data'. *Journal of Ambient Intelligence and Humanized Computing*. 2020, vol. 11, pp. 4743–51.

[32] Nie X., Fan T., Wang B., Li Z., Shankar A., Manickam A. 'Big data analytics and IoT in operation safety management in under water management'. *Computer Communications*. 2020, vol. 154(1), pp. 188–96.

[33] Shankar A., Jaisankar N., Khan M.S., Patan R., Balamurugan B. 'Hybrid model for security-aware cluster head selection in wireless sensor networks'. *IET Wireless Sensor Systems*. 2019, vol. 9(2), pp. 68–76.

[34] Shankar A., Pandiaraja P., Sumathi K., Stephan T., Sharma P. 'Privacy preserving E-voting cloud system based on ID based encryption'. *Peer-to-Peer Networking and Applications*. 2021, vol. 14(4), pp. 2399–409.

[35] Bhardwaj A., Shah S.B.H., Shankar A., Alazab M., Kumar M., Gadekallu T.R. 'Penetration testing framework for smart contract blockchain'. *Peer-to-Peer Networking and Applications*. 2021, vol. 14(5), pp. 2635–50.

[36] Kumar A., Abhishek K., Nerurkar P., Ghalib M.R., Shankar A., Cheng X. 'Secure smart contracts for cloud-based manufacturing using Ethereum blockchain'. *Transactions on Emerging Telecommunications Technologies*. 2020, vol. 33(4).

Chapter 11

Design and analysis of wireless sensor network for intelligent transportation and industry automation

Prabhakar D. Dorge[1], Prasanna M. Palsodkar[2], and Divya Dandekar[3]

This work is based on the wireless sensor networks (WSN), which contain an insufficient number of device nodes, regularly similarly stated nodes or sensors, and sensor knots that are associated with all other wireless communications. There are numerous assumptions or overall possessions of WSNs, and a lot more applications of WSNs around the creation are presented, making it unbearable to protect all their application areas. Applications of WSNs span ecological and animal monitoring, factory and manufacturing monitoring, farming monitoring and mechanization, healthiness monitoring, and many other areas. One of the most characteristics of WSNs is that they are strongly coupled with their application. In this chapter, WI-MAX without wormhole attack is explained, and the related results are explained with their outputs The NS2 evaluation system is applied to production out of all imitations.

11.1 Introduction

A wireless network is an all type of processer net that uses wireless information networks to wad system nodes. Wireless networks are processer networks that are not associated by chains irrespective of the kind. The apple of a wireless network allows originalities to stop the exclusive resources of giving cables into constructions or as an association connecting different apparatus locations. The foundation of wireless systems is the receiver effect, an application to happen on the animal advanced equal of system construction. Wireless skills are different based on the sizes, for the

[1]Department of Electronics and Telecommunication Enginnering, Yeshwantrao Chavan College of Engineering, Nagpur, India
[2]Department of Electronics Engineering, Yeshwantrao Chavan College of Engineering, Nagpur, India
[3]Department of Electronics Engineering, Hochschule Breman University, USA

most part particularly in just how much bandwidth they offer and how distant to one side interactive nodes can be real. Additional significant difference comprises which possible electromagnetic ranges they choose and just how much power they use. In this part, we deliberate four protuberant wireless technologies: Bluetooth, Wi-Fi, Wi-MAX, and 3G cellular wireless. In the segments, we present them in a manner from the straight series to the lengthiest range one; for the most part, usually wireless links are used in these days, which are generally unequal, i.e., together endpoints are typically kinds of nodes. One endpoint, from time to time called the base station, generally has no flexibility but has a connection to the Internet or other systems that join in the conflicting end from the link for the reason that a "client node" can frequently be movable and uses its link to the base station for those with its statements through other nodes.

Multiple-input multiple-output (MIMO) is a technique for multiplying the capacity of a radio link using many transmitting and receiving antennas to utilize multipath propagation. The advantages of using MIMO are increasing link capacity and spectral efficiency. Here we are dealing with multiple radio channels, i.e., the WiMAX-based WSN system will transmit and receive the data through multiple radio channels. Multiple transmitters can transmit data for a particular receiver at a time; such a technique is called multiuser MIMO [1]. By using multiple transmitting and receiving antennas or radio channels, MIMO offers extra special degrees of freedom for data transmission. In a single-user wireless communication system, it has been observed that using the MIMO technique can lead to impressive improvement in capacity and link reliability. The MIMO technique has a great potential to improve the throughput, delay, and jitter performance [2]. MIMO plays a significant role in any wireless communication system. WiMAX uses the MIMO technique in terms of multiple radio channels, which results in an improvement in the performance of WiMAX-based systems.

In today's era of wireless communication systems, the strength and the quality of the received signal by the user is depending upon various factors. Similarly, in the transceiver system, there are several factors that govern the signal strength and quality. Some of these factors are modulation technique, data rate, coding scheme, power constraint, path loss factor, and so on. Now in order to satisfy the need for effective signal transmission and to gain a good signal quality at the receiver or user end, the aforementioned listed parameters have to be adjusted according to the channel parameters. The novel technique employing this strategy is called the link adaptation technique.

In the link adaptation technique, various constraining factors are adjusted or adapted according to the required radio link parameters to provide good-quality signals. Recently, an alternative link adaptation technique called AMC has come up to improve the overall system capacity. AMC allows matching of modulation and coding method along with protocol and signal parameters to those with the conditions on the radio link such as path loss, sensitivity of the receiver, power margin of the transmitter, and so on.

The process of AMC is a dynamic one as the protocol and signal conditions on radio link alter frequently. The main purpose of AMC is to maintain an acceptable bit error rate as well as to make more effective use of channel capacity. Various transmission parameters that can be adapted are data rate, coding rate, error probability and transmitted power.

Other methods can be the assumption of approximately the same channel from TX to RX and from RX to TX in the time-division duplex method. Using link state information that is present in the TX adaptive modulation systems provides an improvement in the rate of transmission.

The AMC concept. As per the AMC concept, here the modulation format is matched according to the SNI ratio for end customers. Here, the channel is made approximately constant by selecting small time–frequency bins, and thus for each time slot, a separate channel is represented by each of these time–frequency bins. The efficient technique will be allowing only one user having the best channel to transmit in each of the parallel channels. For lower values of SINR, the modulation technique used is QPSK with a smaller constellation size of the signal to provide reliability and robust transmission. As the SINR values increase, the modulation techniques with a bigger constellation size of the signal are employed like 8-PSK, 16-QAM, and 64-QAM. For higher values of SINR, the reason for using bigger size of the constellation of the signal is to provide significant modulation rates with lesser values of error probability.

MIMO promises a significant increment in throughput and ranges of wireless communication without any increase in transmit power. A MIMO system relies on techniques such as spatial multiplexing, transmit diversity, and beamforming to improve the quality of transmission, data rates, and received signal gain as well as to reduce interference. Assume a communication system with η_T TX antennas and η_R RX antennas.

$$r_t = Hs_t + v_t$$

Here, $r_t = \left[r_t^1 r_t^2 ... r_t^{nR} \right]^T$ is the receive side signal on time moment t,

$s_t = \left[s_t^1, s_t^2, ..., s_t^{nT} \right]^T$ is the transmitted signal, and v_t is AWGN with unit variance and uncorrelated among the η_R RX antennas. RX antenna i receives a superposition of every transmitted message as of TX j, weighted by the link reply, and a few AWGN is added.

Here, $\eta_R \times \eta_T$ transition matrix is completed from elements $h_{i,j}$ as given:

$$H = \begin{pmatrix} h_{1,1} & ... & h_{1,n_T} \\ ... & .... & ... \\ h_{n_R,1} & ... & h_{n_R,n_T} \end{pmatrix}$$

Here, $h_{i,j}$ represents the complex link coefficient among the jth TX antenna and the ith RX antenna.

The transmitted power is given by

$$P_{tj} = \frac{P}{\eta_T}$$

or $j = 1, 2, ..., \eta_T$

Recently, the requirement for multimedia facilities with large superiority of service requirements has been increasing [2]. The speed of the network depends on multipath propagation and path loss. The key difference between WSN and MANET is the high-speed models, fast-changing topology, and also capability of mobility prediction. The 4×4 MIMO system gives superior performance in the presence of interference. Also, it improves system's capacity.

The sending and receiving sections of the antenna are used to suppress the multi-antenna fading channel. It can take advantage of MIMO channels to improve the wireless channel and double the ability exclusive of growing the bandwidth and transmit power of the antenna. To defeat the troubles of the channel impairments, we used adaptive modulation for MIMO systems. AMC and MIMO increase the information rate of the system. The information of link situation information at the TX is serious for multi-user MIMO, while it is not important for single-user MIMO [3].

In any unplanned network, the nodes are not well known about the topology of the network. Reactive RP is a bandwidth-efficient on-demand routing protocol for *ad hoc* networks. The examples of reactive RPs are *Ad hoc* On-Demand Distance Vector (AODV), *Ad hoc* OnDemand Multipath Distance Vector (AOMDV), and Dynamic Source Routing (DSR).

In case of proactive RP, each node has either one or more than one table that shows the whole network topology. These tables are regularly updated so as to provide advanced information about routing from every node to others. Destination Sequenced Distance Vector (DSDV) is the proactive RP.

The information regarding the topology is transmitted only on-demand by the nodes. AODV uses the shortest path or fastest path for transmission of data. AODV RP is used to find roots from the transmitter to the receiver only on insist, i.e., only when the source node wants to transmit data packets, only then the root is found. This is unipath routing protocol. If the root to the required destination is not available, then the source node sends RREQ to every neighboring node into the system as a result of which it gets many roots to the different destinations from just one root request RREQ message. Ten AODV utilizes target string number for the determination of up-to-date lane and for finding a fresh way to the receiver. The source node receives RREP packets from intermediate nodes that have a valid root to the destination node or else the root replies packets, i.e., RREPs are directly sent by the receiving node to the transmitting node. But in between if the path breaks and the intermediate node identifies it, then it informs the end nodes about the breakage of the path by sending a Root Error message. As a result, the corresponding entry is deleted from the table by the end node. Again now the source node initiates the search of a new path with the new previous destination sequence number and new broadcast identifier. For maintenance of roots in AODV, periodic exchange of HELLO messages is done. Every time when RREQ messages are broadcasted by source nodes to its neighboring nodes, a reverse path is set up, and due to this reverse path, a unique ID is allotted. Every node will check the address of the initiator and this unique ID and rejects the message if it had processed that request. The AODV routing protocol creates a problem during the transmission of data in node-to-node communication [4]. But at the same time, AODV effortlessly overcomes the counting to infinity and Bellman-Ford problems, and it also provides rapid convergence whenever the *ad hoc* network topology is changed [5].

AOMDV RP is used for sensor networks also. This is basically used for linking disjoint paths. As the nodes receive a duplicate root advertisement message, it denotes another route to the receiver.

AOMDV is used for finding node disjoint roots as well as link disjoint roots. For finding node disjoint roots, every RREQ coming through another nearest node of sources presents a node displace lane. For finding several connections to displace roots, the receiver gives a reply to copy of RREQs. As the primary jump is finished, the RREPs go through opposite routes and they are node displace and therefore link put out of place. The paths of every RREP might go through the same midway node at some point except every one of them gets a dissimilar opposite route to the transmitter node in order to make sure disjointness. AOMDV has been verified to be a superior protocol that uses multipath routes. Advantages of AOMDV RP: It is the distributed protocol to discover link disjoint paths. It reduces overhead by providing multiple paths.

Disadvantages of AOMDV routing protocol:

It has additional overhead for route discovery for RREP. Because of periodic route discovery it consumes extra bandwidth.

It emphasizes the issue of improving road safety and transport effectiveness through the use of WSN. Here the authors have considered the issue of safety in vehicular communication and for safety-related applications in WSN; they have surveyed the recent approaches and protocols in WSN. The authentic time route development algorithm is used to ease transfer congestion in city areas. First, the authors have established a hybrid intelligent transportation system and then proposed a novel lane preparation algorithm that outperforms the conventional scattered lane preparation algorithms for spatial utilization. Furthermore, Miao Wang *et al.* designed an efficient coordinated charging strategy. Through this strategy, the authors have achieved improvement in the energy utilization and reduction in the electric vehicles' journey charge: the availability of IPTV services over WSN, communication scenario to verify wireless communication performance and its operating reliability record duplication as a scheme for data division in WSN and also compared various strategies of database replication, and the location Verification Protocol for NLOS (non-line-of-sight) conditions in WSN. Through simulation results, the authors have proved that the NLOS condition can be overcome by using the location verification protocol among the neighboring vehicles, and thus the integrity of localization services for WSN can be secured: the analyzed WSN connectivity in case of limited RSUs (road-side units) deployment as well as provided for enhancement also.

As the path request packet will propagate in the network, if the destination generates the route reply, then it will put the path documentation into the path respond packet from the route request packet. Figures 11.1–11.5 show the path response by the receiving node itself. Adding new metrics and making few changes in the operation of DSR protocol using the fuzzy interface system increase the performance in real-time applications. In some of the applications, the DSR protocol lags behind compared with other reactive routing protocols because if any source has more than

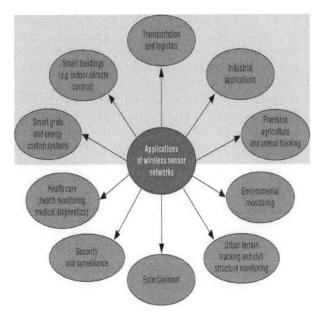

Figure 11.1   Application of WSN

one route in its cache, which route to choose will totally depend on the source. When energy efficiency is considered, the DSR protocol lags behind compared with other reactive routing protocols. The reason behind that is node mobility and node failures.

Advantages of DSR RP:

Paths remain only between nodes that require transmission.

Disadvantages of DSR RP:

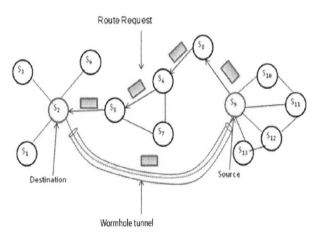

Figure 11.2   ormhole attack

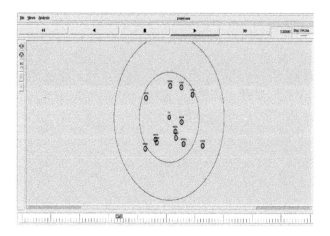

Figure 11.3   Without wormhole attack animator situation

Packet header extents with path length due to source routing.

The middle node may transmit path respond using a stale cached path, thus polluting additional caches.

Here, they have focused on highway WSN scenarios and show that even with a small number of RSUs along the highways, the performance is significantly improved. The authors have put forward a survey of MAC (Media Access Control) protocols for V2V (vehicle-to-vehicle) communications in WSN. The authors have also focused on the benefits and limitations of the various MAC protocols proposed in the survey. In addition to this, they have highlighted some of the challenges of the past proposed MAC protocols and the need for novel solutions. They explained the implementation of the new 17 routing protocol for the WSN environment with handover mechanism and got good results in conditions of speed than other routing protocols. It is used in performance evaluation for multicast transmission in WSN. The new communication strategy is based on conditional transmission for highly dynamic networks like WSNs. The basic idea used here is sending a message with

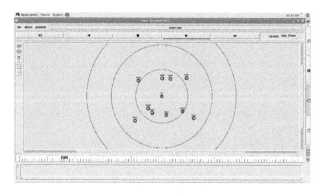

Figure 11.4   Network animator situation with designated nodes

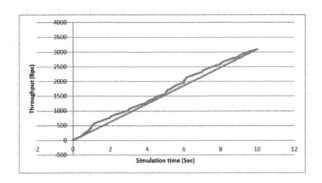

Figure 11.5   Throughput of the simulation system

some condition used for either reception or retransmission instead of transporting addresses or positions. The authors have also compared the performances of proactive and reactive protocols. The authors thoroughly elaborated WSNs and discussed its challenges and future perspectives. They have discussed various applications of WSN as well as suggested measures for further improvement. Furthermore, the authors have determined MTR (Minimum Transmission Range) of various road configurations in WSNs to provide better connectivity.

DSDV has loop-free paths, requires less convergence time, and is more dynamic. At every node, topology information is maintained with the help of tables. DSDV routing protocol can be used for VANET as well as MANET applications. This protocol is simpler and easy to implement than the protocol using vehicle position information, which requires the installations of related devices onto all vehicles on the road. DSDV finds routes in progress for every transmitter and receiver pair and time-to-time exchange topology information to sustain them.

Entry of increasing sequence digit tags helps in keeping the routing table updated. As a result of which, problems of loop formation, counting to infinity hurdle, are avoided and the convergence time is reduced. The routing table is updated by the destination node also by entering a fresh sequence digit that is superior to the prior sequence number.

There are two types of methods for updating the routing tables at each node in DSDV, which are incremental routing table update and full-dump routing table update. In case of incremental routing table update, nodes do not notice a considerable change in local network topology, and this update process takes a single network data packet unit. In case of full-dump routing table update, nodes notice a considerable change in local network topology and it may take more than one network data packet unit.

Advantages of DSDV RP:

- Loop-free paths are guaranteed by the DSDV protocol.
- DSDV has reduced the count to infinity hurdle to a great extent.

- Incremental updates can be used instead of full dump updates to avoid extra traffic.

Disadvantages of DSDV RP:

- Multipath routing is not supported by DSDV.
- It is hard to keep the routing table information for a huge network, as this would lead to overhead resulting in consumption of more Bandwidth.

They designed a high-speed address generator scheme required for address generation in deinterleaver of the WiMAX receiver system. Here, they have proposed a novel Application-Specific Integrated Circuit-based design for address generator, and its modeling has been done using VHDL. The authors have worked on Wi-Fi and also WiMAX technologies. Here the authors have evaluated a multi-vehicle to infrastructure WSN by using Wi-Fi for V2V communication and using WiMAX for the vehicle-to-infrastructure communication. They analyze the WiMAX performance of efficient wireless channels using image and speech transmission. Here they have thoroughly explained the concept of WiMAX system modeling with a proper selection of wireless channels like AWGN, Rayleigh, Racian, and so on so as to control the BER. The operational inference on WSN is 802.16e (WiMAX) and 802.11 p.

Then the authors have analyzed the performance of Wireless Broadband. Here they observed that a large portion of the delay in the handover process is due to the deep computing process occurring during authentication process. WiMAX topology shows that those data rates humiliate with the increase in the distance greater than 10,000 m. The authors proved that the independent MCS level is better than others: the performance of proactive RP in WSN over TCP and CBR connections. The performance is analyzed from parameters like PDR, PLR, and so on. Similar work of performance evaluation of WSN routing protocol is done by Nicholas *et al.* in the field of large-scale urban environment. The routing protocol used for performance evaluation is GPSR, Vehicle-Assisted Data Delivery, and LOUVRE. WiMAX allows more number of users in a short coverage area. While barriers are there, the genuine speed may be below 20 Mbps, but WiMAX can offer safe relief of data and hold mobile subscribers at vehicular mobility. IEEE 802.16e is designed to both achieve high-speed data services and allow mobile users with broadband wireless access solutions. WiMAX enables higher mobility for high-speed data applications.

The number of IFFT and FFT vectors decides the number of subcarriers generated for the given OFDM system. For an OFDM symbol, the orthogonality of subcarriers is given by

$$f_k = \frac{k}{T_{MC}} \quad k = 0, 1, \ldots, N - 1 \tag{11.1}$$

Here, $\frac{1}{T_{MC}}$ is the intercarrier spacing

k' is the number of subcarriers whose frequency is to be calculated.

The corresponding k^{th} subcarrier at frequency f_k can therefore be written as:

$$I_k(t) = e^{j2\pi f_k t} \tag{11.2}$$

For N subcarriers of OFDM symbol after being modulated by transmitter:

$$S(n) = \sum_{k=0}^{N-1} a_k e^{j2\pi \frac{kn}{N}}, \quad 0 \leq n \leq N-1 \tag{11.3}$$

In 3.3, a_k represents data symbols that are properly mapped and are complex in nature.

In an ideal channel where the transmitter and the receiver of the OFDM system are properly synchronized, the received subcarriers sequence $R(n)$ is the same as the transmitted subcarriers sequence, i.e., $R(n) = S(n)$.

So, under these ideal conditions, the demodulated data for the kth subcarrier are given by

$$\hat{a}_{k'} = \frac{1}{N} \sum_{n=0}^{N-1} R(n)\, e^{-j2\pi \frac{k'n}{N}} \tag{11.4}$$

$$= \frac{1}{N} \sum_{n=0}^{N-1} \sum_{k=0}^{N-1} a_k e^{j2\pi \frac{kn}{N}} e^{-j2\pi \frac{k'n}{N}} \tag{11.5}$$

$$= \sum_{k=0}^{N-1} a_k \left(\frac{1}{N} \sum_{n=0}^{N-1} e^{j2\pi \frac{n(k-k')}{N}} \right) \tag{11.6}$$

$$= \sum_{k=0}^{N-1} a_k \delta\left(k - k'\right)$$

$$= a_k$$

The ideal case of the OFDM system in practice does not exist. So, some parameters need to be considered while designing the OFDM system like channel disturbances, oscillator effects, and so on. Also due to the delay in the channel, the OFDM symbols may overlap with each other causing inter-symbol interference (ISI), which results in a change in 3.4. In OFDM symbols, in order to reduce the ISI in dispersive channels, guard intervals are inserted. After modulation d-mapping, the original data will be reconstructed. In this way, the data transmission and reception process is carried out in WiMAX. The technical overview of the WiMAX is given in the following. WSN is the application of MANET that improves traveler's comfort. WiMAX also provides high-level security for data transmission and reception in MANET as well as WSN.

Each vehicular node is capable of receiving, processing, and forwarding the packet. WiMAX base station has sufficient accessible bandwidth, so at a time, it can serve a large number of subscribers and also cover large coverage area range. WiMAX supports the MIMO technique to transmit the data via multiple radio channels. MIMO transmits multiple signals at a time simultaneously. WiMAX has more security than Wi-Fi. Also WiMAX provides a better throughput for high-mobility vehicles. The performance of the WiMAX-based WSN system can be evaluated by various techniques and protocols in which the show of WSN is generally based on RP's.

In today's era of wireless communication systems, the strength and the quality of the received signal by the user are depending upon various factors. Similarly, in the transceiver system, there are several factors that govern the signal strength and quality. Some of these factors are modulation technique, data rate, coding scheme, power constraint, path loss factor, and so on. Now in order to satisfy the need for effective signal transmission and to gain a good signal quality at the receiver or user end, the above-listed parameters have to be adjusted according to the channel parameters. The novel technique employing this strategy is called the link adaptation technique.

In the link adaptation technique, various constraining factors are adjusted or adapted according to the required radio link parameters to provide good-quality signals. Recently, an alternative link adaptation technique called AMC has come up to improve the overall system capacity. AMC allows matching of modulation and coding methods along with protocol and signal parameters to those with the conditions on the radio link such as path loss, sensitivity of the receiver, power margin of the transmitter, and so on.

The process of AMC is a dynamic one as the protocol and signal conditions on the radio link alter frequently. The main purpose of AMC is to maintain an acceptable bit error rate as well as to make more effective use of channel capacity. Various transmission parameters that can be adapted are data rate, coding rate, error probability, and transmitted power.

Other methods can be the assumption of approximately the same channel from TX to RX and from RX to TX in the time-division duplex method. Using link state information that is present at the TX adaptive modulation systems provides an improvement in the rate of transmission.

A benefit of a MIMO system is that without using extra power, multiplexing gain can be enhanced. It uses the highest number of retransmissions suitable for a packet if the earlier transmissions are not successful. Increasing the retry limit improves the system reliability, at the cost of higher packet delay and lower channel throughput. It adapts to the advance antenna technology supporting the MIMO and HARQ to enhance reliability. MIMO can also be used for underground tunnel networks. The MIMO capacity depends on transmission power and traffic load. The MIMO technique can be used to send the data for different sports activities at a time. In mobile communication, the MIMO technique allows frequency use again concept within every cell.

11.2 Wireless sensor network

Figure 11.6 displays the basic sensor network for exchange in a position of discrete, light mass nodes, prepared in large quantity to display the condition or gadget by way of the scale of the fleshly trouble including contamination, heaviness, stickiness,

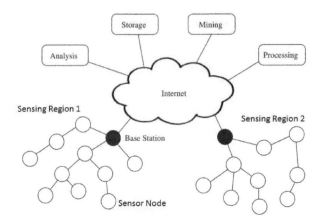

Figure 11.6   Basic stature of WSN

and so forth. The Wi-Fi sensor system is a collection of SNs. The evaluation of storage, mining, and processing of the subsystem of the Internet SNs consists of sensor subsystem, dispensation machine, and message scheme.

11.3   WSN application

It has various applications in this field of WSN. The few applications can be the following.

Military application: WSN is probably an important piece of martial command, control, communication for calculating intellect, battleground surveillance, investigation, and directing systems.

Locale monitoring: In this locale monitoring, the feeler nodes are organized in a section where some experience is to be monitored. At what time the feeler notices the occasion creature observed high temperature and force, and the occasion is stated to one is a BS.

Transference: Genuine-time transfer info is existence composed by WSNs to future supply transport model and attentive drivers of mobbing and transfer problem.

Healthiness application: In the same health application are at the bottom of intrusions for disabled, including patient monitor, indicative, and medicine direction in hospices, tale-monitoring of humanoid physiological information, and tracing and monitoring medics or patients within a hospice.

Ecological sense: The team of ecological feeler networks has residential to cover up lots of applications including air pollution checking, forest fire discovery, greenhouse checking, and landslide detection. This is the type of application of ecology.

Structural monitoring: Wireless sensors are able to be used to observe the association inside constructions and infrastructures such as bridge flyovers, embankment, and tunnel.

Industrialized monitoring: Wireless feeler networks contain industrialized support of technology condition-based repairs as they present important price investments and allow novel function a laity.

Agricultural sector: This wireless network releases the grower as of the conservation of electric wiring in a problematic atmosphere. Irrigation mechanization enables extra effectual water use and compact desecrate.

11.4 Limitations of WSN

1. They have a very slight loading capacity – a few hundred kBs.
2. They have hesitant processing power – 8 MHz.
3. They work in a small variety – devours a lot of power.
4. They need small energy – obliges protocols.

11.5 Literature survey

In this chapter, the wireless networks are vulnerable to many outbreaks, with an outbreak recognized as the loss outbreak. The wormhole outbreak is actual prevailing, and avoiding the attack has been established to be very problematic. In such outbreaks, double or extra malevolent plotting nodes make an advanced level simulated tunnel in the net, which is working to transport packages. It presents an original belief-based structure for classifying and unraveling nodes that generate a wormhole in the system deprived of attractive any cryptographic income. We establish that our arrangement purposes efficiently in the occurrence of malevolent conspiring nodes and do not execute any needless situations upon the system founding and process stage [1].

In this chapter, present the Ad-hoc network vehicular are predicted in to the outcome Wi-Fi knowledge containing of short range, which is grouping of Wi-Fi. Other applicants of prolonged reserves wireless machines are cell, and WI-max. in meant device offers a pair of radio channel in among trans receiver aimed at the printed and response of the information thru using the clue of MIMO expertise. Furthermore, AMC offers a range of variation methods trusting on the sign to finish relation of the channel. These two schemes offer the massive alteration inside the excellence of the current network [2, 3] on this section of the paper Zigbee collection tree be dressed documented Zigbee topology particularly suitable for WSNs impossible to resist low power and maintenance reduce change since it supports sturdy factor rescue schedules [4–8].

11.6 Related work

Figure 11.2 shows that the wormhole outbreak includes the only extra nodes and network between them. The outback node-sized applications or statistics one recover

Table 11.1   Simulation constraints

Constraint	Number
Frequency	2.4 GHz
Bandwidth	20 MHz
Transmission model	TRG propagation
Mac	WiMAX
Nodes	10
Period	10 s
Zone size	500 m × 500 m

and amount them to an additional remotely placed node that allots them neighboring [9–11]. They can then transmit out several types of bouts in contradiction of information circulating flows including discriminating decreasing. The strong factor also displays themselves or masks in a manner. The preceding is showing or naked wormhole outbreak, on the equal although as the concluding is a covered or close to one [12–14].

11.7   Methodology

Simulation parameters are important for the design of any system that provides the information about the nature of the wireless system. Table 11.1 shows the various simulation constraints used to design the wireless communication system. They are decided on the basis of applications that are targeted [15–33].

The QoS parameters of vehicular *ad hoc* networks are important to evaluate the WSN system. Different QoS parameters used in this WSN system are explained below.

11.7.1   Throughput

Throughput is the average rate of successful packet transfer between the transmitter and receiver of any system over a communication channel. Throughput of any network should be as high as possible. Its unit is bps.

Throughput = (Total packets received * Size of packet * 8)/(Time taken for transmission of all packets).

11.7.2   Delay

Delay is the time taken by the packets to transfer from TX to RX. Delay affects due to channel conditions, traffic, improper routing, and so on. Delay is an important performance parameter of any network. Delay shows how fast your data transmission process is carried out. So delay should be as low as possible. Delay is measured in seconds. It is calculated by the following expression.

Delay = Packet receive time − Packet send time

Table 11.2   Result of middling value

Parameters	Quantity
Throughput	1575.204 bps
PDR	77.76%
Delay	1.69×10^{-5} s

11.7.3   Packet delivery ratio

It is defined as the percentage of packets successfully received to RX. To improve PDR, the system should have a low computational requirement and an alternate route should be available if the current link has broken. The packet delivery ratio shows the percentage of packets received at the receiver. So, the packet delivery ratio should be maximum.

Packet Delivery Ratio = ((Total packet received/ Total packet sent) * 100)

11.7.4   Design of WiMAX-based WSN system

This WiMAX-based WSN system is designed using NS 2.34. The designing of the WiMAX-based WSN system is explained in the following.

- The response of any *ad hoc* network is depending on its simulation parameters. To design the WiMAX-based WSN system, the WiMAX parameters play an important role in data transfer. The frequencies used for WiMAX-based WSN systems are 2.5 and 4.5 GHz with a bandwidth of 20 MHz. The WSN system consists of a number of vehicular nodes depending on the application.
- Create a new simulator with trace and NAM file in the write node. NS 2.34 executes the different events on the defined time. So, each event should save in the trace and NAM file, so that both files must be in write mode. Trace file consists of the information about packet send, receive, drop, and forward in the network. It also consists of event time, coordinates of the vehicular nodes, energy, packet size, routing protocol, and IP address of the TX and RX vehicular node. NAM file is the Network AniMator that provides the network animation with all the events.
- Here the new trace format of the wireless communication system is used because this provides more information about the different events and vehicular nodes.
- The vehicular *ad hoc* network changes its topography according to the change in the position of vehicular nodes so that its topography changes continuously. So, initialize the change of topology area as a simulation area.
- Initialize cluster number for each domain. Also create channels and base station.
- Here base station is positioned at the middle of the network, so it can control every vehicular node within its coverage range. To identify the base station in the network, name it BS.

Table 11.3   Comparison of Wi-Fi and WiMAX

Standard	IEEE 802.11 a	IEEE 802.11b	IEEE 802.11 g	IEEE 802.16
Frequency (GHz)	5	2.4	2.4	2.66
Speed (Mbps)	54	11	54	80
Range	50 m	100 m	100 m	50 km
Radio technology	OFDM	DSSS	OFDM (64 channels)	OFDM (256 channels)
Primary application	Wireless LAN	Wireless LAN	Wireless LAN	Broadband Wireless Access

- Create vehicular nodes according to the real-time vehicular system. Each vehicular node has its own source and destination locations. Both the locations should be within its simulation area. The vehicular nodes are moving at some speed, so assign different speeds to each vehicular node. Give different labels to each of the vehicular nodes. Here the vehicular nodes are labeled as V1, V2, V3, and so on.
- Create source traffic. In the WSN system, communication takes place in three different ways, i.e., V2V, base station to vehicle, and vehicle to base station. Any vehicular node can communicate with other according to its requirement. User Datagram Protocol (UDP) agent is used for transmission of data from transmitting node. Connect UDP agents to all transmitting nodes.
- Constant Bit Rate (CBR) agent traffic source is attached to UDP with a packet size of 1,000 bytes and different packet interval times to each of the source vehicular nodes. UDP1 and CBR1 are attached to the same vehicular node so that it will be transmitter or source node.
- Create the NULL agent to sink traffic. Some of the vehicular nodes are receiving nodes, so connect NULL agents to all receivers. The NULL agent will terminate the data to that respective vehicular node.
- Attach two vehicular nodes in which agents UDP and NULL are attached to make pair of transmitter and receiver so that the transmitter node can transmit the data to the receiving node.
- Start and stop the CBR traffic within the simulation time.

11.8   Related results

The function of NAM is to show the animation of static and dynamic nodes with packets transfer, packets loss, position of the nodes, and simulation time scale. NAM also consists of forward, reverse, and stop functions that can be used to see any event that occurred during the simulation at any time instant. The NAM scenarios for various environments are given in the following.

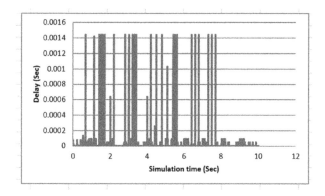

Figure 11.7   Delay among nodes

The situation without wormhole attack animator is shown in

The calculated MANET contains 12 nodes and one base station. The network continuously transmits data or packets or data over. Communication takings residence the portable nodes over Base Station Circles displays that the part of coverage system and the area size is 500 × 500. Figure 11.4 shows the same parameters but in a different way for the zooming animator scenario; it also presents the 10 nodes including one base station.

Figure 11.5 displays the speed of the modeled network in which diagram is planned among simulation time (s) and throughput (bps).

Figure 11.7 displays the delay diagram. The extreme delay is 0.0015 and the lowest delay is intended as 0. The replication time busy to scheme these standards are since 0 to 10 s.

Differentiating the overall sum of packets is traditional on the output nodes. As indicated in Figure 11.8, the package's transfer margin is 1.69 ms. The ordinary price of PDR indicates the model time in seconds; this is the 0–12 range and PDR is measured in ratio, and the all-out variety of the PDR is 100%.

Figure 11.9 shows the middling value of outcomes. The normal throughput range is 1,575.204 bps, which is to be intended. The PDR is 77.76%, and the delay is 1.69×10^{-5} s, which is the last reading in Table 11.2. The comparison of Wi-Fi and WiMax is given in (Table 11.3).

11.9   Conclusion

The designed WSN system is useful for transportation systems as well as industry automation also. This system provides better performance than the existing system. The various simulation parameters show that the designed system provides a high speed of the network for transportation systems as well as for other applications.

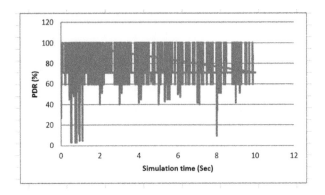

Figure 11.8   PDR network

11.10   Future scope

The investigation carried out in this book chapter leaves an ample scope for the extension of the WiMAX-based WSN system for various environment networks. The performance of the WiMAX-based WSN system can be improved in the future by using the following ways.

The use of hybrid routing protocols in the WiMAX-based WSN system can increase the performance of the network.

Various power reduction techniques can reduce power utilization at the base station.

By using various low-energy-consumption algorithms, the utilization of energy per vehicular node can be reduced.

One can design a WiMAX-based WSN system for a large coverage area network by using multiple relay stations to improve the efficiency.

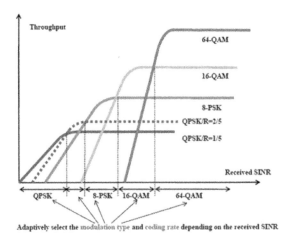

Figure 11.9   Relation of modulation techniques and throughput

It can be concluded that the work under investigation on the design of the WiMAX-based WSN system can be extended toward various applications in the area of intelligent transportation systems. The practical development of an improved WiMAX-based WSN system is one of the major potential research directions in the future.

References

[1] Parmar A., V.B. V. 'Detection and prevention of wormhole attack in WSN using AOMDV protocol'. *7th International Conference on Communication, Computing and Virtualization*; Maharashtra, India, 2016. pp. 700–07.

[2] Dorge P.D., Dorle S.S. 'Design of WSN for improvement of QoS with different mobility patterns'. *6th International Conference on Emerging Trends in Engineering and Technology*; Nagpur, India, 16-18 Dec; 2013.

[3] Dorge P.D., Dorle S.S., Chakole M.B., Research Scholar, G. H. Raisoni College of Engineering, Nagpur, India 'Implementation of MIMO and AMC techniques in wimax network based vanet system'. *International Journal of Information Technology and Computer Science*. 2016, vol. 8(2), pp. 60–68. Available from http://www.mecs-press.org/ijitcs/v8n2.html

[4] Shende S.F., Deshmukh R.P., Dorge P.D. 'Performance improvement in ZigBee cluster tree network'. *International Conference on Communication and Signal Processing (ICCSP)*; Chennai, India, 6-8 Apr; 2017.

[5] Pochhi R.D., Deshmukh R.P., Dorge P.D. 'An efficient multipath RP for cognitive AD hoc networks'. *International Journal of Advanced Electrical and Electronics Engineering*. 2012, vol. 1(3), pp. 1–7.

[6] Meshram S.L., Dorge P.D. 'Design and performance analysis of mobile Ad hoc network with reactive RPs'. *International Conference on Communication and Signal Processing (ICCSP)*; IEEE, Chennai, India, 6-8 Apr; 2017.

[7] Pandilakshmi S., Amar R. 'Detecting and prevent the Wormhole attack using customized evolution'. *International Journal of Innovative Research & Studies*. 2018, vol. 8(4), pp. 1–7.

[8] Ghormare S.N., Sorte S., Dorle S.S. 'Detection and prevention of Wormhole attack in WiMAX based mobile Adhoc network'. *Second International Conference on Electronics, Communication and Aerospace Technology (ICECA)*; Coimbatore, India, 29-31 Mar; 2018.

[9] Siva Ram M.C., Manoj B.S. *Ad hoc wireless networks architecture and protocols, upper saddle river, NJ:* Prentice Hall PTR; 2004.

[10] Gupta S., Kar S., Dharmaraja S. 'WHOP: wormhole attack detection protocol using hound packet'. Presented at The International Conference on INNOVATIONS Technology; Abu Dhabi, United Arab Emirates. IEEE,

[11] Hu Y.-C., Perrig A., Johnson D.B. 'Wormhole Attacks in Wireless Networks'. *IEEE Journal on Selected Areas in Communications*. 2016, vol. 24(2), pp. 370–80.

[12]   ChiuH.S., Lui K.S. 'DelPHI: wormhole detection mechanism for ad hoc wireless networks'. *1st International Symposium on Wireless Pervasive Computing*; Phuket, Thailand, IEEE, 2006. pp. 6–11.

[13]   Chaurasia U.K., Singh V. 'MAODV: modified wormhole detection AODV protocol'. *IEEE*. 2013, pp. 239–43.

[14]   Dorge P.D., Dorle S.S., Chakole M.B., Thote D.K. 'Improvement of qos in WSN with different mobility patterns'. *International Conference on Radar, Communication and Computing*; Tiruvannamalai, India, IEEE, 2012. pp. 206–09.

[15]   Kumar S., Ranjan P., Ramaswami R., Tripathy M.R. 'EMEEDP: eenhanced multi-hop energy efficient distributed protocol for heterogeneous wireless sensor network'. *Fifth International Conference on Communication Systems and Network Technologies*; Gwalior, India, IEEE, 2015. pp. 194–200.

[16]   Kumar S., Ranjan P., Ramaswami R. 'Energy optimization technique for distributed localized wireless sensor network'. *International Conference on Issues and Challenges in Intelligent Computing Techniques (ICICT)*; Ghaziabad, India, IEEE, 2014.

[17]   Chauhan R., Kumar S. 'Packet loss prediction using artificial intelligence unified with big data analytics, internet of things and cloud computing technologies'. *5th International Conference on Information Systems and Computer Networks (ISCON)*; Mathura, India, IEEE, 2021. pp. 1–6.

[18]   Sudhakaran S., Kumar S., Ranjan P., Tripathy M.R. 'Blockchain-based transparent and secure decentralized algorithm'. *International Conference on Intelligent Computing and Smart Communication 2019. Algorithms for Intelligent Systems*; Uttarakhand, India, IEEE, 2020. pp. 327–36.

[19]   Kumar S., Trivedi M.C., Ranjan P., Punhani A., *et al. Evolution of Software-Defined Networking Foundations for IoT and 5G Mobile Networks*. Hershey, PA: IGI Publisher; 2020. p. 350.

[20]   Kumar S., Ranjan P., Radhakrishnan R., Tripathy M.R. 'Energy efficient multichannel MAC protocol for high traffic applications in heterogeneous wireless sensor networks'. *Recent Advances in Electrical & Electronic Engineering*. 2017, vol. 10(3), pp. 223–32.

[21]   Kumar S., Ranjan P., Ramaswami R., Tripathy M.R. 'Resource efficient clustering and next hop knowledge based routing in multiple heterogeneous wireless sensor networks'. *International Journal of Grid and High Performance Computing*. 2017, vol. 9(2), pp. 1–20.

[22]   Kumar S., Cengiz K., Vimal S., Suresh A. 'Energy efficient resource migration based load balance mechanism for high traffic applications IoT'. *Wireless Personal Communications*. 2021, vol. 10(3).

[23]   Kumar S., Cengiz K., Trivedi C.M., *et al.* 'DEMO enterprise ontology with a stochastic approach based on partially observable Markov model for data aggregation and communication in intelligent sensor networks'. *Wireless Personal Communication*. 2022.

[24] Punhani A., Faujdar N., Kumar S. 'Design and evaluation of cubic torus Network-on-Chip architecture'. *International Journal of Innovative Technology and Exploring Engineering*. 2019, vol. 8(6), pp. 2278–3075.

[25] Dubey G., Kumar S., Kumar S., Navaney P. 'Extended opinion lexicon and ML-based Sentiment analysis of tweets: a novel approach towards accurate classifier'. *International Journal of Computational Vision and Robotics*. 2020, vol. 10(6), pp. 505–21.

[26] Singh P., Bansal A., Kamal A.E., Kumar S. 'Road surface quality monitoring using machine learning algorithm' in Reddy A.N.R., Marla D., Favorskaya M.N., Satapathy S.C. (eds.). *Intelligent Manufacturing and Energy Sustainability. Smart Innovation, Systems and Technologies*. 265. Singapore: Springer2022.

[27] Kumar S., Ranjan P., Radhakrishnan R., Tripathy M.R. 'Energy aware distributed protocol for heterogeneous wireless sensor network'. *International Journal of Control and Automation*. 2015, vol. 8(10), pp. 421–30.

[28] Kumar S., Ranjan P., Ramaswami R., Tripathy M.R. 'A utility maximization approach to MAC layer channel access and forwarding'. *Progress in Electromagnetics Research Symposium, Publisher: The Electromagnetics Academy*; Prague, Czech Republic, 2015. pp. 2363–67.

[29] Kumar S., Ranjan P., Ramaswami R., Tripathy M.R. 'An NS3 implementation of physical layer based on 802.11 for utility maximization of WSN'. *International Conference on Computational Intelligence and Communication Networks (CICN)*; Jabalpur, India, IEEE, 2016. pp. 79–84.

[30] Sharma A., Awasthi Y., Kumar S. 'The role of Blockchain, AI and IoT for smart road traffic management system'. *IEEE India Council International Subsections Conference (INDISCON)*; Visakhapatnam, India, 3-4 Oct; 2020. pp. 289–96.

[31] Singh P., Bansal A., Kumar S. 'Performance analysis of various information platforms for recognizing the quality of indian roads'. *10th International Conference on Cloud Computing, Data Science & Engineering (Confluence)*; Noida, India, IEEE, 2020. pp. 63–76.

[32] Kumar S., Ranjan P., Singh P., Tripathy M.R. 'Design and implementation of fault tolerance technique for internet of things (iot)'. *2020 12th International Conference on Computational Intelligence and Communication Networks (CICN)*; Bhimtal, India, IEEE, 2020. pp. 154–59.

[33] Reghu S., Kumar S. 'Development of robust infrastructure in networking to survive a disaster'. *4th International Conference on Information Systems and Computer Networks, ISCON 2019*; Mathura, India, IEEE, 2019. pp. 250–55.

Chapter 12

A review of edge computing in healthcare Internet of things: theories, practices and challenges

Shamik Tiwari[1] and Vadim Bolshev[2,3]

The pandemic has forced industries to move immediately their critical workload to the cloud in order to ensure continuous functioning. As cloud computing expansions pace and organisations strive for methods to increase their network, agility and storage, edge computing has shown to be the best alternative. The healthcare business has a long history of collaborating with cutting-edge information technology, and the Internet of Things (IoT) is no exception. Researchers are still looking for substantial methods to collect, view, process, and analyse data that can signify a quantitative revolution in healthcare as devices become more convenient, and smaller data becomes larger. To provide real-time analytics, healthcare organisations frequently deploy cloud technology as the storage layer between system and insight. Edge computing, also known as fog computing, allows computers to perform important analyses without having to go through the time-consuming cloud storage process. For this form of processing, speed is key, and it may be crucial in constructing a healthcare IoT that is useful for patient interaction, inpatient treatment, population health management and remote monitoring. We present a thorough overview to highlight the most recent trends in fog computing activities related to the IoT in healthcare. Other perspectives on the edge computing domain are also offered, such as styles of application support, techniques and resources. Finally, necessity of edge computing in the era of Covid-19 pandemic is addressed.

[1]School of Computer Science, University of Petroleum and Energy Studies, Dehradun, India
[2]Laboratory of Power Supply and Heat Supply, Federal Scientific Agro engineering Center VIM, Moscow, Russia
[3]Laboratory of Intelligent Agricultural Machines and Complexes, Don State Technical University, Rostov-on-Don, Russia

12.1   Introduction

The IoT has transformed how healthcare solutions operate, and the industry has seen a significant shift away from on-premise hardware and software and towards cloud computing [1]. IoT has spread across a variety of markets, catering to customers on a global scale. From smart voice assistants to smart homes, brands are diversifying their offerings and experimenting with new designs to increase consumer engagement.

IoT devices include gadgets, sensors, actuators, appliances and machines, which are designed for particular purposes and may broadcast data over the Internet or other networks. The IoT is introducing a new layer of complexity to the task of analysing an ever-growing mountain of data in order to improve healthcare [2]. Those who are not physically available in a health institution can use IoT devices to accumulate health indicators such as heart rate, temperature, blood pressure, glucose level and more, reducing the necessity for patients to travel to clinicians by collecting health data themselves. While much of the conversation around big data has focused on the possible shortcomings of Electronic Health Records (EHRs) and the major challenges of intuitive, efficient decision support, the IoT is adding another layer of complexity. Traditional information governance solutions are inadequate to manage this jumbled, unstandardised and poorly defined amount of data, and they are seen undesirably by overloaded, dispassionate health practitioners [3, 4]. Furthermore, the massive size of Patient-Generated Health Data (PGHD) produced each day presents huge problems for already overburdened analytics infrastructures that lack the ability to handle the avalanche of big data coming their way. If information from his wearable sensors don't reach the treatment station in time, a patient in the acute care unit has only minutes before a dip in vital signs leads into a devastating crash. Healthcare organisations frequently utilise cloud-based solutions as the process, service or storage layer between system and insight to allow what is now known as 'real-time analytics'. Data is bulk-uploaded to the cloud, and associated components are discovered and dragged back down into a server for analytics before being submitted to a user interface visualisation [5]. In a perfect world, the operation will only take a few minutes but patient life and quality-of-care judgements cannot be compromised due to time lag. The solution could be found in the edge or fog but not in the cloud. This work provides the details of fog computing including its applications to healthcare IoT. The rest of the chapter consists of sections on cloud computing in healthcare and its limitations, fog computing and its advantages over cloud computing, role of IoT in healthcare, practice of fog computing in healthcare, significance of machine learning in healthcare, integrated impact of IoT, machine learning and fog computing in healthcare, modeling and simulation tools for fog computing, necessities of edge computing in pandemic era and conclusion in that order.

12.2   Cloud computing in healthcare and its limitations

Cloud computing is a computational model that uses the Internet to connect computers, data centres, processors, servers, wired and wireless networks, storage, development tools and even healthcare applications. A cloud service provider may take care

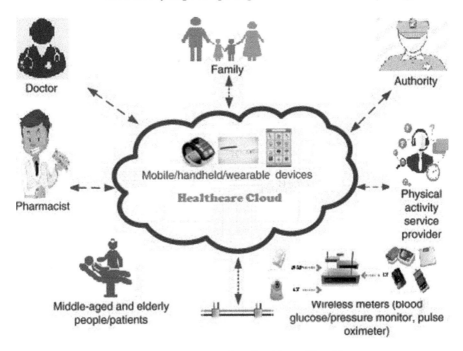

Figure 12.1   Some scenarios for cloud-based healthcare system

of any or all of these needs, including providing equipment, training and ongoing maintenance. Cloud computing can be deployed in different manners, depending on the resources that an organisation demands. The first thing to consider is the deployment model – private cloud, public cloud, hybrid cloud and multicloud depending on the aims of the business use case, each deployment type has strengths and limitations. When deciding on a cloud migration plan, an organisation must weigh all factors [6, 7]. Some scenarios for cloud-based healthcare system are presented in Figure 12.1.

12.2.1   Public cloud

A public cloud is a cloud deployment type in which a vendor owns and operates computational resources that are shared across several tenants through the Internet. A public cloud is an open system that enables customers to access storage or software for freely or on a pay-per-use basis over the Internet. A public cloud is a large data centre that provides all of its users with the same services. The services are available to anyone and are widely used by consumers. Amazon Elastic Cloud Compute (EC2), Google App Engine, IBM Blue Cloud and Azure Services Platform are few examples of common public clouds.

12.2.2   Private cloud

A private cloud (or corporate cloud) is a cloud computing infrastructure in which all equipment/software services are devoted to a single client and only that client has access to them. Private clouds are limited in size and are used by multiple clients who access virtualised services and draw resources from a separate pool of physical computing. With internal hosting and firewalls, the private cloud guarantees that data is private and secure. It also assures that third-party vendors do not have access to functional or critical information. Private clouds include Elastra-private cloud and HP data centres.

12.2.3   Hybrid cloud

A hybrid cloud is one in which services are deployed across multiple contexts. Since nearly no one nowadays relies only on the public cloud, hybrid cloud computing options are becoming increasingly popular. Although hybrid cloud solutions integrate private and public resources in a variety of ways, they frequently use industry-standard technologies like Kubernetes to coordinate container-based services. Google Anthos, Azure Stack, AWS Outposts, Azure Arc and VMware Cloud on AWS are other examples.

12.2.4   Community cloud

The phrase 'community cloud computing' refers to a shared cloud computing service environment geared towards a small number of businesses or employees. Technically, community cloud is a multitenant platform that is only available to a limited number of customers. It can be shared by organisations with similar computing concerns and mutual interests. Ventures, corporate organisations, research groups and tenders are the greatest candidates for this form of cloud computing. This allows community cloud users to understand and analyse market requirements upfront.

Many EHRs are actually housed on conventional client–server architectures. IoT has also aided in the simplification of operations in this area, making the process much more effective and patient-centric than it was a decade ago. Healthcare activities can be made much more convenient and cost-effective by implementing cloud computing solutions [8].

The cloud provides on-demand computing by deploying, accessing and utilising networked information, software and services using cutting-edge technology. However, there are certain drawbacks of cloud computing in healthcare.

- **Connectivity:** While cloud computing requires connectivity to the cloud, some IoT systems must function even if the link is temporarily unavailable.
- **Bandwidth:** Cloud computing assumes that there is enough bandwidth to collect data, but for industrial IoT applications, this may be an excessively optimistic assumption.

- **Centralised analytics:** Cloud computing centralises analytics, thus determining the system's lower bound response time. Some IoT applications would be unable to wait for data to be sent to the cloud, analysed and insights to be returned.
- **Security:** Existing data security systems in cloud computing, such as encryption, have failed to secure data from attackers.

12.3 Edge computing and its advantages over cloud computing

Data processing, analytical and computational skills are brought nearer to the network's edge with edge computing. These are the so-called 'things' in the context of an IoT network. There is some ambiguity about the use of these two words in the IoT industry [9]. Others see a slight difference in that the calculation is performed differently in a fog or edge scheme, but they are also used interchangeably. Edge computing, also known as fog computing, enables computers to perform essential analytics without relying on the inefficient cloud storage method. For this form of processing, speed is important, and it could be crucial to creating the IoT in healthcare truly effective for patient interaction, nursing, healthcare management and remote health assistance. Fog computing is a distributed computing model that sits between cloud data centres, IoT computers and sensors as an intermediary layer [10, 11]. It offers cloud-based services with computing, networking and storage capabilities that can be applied closer to IoT devices and sensors. Cisco introduced fog computing in 2012 to handle the problems that IoT applications face in traditional computing environments. IoT devices and sensors, as well as real-time and latency-sensitive service specifications, are widely spread at the network's edge. Cloud data centres are physically centralised, and they regularly struggle to meet the storage and handling demands of billions of globally dispersed IoT devices and sensors. As a result, the network is congested, service delivery is late and the quality of service is weak [12, 13]. Figure 12.2 presents edge and cloud computing with end point devices. Table 12.1 assesses cloud computing and edge/fog computing.

12.3.1 Advantages of edge/fog computing

For IoT, big data and real-time analytics, edge and fogging methods offer numerous benefits. The advantages of edge computing over cloud computing are as follows:

- **Low latency**: The latent of edge/fog computing to improve network efficiency by decreasing latency is its most substantial benefit. The information collected by IoT edge computing devices does not have to move near as far as it would in a standard cloud architecture because the data is processed locally or in nearby edge data centres.
- **Low bandwidth requirement**: Because data is collected at multiple locations rather than being sent all at once to a single destination via a single channel, there are no bandwidth constraints.

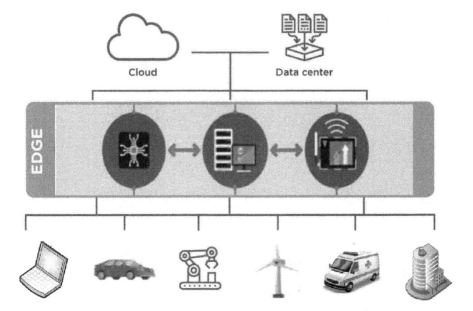

Figure 12.2   Edge and cloud computing with endpoint devices

- **High reliability:** Due to a network of interconnected channels, a loss of connection is impossible.
- **High security:** In a complex distributed system, a large number of nodes, resulting in excellent security, process data.
- **Improved user experience:** Users are satisfied because they receive immediate responses and there are no downtimes.
- **Power efficiency:** Low-power protocols like as Bluetooth, Zigbee and Z-Wave are used by edge nodes, which make it power efficient.

12.3.2   Disadvantages of edge/fog computing

Although the technology has no apparent flaws, there are a few flaws to be aware of:

- **A more complicated approach:** Fog is a data processing and storage device that is applied as a layer.
- **Additional costs:** Edge devices such as routers, hubs and gateways may be purchased by companies.
- **Scalability:** Fog's scalability is reduced compared with the cloud.

Table 12.1   Assessment of cloud computing and edge/fog computing

Parameters	Cloud computing	Edge/fog computing
Latency	High latency in terms of network	Low latency in terms of network
Speed	Access speed is high depending on Virtual machine (VM)connectivity	High even more compared with cloud computing
Processing power	Superior and advanced processing capabilities	Lesser processing capabilities
Scalability	High	Lesser compared with cloud computing
Storage	High	Low
Data processing point	Central cloud server	Located near the sensors on the devices to which the sensors are attached, or on a gateway system
Distance between client and server	Multiple hops	Single hope
Security	Undefined	Possible to define
Vulnerability	High chance	Low chance
Location alertness	No	Yes
Data integration	Data from many sources can be combined	Data from a variety of sources and devices can be combined
Geodistribution	Centralised	Distributed
Responsiveness	Low	Fair
Support of mobility	Limited	Available
Type of last mile connectivity	Leased line	Wireless
Number of server nodes	Limited	Extensive
Real-time communications	Provided	Provided
Purpose	It is best for long-term, in-depth data analysis	Best suited for real-time response analysis that requires fast analysis

12.4   IoT in healthcare

Due to IoT-enabled products, remote monitoring in the healthcare business is now possible, which helps retain patients safe and secure while driving doctors to deliver superior treatment. As communications with doctors have become simple, rapid and more successful, patients' involvement and enjoyment have improved. Furthermore, remote patient control is beneficial [14, 15]. IoT devices provide a plethora of new opportunities for healthcare providers to monitor their patients' health as well as for individuals to monitor their own health. As a result, the numerous wearable IoT devices offer a number of benefits and challenges to both healthcare providers and patients. Figure 12.3 shows

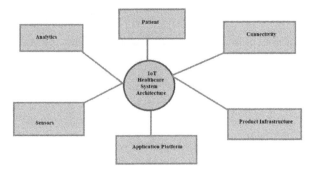

Figure 12.3   Component of IoT-enabled healthcare system

components of IOT enabled healthcare system. Some prominent examples of IoT applications for healthcare are as follows:

- depression and mood monitoring
- glucose monitoring
- ECG monitoring
- PCG monitoring
- remote patient monitoring
- heart rate monitoring
- body hygiene monitoring
- robotic surgery

IoT can play a critical role in smart hospitals, for example. By integrating IoT technologies into the healthcare sector, it can change almost all of these situations. Utilising blockchain and smart contracts, inefficient large paper registries can be substituted by an automated, centralised database. Submissions can be received, queues can be controlled and staff members may be tracked in real time via smartphones with an all-encompassing processing system. Using blockchain and smart contracts, any equipment can be continuously controlled and maintained.

12.5   Edge computing in healthcare

The availability of critical data and real-time data analysis is beneficial to every firm. These variables, on the other hand, could spell the change between life and loss in the healthcare. The vast bulk of processing remains to take place in the cloud or at single-site data centres. Analysing data from a distance, particularly from the latter, presents a number of challenges. Congestion of bandwidth, high latency and low reliability are examples of these issues [16, 17]. Even with today's 4G LTE networks, these problems will still arise as every second counts. Edge/fog computing seeks to solve these problems by taking data processing closer to the data collection devices. This is particularly useful in cases where data must be acted on right away, such as in healthcare. There isn't time to upload it to the cloud and process it when every second counts.

Improved security, quicker accessibility to real-time data and transmission efficiency are the three significant benefits of edge computing. Because each edge data centre handles less data, the security of health records can be improved. Because the amount of potentially sensitive data in each site is less, malicious hackers will have a tougher time compromising critical resources or infecting the existing network. Establishing a closed-loop system in an intensive care unit (ICU) that includes smart systems to detect acutely ill patient can help healthcare professionals react in condition more quickly is an example of edge computing in action. In an ICU, edge computing is performed by attaching sensors to modest, local control systems that manage computation and transmission. Organisations can realise the following advantages after they have precisely articulated what they really want to aim from edge computing and what they have to do to enable it:

- The proximity and efficiency of data
- Integration of IoT data and healthcare provider systems
- Data about patient health that is more accurate and up to date
- Medical gadgets such as insulin pumps, smart glasses and pacemakers are used to monitor patients
- Telemedicine
- Wearables and application support that monitor a variety of health indicators

12.6   Machine learning in healthcare

Machine learning (ML) is a sort of data analysis that uses artificial intelligence (AI) to build analytical models. It is a subfield of AI centred on the idea that robots can learn from data, see patterns and create decisions with minute to not at all human intervention. ML refers to a system's potential to 'learn' by identifying patterns in huge datasets. In other words, the 'solutions' generated by ML algorithms are statistical conclusions drawn from very big datasets. The ability to collect, distribute and deliver data is becoming increasingly important as digitalisation disrupts every sector, including healthcare [18, 19]. ML, big data and AI will all assist in overcoming the obstacles that large quantities of data present.

ML is a branch of AI that includes the methods that permit machines to infer implication from historical data and design intelligent systems. However, deep learning (DL) is a subset of ML that enables machines to comprehend extremely complex problems. DL is a relatively new branch of AI based on artificial neural networks. We can classify DL algorithms as a subsection of ML since they require data to learn and solve issues. Figure 12.4 provides machine learning and allied areas.

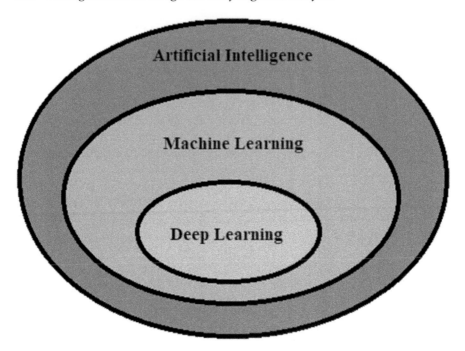

Figure 12.4   ML and allied areas

Healthcare organisations can use ML to meet rising patient demands, optimise procedures and cut costs. ML advancement at the bedside will assist healthcare practitioners in detecting and treating illness more quickly, with greater precision and with more personalised treatment [20, 21]. Some prominent applications of ML in healthcare are as follows:

- Identification of diseases and diagnosis
- Medical imaging
- Drug discovery and manufacturing
- Personalised medicine/treatment
- Predicting diseases
- Medical research
- Smart health records
- Identify relationship between disease and symptoms
- Robotic surgery

In healthcare, AI and ML are still in their infancy. Adoption on a big scale has yet to occur. In order to be effective in the healthcare industry, AI and ML must have the support of healthcare medical specialists and doctors.

However, a lot of money is being invested in AI in healthcare, and it is growing quickly. AI in healthcare is now targeted at improving patient outcomes, balancing

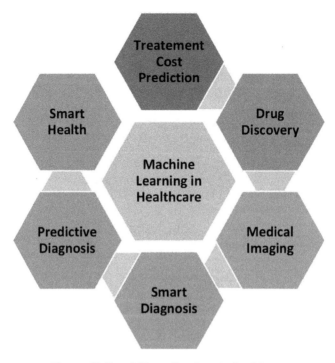

Figure 12.5   ML applications in healthcare

the interests of multiple stakeholders, enhancing availability and lowering healthcare expenditures. Moreover, in the coming years, AI and ML, as well as methods supported by data science and DL will play a much more holistic role in advancing healthcare. Figure 12.5 presents machine learning applications in healthcare domain.

DL algorithms are not only remarkably precise but also extremely quick. Studies have discovered a deep neural network capable of identifying some neurological brain diseases faster and more accurately than radiologists, such as stroke and brain bleeding. In few seconds, the system examines the image, evaluates its contents and alarms in cases of a problematic clinical finding. In neurological settings, 'time is brain'. In other words, in the diagnosis of patients' neurological disorders, a quick reaction is crucial; any methods that reduce the time it takes to diagnose a patient may result in a better outcome. DL is most commonly used in medical imaging. A representative of DL applications in the medical imaging is provided below. These are only a small number of applications, and it will continue to grow over time. It gives an indication of the long-term influence of DL in the medical imaging sector today.

- Diabetic retinopathy
- Brain tumour
- Alzheimer disease
- Tracking tumour growth
- Breast cancer

- Covid-19-related lung abnormalities
- Skin cancer, etc.

12.7   Integrated role of IOT, ML and edge computing in healthcare

Connected healthcare is gaining significant attention from academics, governments, industry and the healthcare community as smart sensory media, objects, edge analytics, AI and cloud technologies advance. Patients now need a comprehensive and specialised smart healthcare system that is customised to their individual health needs, thanks to the introduction of emerging technology and the quick pace of human life. Edge/fog computing, in conjunction with 5G networks, AI and cutting-edge smart IoT sensors, enables sophisticated, real-time healthcare applications that are low on energy and low on latency. While researchers have done substantial development in the study of edge-AI and IoT for health services on their own, there has been little focus on developing cost-effective and inexpensive smart healthcare services. The linked healthcare industry's edge-AI-driven IoT has the potential to change many aspects of our industry [22].

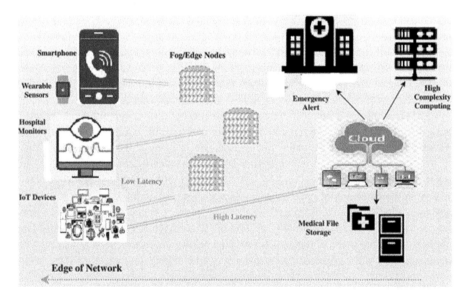

Figure 12.6   Integrated role of IOT, ML and edge computing in healthcare. The edge computing paradigm brings processing closer to physical IoT equipment, which serves as a vital midway for lowering latency and conserving bandwidth in the cloud.

Following are some case studies where integrated role of IOT, ML and edge/ fog computing in healthcare can be applied. Figure 12.6 discusses integrated role of IOT, ML and edge computing in healthcare.

12.7.1 Patient care during surgical procedure

Edge/fog computing has the potential to alter operating theatres in hospitals. In the past, a nurse or two would have to be present in the operating room, maintaining meticulous records and charting each action being taken by the surgeon and his or her staff. Software that can log each action is now available, thanks to the deployment of cameras and other edge computing devices. This helps to save time for nurses and eliminates the potential for human error. Nurses and surgeons are able to focus on the patient.

12.7.2 Patient care at home

Most do not have easy access to high-quality healthcare. From the comfort of their own homes, edge data centre technologies can enable patients receive better treatments and more accurate diagnoses. While this was formerly assumed to only assist residents in distant places, the Covid-19 pandemic has educated us that there are a variety of other reasons that people may be unable to evacuate their families and seek medical attention in a hospital. Wearable sensors that patients can wear in their homes benefit from edge/fog computing. These sensors can collect data on patient health and deliver precise faced by healthcare practitioners as it becomes available. m-Health discussions benefit from edge data centre services as well. Drone deliveries of medical supplies and lab specimens are also possible, thanks to cutting-edge equipment.

12.7.3 Patient care in ambulance

For in-hospital physicians and nurses, predicting a patient's health when they arrive for care via ambulance is no longer a guessing game. First services used to be able to relay certain critical information by radio. Today's cutting-edge sensors and systems can send live ambulance surveillance video to doctors, giving emergency room professionals real-time patient information. The team can adequately position for the patient's presence with this knowledge.

12.8 Modelling and simulation tools for edge/fog computing

As attention in edge/fog computing grows, so does the demand for simulation platforms to facilitate the development and evaluation of edge computing systems. In many cases, in addition to real-world solutions, simulations are needed to examine the behaviour of composite IoT-edge-cloud systems or to create modern, effective data analytics solutions. Several simulators for examining distributed systems, especially IoT and cloud systems are available these days for researchers. Some prominent tools for simulation of fog and edge computing are listed below [23, 24].

- iFogSim
- FogTorch
- FogTorchPi
- FogNetSim++
- FogBed
- MaxiNet
- EmuFog
- Yet Another Fog Simulator
- IoTSim
- FogExplorer
- RECAP
- EdgeCloudSim
- Sleipnir

iFogSim is the most popular of these tools. iFogSim is a Java-based open-source simulation programme based on Java for simulating fog communications environments. It was developed at the Cloud Computing and Distributed Systems Lab, University of Melbourne. It's features include mobility support and migration management, dynamic distributed clustering, microservice orchestration and full compatibility with CloudSim The iFogSim architecture, as shown in Figure 12.7, is made up of layers that are in charge of different tasks. At the bottom of the layer is the IoT devices, for example, actuators and sensors that interact with the real world, indicating whether they are data producers or sinks. To mimic more complex equipments, such as environmental sensors, smart cameras and mobile vehicles, these components can be tweaked to mimic the effects of collecting data or performing actions. Fog endpoints, according to iFogSim, are any network element that can host application modules. Figure 12.8 presents iFogSim   simulation   architecture.

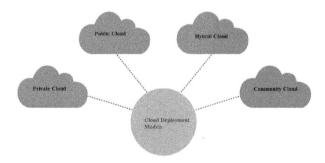

Figure 12.7   Cloud deployment models

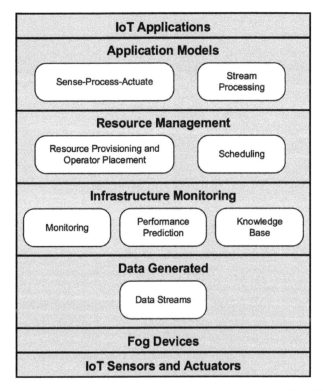

Figure 12.8   iFogSim simulation architecture (adapted from [25])

12.9   Edge computing in Covid-19 pandemic era

The Covid-19 pandemic and accompanying lockdowns have prompted significant adjustments in our lifestyles, as well as exposing major flaws in the broader network systems that sustain us. More remote work, virtual collaboration and increasing bandwidth requirements are just a few of the changes [26]. However, the flaws, such as wired networks that have slowed due to increased load, must be addressed. Due to the pandemic, organisations have been obliged to hastily migrate critical workloads to the cloud in order to maintain business continuity. As cloud computing gains pace and businesses hunt for ways to increase their network, storage and agility, edge computing has shown to be the best alternative. Every industry is being put to the test as the globe prepares for the continued effect of the Covid-19 pandemic [27, 28].

As the health industry re-evaluates their long-term network needs based on their experience tackling the Covid-19 pandemic, edge computing is now emerging as the forefront and crucial pillar of the network architecture to accommodate this new distributed workforce and effectively control the rising universe of sensors and devices at the edge of their networks [29, 30]. Edge computing can support the pandemic era in following manners.

- Creating the self-contained healthcare centres
- Providing opportunities for new health workers
- Increasing the impact of health Industry 4.0
- Speedy diagnosis of Covid-19 patients
- Distant intensive care of Covid-19 patients in quarantine institutions and home isolation
- Quick analysis of Covid-19 patient data
- Securing medical records
- Edge/fog computing–based solutions for mobile applications and mobile payments

12.10   Challenges of edge computing

Data processing for IoT achieves somewhat efficiency due to edge/fog computing. It adds to the organisation's coordinated and accurate execution. However, along with the nice stuff, there are some severe difficulties to deal with. The following are some of the major issues that arise with implementing edge-computing technologies [31–33].

- Data centres acquire higher bandwidth under the conventional asset distribution model, while endpoints get less. Because edge data processing necessitates a large amount of bandwidth for optimised and efficient workflow, the dynamics of edge computing altered intensely. Retaining a balance between the two while achieving decent performance is the issue.
- Upgrades to edge devices or services might go wrong, resulting in clusters or devices failing.
- Edge/fog computing raises the significance of the physical setting and computing environment for data collection and processing. Organisations must have a position in local data centres to resulting optimal workload and give reliable result [25, 34–38].
- The set of modules in most servers is distributed and placed high off the ground. Edge Computing (EC) on the other hand, usually brings all systems closer to the computational areas. This causes a conflict because the business server must consider the edge server during computation.
- It becomes more difficult to detect and oversee when firms install ever more edge nodes to oversee a larger range of processes. Devices may eventually exceed the edge's bounds, causing bandwidth saturation and compromising the security of numerous devices. IoT traffic raises delay as it expands, and when data is transferred untreated, it might endanger security [39–44].
- Because of the multiple edge receivers located at various distances from the data centre, troubleshooting and repairing any issues that arise in the framework necessitate a significant amount of logistical as well as manual input, raising the cost of maintenance.

- Edge devices are frequently ignored by security-conscious personnel, and many have inadequate password policies. Hackers have devised advanced methods for breaching password schemes [45–49].
- Integrated data and network security practices are possible due to a centralised cloud infrastructure. On the other hand, EC/Fog computing (FC) necessitates implementing similar policies for remote servers, despite the fact that security perimeter and traffic conditions are more difficult to evaluate.
- A centralised cloud architecture can be integrated with a system-wide data loss protection solution. Edge/fog computing's decentralised architecture necessitates specialised control and maintenance tools to manage information at the edge.
- Contain local storage to enable high-performance and low-latency data processing, as well as connections to remote storage solutions.
- Data access and storage controls must be handled differently in the edge/fog computing framework. While centralised infrastructure provides for consistent regulations, edge/fog computing necessitates constant monitoring of each 'edge' location.
- While safeguarding patient data may come at a steep price to the sector, it is an important duty for healthcare to play. It is crucial not just for the protection of personal patient information but also for ensuring compliance with legislation [50–52].

In order for 'the edge' to become as widespread in the business world as 'the cloud', plenty of technical difficulties must be overcome. Those include production of small devices with large computing power, software that allows businesses to remotely control and maintain an unlimited number of edge devices from anywhere in the globe and additional security techniques and protocols to ensure things protected. Red Hat, Amazon, Microsoft, IBM, Nutanix and Cloudera, for example, are all continuously trying to solve these issues and have built their own edge solutions.

12.11   Conclusion

The transition to edge/fog computing solutions is now and will continue to be a healthcare necessity, particularly as organisations begin to implement post-Covid recovery approaches. Living on the edge will soon become the norm in any organisation, both as a result of and in spite of the pandemic's impact on healthcare industry. Existing physical equipment will be transformed from a single-function activity to an aggregation of processes, inputs and outputs using edge/fog computing. Merging these different processes, inputs and outputs in a number of ways will result in a plethora of resolutions as well as hundreds of operational and commercial models, accelerating the Industrial 4.0 Revolution in post-Covid era. This chapter provides a comprehensive analysis to highlight the most recent advancements in fog computing activities in healthcare related to the IoT. Other aspects of the edge/fog computing area, such as application support styles, methodologies and resources, are also discussed. Finally, the importance of edge/fog computing in the context of the Covid-19 pandemic is discussed. Future research should concentrate on improving present edge tools, and there is a pressing necessity for the development of a strong computationally edge intelligent devices and model for tackling pandemic.

References

[1]   Wu Q., He K., Chen X. 'Personalized federated learning for intelligent IoT applications: a cloud-edge based framework'. *IEEE computer graphics and applications*. 2020, vol. 1, pp. 35–44.

[2]   Stoyanova M., Nikoloudakis Y., Panagiotakis S., Pallis E., Markakis E.K. 'A survey on the Internet of things (IoT) forensics: challenges, approaches, and open issues'. *IEEE Communications Surveys & Tutorials*. 2020, vol. 22(2), pp. 1191–221.

[3]   Abrahão M.T.F., Nobre M.R.C., Gutierrez M.A. 'A method for cohort selection of cardiovascular disease records from an electronic health record system'. *International journal of medical informatics*. 2017, vol. 102, pp. 138–49.

[4]   Agniel D., Kohane I.S., Weber G.M. 'Biases in electronic health record data due to processes within the healthcare system: retrospective observational study'. *BMJ*. 2018, vol. 361, p. k1479.

[5]   Baumann L.A., Baker J., Elshaug A.G. 'The impact of electronic health record systems on clinical documentation times: a systematic review'. *Health Policy*. 2018, vol. 122(8), pp. 827–36.

[6]   Tiwari S. 'An ensemble deep neural network model for onion-routed traffic detection to boost cloud security'. *International Journal of Grid and High Performance Computing*. 2021, vol. 13(1), pp. 1–17.

[7]   Green D.R. Cloud Computing in Healthcare: Understanding User Perception, Organizational Operations, and IT Costs to Be Successful in the Cloud. [Doctoral dissertation]. Northcentral University; 2020.

[8]   Mourya A.K., Idrees S.M. 'Cloud computing-based approach for accessing electronic health record for healthcare sector'. *Microservices in Big Data Analytics*. Singapore: Springer; 2020. pp. 179–88.

[9]   Dong P., Ning Z., Obaidat M.S., *et al.* 'Edge computing based healthcare systems: enabling decentralized health monitoring in Internet of medical things'. *IEEE Network*. 2020, vol. 34(5), pp. 254–61.

[10] Amin S.U., Hossain M.S. 'Edge intelligence and Internet of things in healthcare: a survey'. *IEEE Access*. 2020, vol. 9, pp. 45–59.

[11] Patra B., Mohapatra K. 'Cloud, edge and fog computing in healthcare'. *Intelligent and Cloud Computing*. Singapore: Springer; 2021. pp. 553–64.

[12] Verma P., Fatima S. 'Smart healthcare applications and real-time analytics through edge computing' in *Internet of things use cases for the healthcare industry*; 2020. pp. 241–70.

[13] Yaraziz M.S., Bolhasani H. 'Edge computing applications for IoT in health-care: A systematic literature review'. *In Review*. 2021.

[14] Haghi Kashani M., Madanipour M., Nikravan M., Asghari P., Mahdipour E. 'A systematic review of IoT in healthcare: applications, techniques, and trends'. *Journal of Network and Computer Applications*. 2021, vol. 192(5) 103164.

[15] Dang L.M., Piran M.J., Han D., Min K., Moon H. 'A survey on internet of things and cloud computing for healthcare'. *Electronics*. 2019, vol. 8(7), p. 768.

[16] Singh A., Chatterjee K. 'Securing smart healthcare system with edge comput-ing'. *Computers & Security*. 2021, vol. 108(1) 102353.

[17] Mulimani M.S., Rachh R.R. 'Edge computing in healthcare systems'. *Deep Learning and Edge Computing Solutions for High Performance Computing*. Cham: Springer; 2021. pp. 63–100.

[18] Qayyum A., Qadir J., Bilal M., Al-Fuqaha A. 'Secure and robust machine learning for healthcare: a survey'. *IEEE Reviews in Biomedical Engineering*. 2020, vol. 14, pp. 156–80.

[19] Saleem T.J., Chishti M.A. 'Exploring the applications of machine learning in healthcare'. *International Journal of Sensors, Wireless Communications and Control*. 2020, vol. 10(4), pp. 458–72.

[20] Tiwari S. 'Dermatoscopy using multi-layer perceptron, convolution neural network, and capsule network to differentiate malignant melanoma from be-nign nevus'. *International Journal of Healthcare Information Systems and Informatics*. 2021, vol. 16(3), pp. 58–73.

[21] Sharma S., Tiwari S. 'COVID-19 diagnosis using X-ray images and deep learning'. *International Conference on Artificial Intelligence and Smart Systems (ICAIS)*; Coimbatore, India, IEEE, 2021. pp. 344–49.

[22] Darwish A., Hassanien A.E., Elhoseny M., Sangaiah A.K., Muhammad K. 'The impact of the hybrid platform of Internet of things and cloud computing on healthcare systems: opportunities, challenges, and open problems'. *Journal of Ambient Intelligence and Humanized Computing*. 2019, vol. 10(10), pp. 4151–66.

[23] Ning H., Li Y., Shi F., Yang L.T. 'Heterogeneous edge computing open plat-forms and tools for Internet of things'. *Future Generation Computer Systems*. 2020, vol. 106, pp. 67–76.

[24] Ranjan R., Villari M., Shen H., Rana O., Buyya R. 'Software tools and tech-niques for FOG and edge computing'. *Software: Practice and Experience*. 2020, vol. 50(5) 473–5.

[25] Gupta H., Vahid Dastjerdi A., Ghosh S.K., Buyya R. 'iFogSim: a toolkit for modeling and simulation of resource management techniques in the Internet of things, edge and FOG computing environments'. *Software: Practice and Experience*. 2017, vol. 47(9), pp. 1275–96.

[26] Javaid M., Khan I.H. 'Internet of things (IoT) enabled healthcare helps to take the challenges of COVID-19 pandemic'. *Journal of Oral Biology and Craniofacial Research*. 2021, vol. 11(2), pp. 209–14.

[27]   Sufian A., Ghosh A., Sadiq A.S., Smarandache F. 'A survey on deep transfer learning to edge computing for mitigating the COVID-19 pandemic'. *Journal of Systems Architecture*. 2020, vol. 108(4), p. 101830.

[28]   Rahman M.A., Hossain M.S. 'An internet-of-medical-things-enabled edge computing framework for tackling COVID-19'. *IEEE Internet of Things Journal*. 2021, vol. 8(21) 15847–54.

[29]   Tiwari S., Jain A. 'Convolutional capsule network for COVID-19 detection using radiography images'. *International Journal of Imaging Systems and Technology*. 2021, vol. 31(2), pp. 525–39.

[30]   Kong X., Wang K., Wang S., *et al.* 'Real-time mask identification for COVID-19: an edge-computing-based deep learning framework'. *IEEE Internet of Things Journal*. 2021, vol. 8(21) 15929–38.

[31]   Varghese B., Wang N., Barbhuiya S., Kilpatrick P., Nikolopoulos D.S. 'Challenges and opportunities in edge computing'. *IEEE International Conference on Smart Cloud (SmartCloud)*; New York, NY, USA, IEEE, 2016. pp. 20–26.

[32]   Xiao Y., Jia Y., Liu C., Cheng X., Yu J., Lv W. 'Edge computing security: state of the art and challenges'. *Proceedings of the IEEE*. 2019, vol. 107(8), pp. 1608–31.

[33]   Liu S., Liu L., Tang J., Yu B., Wang Y., Shi W. 'Edge computing for autonomous driving: opportunities and challenges'. *Proceedings of the IEEE*. 2019, vol. 107(8), pp. 1697–716.

[34]   Haidar M., Kumar S. 'Smart healthcare system for biomedical and health care applications using aadhaar and blockchain'. *5th International Conference on Information Systems and Computer Networks (ISCON)*; Mathura, India, IEEE, 2022. pp. 1–5.

[35]   Kumar S., Ranjan P., Radhakrishnan R., Tripathy M.R. 'Energy efficient multichannel MAC protocol for high traffic applications in heterogeneous wireless sensor networks'. *Recent Advances in Electrical & Electronic Engineering*. 2017, vol. 10(3), pp. 223–32.

[36]   Kumar S., Ranjan P., Ramaswami R., Tripathy M.R. 'Resource efficient clustering and next hop knowledge based routing in multiple heterogeneous wireless sensor networks'. *International Journal of Grid and High Performance Computing*. 2017, vol. 9(2), pp. 1–20.

[37]   Punhani A., Faujdar N., Kumar S. 'Design and evaluation of cubic torus network-on-chip architecture'. *International Journal of Innovative Technology and Exploring Engineering (IJITEE), 1672-1676*. 2019, vol. 8(6).

[38]   Dubey G., Kumar S., Kumar S., Navaney P. 'Extended opinion lexicon and ML-based Sentiment analysis of tweets: a novel approach towards accurate classifier'. *International Journal of Computational Vision and Robotics*. 2020, vol. 10(6), pp. 505–21.

[39]   Kumar S., Ranjan P., Radhakrishnan R., Tripathy M.R. 'Energy aware distributed protocol for heterogeneous wireless sensor network'. *International Journal of Control and Automation*. 2015, vol. 8(10), pp. 421–30.

[40] Singh P., Bansal A., Kamal A.E., Kumar S. 'Road Surface Quality Monitoring Using Machine Learning Algorithm' in Reddy A.N.R., Marla D., Favorskaya M.N., Satapathy S.C. (eds.). *Intelligent Manufacturing and Energy Sustainability. Smart Innovation, Systems and Technologies*. 265. Singapore: Springer; 2022.

[41] Sharma A., Awasthi Y., Kumar S. 'The role of blockchain, AI and iot for smart road traffic management system'. *Proceedings of the IEEE India Council International Subsections Conference, INDISCON 2020, Publisher: IEEE, Visakhapatnam, India*; 2020. pp. 289–96.

[42] Kumar S., Ranjan P., Singh P., Tripathy M.R. 'Design and implementation of fault tolerance technique for internet of things (iot)'. *Proceedings – 2020 12th International Conference on Computational Intelligence and Communication Networks, CICN 2020, Publisher: IEEE, Bhimtal, India*; 2020. pp. 154–59.

[43] Singh P., Bansal A., Kumar S. 'Performance analysis of various information platforms for recognizing the quality of indian roads'. *Proceedings of the Confluence 2020 – 10th International Conference on Cloud Computing, Data Science and Engineering*; Noida, India, IEEE, 2020. pp. 63–76.

[44] Chauhan R., Kumar S. 'Packet loss prediction using artificial intelligence unified with big data analytics, internet of things and cloud computing technologies'. *5th International Conference on Information Systems and Computer Networks (ISCON)*; India, Mathura, 2021. pp. 1–6.

[45] Reghu S., Kumar S. 'Development of robust infrastructure in networking to survive a disaster'. *4th International Conference on Information Systems and Computer Networks, ISCON 2019*; Mathura, India, IEEE, 2019. pp. 250–55.

[46] Kumar S., Ranjan P., Ramaswami R., Tripathy M.R. 'An NS3 implementation of physical layer based on 802.11 for utility maximization of WSN'. *Proceedings of the International Conference on Computational Intelligence and Communication Networks, CICN 2015*; 2016. pp. 79–84.

[47] Kumar S., Ranjan P., Ramaswami R., Tripathy M.R. 'A utility maximization approach to mac layer channel access and forwarding'. *Progress in Electromagnetics Research Symposium*; The Electromagnetics Academy, 2015. pp. 2363–67.

[48] Kumar S., Ranjan P., Ramaswami R., Tripathy M.R. 'EMEEDP: enhanced multi-hop energy efficient distributed protocol for heterogeneous wireless sensor network'. *Proceedings of the 5th International Conference on Communication Systems and Network Technologies, CSNT*; Gwalior, India, IEEE, 2015. pp. 194–200.

[49] Kumar S., Ranjan P., Ramaswami R. 'Energy optimization in distributed localized wireless sensor networks'. *Proceedings of the International Conference on Issues and Challenges Intelligent Computing Technique (ICICT)*; Ghaziabad, India, IEEE, 2014.

[50] Sudhakaran S., Kumar S., Ranjan P., Tripathy M.R. 'Blockchain-based transparent and secure decentralized algorithm'. *International Conference on Intelligent Computing and Smart Communication. Algorithms for Intelligent Systems*; Springer: Singapore; 2020.

[51]   Kumar S., Trivedi M.C., Ranjan P., Punhani A. *Evolution of Software-Defined Networking Foundations for IoT and 5G Mobile Networks*. Hershey, PA: IGI Publisher; 2020. p. 350.

[52]   Kumar S., Cengiz K., Vimal S., Suresh A. 'Energy efficient resource migration based load balance mechanism for high traffic applications IoT'. *Wireless Personal Communications*. 2021, vol. 10(3).

Chapter 13

Image Processing for medical images on the basis of intelligence and biocomputing

M. Mohammed Mustafa[1], S. Umamaheswari[2], and Korhen Cengiz[3]

Intelligence in medical imaging explores how intelligent computing can create a large amount of changes to existing technology in the field of medical image processing. The book presents various algorithms, techniques, and models for integrating medical image processing with artificial intelligence (AI) and biocomputing. Bioinformatics solutions lead to an effective method for processing the image data for the purpose of retrieving the information of interest and collecting various data sources for extracting the knowledge. Moreover, image processing methods and techniques help scientists and physicians in the medical field with diagnosis and therapies. It describes evolutionary optimization techniques, support vector machines (SVMs), fuzzy logic, a Bayesian probabilistic framework, a reinforcement learning-based multistage image segmentation algorithm, and a machine learning (ML) approach. It discusses how these techniques are used for image classification, image formation, image visualization, image analysis, image management, and image enhancement. The term "medical image processing" illustrates the provision of digital image processing, particularly for medicine. Medical imaging intends to identify internal structures hidden in the human body. It helps to find abnormalities in the body. Digital images can be processed effectively, also evaluated, and utilized in many circumstances concurrently with help of suitable communication protocols.

13.1 Introduction

The motive for the primary image processing was modified to enhance the huge image. It is modified to goal human beings to enhance the seen effect of people. In

[1]Department of Information Technology, Sri Krishna College of Engineering & Technology, Coimbatore, Tamilnadu, India
[2]Department of Information Technology, C. Abdul Hakeem College of Engineering & Technology, Melvishsaram, Tamilnadu, India
[3]College of Information Technology, University of Fujairah, UAE

image processing, the middle is a low and huge image, and the output is an image with top-notch progress. Common image processing consists of image enhancement, restoration, encoding, and compression. First-a-hit software program became the American Jet Propulsion Laboratory. They used image processing techniques, which protected geometric correction, gradation transformation, noise removal, etc.

13.1.1　What is an image?

Practically, each scene around us is bureaucratic, and this is concerned with photo processing. A photo is shaped through two-dimensional analog and virtual signs that carry color facts organized alongside x and y spatial axis.

13.2　Image processing

Image processing is a technique to carry out a few operations on an image, with the purpose to get a superior image or extract a few beneficial records from it.

In general terms, manipulating an image to amplify the same to induce information out of it is called image processing.

There are two styles of image processing, which are as follows:

- analog image processing, which is used for recycling photos, printouts, and other image hard clones
- digital image processing, which is used for manipulating digital images with the help of complex algorithms

The main purposes of image processing are as follows:

- representing reused data in a visual way one can understand, for example, giving a visual form to unnoticeable objects
- to ameliorate the reused image quality, image stropping and restoration work well
- image recuperation helps in searching images
- helps to measure objects in the image
- with pattern recognition, it becomes easy to classify objects in the image, detect their position, and get an overall understanding of the scene

13.2.1　Equivalent image processing

Analog image processing is carried out on analog alerts, and its methods are the simplest two-dimensional alerts. The snapshots are manipulated with the aid of using electric alerts. In analog image processing, analog alerts may be periodic or nonperiodic. Examples of analog snapshots are TV snapshots, images, paintings, clinical snapshots, etc. [1].

13.2.2 Digital image processing

Virtual image processing is carried out on virtual images (a matrix of small pixels and elements). For manipulating the images, there are some software programs and algorithms, which are carried out to carry out changes. Digital image processing is one of the quickest developing enterprises which impacts everyone's life. Examples of virtual images are processing, image recognition, video processing, etc.

13.2.3 Digital image

A virtual image is an illustration of a two-dimensional image as a fixed set of virtual values, referred to as image factors or pixels.

Common image formats are as follows:

- one sample per point (grayscale or B&W)
- two samples per point (green, red, and blue)
- three samples per point (green, blue, red, and "Alpha")

13.2.4 Applications of color models

Red, Green, Blue (RGB) model for color monitor and color video camera CMY mode included for color printing HIS mode included for color image processing YIQ mode included for color image transmission.

Digital photo processing represents the usage of a personal computer (PC) to govern images through an algorithm. Analog photo processing allows a far wider form of algorithms to be applied to enter statistics and might keep away from issues together with noise and distortion at some point of processing. Since images are defined in phrases of dimensions, digital photo processing may be modeled in the shape of a multidimensional system. Screening of huge numbers of people is the want of the hour to minimize the unfolding of ailment within the community. Real-time Polymerase chain reaction (PCR) is a widespread diagnostic device getting used for pathological checking out. But the growing wide variety of fake check effects has opened the route for exploration of opportunities for checking out tools. Chest X-rays of Covid-19 patients affected by pneumonia, tuberculosis, and chronic bronchitis have proved to be a crucial opportunity indicator in disease screening. But again, accuracy relies upon radiological expertise [2].

13.2.5 Applications of digital image processing

The use of virtual photograph manner strategies has exploded, and that they are presently used for various duties altogether in variety of regions, such as image enhancement and restoration, medical field, remote sensing, transmission and coding, machine/robot vision, color processing, pattern recognition, video processing, and microscopic images.

13.2.6   *Fundamental steps in digital image processing*

Step 1: Image acquisition

The photograph is captured via means of a device (e.g., camera) and digitized if the output of the digital or sensor isn't perpetually in virtual form, using the analog-to-virtual device [3–8].

Step 2: Image enhancement

The method of manipulating an image in order that the end result is greater appropriate than the unique for particular applications. The concept behind enhancement strategies is to convey information that might be hidden, or easy to spotlight the positive functions of a hobby in an image.

Step 3: Image restoration

It improves the arrival of associate degree image – tend to be mathematical or probabilistic models. Enhancement, on the choice hand, is entirely on human subjective selections regarding what constitutes a "good" sweetening result.

Step 4: Color image processing

Use the shade of the image to extract the capabilities of the hobby in a very image. Color modeling and process in a virtual space plays an important role in image processing.

Step 5: Wavelets

These are the muse of representing photos in various stages of resolution. It is used for image facts compression whereby photos are divided into smaller regions.

Step 6: Compression techniques

These are used for decreasing the garage required to keep an image or the bandwidth required to transmit it.

Step 7: Morphological processing

Tools for extracting photographic additives that can be useful in the illustration and outline of the shape. In this step, there may be a transition from approaches that generate images, to approaches that emit photographic attributes [9–12].

Step 8: Image segmentation

Segmentation approaches break down an image into its building blocks or objects. Important tip: The better the segmentation, the more likely the popularity to succeed.

Step 9: Representation and description

Representation: select whether or not the records should be represented as a boundary or as an entire region. It continuously follows the exit from a segmentation phase. Representation of limits: focus on the characteristics of the external form, as well as angles and inflections. Representation of the region: focus on internal properties, as well as the texture or shape of the skeleton. Transform raw recordings into a suitable form for further processing on PC. Descriptive offerings with extractive attributes that determine certain quantitative hobby records are fundamental to differentiate elegance of one object from another.

Step 10: Object recognition

The method of labeling an item, based primarily on the facts, is provided by its description. Recognition is the method of assigning a tag, such as a "vehicle" to an item, based primarily on its descriptors.

13.2.7   Components of an image processing system

1. Image sensors

    The first is the bodily instrument, which is sensitive to the electricity radiated using the object that one wishes to visualize (sensor). The second, called a digitizer, is a tool for transforming the output of the body detection tool into a virtual shape [13–19].

2. Specialized image processing hardware

    It typically includes the digitizer, mentioned earlier, as well as hardware that performs several primitive operations, including a mathematical good judgment unit (ALU), which reproduces mathematical and logical operations in parallel to the entire images. This form of hardware is sometimes known as the front-end subsystem, and its biggest distinguishing feature is speed. In other words, this unit performs features that require statistical processing speeds that the standard laptop computer cannot handle.

3. Image processing software

    Image processing software includes specialized modules that perform unique tasks. A well-designed package also includes the functionality to allow the person to write code that, at a minimum, uses specialized modules.

4. Mass storage capability

    Mass garage functionality is a necessity in an image processing program. And an image of size 1,024 × 1,024 pixels requires a megabyte of garage area if the image is not always compressed. The digital garage for image processing programs falls into three main categories: short-term archiving for use during processing, online archiving for relatively quick recall, and archiving characterized by infrequent access.

5. Image displays

    Presentations used today are mainly color television screens (ideally a flat screen). Monitors are pushed through the image outputs, and the images show playing cards which are an essential part of a PC system.

6. Hardcopy devices

    Used for recording images, they consist of laser printers, film cameras, heat-sensitive devices, inkjet gadgets, and virtual gadgets, which include optical discs, cameras, and Compact Disk-Read Only Memory (CD-ROM).

7. Networking

    It is a kind of default characteristic on any transportable device in use to-day. Due to the large quantity of data inherent in photograph processing software program packages, the essential aim of photograph transmission is bandwidth. In devoted networks, this isn't always typically usually a problem; however, communications with far-flung websites in the community aren't usually as efficient.

13.3   Medical imaging

Medical imaging is the technique used to achieve pictures of the frame elements for scientific applications, makes use of it on the way to perceive or examine diseases. There are masses of heaps of imaging strategies completed every week worldwide. Medical imaging is developing swiftly due to developments in image graph processing techniques including image graph recognition, assessment, and enhancement. Image processing will grow the percentage and amount of detected tissues. There are many straightforward and complicated image graph assessment techniques within the medical imaging field. They are also explaining a way to exemplify photo interpretation demanding situations and the usage of distinct photo processing algorithms which include k-means, ROI primarily based on segmentation, and watershed strategies.

13.4   Deep learning techniques

Deep learning strategies, especially convolutional neural networks (CNNs), have confirmed success in clinical imaging classification. Many, one-of-a-kind CNN architectures have been investigated on images of chest X-rays for prognosis of sickness (Figure 13.1). These fashions were preskilled at the keras and tensor waft ImageNet database with the aid of lowering the use for big education units as they have got preskilled weights. Its changes discovered that CNN primarily based on architectures has the capability for prognosis of sickness. Several types of current in-depth study strategies including Convolutional Neural Community (CNN), Vanilla Neural Community, Fully Neural Community-Based Visible Geometry Organization (VGG), and Pill Community are implemented for the prediction of lung disease. Simple CNN has terrible overall performance for rotated, tilted, or non-normal image orientation. Recently, in-depth study has proven brilliant capability while implementing clinical images for sickness detection, inclusive of lung sickness.

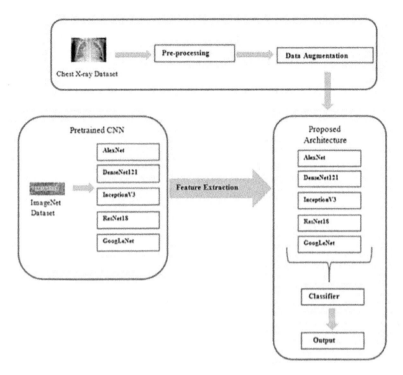

Figure 13.1   The architecture of image processing using deep learning

Lung sickness refers to problems that have an effect on the lungs, the organs that enable us to breathe. Breathing trouble due to lung sickness may also save the frame from getting sufficient oxygen. Lung sickness is the first-rate challenge for human beings, and many people lose their life due to lung sickness. In general, the CNN set of rules is getting used for image classification and popularity due to its excessive accuracy.

In this modern day ever transcending world, wherein the generation is converting loads of one-of-a-kind fields and industries, human beings nevertheless now no longer create an entire benefit of generation in diverse industries. The foremost cause for this will be that maximum of the engineers as a minimum the bulk of them are absolutely dedicated to laptop technological know-how, which regard a sequence of hate or problem attitude for the programmer; however, there are few who clearly desire to make large adjustments in the clinical region and in fact make novel improvements within the field.

In current years, a lot of such computer-aided diagnoses (CAD) structures are designed for the analysis of numerous diseases. Most lung cancer detection at an early degree has come to be very critical and additionally very clean with image processing and deep gaining knowledge of strategies. The lung-affected person computer tomography (CT) test images are used to classify the lung nodules and to stumble on the malignancy stage of those nodules. The CT test images may be segmented with the use of U-Net architecture. Globally, pneumonia is the maximum critical motive of loss of life, although it is a vaccine-preventable ailment. It may be detected by studying chest X-rays. Analyzing chest X-rays is a hard assignment and calls for precision. A higher and superior synthetic intelligence device for pneumonia detection can move in an extended manner to lowering the mortality price and growing lifestyle expectancy. A deep neural community version primarily based on CNNs and residual community together with strategies of figuring out the most reliable differential quotes, the use of cosine annealing and stochastic gradient with restarts to reap a green, and enormously correct community with a view to assisting stumble on and are expecting the presence of pneumonia with the use of chest X-rays.

Lung disease is a common occurrence at some point in the world. These embrace persistent clogging pneumonic upset, pneumonia, asthma, tuberculosis, fibrosis, etc. Timely analysis of respiratory organ ailment is essential. Many image processing and gadget gaining knowledge of fashions had been evolved for this purpose. Millions of human beings have developed coronary heart ailment each year, and coronary heart ailment is the most important cause of fatality of both women and men in the United States and across the world. The World Health Organization (WHO) analyzed that 12 million deaths take place globally because of heart diseases. In nearly every 34 seconds, the coronary heart ailment kills one person in the world. Medical analysis performs critical functions and complex assignments that require to be done efficaciously and accurately. To lessen fee for attaining medical exams, the appropriate PC primarily based on statistics and choice guide need to be aided. Data mining is using software program strategies for locating styles and consistency in units of records. Also, with the appearance of records mining during the final decades, there is a massive possibility to permit computer systems to at once assemble and classify the specific attributes or classes.

A deep neural network model based primarily on CNNs and residual networks collectively with reliable maximum differential rate identification techniques using cosine annealing and stochastic gradient with restarts to obtain an inexperienced and distinctly precise network that helps to meet and anticipate the presence of pneumonia in chest X-rays. Lung disorder is not an unusual place at an unspecified time in the future of the world. These include continuous obstructive pulmonary disorders, pneumonia, asthma, tuberculosis, fibrosis, etc. Rapid assessment of lung disorders is essential. Many models of image processing and machine mastering have been advanced for this purpose. Millions of humans have emerged with some shape of coronary heart disorder every year, and coronary heart disorder is the maximum cause of death of both women and men in the United States and throughout the world. The WHO analyzed that 12 million deaths take place globally due to heart diseases. In almost every 34 seconds, the coronary heart disorder kills one man or woman in the world. Medical evaluation plays a vital characteristic; however, complicated project wants to be achieved successfully and accurately. To reduce rate for achieving scientific checks, an appropriate laptop-based definite information and desire manual need to be aided. Data mining is the use of software program application techniques for finding patterns and consistency in devices of data. Also, with the advent of data mining during the final decades, there is a big opportunity to allow PC structures to gather and classify the unique attributes or classes.

13.4.1   Uses of image processing

1. Image correction, stropping, and resolution Correction

   Frequently, we wish we could make old images more. And that is possible currently. Zooming, stropping, edge discovery, and high dynamic range edits all fall under this order. All these ways help in enhancing the image. Utmost editing software and image correction law can do these effects fluently.

2. Pollutants on editing apps and social media

   Utmost editing apps and social media apps give pollutants these days.

   Pollutants make the image look more visually charming. Pollutants are generally a set of functions that change the colors and other aspects in an image that make the image look different. Pollutants are an intriguing operation of image processing.

3. Medical technology

   In the medical field, image processing is used for colorful tasks such as Positron emmission tomography (PET) checkup, X-ray imaging, medical CT, UV imaging, cancer cell image processing, etc. The preface of image processing to the medical technology field has greatly bettered the diagnostic process.

4. Computer/machine vision

   One of the most intriguing and useful operations of image processing is in the computer vision. Computer vision is used to make the computer see, identify effects, and process the whole terrain as a whole. The important use of computer vision is self-driving buses, drones, etc. Computer vision helps in handicap discovery, path recognition, and understanding the terrain.

5. Pattern recognition

   Pattern recognition is a part of image processing that involves AI and machine literacy. Image processing is used to find out colorful patterns and aspects in images. Pattern recognition is used for handwriting analysis, image recognition, computer-backed medical opinion, etc.

6. Video processing

Video is principally a fast movement of images. Colorful image processing ways are used in video processing. Some styles of video processing are noise junking, image stabilization, frame rate conversion, detail improvement, etc.

13.5   Convolutional neural network

A CNN is crafted from one or more convolutional layers (regularly with a subsampling step) as soon as that is observed through technique of manner of one or more wholly related layers as accomplice diploma exceeding in a powerful multilayer neural community. The shape of a CNN is supposed to require a gain of the second one shape of an input image (or absolutely distinct two-dimensional input which includes a speech signal). This may be completed with near connections and tied weights found through the manner of many forms of pooling which ends up in translation-invariant features. Another gain of CNNs is that they are simpler to train and feature numerous fewer parameters than wholly related networks with the same form of hidden units. The data are preprocessed which include image reshaping, resizing, and conversion to array form. A similar system is also accomplished on the test image. A database complete of approximately 4,000 one every of a kind plant species is obtained, out of that, any photograph is likewise used as a test photograph for the software bundle program.

The training database is used to teach the version (CNN) so that it can select the control image and the disease it has. CNN has unique levels which could be Convolution2D, MaxPooling, and fully related. Once the version is successfully activated, the software can detect the disease if the plant species is contained in the database.

After a fulfillment training and preprocessing, evaluation takes a look at image, and skilled model takes area to anticipate the contamination.

1. This model will be a successive model having a chain of layers to transform equal preceding period image proper right into a carry out set for similar processing.
2. The number one layers of this model M are the convolutional layer with 128 filters, and Relook because of the activation feature.
3. The 0.33 layer is that the Gamma hydroxybutrayte (GHB) pooling layer, so it is going to lessen the dimensions of the convoluted image through manner of (2, 2).
4. It yet again offers in addition convolutional layers can have 256 filters and rectified linear unit (ReLU) because of the activation feature.
5. The sixth layer is that the GHB pooling layer with a pool length of (2, 2).
6. A convolutional layer with 384 filters and ReLU activation feature is delivered to the version.
7. The following layer is once more a convolutional layer with 256 filters and ReLU activation feature.
8. Then it is a max pooling layer ascertained via means of dropout fee 0.2.

9. Then this version has brought one further layer to flatten the output of the on top of designed convolutional neural community version.
10. This destruction system will deliver the perform set for every image within the form of output.
11. Now, this version has utterly connected layers so it will be used for the kind of photos entirely at the generated function set.
12. This dense layer acts as a result of the hidden layer of the artificial neural community having 512 hidden neurons, and also the activation feature is ReLU. This version is an intended one among these manners that every entered somatic cell is connected to every completely different hidden neuron forming a very connected layer.
13. It is one further completely related layer that acts as a result of the output layer of the artificial neural community having three output neurons. The range of output neurons is regularly looking on the classes. It makes use of SoftMax activation feature.
14. The output of this residue is that the anticipated magnificence label that is to assess the final accuracy of this version.

The CNN algorithm is being used for image classification and recognition because of its high accuracy. Initially, the problem statement has been studied and analyzed the dataset, then apply machine learning and deep learning to predict whether the patient has lung disease or not. In this current ever-transcending world, where technology is changing a lot of different fields and industries, people still not making complete advantage of technology in various industries. The main reason for this would be that most of the engineers are completely committed to computer science, which regard a series of hate or difficulty mindset for the programmer, but there are few who really want to make big changes in the medical sector and actually make novel advancements in the field.

13.6   Convolution layers

From Figure 13.2, the convolutional layer includes a tough associate in nursing quick of filters whose parameters need to be learned. The height and weight of the filters are smaller than those of the enter extent. Every filter is convolved with the enter extent to cipher an activation map factory made from neurons. In numerous words, the clear out is softened throughout the breadth and peak of the middle, and also the dot merchandise between the enter and clear out is computed at each spatial position.

Automatically detecting diseases and obtaining correct diagnoses through X-ray medical images have become a new research priority in the field of computer science and AI, as the expense of manual labeling and classification continues to rise. However, the quality of a standard radiograph is insufficient for most activities, and traditional approaches are inadequate for dealing with large pictures. To detect pneumothorax from chest X-ray images, we present a feature fusion CNN model. To

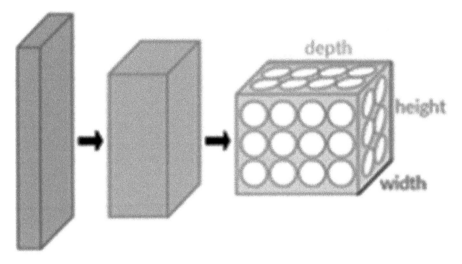

Figure 13.2   The structure of the convolutional layer

begin, two methods are used to improve the preprocessed image samples. The final classification is then implemented using a feature fusion CNN model that combines the Gabor features with the additional information collected from the images.

Furthermore, the CNN has made significant progress in the recognition of patterns in images, particularly in medical imaging. Designing an image-feature extractor is crucial in traditional CAD techniques. This is, however, a challenging task. A CAD approach that employs CNN, on the other hand, does not necessitate the employment of an image-feature extractor. We used CNN to create an image-based Computer Aided Design X (CADx) for differential diagnosis of lung anomalies including lung nodules and diffuse lung illnesses in this work. CNN performs admirably in the classification of natural photos. As a result, numerous studies have been conducted on the differential diagnosis of lung anomalies such as lung nodules and diffuse lung illnesses. CNNs or ConvNets are a type of deep neural network used to analyze visual imagery in deep learning. Based on the shared weight architecture of the convolution kernels that shift over input features and produce translation equivariant responses, they are also known as shift in variant or space invariant artificial neural networks (SIANN). Surprisingly, most convolutional neural networks are equivariant rather than invariant under translation. They can be used in computer vision and pattern recognition, recommender systems, classification, image segmentation, medical image analysis, natural language processing, central nervous system interfaces, and financial time series, to name a few applications.

Step 1: The first step is to do a convolution operation. The convolution operation is the initial step in our attack strategy. We will discuss about feature detectors in this stage, which are essentially the neural network's filters. We will also discuss about feature maps, including how to learn the parameters of such maps, how to recognize patterns, the layers of detection, and how to map out the results.

Step 1a: ReLU layer will be used in the second half of this process. We will discuss about ReLU layers and how linearity works in the context of CNNs. It is not vital to understand CNNs but it is never a bad idea to brush up on your skills.

Step 2: Pooling is the next step. Pooling will be covered in this section, and we will learn how it works in general. However, our nexus will be a special form of pooling: maximum pooling. However, we will go over a variety of ways, including mean (or sum) pooling. This section will conclude with a demonstration using a visual interactive tool that will undoubtedly clarify the entire subject.

Step 3: Flattening is the third step. When working with CNNs, there will be a brief discussion of the flattening process and how we move from pooling to flattened layers.

Step 4: Complete the connection, and everything we have discussed so far will be combined in this section. By learning this, you will gain a better understanding of how CNNs work and how the "neurons" that are eventually formed learn to classify photos.

The output extent of the convolutional layer is received via manner of means of stacking the activation maps of all filters aboard the intensity dimension. Since the breadth and peak of each filter out are intended to be smaller than the entire, every nerve cell within the activation map is simplest involving tiny low close space of the enter extent. In numerous words, the receptive subject length of every neuron is small and is a clone of the clear out length. The nearby property is influenced via way of means of the structure of the animal visible cortex whereby the receptive fields of the cells are small. The nearby property of the convolutional layer permits the community to check filters that maximally reply to a close-by space of the enter, consequently exploiting the spatial nearby correlation of the enter (for AN enter image, a constituent is further correlated to the within sight pixels than to the remote pixels). In addition, as a result, the activation map is received via manner of means of acting convolution among the filter out and also the larger, the clear out parameters are shared for all nearby positions. The load sharing reduces the large choice of parameters for performance of expression, performance of learning, and precise generalization.

The accuracy of the version is excessive while compared with different category methods.

1. The version is computationally powerful and simple.
2. Due to actual time implementation, it will increase financial value.

After categorizing the photos based mostly on elegance labels, process the facts to fit in our model with the usage of CNN and educate the CNN based mostly on training photos. CNN is proposed on this artwork for the elegance of the leaves inflamed with the brilliant sorts of fungal disease. The education snapshots have been taken for the beauty labels. Training a CNN is the exercising of going for walk education examples through the version from the input layer to the output layer concurrently developing a prediction and identifying the effects or errors. If the prediction is incorrect then it is over again propagated in opposite order, that is, from final layer to first layer.

13.6.1   Training phase

During the training segment, the version's inner weights are mechanically up to date over numerous iterations. External elements including the training method, structure, regularization techniques, or the rate of the hyperparameters have an effect on this training process. Comparing research and their consequences to extract insights on the way to outline the training segment is complex due to the reality that they do not use the identical records and do not offer all of the parameters required to breed their experiments.

13.6.2   Training strategies

There are techniques to educate a CNN: from scratch or with switch studying. Transfer studying is at the same time as a community is preinformed on a massive set of photos (e.g., ImageNet and its 1.2 million photos in 1,000 classes) is used and tailored to three distinctive tasks. This shape of studying is enabled through way of method of the fact that the primary layers of CNNs take a look at common low-diploma functions that aren't splendor unique.

In practice, this model is finished using the community weights from preceding education. Using switch analyzing permits us to apply CNNs even though the quantity of education data is limited, that is frequently the case within the context of crop illnesses identification. This approach allows to benefit more generalizability, because of the truth that the community had formerly located to address lot of examples. It is likewise a manner to keep in phrases of computing time and capacity. There are tactics to carry out switch analyzing: via feature extraction and fine-tuning. Feature extraction is composed in maintaining the weights of a preinformed version intact, and using the embedding it produces to educate a modern classifier at the cause dataset. Fine-tuning is composed with in the usage of the weights of a preinformed version to initialize the version after which education all or a part of those weights at the cause dataset. Choosing one approach or the opportunity is primarily based upon the proximity among each of the supply and cause datasets (in case they are very close, feature extraction can be sufficient), however, on the scale of the cause dataset. Training a big quantity of layers with a small dataset can also furthermore boom the danger of over becoming. Training from scratch is at the same time as the community weights aren't inherited from a preceding version, however, are as a substitute randomly initialized. It calls for a bigger education set, and the over becoming danger is better for the reason that community has no revel in preceding education periods and so needs to depend upon the input data to outline all its weights. However, this technique permits us to outline a problem-particular community form that may enhance the performance. These problem-particular architectures may be developed, as an example, to address more than three caseation channels, multiscale dimensions, or to combine multiple fashions informed differently (with diverse hyperparameters or datasets).

13.6.3   CNN performance

A characteristic fusion convolutional neural community (CNN) version may be used to locate pneumothorax from chest X-ray photos. In this version, the preprocessed image samples are stronger via means of strategies. Using CNN and regions with CNN features (R-CNN), the convolutional neural community (CNN) has delivered approximately a step forward in sample reputation of photos which includes scientific photos. In ordinary CAD algorithms, designing an image-function extractor is important. However, this mission is hard. On the other hand, a CAD set of guidelines through the manner of use of CNN does not usually require the image-function extractor. In this version, an image-based CADx can be advanced for differential diagnosis of lung abnormalities inclusive of lung nodules and diffuse lung ailments through the way of the use of CNN. CNN shows immoderate general overall performance for a class of natural photos. Therefore, many researchers have studied about differential diagnosis of lung abnormalities including lung nodules and diffuse lung ailments; on the other hand, a manner of R-CNN became proposed for the detection of devices including persons and animals in natural photos. Therefore, an image-based Computer assisted data entry (CADe) additionally may be used for the detection of lung abnormalities including lung nodules and diffuse lung ailments through the way of the use of R-CNN.

13.6.3.1   Interstitial lung disease detection

The usage of CNN in a large variety of lung texture styles of sickness may be discovered in CT experiment photos. These snapshots are the intermix of several patterns, and for that reason, it becomes very tough for radiologists to differentiate them and diagnose the illness. One manner of fixing this hassle is the discovery of CNN. CNN is usually used for sample magnificence and photo popularity systems. They have completed an entire lot tons much fewer mistakes in the database, and photo magnificence using CNN became exceedingly fast. Interstitial lung infection is a time period that incorporates wonderful forms of lung infection. Insterstitial lung illnesses (ILDs) have an effect on the insterstitial, that is, the part of the lung's anatomic form. Lung tissue characterization is the critical element of a CAD device for the detection of ILDs. Thus, using CNN, interstitial lung infection detection offers the correct results. This version includes CNN having seven layers with a local binary sample as a function extractor. The execution of sophistication exhibited the capability of CNNs in studying lung patterns. In our corpus, 15 research studies (79%) used switch studying and 7 research studies (37%) informed a version from scratch. Choosing a schooling technique is primarily based upon technical (quantity of photos, computing capacity) and thematic (availability of the proper form or of preinformed weights properly best with the records used) troubles in comparison with three schooling techniques on six CNN architectures (AlexNet, DenseNet-169, Inception v3, ResNet-34, SqueezeNet-1.1, and VGG13). They used the Plant Village dataset augmented with the elegant facts. Two techniques used switch studying: function extraction and whole fine-tuning. In one of the three techniques, the community came to be informed from scratch. The accuracies were obtained at the validation set and the schooling time. For the six architectures, fine-tuning gave very brilliant precision (from 99.2% for SqueezeNet to 99.5% for VGG13). The instances required for fine-tuning and for schooling from scratch are close (from 1.05 to 5, 64 h for fine-tuning and from 1.05 to 5, 91 h on the equal time as informed from scratch). The function extraction technique had the bottom schooling instances (from 0.85 to 3, 63 h). Overall, from scratch and switch-studying should recognize and must not be visible as without a doubt together for the fantastic techniques.

Gao *et al.*'s artwork assign a single ILD class label without delay upon whole axial CT test photographs but without preprocessing the reap ROIs. While reading the lung ailments photo database, with segmentation masks, a variety of CT test photographs are located with or more illness labels. The efficiency of deep gaining knowledge is a subfield of device gaining knowledge regarding algorithms stimulated via means of the feature and shape of the brain. Recent traits in device gaining knowledge, in particular, aid the identity, quantification, and category of styles in scientific photos. These traits had been made feasible because of the capacity of deep gaining knowledge of two discovered capabilities simply from data, as opposed to hand-designed capabilities primarily based on domain-precise knowledge. Deep-gaining knowledge is turning speedily into country of the art, mainly to step forward overall performance in several scientific applications. Consequently, those improvements help clinicians in detecting and classifying positive scientific situations efficiently. Deep neural community fashions have conventionally been designed, and experiments had been finished upon them by means of human specialists in a persevering manner with the trial-and-mistakes technique. This system needs giant time, know-how, and resources. To triumph over this problem, a unique, however, easy version is brought to routinely carry out the most advantageous category responsibilities with a deep neural community structure. The neural community structure turned into especially designed for pneumonia image category responsibilities. This approach is primarily based on the convolutional neural community set of rules, using a hard and fast set of neurons to convolve on a given image and extract applicable capabilities from them. Demonstration of the efficacy of the proposed approach with the minimization of the computational fee as the focal point becomes done compared with the exiting modern lung illness class networks. Lung infection detection is commonly offered by classifying an image graph into healthy lungs or infection-inflamed lungs. The lung infection classifier, every now and then known as a version, is acquired through training. Training is the tool wherein a neural community learns to apprehend a category of photos. Using deep getting to know, it is miles feasible to train a version that can classify photos into their respective beauty labels. Therefore, to use deep getting to know for lengthy infection detection, Step 1 is to collect photos of lungs with the infection to be classified. The second step is to train the neural community till it can recognize the illnesses. The very last step is to classify new photos. Here, new images are unseen through the way of the version earlier than the established in the version, and the version predicts the beauty of these photos.

However, the process of deep learning applied to spot respiratory organ diseases from medical images is described. There are three main steps: (1) image preprocessing, (2) coaching, and (3) classification.

13.6.3.2   Image preprocessing

Image processing is a technique to carry out a few operations on an image, with a purpose to get an additional image or to extract a few beneficial facts from it. It is a form of sign processing wherein input is an image and output can be an image or characteristics/competencies related to that image. Nowadays, photo processing is among unexpectedly growing technologies. Image processing essentially consists of the subsequent three steps:

1.   importing the dataset image through image acquisition tools
2.   analyzing and manipulating the dataset image
3.   output wherein end result may be altered image or record, this is primarily based on image analysis

13.6.3.3   Training

Deep mastering neural community fashions discover ways to map inputs to outputs given an education dataset of examples. The education procedure entails locating a fixed weight within the community that proves to be appropriate, or appropriate enough, at fixing the unique problem. Training is the procedure wherein a neural community learns to understand a category of images. We need to teach the neural community till it may understand the diseases. This is the vital section of the machine as this section makes a decision on the accuracy and overall performance of the machine.

13.6.3.4   Classification

The very last section is the type of the images. In our machine, the type is of the underneath types, such as (1) healthy, (2) pneumonia, (3) tuberculosis, and (4) Covid-19. While importing the image, our skilled version classifies the image into someone of the above diseases. This approach has the subsequent advantages:

1.   use higher and optimized facts of scans to supply an awful higher consequences
2.   increase overall performance of utility computation usage
3.   hyper rapid consequences without taking an awful computation from locale
4.   accurate consequences
5.   clear generalized record in my view dispatched to user

13.6.4   Convolutional neutral networks with AI

CNN can be a subfield of synthetic intelligence (AI). In deep learning, a CNN or ConvNet is a category of deep neural networks, administrated to studying visual imagery. They are also referred to as SIANN, due to their shared-weights shape and translation changelessness characteristics. There are several programs in image and video recognition, recommender systems, image classification, clinical image analysis, seasoned language processing, and financial time series. CNNs are regularized variations of multilayer perceptron. Multilayer perceptions commonly counsel fully connected networks, that is, each somatic cell in a single layer is hooked up to all or any neurons within the next layer. The "absolute connectedness" of these networks makes them in danger of over changing into records. Typical strategies of regularization encompass some form of significance dimension of weights to the loss function. CNNs take further ordinary unprecedented a rare methodology toward regularization. They take gain of the hierarchical sample in records and collect more difficult designs with the usage of smaller and fewer complicated styles. Therefore, on the scale of connectedness and complexity, CNNs are at the decrease extreme (Figure 13.3). Convolutional networks are aroused with the aid of exploitation organic procedures, in this the property sample among neurons resembles the leader of the animal visible cortex. Individual animal tissue neurons reply to stimuli handiest in a very restricted space of the field of regard known as the receptive field. The receptive fields of assorted neurons partially overlap such that they cowl the entire visual view.

13.6.5   CNN layers

The CNN layer consists of a 32×32×3 image with a 5×5×3 filter and an activation map that is used to slide over all the spatial locations.

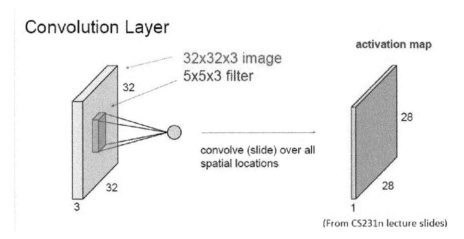

Figure 13.3   The CNN layers with the activation map

13.6.6   CNN image classifier

The classification of rubbish into recyclable and nonrecyclable is carried out by the use of the CNN classifier. This classifier makes use of the CNN set of rules for less complicated identity and separation of rubbish from the organization and for less complicated separation into respective sections. The dataset is the collection of daily-existence wastages like plastic, metal, meals gadgets, etc. Around 450–500 pattern pictures are feed into the dataset for higher capability of set of rules. Each pattern is zoomed, differed in width and height, mild stage over the object, and a few greater versions in order that the processing of photo may be made with proper stage of accuracy.

The convolutional layer works in the following manner – the layer gets a few input volume, in this example a photo for you to have a particular height, width, and intensity. There are filters gift which might be essentially matrices which might be initialized with random numbers at first. The filters are small spatially, however, have intensity identical as channels of the input photo. For RGB, the filters could have intensity 3; for grayscale, the tilters could have intensity 1; and so on. The filter is convolved over input volume. It slides spatially through the photo and computes dot product for the duration of the photo. The filters come to be generating activation maps for the input photo.

13.6.6.1   Classification

The set of rules works in a two-segment cycle, the ahead by skip and returned propagation. During the ahead by skip, the photo is handed to each of the above layer, and the output is calculated. The anticipated output is in comparison with the real output, and the mistake is calculated. After the mistake is calculated, the set of rules then adjusts the weights, that is, the spatial values of each of the filters and the biases as much as the primary enter layer. This adjustment of the weights or the spatial values of the filters is the returned propagation segment. This returned propagation segment is used at the side of optimization strategies together with gradient descent to decrease the mistake as a great deal as possible.

13.6.6.1.1   CNN-based finger-vein extraction

Existing methodologies separate vein patterns by expecting that they create disseminations, for example, valleys and line portions. In this segment, a CNN is straightforwardly prepared to demonstrate the dissemination of vein pixels with practically no quality dispersion suspicion. To begin with, we name every pixel of a preparation image as one or the other vein or foundation in view of the joined result of a few standard check frameworks. For each labeled pixel, a window focused on it is contributed to CNN for preparing. Assuming that a window stretches out external to the image limit, the missing pixels are incorporated by reflecting. The result of the last CNN layer is deciphered as the probability of the fix place pixel to have a place with a vein pattern. Applying CNN to every one of the pixels thusly, the vein patterns are separated in view of a probability edge. The subsequent binarized images are thus utilized for finger vein check.

Microscopy is a key innovation driving biological disclosure. These days, microscopy-based logical discoveries should be validated by quantitative image analysis

ML is a computational approach to distinguishing patterns in a provided dataset to make inductions in another, comparable dataset. A traditional textbook model is the machine recognition of handwriting-like postal addresses on envelopes. Lately, conventional article recognition has made colossal advances and is presently moving toward human precision. Customarily, visual perception by specialists has been directed to analyze plant illnesses. Nonetheless, there is a risk for blunder because of abstract insight. In this unique circumstance, different spectroscopic and imaging strategies have been read up for identifying plant infections. In any case, they require exact instrument and bulky sensors which lead to significant expense and low effectiveness. All things considered, by and large, customary ML approaches, for example, SVM and K-means clustering have complex image preprocessing and highlight extraction steps, which lessen the efficiency of illness determination.

13.7   Deep learning for lung disease detection

Lung disease detection generally entails categorizing an image as healthy or disease-infected. Training is used to create the lung disease classifier, also known as a model. The process by which a neural network learns to recognize a class of images is known as training. Deep learning can be used to train a model that can classify images based on their class labels. As a result, the first step in using deep learning for lung disease detection is to collect images of lungs with the disease to be classified. The neural network will then be trained until it can recognize the 14 diseases. The last step is to categorize new images.

In this case, the model is shown in new images that it has never seen before, and it predicts the class of those images.

The method for using deep learning to identify lung diseases from medical images is described. There are three major steps:

1. preprocessing of images
2. education
3. categorization

13.7.1   Preprocessing of images

Image processing is a method of performing operations on an image in order to improve it or extract useful information from it. It is a type of signal processing in which the input is an image, and the output can be an image or image characteristics/features. Image processing is one of today's fastest growing technologies.

In our proposed system, scanned lung X-ray images are preprocessed, and the output is disease prediction. This is accomplished by analyzing the characteristics of the image that we upload.

The three basic steps in image processing are as follows:

- importing the dataset image using image acquisition software
- analyzing and manipulating the dataset image
- output, which can be an altered image or a report based on image analysis

13.7.2 Training

Given a training dataset of examples, deep learning neural network models learn to map inputs to outputs. The training process entails locating a set of weights in the network that is good, or good enough, at solving the specific problem.

Training data for ML is an important input to algorithms that comprehend and memorize information from such data for future prediction. However, various aspects emerge during the ML development process, without which various critical tasks cannot be completed. Training data is the foundation of any AI or ML project; without it, it is impossible to train a machine that learns from humans and predicts for humans.

The process by which a neural network learns to recognize a class of images is known as training. We must train the neural network until it can recognize diseases. This is the most important phase of the system because it determines the system's accuracy and performance.

13.7.3 Classification

Image classification entails extracting features from an image in order to identify patterns in a dataset. Using an Artificial neural network (ANN) for image classification would be extremely computationally expensive due to the extremely large trainable parameters.

The images are classified in the final stage. The classification in our system is of the following types.

1. Normal
2. Pneumonia (19th)
3. Tuberculosis
4. Covid-19

While uploading the image, our trained model classifies it as one of the diseases listed above. We use better and optimized scan data in the proposed system to produce much better and optimized results. Our system improves application performance when it comes to computation usage.

It generates hyperfast results without requiring much computation from local, which saves lives at an earlier stage, and it generates accurate results. The results produced are highly accurate.

13.8   Conclusion

Comparison with alternative approaches in image category, CNNs trounce standard image process ways in varied applications. This well-liked fashion is likewise discovered within the machine-driven identity of crop illnesses. A number of the chosen analysis as compared with the performance received with CNNs to it is of various strategies. Altogether of these research studies, the CNN outcomes are more than the others. The fine outcomes received for a CNN and for a chance technique in research that created a comparison.

The distinction of accuracy ranged from 3% to 28.89% using feature fusion CNN. With the boom of lung illnesses in patients, routinely detecting illnesses and acquiring correct prognosis through the X-ray scientific photos turn out to be the brand new studies recognition within the discipline of PC technological know-how and synthetic intelligence to shop the sizable price of guide labeling and classifying. However, the high satisfaction of not unusual place radiograph is't pleased for the maximum responsibilities, and conventional strategies are poor to cope with the large photos.

References

[1]   Kumar S., Ranjan P., Ramaswami R., Tripathy M.R. 'EMEEDP: enhanced multi-hop energy efficient distributed protocol for heterogeneous wireless sensor network'. *Proceedings of the 5th International Conference on Communication Systems and Network Technologies, CSNT 2015*; Gwalior, India, IEEE, 2015. pp. 194–200.

[2]   Kumar S., Ranjan P., Ramaswami R. 'Energy optimization in distributed localized wireless sensor networks'. *Proceedings of the International Conference on Issues and Challenges Intelligent Computing Technique (ICICT)*; Ghaziabad, India, IEEE, 2014.

[3]   Chauhan R., Kumar S. 'Packet loss prediction using artificial intelligence unified with big data analytics, internet of things and cloud computing technologies'. *5th International Conference on Information Systems and Computer Networks (ISCON)*; Mathura, India, IEEE, 2021. pp. 1–6.

[4]   Sudhakaran S., Kumar S., Ranjan P., Tripathy M.R. 'Blockchain-based transparent and secure decentralized algorithm'. *International Conference on Intelligent Computing and Smart Communication 2019. Algorithms for Intelligent Systems*; Singapore: Springer; 2020.

[5]   Kumar S., Trivedi M.C., Ranjan P., Punhani A. *Evolution of Software-Defined Networking Foundations for IoT and 5G Mobile Networks*. Hershey, PA: IGI Publisher; 2020. p. 350.

[6]   Kumar S., Ranjan P., Radhakrishnan R., Tripathy M.R. 'Energy efficient multichannel MAC protocol for high traffic applications in heterogeneous wireless sensor networks'. *Recent Advances in Electrical & Electronic Engineering*. 2017, vol. 10(3), pp. 223–32.

[7]   Kumar S., Ranjan P., Ramaswami R., Tripathy M.R. 'Resource efficient clustering and next hop knowledge based routing in multiple heterogeneous wireless sensor networks'. *International Journal of Grid and High Performance Computing*. 2017, vol. 9(2), pp. 1–20.

[8]   Kumar V., Arablouei R., Cengiz K., Vimal S., Suresh A. 'Energy efficient resource migration based load balance mechanism for high traffic applications IoT'. *Wireless Personal Communications*. 2022, vol. 10(3), pp. 1623–44.

[9]   Kumar S., Cengiz K., Trivedi C.M., *et al.* 'DEMO enterprise ontology with a stochastic approach based on partially observable Markov model for data aggregation and communication in intelligent sensor networks'. *Wireless Personal Communication*. 2022.

[10] Punhani A., Faujdar N., Kumar S. 'Design and evaluation of cubic torus Network-on-Chip architecture'. *International Journal of Innovative Technology and Exploring Engineering (IJITEE)*. 2019, vol. 8(6).

[11] Dubey G., Kumar S., Kumar S., Navaney P. 'Extended opinion lexicon and ML-based Sentiment analysis of tweets: a novel approach towards accurate classifier'. *International Journal of Computational Vision and Robotics*. 2020, vol. 10(6), pp. 505–21.

[12] Singh P., Bansal A., Kamal A.E., Kumar S. 'Road surface quality monitoring using machine learning algorithm' in Reddy A.N.R., Marla D., Favorskaya M.N., Satapathy S.C. (eds.). *Intelligent Manufacturing and Energy Sustainability. Smart Innovation, Systems and Technologies*. 265. Singapore: Springer; 2022.

[13] Kumar S., Ranjan P., Radhakrishnan R., Tripathy M.R. 'Energy aware distributed protocol for heterogeneous wireless sensor network'. *International Journal of Control and Automation*. 2015, vol. 8(10), pp. 421–30.

[14] Kumar S., Ranjan P., Ramaswami R., Tripathy M.R. 'A utility maximization approach to MAC layer channel access and forwarding'. *Progress in Electromagnetics Research Symposium, Publisher: The Electromagnetics Academy*; 2015. pp. 2363–67.

[15] Kumar S., Ranjan P., Ramaswami R., Tripathy M.R. 'An NS3 implementation of physical layer based on 802.11 for utility maximization of WSN'. *Proceedings of the International Conference on Computational Intelligence and Communication Networks, CICN 2015*; Jabalpur, India, IEEE, 2016. pp. 79–84.

[16] Sharma A., Awasthi Y., Kumar S. 'The role of blockchain, AI and iot for smart road traffic management system'. *Proceedings of the IEEE India Council International Subsections Conference, INDISCON 2020*; Visakhapatnam, India, IEEE, 2020. pp. 289–96.

[17] Singh P., Bansal A., Kumar S. 'Performance analysis of various information platforms for recognizing the quality of indian roads'. *Proceedings of the Confluence 2020 – 10th International Conference on Cloud Computing, Data Science and Engineering*; Noida, India, IEEE, 2020. pp. 63–76.

[18] Kumar S., Ranjan P., Singh P., Tripathy M.R. 'Design and implementation of fault tolerance technique for internet of things (iot)'. *Proceedings of the 12th*

International Conference on Computational Intelligence and Communication Networks, CICN 2020; Bhimtal, India, IEEE, 2020. pp. 154–59.

[19] Reghu S., Kumar S. 'Development of robust infrastructure in networking to survive a disaster'. *4th International Conference on Information Systems and Computer Networks, ISCON 2019*; Mathura, India, IEEE, 2019. pp. 250–55.

Chapter 14

IoT-based architecture for smart health-care systems

S P Rajamohana[1], Zbigniew M Wawrzyniak[2], T A Deva Priyan[3], V Rajeevan[3], N Vaibhav Ram[3], J Vinith[3], J Keerthanaa[3], and Priyanka Raj[3]

Internet of Things (IoT) provides a pathway for connecting physical entities with digital entities using devices and communication technologies. The rapid growth of IoT in recent days has made a significant influence in many fields. Healthcare is one of those fields which will be hugely benefited by IoT. IoT can resolve many challenges faced by patients and doctors in healthcare. Smart health-care applications allow the doctor to monitor the patient's health state without human intervention. Sensors collect and send the data from the patient. Recorded data are stored in a database that enables medical experts to analyze those data. Any abnormal change in the status of the patient can be notified to the doctor. This chapter aims to study different research works made on IoT-based health-care systems that are implemented using basic development boards. Various hardware parameters of health-care systems and sensors used for those parameters are explored. A basic Arduino-based health-care application is proposed using sensors and global system for mobile communication (GSM) module.

14.1   Introduction

In recent years, population growth has caused many problems in the health sector [1]. On average, around 523 million people suffered through a heart attack in a year. Doctors cannot provide treatment for them. People who have heart attack has an average age of greater than 50 years [2]. So, constant monitoring is required for these kinds of diseases. A smart health-care application helps in this scenario. The elder people who cannot travel often can be benefited through this application. It

[1]Department of Computer Science & Engineering, Pondicherry University, Coimbatore, India
[2]Faculty of Electronics and Information Technology, Warsaw University of Technology, Warsaw, Poland
[3]Department of Information Technology, PSG College of Technology, Coimbatore, India

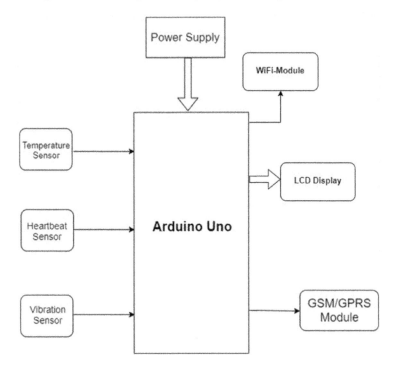

Figure 14.1   Block diagram of the proposed system

is also helpful for those children and babies whose both parents have to work [3]. One of the main advantages of this smart health-care application is that it will be more helpful for those diseases that take more time to cure and that do not have a cure [4].

IoT provides a huge benefit in the health sector. It is used to track and monitor the patients closely from a remote location. Sensors such as heartbeat sensors, pressure sensors, and temperature and humidity sensors are used to record values from the patients. These values are processed for further analysis to produce better results. The results that were produced are helpful for further treatment and are stored in a secured manner [5]. The whole process of storing the values from the sensor can be done without human intervention.

The connection between wired and intelligent physical devices creates the major part of the IoT. These devices are capable of performing many functions such as storing information, collecting information, and also for its processing. These instruments have further usages such as communication between applications and the sensors, Internet connectivity, and so on. This smart care health application provides better accuracy and results than the traditional methods as there are no human interventions here. It is also proved to be economically better than traditional patient monitoring [6].

Traditional health-care monitoring requires more human intervention. Humans make mistakes, and the cost of the traditional method is high. The manpower involved here is also high.

IoT is used here to address these issues. As the application is automated and works without any human intervention, the chances of mistakes during this process are very less. The cost of this IoT-based patient monitoring is also very less because of no manpower and the analysis can be done from a remote area [7]. The most important advantage of IoT is that it will be more helpful in emergency conditions. The analyzed data will be useful to predict those emergency conditions well before the seriousness. Thus, smart health-care applications will be able to reduce the seriousness of those conditions [8]. The Figure 14.1 represents the block diagram of the proposed system.

14.2 Literature survey

S.No.	Author and publication year	Proposed framework or prototype description	Used hardware components	Used software components	Communication module	Limitations
1.	Uday Kumar *et al.* (2020) [8]	This paperwork proposes a smart healthcare patient data and security system to monitor patient health-care data like temperature and blood pressure. The patient data are uploaded to the Cloud server.	✓ Arduino ✓ Blood pressure sensor ✓ DS18B20 Temperature sensor	✓ Arduino IDE ✓ Embedded C language ✓ Thingspeak Server	✓ GSM/GPRS module	Data stored in radio frequency identification (RFID) tags are not secure. Strong encryption strategies should be used to secure data in the cloud servers.
2.	Vajubunissa Begum *et al.* (2020) [2]	This paper aims at helping cardiac patients by continuously collecting and monitoring the health status of the former using sensors. This framework also provides an ECG graph of the patient's heart rate.	✓ Arduino UNO ✓ Temperature sensor (LM 35) ✓ Humidity sensor (DHT 11) ✓ ECG sensor (AD8232) ✓ Heart rate monitor sensor (MAX 30105) ✓ Body position sensor (ADXL 335) ✓ Raspberry Pi	✓ Arduino IDE ✓ Embedded C language ✓ Python language	✓ Wi-Fi module ✓ Bluetooth module	The data collected from this sensor are not secured. The cost of this system setup is high.
3.	Milon Islam *et al.* (2020) [9]	This paperwork is about a smart health-care application using five sensors. Error percentage in these five sensors is also analyzed in this application.	✓ ESP 32 (node MCU) module ✓ Heartbeat sensor ✓ Body temperature sensor (LM35) ✓ Room temperature sensor (DHT11) ✓ CO Sensor (MQ 9) ✓ CO2 Sensor (MQ 135)	✓ Thingspeak Server ✓ Arduino IDE	✓ Wi-Fi module	This system is bulkier, so it is not flexible to work with.
4.	Dahlia Sam *et al.* (2020) [3]	This article proposes a working IoT-based architecture that is capable of monitoring the health of any patient by using sensors and microcontrollers during the pandemic situation. So, by reducing the unnecessary expenses for doctor and hospital visits.	✓ Microcontroller (ATMega328P) ✓ Arduino UNO ✓ Temperature sensor (LM35) ✓ Blood pressure sensor	✓ Arduino IDE ✓ Cloud database	✓ GSM module	The limitation in this system is the need for excess wires for connection between the devices.

S.No.	Author and publication year	Proposed framework or prototype description	Used hardware components	Used software components	Communication module	Limitations
5.	Seena Naik *et al.* (2019) [10]	This journal paper gives the implementation of Raspberry Pi and IoT in the health system. The various sensors gather the body health parameters information for the diagnosis by connecting with Raspberry Pi, which is associated with the cloud and displayed on the LCD.	✓ECG sensor ✓Raspberry Pi ✓Respiration sensor ✓Acceleration sensor ✓Temperature sensor ✓Blood pressure sensor ✓Heartbeat sensor	✓Cloud database ✓Raspbian OS	✓GSM module	There are no limitations mentioned in this paper.
6.	Suneeta S. Raykar *et al.* [2019] [11]	The proposed framework in this paper is ALERT (android-based health enabled remote terminal). The system is built using node MCU with various sensors for monitoring the oxygen level, heart-pumping rate, body temperature levels.	✓Node MCU ✓Max30105 oxygen saturation sensor ✓ECG sensor AD-8232 ✓Max30102 pulse rate body temperature sensor	✓ThingSpeak Cloud ✓Arduino IDE	✓API developed using MIT App inventor	The developed framework allows the medical experts to examine and provide advice to one patient at a time. This limitation has to be changed to multi-user accessibility.
7.	PandiaRajan Jeyaraj *et al.* (2019) [12]	The proposed IoT health-care system is combined with some deep learning algorithms and sensor networks. The model collects the data from the patients with the help of sensors and stores them in a cloud server. Further, the data are analyzed and visualized using the DCNN algorithm that was developed for learning and using WEKA analysis is done.	✓EEG sensor ✓ECG sensor Temperature sensor ✓Pulse rate sensor ✓NI-myRIO processor	✓Cloud for data storage ✓WEKA	–	The proposed model classifies or states the patient Figure 14.1 as more generically like abnormal, normal, and subnormal rather than providing some medical assistance. Even though the proposed system provides reliable and high accuracy health status prediction, it does not provide any portal for the user (patient) and medical expert and communication platform.
8.	Subasish Mohapatra *et al.* (2019) [6]	This paperwork proposes a health-care system using Arduino, collects the data from various sensors, and stores the data into the cloud database using a Wi-Fi module.	✓Arduino ✓Heartbeat sensor ✓DS18B20 Temperature sensor ✓ESP8288 (Wi-Fi module)	✓Cloud Server ✓Embedded C language ✓Arduino IDE	✓Wi-Fi module	There are no limitations mentioned in this paper.
9.	Abhishek Kumar *et al.* (2018) [7]	This paperwork presents a health-care monitoring system to monitor temperature and heartbeat using sensors. This system also has a web camera on the patient's side.	✓Raspberry Pi ✓DS18B20 Temperature sensor ✓Heartbeat sensor ✓Analog-to-digital converter (MCP3008) ✓Web camera	✓Thingspeak server ✓Raspbian OS ✓HTML ✓Blynk	✓Wi-Fi module	This system is not scalable to add more sensors, and it also has many wired connections that make the system less flexible.
10.	Shubham Banka *et al.* (2018) [13]	This paperwork is about a smart health-care system using Raspberry Pi. This system collects various details from the sensor and is capable of intimating these details to the patient's family and doctor.	✓Raspberry Pi ✓Temperature sensor (LM35) ✓Heartbeat sensor ✓Vibration sensor ✓BP sensor	✓Raspbian OS	✓Wi-Fi module ✓GSM module	There are no limitations mentioned in this paper.

S.No.	Author and publication year	Proposed framework or prototype description	Used hardware components	Used software components	Communication module	Limitations
11.	C. Senthamilarasi, *et al.* (2018) [14]	This journal presents a real-time patient monitoring system interconnected with IoT to evaluate the performance and practicability of the systems. This procedure helps to monitor the patient's healthcare continuously based on some parameters. This method will be supported by Arduino UNO with a cloud database.	✓ Arduino UNO ✓ ECG sensor ✓ Temperature sensor ✓ Heartbeat sensor	✓ Cloud Server ✓ Arduino IDE ✓ Embedded C language	✓ Wi-Fi module	There are no limitations mentioned in this paper.
12.	Swaleha Shaikh *et al.* (2017) [15]	This paperwork proposes a smart health-care monitoring system using Raspberry Pi and a cloud database to effectively monitor the patients.	✓ Raspberry Pi ✓ LM35 (temp sensor) ✓ Heart rate sensor ✓ Blood pressure sensor ✓ Accelerometer	✓ Cloud Server ✓ Raspbian OS	✓ Wi-Fi module	Security concerns over the patient's sensitive data.
13.	Tarannum Khan *et al.* (2017) [16]	This paperwork presents a patient monitoring application using Arduino UNO. The stored data are also presented through the android application.	✓ Arduino UNO ✓ Temperature sensor ✓ Heartbeat sensor ✓ SD card	✓ Arduino IDE ✓ Embedded C Language ✓ Blynk Application	✓ Wi-Fi module	The data that are uploaded on the cloud is insecure.
14.	Shreyaasha Chaudhury *et al.* (2017) [5]	This paperwork presents a health-care application that monitors health parameters through sensors. An audio signaling device and message service are attached to the system to indicate emergencies.	✓ Arduino UNO ✓ Temperature sensor (LM35) ✓ ECG sensor ✓ Heart rate monitor sensor	✓ Arduino IDE ✓ Embedded C language ✓ HTML	✓ Wi-Fi module ✓ GSM module	The data stored in the cloud are insecure, and the cost of this system is also high.
15.	Niharika Kumar (2017) [17]	This paper proposes a smart frame for a healthcare system that uses architecture protocols of the 6LoWPAN protocol and IEEE 11073, which is associated with cloud networks.	✓ Arduino UNO ✓ Gyroscope ✓ ECG sensor ✓ Temperature sensor ✓ Heart rate sensor	✓ Arduino IDE ✓ Embedded C Language ✓ HTML	✓ Wi-Fi module	The cost of this proposed system is high.
16.	Fatima Alshehri *et al.* [2020] [18]	This paper provides a detailed survey about smart healthcare. This paper includes various methods for smart healthcare like the IoT, Internet of medical things, and artificial intelligence.	–	–	–	–
17.	Yasmeen Shaikh *et al.* (2018) [19]	This paperwork proposes several methods for providing health-care solutions using IoT. The major methods discussed in this paper are RFID and named data networking.	–	–	–	–
18.	Wei Li *et al.* (2020) [20]	This paper is about a survey that explores the different possibilities of implementing smart healthcare using machine-learning and big data analysis.	–	–	–	–
19.	Ramakrishna Hegde *et al.* (2021) [21]	The proposed system is to monitor the daily health-related activities of a patient and report to the doctors through the internet with a different approach.	–	–	–	–

S.No.	Author and publication year	Proposed framework or prototype description	Used hardware components	Used software components	Communication module	Limitations
20.	Hongxu Zhu *et al.* (2019) [22]	This paper framework is about the various phases in healthcare with IoT along with the management of patient health data and having an oriented management system.	–	–	–	–
21	Durga Amarnath M. Budida *et al.* (2017) [23]	This paperwork proposes an end to end well-organized health application. The proposed framework uses ATMEL microcontroller as the main processor. It uses HTML for organizing the web pages and uses SQL for storing the data.	✓ Microcontroller ATMEL 89s52 ✓ Temperature sensor ✓ Pulse rate sensor ✓ RS-232 ✓ Analog-to-digital converter ✓ Voltage regulator IC-7805	✓ SQL ✓ HTML	✓ Wi-Fi module	The proposed system is outdated and requires regular maintenance.
22	Kavita Jaiswal *et al.* (2017) [24]	This paper is about a health-care monitoring system which uses Raspberry Pi as a main microcontroller. It uses a Docker container and a DBMS to manage the data created.	✓ Raspberry Pi ✓ Temperature sensor ✓ ECG ✓ Blood ✓ Pressure sensor	✓ SQL ✓ Docker	✓ Wi-Fi module	The proposed system is costly since it has a server that has a docker container and a database.
23	Gowrishankar, S. M.Y. Prachita *et al.* (2017) [25]	This paper uses sensors to collect the state of the heart and body temperature with different test cases and provides an alert message using an LCD monitor.	✓ Pulse sensor ✓ LM 35 ✓ Temperature sensor ✓ Arduino UNO	✓ ESP8266 module	✓ Wi-Fi	Data transfer between devices must be fast enough with minimized delay response, sensor module should extract accurate readings, and two different sensors must be used and should be under little control of microcontroller to be accurate in output.
24	Mayur, Suraj, Shubham, Nikhil *et al.* (2016) [26]	The paper proposes a portable ECG monitor where the heart rate will be collected and sent to an android phone. The Android phone is using a detection algorithms to find out the abnormality.	✓ ECG monitor, Android phone	✓ NA	✓ Mobile data/Wi-Fi module	Wi-Fi module is used to transfer and monitor data, so connectivity must be constant and very fast enough to avoid delay. Sensor module should extract accurate readings. Data are stored in the server.
25	Manisha, Mamidi (2016) [27]	This paper proposes a method to record the patient's heart and pulse rate which is further analyzed using big data analytics.	✓ MI Band 2, android phone, big data analytics	✓ NA	✓ Mobile data/Wi-Fi module	The response time is limited, when the micro-controller transmits the information the encoder must respond immediately and it needs precise decoding.

The detailed literature survey analysis is given in Table 14.1.

14.3 Related works

Uday Kumar *et al.* [8] proposed Arduino-based patient monitoring system that stores patient details such as blood pressure and temperature. The author implemented this system by using a temperature sensor to monitor temperature and a blood pressure sensor to monitor blood pressure. Patient data that are collected through sensors are stored in radio frequency identification (RFID) tags and are also uploaded in the cloud. The stored data will be useful to doctors to analyze patients' conditions. This system has GSM/General Packet Radio Service (GPRS) module to alert emergencies to the patient's side by short message services (SMS).

Vajubunnisa Begum *et al.* [2] proposed a health-care monitoring system specially designed for cardiac patients using Raspberry Pi. The data are collected through the sensors such as temperature sensors, heartbeat sensors, ECG sensors, and body position sensors. Wi-Fi module is used for sending the collected data from sensors to the cloud. The data are also transferred to the doctor's side using the Bluetooth module. Serial plotter software is used to plot the stored data collected from the ECG sensor. The analyzed result from the sensor is displayed on the LCD.

Milon Islam *et al.* [9] proposed IoT-based health-care application using Node MCU (which is also known as ESP 32). Five sensors collected patient's data and there are a heartbeat sensor to monitor heartbeat, a room-temperature sensor to monitor room temperature, a body temperature sensor to monitor temperature, an MQ9 sensor to monitor CO gas, and an MQ135 sensor to monitor CO_2 gas.

Dahlia Sam *et al.* [3] proposed an Arduino-based model patient monitoring system to monitor the patient's situation. Patient monitoring is done using a temperature sensor for monitoring body temperature and an optical sensor that measures heartbeat in pulsates. These sensors send the digital signals to the Arduino UNO, and sensor data through a Wi-Fi module and can be accessed through the cloud by doctors and also relatives.

Seena Naik *et al.* [10] have proposed a framework by implementing a working model that monitors and checks a patient's health condition even from a distance in a cheap way using an ECG sensor, temperature sensor, and heartbeat sensor conditioned by Raspberry Pi. All the digital signals will be transmitted to the Raspberry Pi and stored in a database accessed by the cloud. The details will be sent to the health specialist via the Wi-Fi module.

Suneeta S. Raykar *et al.* [11] have proposed a duplex communication system that provides a gateway to monitor various health parameters. The data will be recorded using a sensor and sent to the ThingSpeak cloud. The medical experts will use the data to make decisions on the patient's health. They can also give medical recommendations based on that data. The recommendations that are given by the medical experts can be seen by the patient through an android application that is developed using MIT App inventor. It also suggests future modifications that can be made for the proposed framework.

PandiaRajan Jeyaraj *et al.* [12] have proposed a patient monitoring system along with a deep learning algorithm for making an accurate prediction based on the patient collected data. The system collects various data such as EEG, ECG, body temperature, and vital signs. The data are connected using an intelligent sensor network, and then the data are stored using central cloud storage with the help of the myRIO processor along with a Wi-Fi module. The data from the cloud are taken, classified using WEKA, and analyzed using a Deep Convolutional Neural Network (DCNN) learning algorithm. The model provides results with 97.2% prediction accuracy.

Swaleha Shaikh *et al.* [6] proposed an application that observes the patient's health conditions with Raspberry Pi at its heart. This framework presents a system in which the data are collected using embedded sensors that are wearable, and the health status of the patient is monitored concerning some parameters dynamically. The collected data are then transmitted to the Raspberry Pi, which will process and analyze the data. These data that have been analyzed by the processor are stored in the cloud. The stored results are then used by the doctors when the details of the patient are needed.

Abhishek Kumar *et al.* [7] proposed a smart health-care application using Raspberry Pi. Raspberry Pi is connected with a temperature sensor to monitor temperature and heartbeat sensors to monitor the heartbeat. The input from the sensor is processed in Raspberry Pi and displayed on LCD. The data are then sent to the cloud by using Raspberry Pi that enables doctors to continuously monitor the status of the patient. The patient's side has a web camera that helps the doctor to monitor the patient. Both Web and android application is used to present the data collected through the sensor.

Shubham Banka *et al.* [13] proposed a smart health-care monitoring system using Raspberry Pi. The author implemented this system using a temperature sensor, heartbeat sensor, BP sensor, and vibration sensor to monitor the patient's temperature, heartbeat, BP, and shivering of the patient. The data collected from the sensor are stored and are presented through the web user interface. A GSM module is attached to inform the critical situations of the patients through SMS.

Senthamilarasi *et al.* [14] proposed a model for monitoring patients' healthcare by Arduino UNO. The real-time implementation of health-care applications uses a temperature sensor for body temperature, ECG for heartbeat, and a heartbeat sensor for heartbeat rate monitoring. These sensors send the signal to the Arduino UNO, and sensor data can be monitored by any smart device that is interconnected with the cloud database, which acts as a server for communication. The paper also discusses the recent advancements in the IoT-based health-care eco-system.

Subasish Mohapatra *et al.* [15] implemented a health-care monitoring system using Arduino. This model uses a temperature sensor and pulse sensor that are connected to the Arduino. The health parameters given by the sensors are then stored in the cloud database by using Wi-Fi module. This cloud database processes the data provided by the sensors and if the data exceeded the threshold value, it makes an emergency call to the concerned doctor with the current health status of the patient and with a full detailed medical report, so that the doctor suggests a proper health-care measures to be taken in case of critical health conditions.

Tarannum Khan *et al.* [16] proposed an Arduino-based patient monitoring system to monitor the health of the patients. The patient's details are collected using two sensors that are temperature sensor and heartbeat sensor to monitor temperature and heartbeat. An LCD screen is used to display the monitored details. The collected details are uploaded on the server and are converted into JSON links for visualizing in an android application.

Shreyaasha Chaudhury *et al.* [5] proposed a patient monitoring system using the IoT. The author implemented this system using Arduino UNO, temperature sensor, ECG sensor, and heartbeat sensor to monitor the patient's health parameter. The data collected through the sensors are monitored and analyzed by the doctor. Abnormal changes in the health parameters are notified to the doctor using a buzzer and SMS. The data collected are stored in a database and are present through a simple web page.

Niharika Kumar [17] gave a framework end-to-end health-care system associated with Arduino UNO. The implementation of the health-care application system uses a temperature sensor for body temperature, ECG for heartbeat, gyroscope for sense angular velocity, and heartbeat sensor for the heartbeat rate monitoring. These sensors send the signal to the Arduino UNO, which is connected to the Internet and acts as the communication media between the IoT devices and exhibit devices such as a computer system or phones.

Durga Amarnath M. Budida *et al.* [23] proposed a health-care system that uses ATMEL 89s52 microprocessor as its base. The system contains a login to validate the user who can access the system. The data are sent from microprocessor to other computers in the hospital side using Wi-Fi module. The system has a temperature sensor and a pulse rate sensor to monitor the patient's health, and it also requires analog to digital convertor. This convertor will convert the analog to digital on which the microprocessor works.

Kavita Jaiswal *et al.* [24] implemented a Raspberry Pi-based health monitoring system that is used to monitor the health condition of a patient from a remote location. This system uses a Docker container to manage the data that are collected and also uses a Database to store the data about the patient. Once the data is stored, it can be accessed by multiple users who can be benefitted.

Gowrishankar *et al.* [25] proposed and designed a framework that determines the human body temperature and heartbeat of the patient, then it redirects the data to the server end by using a cost-efficient microcontroller with great effect. It uses three different sensors, such as pulse sensors, heartbeat sensor, and temperature sensor, and they are controlled by the microcontroller.

14.4   Hardware components and sensors

14.4.1   Development boards

Development boards are circuit boards used to test sensors and act as an interface between the sensors and the processing units. The development boards used in the above research paper works are Arduino UNO, Raspberry Pi, NI-my RIO processor, and Node MCU ESP8266.

14.4.1.1   Arduino UNO

Arduino UNO is an open-source microcontroller development board used widely in IoT projects. The major benefits of using Arduino are low cost and flexibility. The Arduino UNO is used to monitor the health parameters in healthcare applications proposed in References 2, 3, 8. In Reference 2, Arduino is used for developing a health-care application for an electrocardiogram to detect the electrical signals of our heart.

14.4.1.2   Raspberry Pi

Raspberry Pi is a single-board computer that allows us to connect and explore with different sensors. In References 6, 7, 10, the health-care application is built upon the Raspberry Pi platform. In Reference 2, the smart health-care application is implemented in both the Arduino and Raspberry Pi platforms to compare the efficiency. Raspberry Pi gave better results than the Arduino in the patient monitoring system proposed in Reference 2.

14.4.1.3   NI-my RIO processor

NI-my RIO processor is an evaluation board that is used to create an application using the microprocessor present in it. In Reference 12, patient monitoring is done with the help of NI-my RIO processor. The data collected here are stored and analyzed using machine learning algorithms.

14.4.1.4   Node MCU ESP 8266 module

Node MCU is an open-source development board and is extensively known for its Wi-Fi chip present in it. Node MCU is used as a development board in the health-care monitoring system proposed in References 9 and 11.

14.4.2   Sensors

14.4.2.1   Blood pressure sensor

The blood pressure sensor is capable of monitoring the blood flow of a patient. The pressures created in the blood flow are detected and converted to electrical signals. Blood pressure is an important factor when considering a person's health. This sensor is used in the patient monitoring system proposed in References 7, 8, 10 to study the blood pressure of the patient.

14.4.2.2 Temperature sensor (DS18B20)

The temperature of the place and patient is one of the considering factors that can affect a patient's health. This temperature sensor is digital, programmable, and also follows a single wire protocol. The temperature of the patient is collected using this sensor in frameworks proposed in References 7–9 to monitor the patient's temperature.

14.4.2.3 Temperature sensor (LM35)

Temperature sensor (LM35) works on the principle of the diode. The output is in the form of voltages. This temperature sensor helps take into account the temperature required for the patient's health. This temperature sensor is used in the health-care application proposed in References 3, 9, 12.

14.4.2.4 Humidity sensor (DHT11)

Humidity sensor acts as a digital temperature sensor as well as a humidity sensor. It gives a digital signal as output by measuring the air humidity. This sensor is used to study the room temperature in the patient monitoring system proposed in Reference 9.

14.4.2.5 ECG sensor (AD-8232)

ECG sensor is used to monitor heartbeats. The condition and activity of heart pumping and vibrations are measured and electrically converted to a signal that can be monitored on a display. In References 2, 11, 12, the activity of the heart is monitored using an ECG sensor.

14.4.2.6 Heart rate monitor sensor (MAX 30105)

Heart rate monitor sensor (MAX 30105) is used for heartbeat plotting and heart rate monitoring. It has three LEDs for pulses and detects the reflection accordingly. Heart rate is monitored using this sensor in frameworks proposed in References 2, 9, 10 to monitor heart rate.

14.4.2.7 Body position sensor (ADXL 335)

The body position sensor is also called an accelerometer. The output of this sensor is analog voltages that are proportional to the acceleration. By measuring the acceleration, it can identify the position or angle of the vibration. This sensor is used in health-care applications proposed in frameworks [2, 10, 15] to determine the body position of the patient.

14.4.2.8 CO sensor (MQ 9)

CO sensor is used for gas leakage detection, such as LPG, CO, CH4. Its sensitivity can be adjusted by using a potentiometer. It has a fast response time and high sensitivity. In Reference 9, this sensor is used to monitor CO gas.

14.4.2.9 CO_2 sensor (MQ 135)

In CO_2 sensor (MQ 135), the sensitivity can be set by using a potentiometer. It can read gases such as ammonia nitrogen, oxygen, and also alcohol. Not like MQ9, it is capable of detecting more harmful gases. This sensor is used in the patient monitoring system proposed in Reference 9.

14.4.2.10 Respiration sensor

A respiration sensor is used for giving the output of respiration vibration in the form of a wave. As the breathing of the patient takes place, a respiratory waveform can be shown in the display. In Reference 10, this sensor is used to monitor the patient's respiration.

14.4.2.11 Pulse rate body temperature sensor (MAX 30102)

Pulse rate body temperature sensor is a heart rate monitor biosensor and also a pulse oximetry sensor. It measures the heart rate of the patient and also the hemoglobin level of a patient by measuring oxygen. This sensor is used in frameworks proposed in References 11, 12 to monitor the pulse rate.

14.4.2.12 Vibration sensor

The vibration sensor works in the same way as the pulse sensor, but it measures the vibration in terms of frequency. This is used to detect any breakdowns or imbalances present in the patient. This sensor is used in the patient monitoring system proposed in Reference 13 to monitor the shivering of patients.

14.4.2.13 Gyroscope sensor

Shortly known as a gyro sensor, gyroscope can measure angular velocity. This sensor can be used for maintaining the stability of a patient and measuring the level of effectiveness. In Reference 17, this sensor is used to maintain the stability of the patient.

14.4.3 Other modules

14.4.3.1 Radio frequency identification

RFID is a technology that is used to automatically identify and collect information about a particular object. RFID uses radio waves to identify and collect data about the object. In Reference 8, RFID technology is used to store a particular patient's details in RFID tags.

14.4.3.2 GSM/GPRS module

GSM/GPRS module is the communication module that is used to establish a connection with mobile mostly in Arduino-based frameworks. The GSM module is capable of sending SMS, and the GPRS module is used for providing network connectivity.

This module is used in health-care systems proposed in References 3, 8, 10 to notify the doctors during emergencies.

14.5   Proposed work

The proposed health-care application uses Arduino at its heart which is a microcontroller capable of articulating multiple sensors. Arduino development boards have the power of transforming the data provided to them. The system uses three sensors to monitor the health of the patients. The sensors are a temperature sensor, heartbeat sensor, and pressure sensor [28]. Many varieties of temperature sensors are used to read the temperature from patients. The temperature sensor used in this proposed framework is LM 35. A heartbeat sensor is used for monitoring the heartbeat of the patient. The vibration sensor is capable of checking the shivering of the patient. The data collected from Arduino are constantly monitored. The GSM module sends messages to doctors when the patient's state is critical. The LCD is used to display the temperature, heartbeat, and vibration status of a patient. The data can also be accessed online with the help of a Wi-Fi module [27, 29–43].

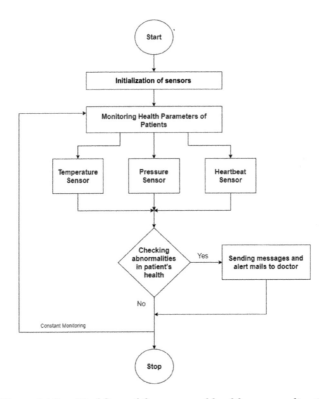

Figure 14.2   Workflow of the proposed health-care application

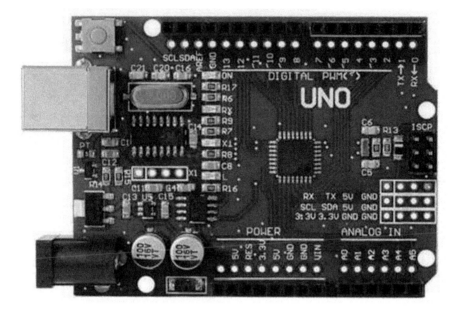

Figure 14.3   Arduino UNO

The workflow of the proposed system is shown in Figure 14.2. The objective of this work is to monitor the patient's health parameters continuously. This system uses an Arduino microcontroller for interfacing different sensors [44–47]. First, the sensor modules are initialized. The code should be written in Arduino IDE using embedded C language for these sensor modules. The code is compiled and verified to check the errors. In case of any errors, the code is modified appropriately. Once the code is error-free, it is uploaded to the Arduino development board. The health parameters such as temperature, pressure, and heartbeat are red using sensors. The data collected from the patient are now processed. If there exist any abnormalities in a patient's health, messages are sent to the doctor with the help of the GSM module [3, 8, 10].

14.5.1   Hardware components used

14.5.1.1   Arduino

The microcontroller used for the project is Arduino UNO. It has 6 analog pins and 14 digital pins. It is cheaper and has many user-friendly features. It has simple architecture and supports higher input/output drive strength (Figure 14.3).

14.5.1.2   Temperature sensor

The temperature sensor used in this project is LM-35. It has three terminals, namely VCC, GND, and OUT. It can measure temperature ranging between –55 and 150°C. It measures analog voltage that is proportional to the temperature. We can convert

Figure 14.4   Temperature sensor

the analog voltage to digital format for readability purposes. The temperature sensor is shown in Figure 14.4.

14.5.1.3   Heartbeat sensor

A heartbeat sensor is used to measure the heartbeat/pulse of a human. It is also known as a pulse sensor and can detect the heart rate of a person 3 feet away. The sensor detects the heartbeat with the help of passing green light on the finger and the methodology is known as photoplethysmogram. The patient's or user's fingerprint is kept on the front side of the sensor (heart-shaped side) and an LED to indicate the functioning of the sensor [48]. On the backside, we have resistors, diodes, microchips, and capacitors. The sensor can handle 3.3–5 V and a current of 4 mA. It has three male header connectors—one for VCC, another for GND, and another for signal output—that is connected to the analog input of the Arduino board. The heartbeat sensor is depicted in Figure 14.5.

14.5.1.4   Vibration sensor

We are using vibration sensor module SW-420 to check the shivering level of the patient. This sensor can detect the vibration in the human body beyond a specified limit/threshold. It has three pins Vcc, GND, and a digital output pin. It is combined with an LM393 comparator to detect the vibration. A potentiometer is present to adjust the threshold of vibration to detect. The vibration sensor is shown in Figure 14.6.

14.5.1.5   GSM/GPRS module

GSM/GPRS module is responsible for the communication between the development board and the network. GSM module allows the users to send messages by using SMS. GPRS module is an advancement in the GSM module that allows the user to connect to the Internet. The GSM module is depicted in Figure 14.7.

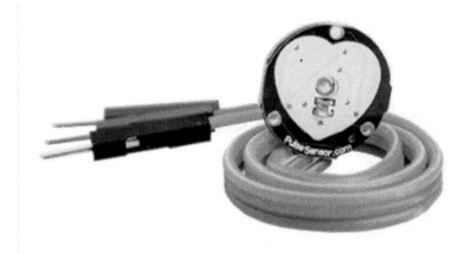

Figure 14.5   Heartbeat sensor

14.5.1.6   LCD display

The LCD of the Arduino is used to display the content from the Arduino board. It is a 16 × 2 LCD module that has four connection ports. These ports are responsible for connection purposes. This display is capable of displaying 16 characters in 2 lines. The LCD is shown in Figure 14.8.

Figure 14.6   Vibration sensor

Figure 14.7   GSM/GPRS module

14.5.1.7   Wi-Fi module (ESP8266)

ESP8266 module helps the microcontroller to connect with Wi-Fi network. It is an SOC (System On-chip) integrated with a TCP/IP protocol stack, which can provide microcontroller access to any type of Wi-Fi network. This can also host an application individually. ESP8266 module generally has 16 GPIO pins. It also allows us to enable connections such as SPI, I2C, UART, and PWM pins. Figure 14.9 shows Wi-Fi module [49].

Figure 14.8   LCD display

Figure 14.9   ESP8266 module

14.6   Implementation and results

The proposed system is implemented using the Proteus application. The different components used in this application are connected to the Arduino. The block diagram of the proposed system is demonstrated in Figure 14.2. The sensor modules used in the system are connected to the Arduino development board using wires. Each sensor used in this system contains a V_{cc} and a ground. These connections are provided to the sensors. The output pin of the LM35 sensor is connected to A0 of the Arduino board. The output pin of the heartbeat sensor is connected to A2 of the Arduino board. D0 of the Arduino board is connected to the output pin of the vibration sensor. Virtual terminal in Proteus is used to display the output of the proposed system. The RX pin of the serial monitor is connected to D1 of Arduino. The GSM module contains two pins, RX and PX. The RX pin and TX pin of the GSM module is connected to D2 and D3 of the Arduino board, respectively. The circuit diagram of the proposed system is shown in Figure 14.10.

The code for the proposed system is compiled and executed in the Arduino IDE. The hex file of the executed code is uploaded to the Arduino board that is the

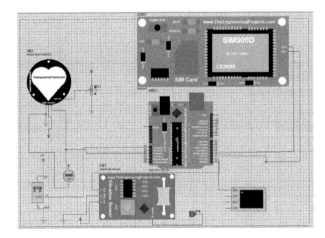

Figure 14.10   The circuit diagram of an implemented system in Proteus

program file of the board. The program file of the GSM module is uploaded in it. The proposed system is simulated to view the results.

The data collected from the sensors are displayed on the virtual terminal. First, the temperature is displayed in two units, and they are Celsius and Fahrenheit. The output from the vibration sensor is either the patient is normal or the patient is shivering. The heartbeat sensor gives heartbeats per minute. If the patient is normal, then there will be no alert messages sent to the doctor's side. The data displayed are shown in Figure 14.11.

Each parameter is set to a threshold value. When the data recorded from the sensor exceed the threshold value, alert messages are sent to the doctor. The threshold

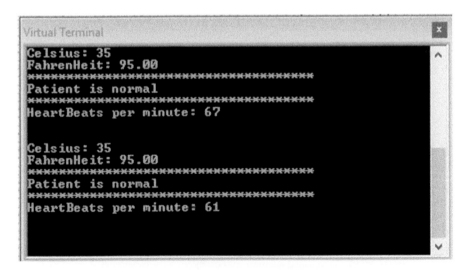

Figure 14.11   Data displayed in virtual terminal

Figure 14.12   Alert message sent to doctor's side

value for the temperature sensor is 101 °F. If the temperature value exceeds the given value, then the alert messages are sent to the doctor using the GSM module. In the same way, the threshold value of the heartbeat sensor is 50. If the heartbeats per minute reduce below 50, then the alert messages should be sent to the doctor's number. The alert message is shown in Figure 14.12.

Figure 14.13 shows the temperature reading of the patient collected during different times of the day. For this particular patient, the temperature value is between 98.2 and 98.9 °F.

The heartbeat of the patient recorded using sensors is shown in Figure 14.14. . The heartbeats of the patient vary from range 69 to 72.

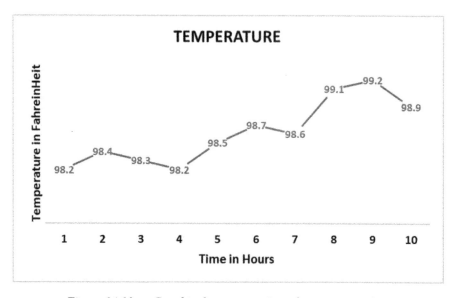

Figure 14.13   Graphical representation of temperature data

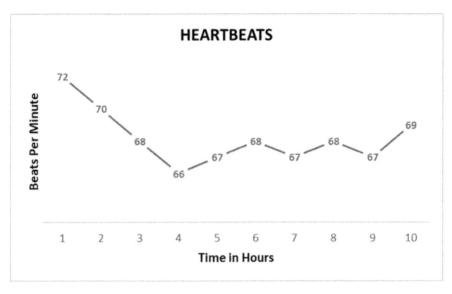

Figure 14.14   Graphical representation of heartbeat data

14.7 Conclusion

IoT combined with the health-care sector has proved to make remote monitoring of patients possible and effective. It unleashes the power and possibility to keep the patients healthy and also empower the medical experts to deliver instant care to the patients. It also prevents unnecessary admission in hospitals since every single change in their body is being collected at an early stage and remedies can be provided superlatively.

IoT in the health-care system is proving to be significantly effective and the outcome is very much beneficial, not only to the patients but also to the medical experts and hospitals. This paper deals with various health-care monitoring systems that have been developed using IoT and provides an extensive survey on the same. It briefs about different designs for the health-care system. Also, the different types of IoT components used for building the system, their limitations, and support provided by each type of design have been extensively discussed. An Arduino-based application is simulated on the Proteus application.

References

[1]   Zhu H., Wu C.K., Koo C.H., *et al.* 'Smart healthcare in the era of Internet-of-Things'. *IEEE Consumer Electronics Magazine*. 2019, vol. 8(5), pp. 26–30.
[2]   Vajubunnisa Begum R., Dharmarajan K. 'Smart healthcare monitoring system in IoT'. *European Journal of Molecular & Clinical Medicine*. 2020, vol. 7(4).

[3] Dahlia Sam S., Srinidhi V., Niveditha R., Amutha S. 'Progressed IOT based remote health monitoring system'. *International Journal of Control and Automation*. 2020, vol. 13(2s).

[4] Baker S.B., Xiang W., Atkinson I. 'Internet of things for smart healthcare: technologies, challenges, and opportunities'. *IEEE Access*. 2017, vol. 5, pp. 26521–44.

[5] Chaudhury S., Paul D., Mukherjee R., Haldar S. 'Internet of thing based health-care monitoring system'. *2017 8th IEEE Annual Information Technology, Electronics and Mobile Communication Conference (IEMCON), Publisher: IEEE, Vancouver, BC, Canada*; IEEE, 2017.

[6] Mohapatra S., Mohanty S., Mohanty S. *Smart healthcare: an approach for ubiquitous healthcare management using iiott, Editor(s): Nilanjan Dey, Himansu Das, Bighnaraj Naik, Himansu Sekhar Behera, in advances in ubiquitous sensing applications for healthcare, big data analytics for in-telligent healthcare management, academic press, 2019, 175-196, ISBN 9780128181461*. Elsevier; 2019.

[7] Kumar A., Chattree G., Periyasamy S. *Smart healthcare monitoring system, wireless personal communications, 453–463 (2018). https://doi.org/10.1007/s11277-018-5699-0*. Vol. 101. Springer; 2018. pp. 453–63.

[8] Uday Kumar K., Shabbiah S., Rudra Kumar M. 'Design of high-security smart health care monitoring system using IoT'. *International Journal of Emerging Trends in Engineering Research*. 2020, vol. 8(6).

[9] Islam M.M., Rahaman A., Islam M.R. 'Development of smart healthcare monitoring system in IoT environment'. *SN Computer Science*. 2020, vol. 1(3), p. 185.

[10] Seena Naik K., Sudarshan E. 'Smart healthcare monitoring system using raspberry Pi on IoT platform'. *ARPN Journal of Engineering and Applied Sciences*. 2019, vol. 14(4).

[11] Raykar S.S., Suneeta S., Shet V.N. 'Design of healthcare system using iot enabled application'. *Advanced Materials for Clean Energy and Health Applications, Today: Proceedings, Volume 23, Part 1, 2020, Pages 62-67*. 2019.

[12] Rajan Jeyaraj P., Nadar E.R.S., Jeyaraj P. 'Smart-monitor: patient monitoring system for IoT-based healthcare system using deep learning'. *IETE Journal of Research*. 2019, vol. 16(1), pp. 1–8.

[13] Banka S., Madan I., Saranya S.S. 'Smart healthcare monitoring using IoT'. *International Journal of Applied Engineering Research*. 2018, vol. 13(15).

[14] Senthamilarasi C., Jansi Rani J., Vidhya B., Atitha H. 'A smart patient health monitoring system using IoT'. *International Journal of Pure and Applied Mathematics*, vol. 119(16).

[15] Shaikh S., Chitre V. 'Healthcare monitoring system using iot'. *International Conference on Trends in Electronics and Informatics ICEI, Publisher: IEEE, Tirunelveli, India, DOI: 10.1109/ICOEI.2017.8300952*; 2017.

[16] Khan T., Chattopadhyay M.K. 'Smart healthcare monitoring system'. *IEEE, International Conference on Information, Communication, Instrumentation*

and Control (ICICIC), Publisher: IEEE, Indore, India, DOI: 10.1109/ ICOMICON.2017.8279142; 2017.

[17] Kumar N. 'IoT architecture and system design for healthcare systems'. *International Conference on Smart Technology for Smart Nation IEEE, Publisher:IEEE, Bengaluru, India, DOI: 10.1109/ SmartTechCon.2017.8358543*; 2017.

[18] Alshehri F., Muhammad G. 'Comprehensive survey of the IoT and AI-Based smart healthcare'. *IEEE Access: Practical Innovations, Open Solutions*. 2021, vol. 9, pp. 3660–78.

[19] Shah Y., Parvati V.K., Biradar S.R. 'Survey of smart healthcare systems using internet of things (iot)'. *2018 International Conference on Communication, Computing and Internet of Things (IC3IoT), Publisher: IEEE, Chennai, India, DOI:10.1109/IC3IoT.2018.8668128*; IEEE, 2018.

[20] Li W., Chai Y., Khan F., *et al.* 'A comprehensive survey on machine learning-based big data analytics for IoT-enabled smart healthcare system'. *Mobile Networks and Applications*. 2021, vol. 26(1), pp. 234–52.

[21] Hegde R., Ranjana S., Divya C.D. 'Survey on development of smart healthcare monitoring system in iot environment'. *Fifth International Conference on Computing Methodologies and Communication, Publisher: IEEE, Erode, India, DOI: 10.1109/ICCMC51019.2021.9418405*; ICCMC, 2021.

[22] Zhu H., Wu C.K., Koo C.H., *et al.* 'Smart healthcare in the era of Internet-of-Things'. *IEEE Consumer Electronics Magazine*. 2019, vol. 8(5), pp. 26–30.

[23] Budida D.A.M., Mangrulkar S. D.R. 'Design and implementation of smart healthcare system using iot'. *International Conference on Innovations in Information*; Embedded and Communication Systems (ICIIECS), Publisher: IEEE, Coimbatore, India, DOI: 10.1109/ICIIECS.2017.8275903, 2017.

[24] Jaiswal K., Sobhanayak S., Mohanta B.K., Jena D. 'IoT-cloud based framework for patient's data collection in smart healthcare system using raspberry-pi'. *International Conference on Innovations in Information, Embedded and Communication Systems (ICIIECS), Publisher: IEEE, Ras Al Khaimah, United Arab Emirates, DOI: 10.1109/ICECTA.2017.8251967*; 2017.

[25] Gowrishankar S.M.Y., Prakash P.A. 'IoT based heart attack detection, heart rate and temperature monitor'. *International Journal of Computer Applications, 26-30, DOI: 10.5120/Ijca2017914840, July 2017*. 2017, vol. 170(5).

[26] Arith B., Deepak K.C., Sathish K., Aboobacker S., Kumar A. 'Heartbeat sensing and heart attack detection using internet of things: IoT'. *International Journal of Engineering Science and Computing*. 2017, vol. 7(14), pp. 6662–6.

[27] Manisha M., Neeraja K., Sindhura V., Ramya P. 'IoT on heart attack detection and heart rate monitoring'. *International Journal of Innovation in Engineering and Technology (IJIET)*. 2020.

[28] Jaiswal K., Sobhanayak S., Turuk A.K., Bibhudatta S.L., Mohanta B.L., Jena D. 'An IoT-cloud based smart healthcare monitoring system using the container-based virtual environment in Edge device'. *International Conference on Emerging Trends and Innovations in Engineering and*

Technological Research (ICETIETR)*; Ernakulam, India, 11–13 July 2018; 2018. pp. 1–7.

[29] Kumar S., Ranjan P., Ramaswami R. 'EMEEDP: enhanced multi-hop energy efficient distributed protocol for heterogeneous wireless sensor network'. *Proceedings – 2015 5th International Conference on Communication Systems and Network Technologies CSNT*; Gwalior, India, 04–06 April 2015; 2015. pp. 194–200

[30] Kumar S., Rao A.L.N., Ramaswami R. 'Energy optimization in distributed localized wireless sensor networks'. *Proceedings of the International Conference on Issues and Challenges Intelligent Computing Technique (ICICT)*; Ghaziabad, India, 07–08 February 2014; 2014. pp. 350–5.

[31] Chauhan R., Kumar S. 'Packet loss prediction using artificial intelligence unified with big data analytics, Internet of things and cloud computing technologies'. *5th International Conference on Information Systems and Computer Networks (ISCON)*; 2021. pp. 01–6.

[32] Sudhakaran S., Kumar S., Ranjan P., Tripathy M.R. 'Blockchain-based transparent and secure decentralized algorithm'. *International Conference on Intelligent Computing and Smart Communication 2019. Algorithms for Intelligent Systems*; Springer, Singapore; 2019.

[33] Kumar S., Trivedi M.C., Ranjan P. *Evolution of software-defined networking foundations for iot and 5G mobile networks,publisher: IGI, DOI: 10.4018/978-1-7998-4685-7, ISBN13: 9781799846857*; 2020. p. 350.

[34] Kumar S., Ranjan P., Radhakrishnan R., Tripathy M.R. 'Energy efficient multichannel MAC protocol for high traffic applications in heterogeneous wireless sensor networks'. *Recent Advances in Electrical & Electronic Engineering*. 2017, vol. 10(3), pp. 223–32.

[35] Kumar S., Ranjan P., Ramaswami R., Tripathy M.R. 'Resource efficient clustering and next hop knowledge based routing in multiple heterogeneous wireless sensor networks'. *International Journal of Grid and High Performance Computing*. 2017, vol. 9(2), pp. 1–20.

[36] Kumar S., Cengiz K., Vimal S., Suresh A. 'Energy efficient resource migration based load balance mechanism for high traffic applications IoT'. *Wireless Personal Communications*. 2021, vol. 10(3).

[37] Kumar S., Cengiz K., Trivedi C.M., *et al.* 'DEMO enterprise ontology with a stochastic approach based on partially observable Markov model for data aggregation and communication in intelligent sensor networks'. *Wireless Personal Communication*. 2022.

[38] Punhani A., Faujdar N., Kumar S. 'Design and evaluation of cubic torus network-on-chip architecture'. *International Journal of Innovative Technology and Exploring Engineering (IJITEE)*. 2019, vol. 8(6), pp. 2278–3075.

[39] Dubey G., Kumar S., Kumar S., Navaney P. 'Extended opinion lexicon and ML-based sentiment analysis of tweets: a novel approach towards accurate classifier'. *International Journal of Computational Vision and Robotics*. 2020, vol. 10(6), pp. 505–21.

[40] Singh P., Bansal A., Kamal A.E., Kumar S. 'Road surface quality monitoring using machine learning algorithm' in Reddy A.N.R., Marla D., Favorskaya M.N., Satapathy S.C. (eds.). *Intelligent Manufacturing and Energy Sustainability. Smart Innovation, Systems and Technologies*. 265. Singapore: Springer; 2022.

[41] Kumar S., Ranjan P., Ramaswami R., Tripathy M.R. 'Energy aware distributed protocol for heterogeneous wireless sensor network'. *International Journal of Control and Automation*. 2015, vol. 8(10), pp. 421–30.

[42] Kumar S., Ranjan P., Ramaswami R., Tripathy M.R. 'A utility maximization approach to MAC layer channel access and forwarding'. *Progress in Electromagnetics Research Symposium*. 2015, vol. 2015, pp. 2363–7.

[43] Kumar S., Ranjan P., Ramaswami R., Tripathy M.R. 'An NS3 implementation of physical layer based on 802.11 for utility maximization of WSN'. *Proceedings – 2015 International Conference on Computational Intelligence and Communication Networks, CICN 2015*; 2016. pp. 79–84.

[44] Sharma A., Awasthi Y., Kumar S. 'The role of Blockchain, AI and IoT for smart road traffic management system'. *Proceedings – 2020 IEEE India Council International Subsections Conference, INDISCON 2020*; 2020. pp. 289–96.

[45] Singh P., Bansal A., Kumar S. 'Performance analysis of various information platforms for recognizing the quality of indian roads'. *Proceedings of the Confluence 2020 – 10th International Conference on Cloud Computing, Data Science and Engineering, Publisher: IEEE, Noida, India, DOI: 10.1109/Confluence47617.2020.9057829*; 2020. pp. 63–76.

[46] Kumar S., Ranjan P., Singh P., Tripathy M.R. 'Design and implementation of fault tolerance technique for Internet of things (IoT)'. *Proceedings – 2020 12th International Conference on Computational Intelligence and Communication Networks, CICN 2020*; 2020. pp. 154–9.

[47] Reghu S., Kumar S. 'Development of robust infrastructure in networking to survive a disaster'. *2019 4th International Conference on Information Systems and Computer Networks, ISCON 2019, Publisher: IEEE, Mathura, INdia, 10.1109/ISCON47742.2019.9036244*; 2019. pp. 250–55.

[48] Kumar A., Krishnamurthi R., Nayyar A., Sharma K., Grover V., Hossain E. 'A novel smart healthcare design, simulation, and implementation using healthcare 4.0 processes'. *IEEE Access*. 2020, vol. 8, pp. 118433–71.

[49] Sundaravadivel P., Kougianos E., Mohanty S.P., Ganapathiraju M. K. 'Everything you wanted to know about smart health care'. *IEEE Consumer Electronics Magazine, pp. 18-28, Jan. 2018, Doi: 10.1109/MCE.2017.2755378*. 2018, vol. 7(1).

Chapter 15

IoT-based heart disease prediction system

Rajamohana S P[1], Zbigniew M Wawrzyniak[2], Krishna Prasath S[3], Shevannth R[3], Raja Kumar I[3], Mohammed Rafi M[3], and T Hariprasath D[3]

In India, almost 80% of patients who die from heart disease do not receive adequate care. This is a challenging task for doctors because they often seem unable to make an accurate diagnosis. This condition is extremely expensive to treat. The proposed solution uses data mining technologies to simplify the decision support system in order to increase the cost-effectiveness of therapy. To oversee their patients' care, most hospitals use a hospital management system. Unfortunately, many of these tools do not employ large amounts of clinical data to derive useful information. Because these systems generate a considerable amount of data in many embodiments, the data is rarely accessed and remains unusable. As a result, making sensible selections requires a lot of effort during this procedure. The process of diagnosing a disease currently entails identifying the disease's numerous symptoms and characteristics. This research employs a number of data mining approaches to assist with medical diagnostics.

15.1 Introduction

Heart diseases are becoming the leading cause of death [1]. We can use health-care data from several hospitals to train a machine learning system to forecast the occurrence of health illnesses. Machine learning is highly regarded in health care because of its ability to process massive datasets faster than humans [2]. Predicting this outcome would help the doctor plan and deliver better care. It is a structure that uses a historical cardiac database to predict heart disease. Health-related signals including blood pressure, heart rate, chest discomfort, blood sugar, and cholesterol are among the input signals. Two additional factors that are also effective in achieving

[1]Department of Computer Science & Engineering, Pondicherry University, Karaikal, India
[2]Department Electronics and Information Technology, Warsaw University of Technology, Warsaw, Poland
[3]Department of Information Technology, PSG College of Technology, Coimbatore, Tamil Nadu, India

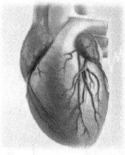

Coronary artery

Arteries that supply
oxygen and blood
to the heart
become narrow

Arrhythmia
Abnormal
heart rhythm

Heart valve

One or more of the valves in
the heart are not working well

Heart failure

Heart does not have enough
strength to pump

Heart muscle

Congenital heart

Children may with this disease

Heart walls become thick or
heart becomes enlarged

Figure 15.1   Types of heart diseases and their symptoms

the desired outcomes are smoking and obesity, both of which are recognized as significant heart disease symptoms. To obtain the findings, classification techniques like decision trees and random forests are used along with the data.

The health-care industry gathers a massive amount of data about health-care services. Unfortunately, it often lacks practical information that could aid in making sound judgments. This work created a revolutionary data mining system capable of detecting and forecasting cardiac problems.

The outcome of paper demonstrates that each process has its own unique capability in reaching the stated mining objectives [1]. IHDPS can provide answers to the complex concerns of what if traditional decision-making networks could not use medical files such as age, while blood sugar and blood pressure can predict that patients will develop heart disease, thereby providing valuable information [3].

As a result, data mining helps to achieve natural evolution in the medical field [2]. Deep learning is one of the most often utilized methods for the diagnosis of cardiac problems, along with machine learning and neural networks. The section that follows provides a brief description of each [3].

15.1.1   Deep learning

The problem in function of heart due to different circumstance is titled as a heart disease. Some of the familiar heart diseases are congestive heart failure, cardiac arrest, arrhythmia, stroke, coronary artery disease (CAD), and congenital heart disease as shown in Figure 15.1. How heart disease varies establish on its type and its symptoms are shown in Figure 15.2.

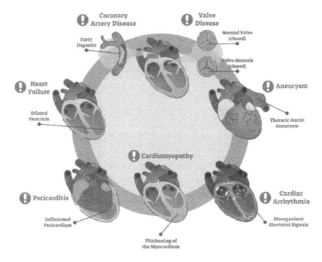

Figure 15.2   Heart disease

The indication to forecast the heart disorder based on the type of heart disorder symptoms depends on its heart disorder. For example, high blood pressure is one of the indications for coronary artery for all the people with similar symptom, the other may differ having the symptom of chest pain. The doctor confirms the heart disease with the diagnosed report of the patient and several other frameworks. Some of the most usual heart disorder symptoms and its types are listed in Table 15.1 and Figure 15.1.

Table 15.1   Heart disease factors with symptoms

Heart disease: risk factors	Heart disease: symptoms
Age	Discomfort, pressure or heaviness
Sex	Pain in the chest or arm, or below the breastbone
Family history	Discomfort burning to the back, jaw, throat, or arm
Smoking	Fullness, indigestion, or choking feeling
Poor diet	Sweating, nausea, vomiting, or dizziness
High blood pressure	Extreme weakness, anxiety, or shortness of breath
High blood cholesterol level	Rapid or irregular heartbeats
Diabetes	
Obesity	
Physical inactivity	
Stress	
Poor hygiene	

15.2   Related work

Only a few healthcare sectors employ clinical data for predictive purposes, and even those that do may be limited by a plethora of patient organizational constraints. Literature surveys are mentioned in Table 15.2. Predictions are based on a doctor's intuition rather than extensive research from a scientific database. Incorrect therapy caused by a faulty diagnosis poses a severe threat to the clinical profession. To solve these challenges, the following part provided and discussed a data mining strategy helped by scientific statistics.

Gowrishankar *et al.* (2017) proposed a framework that estimates and determines the case's human body temperature and heartbeat, then redirects the data to the customer or server end using a low-cost microcontroller. It employs three distinct sensors (pulse, heartbeat, and temperature sensors), all of which are heavily controlled by the microcontroller.

Balamurugan *et al.* (2017) proposed a framework that uses an Arduino, plus, and a heartbeat sensor to determine the patient's pulse and analyze the data to determine whether the patient is healthy or at risk of having a heart attack [44].

Manisha *et al.* (2016) proposed a system that assists elderly persons who are constantly producing heart diseases or heart attacks by tracking their cardiac abnormalities and sending an alert alarm to the user's or the surrounding person's mobile phone using a gadget [52]. Additionally, it analyses the heartbeat's data set. It also makes use of big data analytics, which through utilizing various tools and regulations fosters an environment that is open to customers.

Polu *et al.* (2019) proposed a system that assists to lower deaths brought by heart disorder since the main reason of heart disorder deaths is expected due to wait time and proper treatment. It can be bypassed since the technology will notify the doctor of his present location and ECG report.

Patel *et al.* (2014) proposed an article that says angina is very significant for the sufferer. The sufferer may be saved if additional care and medical assistance are provided within an hour. To quickly identify heart conditions utilizing the algorithm and the crucial therapy. A gaming gadget can also serve as lifesaving equipment in this way. If put into practice, this concept is quite helpful.

Ashrafuzzaman *et al.* (2013) proposed a method that teaches us how to identify heart problems by heartbeat and blood data. This technique for identifying heart issues is highly accurate. With the help of this technique for capturing heart frequencies, we could identify a number of heart-related conditions. In addition to heart attacks, it can detect abnormal blood, heart obstruction, and valve circulation. This is because the heartbeat was captured. It is now capable of identifying heart issues. Based on heart frequencies, our technology will assist in the early detection of cardiac issues.

Bo Jin, Chao Che *et al.* (2018) proposed a neural network-based model where the trial and early diagnosis of the heart complaint were performed using electronic health record (EHR) data from real-world datasets related to ischemic heart disease in this research [29]. We used one-hot encoding and word vectors, which are the

Table 15.2   Related works

S. No.	Author and publication year	Proposed framework	Used hardware and software components	Algorithms used	Communication module	Limitations
1	Gowrishankar *et al.* (2017) [4]	This paper uses sensors to collect the state of the heart and body temperature with different test cases and provides an alter message using LCD monitor.	LM35, Pulse-sensor, Arduino UNO, temperature sensor	NA	ESP8266 (Wi-Fi module)	• Data transfer between devices must be fast enough with minimized delay response,sensor module should extract accurate readings, two different sensors must be used and should be under the control of microcontroller to be accurate in output.
2	Aboobacker *et al.* (2017) [5]	This paper presents a method to detect the heart rate of the patient, store them, and make analysis based on the sensed data. It provides results as if a person is healthy or not/if he has a chance of getting heart attack.	Pulse sensor, Arduino UNO	NA	Wi-Fi module	• Pulse sensor must detect the pulse precisely and accurately.

(Continues)

Table 15.2 Continued

S. No.	Author and publication year	Proposed framework	Used hardware and software components	Algorithms used	Communication module	Limitations
3	Manisha et al. (2016) [6]	This paper presents a method where the proposed system records heart rate and pulse rate and uses big data analysis to do analysis	MI Band 2, Android phone, big data analytics	NA	Mobile data/Wi-Fi module	• Encoder must respond immediately as the microcontroller transmits info, decoder/decoding must be accurate to get an actual output.
4	Subbalakshmi et al. (2020)ok [7]	The paper proposes a portable ECG monitor where the heart rate will be collected and sent to Android phone. In the phone using detection algorithms, abnormality will be recorded and message to ambulance will also be sent if needed.	ECG monitor, Android phone	NA	Mobile data/Wi-Fi module	• Wi-Fi module is used to transfer and monitor data so connectivity must be constant and fast enough to avoid delay. Sensor module should extract accurate readings. Data are stored in the server.

(Continues)

Table 15.2 *Continued*

S. No.	Author and publication year	Proposed framework	Used hardware and software components	Algorithms used	Communication module	Limitations
5	Ashrafuzzaman *et al.* (2014) [8]	This paper proposes a device "Kinect" that monitors heart rate and few other parameters and detects heart attack. It also sends alert messages to emergency contacts and makes a Skype call to hospital if needed.	Kinect, Xbox one	NA	Wi-Fi module	• Device detection of heartbeat must be precise and accurate otherwise it will SMS triggering alert about the observer will be activated and sent to his/her friends and family.
6	Ashrafuzzaman *et al.* (2013) [9]	This paper says about how to detect blood and heart rate and using heart rate recoding detect heart attacks, heart blockage, abnormal blood, and valve circulation.	Smartphone	NA	Wi-Fi module	• Heart rate calculation must be accurate. • Noise-free environment is required that is not favourable mostly.
7	Jin *et al.* (2018) [10]	The paper uses sequential data modeling to predict heart disorder.	Pulse-sensor, LM35 temperature sensor, Arduino UNO (wearable sensors), database	LSTM	ESP8266 Wi-Fi module	• Techniques in the future to classify and predict heart diseases. • These techniques maybe less speed and accuracy.

(Continues)

Table 15.2 Continued

S. No.	Author and publication year	Proposed framework	Used hardware and software components	Algorithms used	Communication module	Limitations
8	Javeed *et al.* (2017) [11]	The article presents a solution for by using optimized algorithms.	Heart disease data set	Enhanced random forest model, random search	NA	• Many trees make the algorithm slow and ineffective.
9	Sarangi *et al.* (2015) [12]	The article presents a solution by using hybrid techniques.	Heart disease data set	Hybrid algorithms (GA and neural networks)	NA	• The used algorithms have too many parameters for somebody non expert in data mining.
10	Mamatha and Shaicy (2019) [13]	The article presents a solution by using data mining for identify.	Heart disease data set	Support vector machine	NA	• SVM is not apt for larger data sets.
11	Bahrami and Shirvani [14]	The article presents a solution by using data mining for identify using KNN, SVO classifiers.	Heart disease data set	ICD, KKN	NA	• Accuracy depends on the quality of the data.
12	Bhuvaneswari and Kalaiselvi (2012) [15]	The article presents steps for identify facts based on patient reports.	Arduino and heart disease data set	Naive bayes, neural network, decision trees	NA	• Naive Bayes suppose that all features are unique, rarely happening in real time.
13	Subbalakshmi *et al.* (2011) [7]	The article presents a solution for using a Decision Support.	Heart disease data set	DSHDPS, Cleveland Database Naive Bayes	NA	• This algorithm is also notorious as a lousy estimator.

(Continues)

Table 15.2 Continued

S. No.	Author and publication year	Proposed framework	Used hardware and software components	Algorithms used	Communication module	Limitations
14	Jabbar *et al.* (2011) [16]	The article is to learn, develop and identify a network by implement associative rules.	Heart disease data set	Cluster and association rule mining algorithms	NA	• They have limitation execution time.
15	Arabasadi *et al.* (2017) [17]	The article presents a solution for a proposed hybrid identification model such as genetic and ANN algorithm.	Heart disease data set	ANN	NA	• The greater computational burden, black box nature, proneness to overfitting, and the empirical nature of model development.
16	Ambekar and Phalnikar (2018) [18]	The article presents a solution for a proposed disease risk prediction using CNN-UDRP algorithm.	Heart disease data set	Naïve Bayes, KNN algorithm	NA	• Naïve Bayes assumes that all traits are one of a kind and that they only occur infrequently in real time.

(Continues)

Table 15.2 Continued

S. No.	Author and publication year	Proposed framework	Used hardware and software components	Algorithms used	Communication module	Limitations
17	Ana and Krishna (2017) [19]	The article presents a solution for disease prediction for stoke patients using wearable sensors in IOT.	Heart disease data set	Naive Bayesian, KNN, and Tree based	NA	• The multiple algorithms are performed that increase a rise factor of giving an improper information about the patient.
18	Gupta *et al.*(2019) [20]	This article presents that KNN has the best results comparatively to other algorithms.	Heart disease data set	KNN, SVM, decision tree	NA	• A real-time heart disease prediction system for proactive health monitoring is not present.
19	He (2020) [21]	Data are collected from wearable IoT devices for 24 hours and analysis is made in the cloud.	Heart disease data set	KNN	Smart watches	• The prediction should be done in time series manner so the time consumption is relatively high.
20	Shaikh *et al.* (2015) [22]	The article presents a solution using data mining technics and is implement as a Java application.	Heart disease data set and Java Swing	KNN, Bayesian	NA	• The system cannot handle different kinds of traits.

(Continues)

Table 15.2   Continued

S. No.	Author and publication year	Proposed framework	Used hardware and software components	Algorithms used	Communication module	Limitations
21	Ganesan (2019) [23]	In this article, they have presented to diagnose heart disease using a cloud and IoT-based model.	Heart disease data set and IoT model	Classification	Wi-Fi Module	• Predictions should be made in a time series format, since this reduces the amount of time required.
22	Binsalman (2018) [24]	This paper proposed a remote monitoring a heart disease patient.	NA	Sensors	Wi-Fi module	• It is used to monitor a pre-heart disease patient only.
23	Bhat (2020) [25]	In this paper, they have automated the real-time medical diagnosis patient.	Heart disease data set	Convolutional neural network	NA	• There is a time restriction on how long they can execute.
24	Pooja Arjun (2020) [26]	In this article, the author has proposed an automated system to monitor the heart disease patient.	NA	Sensors	Wi-Fi module	• It is only used to monitor a patient who is in the early stages of cardiac disease.

(Continues)

Table 15.2 Continued

S. No.	Author and publication year	Proposed framework	Used hardware and software components	Algorithms used	Communication module	Limitations
25	Raju *et al.* (2022) [27]	With the use of Edge-Fog-Cloud computing, the author has tried to present a revolutionary smart healthcare model in this study.	Heart disease data set	GSO-CCNN	NA	• The accuracy is maintained at the first learning percentages, as it is with other algorithms, and it requires greater learning percentages to raise it.

core ideas of an extended memory network model, to model the diagnostic events and read coronary failure events [11]. We usually use the findings to show how crucial it is to value the successional structure of clinical records [7].

Ashir Javeed *et al*. (2019) proposed an arbitrary timber model and an arbitrary quest algorithm to identify cardiovascular disease (RSA). This model is intended to be used in conjunction with a grid quest algorithm.

Srikanta Pattnaik *et al*. (2015) proposed a cost-effective model using the genetic algorithm optimizer technique where the weights were reformed and fed as an input into the specified network. Ninety percent accuracy was achieved using a hybrid technique combining GA and neural networks.

Mamatha Alex P *et al*. (2019) proposed a system that makes use of KNN, ANN, SVM, and Random Forest techniques. ANN [10] compares all of these data mining to prognosticate the advanced delicacy of the heart complaint diagnosis.

Boshra Bahrami *et al*. (2020) proposed a colorful bracket methodology was used in this study to determine the cause of a cardiovascular problem. Classification algorithms such as SVO, Decision Tree, and KNN are used to partition the datasets [11]. Following the bracket and performance evaluation, the Decision tree is regarded as the most fashionable option from the dataset for cardiovascular complaint vaccination.

Bhuvaneswari *et al*. (2018) proposed a system that investigates prior experience and predicts the level of an object among all objects using the Naive Bayes classification. The Naive Bayesian and Back Propagation Neural Network categorization algorithms were used in the proposed work [22]. In the supervised learning environment, the Naive Bayesian classification is utilized to train very effectively, and the prior backend is formed by Bayesian rules based on the precise structure of the probability model.

Chinna Rao *et al*. (2019) proposed a Decision Support in Heart Disorder Identification Network (DSHDPS) using the nave processing modeling technique [38]. Heart disease indicators like sex, age, blood pressure, and chest discomfort can forecast a victim's likelihood of having a heart issue. Ti functions as an online application with a questionnaire. Prior to this, the UCI Cleveland database was used to gather data on heart victims. The nave technique is preferable for identifying cardiac problems for the reasons listed below: We can obtain a better classification technique when the amount of data is substantial, the dimensions are distinct from one another, and the model is compared to other models. Notwithstanding its simplicity, naive algorithms frequently outperform more intricate ones [13].

Jabbar *et al*. (2019) developed a vatication system using associative rules and a novel method that combines the concept of sequence figures and clustering heart attract vatication in this study. The first datasheet of heart complaint cases was converted into double format using this method, and the proposed system was applied to double transitional data. A data set of heart complaint cases with 14 essential dimensions was extracted from the UCI depository's Cleveland database. Cluster Based Association Rule Mining Grounded on Sequence Number (CBARBSN) is the name of the algorithm. In rule mining, support is a fundamental guideline. To be included in a commonly used item collection, an item must meet the support criteria.

In this investigation, the valid data table is separated based on cluster fractions (disjoint subsets of the factual valid table), and each item's Seq.No and Seq.ID are predetermined. Frequent item sets have been identified in various clusters based on Seq.ID, with the most common frequent item set designated as the general item set. Maximum heart rate > 100, trial blood pressure > 120, old peak > 0, age > 45, and Thal > 3 indicate a heart attack (frequent item set plant in both clusters in this trial) [23]. When compared to the preliminary developed system, our proposed algorithm has a lower prosecution time to mine rules (i.e., 0.879 ms when support is 3), and the prosecution time changes dramatically as support increases.

Zeinab Arabasadi *et al.* (2017) proposed a mongrel opinion network for coronary roadway complaints based on the Videl ANN machine literacy algorithm and inheritable algorithms. The Z-Alizadeh Sani dataset was used in this study, which contains 303 case records with 54 features (only 22 were included in the trial), including 216 cases with coronary artery disease (CAD) [33]. The weights of the artificial neural network were linked using an inheritable technique first, and then the ANN model was developed using training data. This sample ANN employs a feedforward technique with one input and one output subcaste, as well as one hidden subcaste with five neurons. The system was evaluated in this trial using a 10-fold cross-confirmation method. We can see from the data that our proposed model outperformed a simple ANN model in terms of delicacy. We also put our model to the test in four other well-known cardiac complaint data sets, with mixed results. In comparison to an ANN model, our proposed model has a high level of delicacy.

Sayali Ambekar *et al.* (2018). created a Neural Network technique that predicts a patient's disease using a CNN-UDRP algorithm in structured data. This study employs a real-time dataset of cardiac illness. They compared the results of the KNN and Naive Bayes algorithms and discovered that the accuracy of the NB algorithm is 82%, which is higher than the accuracy of the KNN algorithm. They were able to forecast disease risk with structured data with a 65 % accuracy [6]. They were able to achieve accurate disease risk prediction as an output by supplying accurate sickness risk prediction as input, providing us with a greater understanding of the level of disease risk prediction. The risk of heart disease is classified as low, high, or medium [12]. Disease risk prediction can now be done in a short amount of time and at a low cost thanks to this approach [6].

By adjusting the risk factors associated with the disease, ANA *et al.* (2017) suggested an ensemble classifier that may be utilized as a general prediction model for a range of diseases. The system is made up of a microcontroller that is linked to a number of wearable sensors and the cloud [8]. Sensors record input values, which are subsequently saved in the cloud and used to generate an alarm message [28]. When a critical level is reached, the system predicts the onset of sickness, allowing the clinician to take appropriate measures. They investigated the accuracy of various classification methods as well as ensemble classifiers in this study [8]. The findings imply that ensemble classifiers are superior to other methods for making predictions.

Anashi Gupta *et al.* (2019) conducted a result analysis and determined that their model uses KNN as the training method for classifying individuals with "a chance of heart disease" and "no chance of heart disease." In this case, KNN outperforms well in terms of accuracy, sensitivity, and miss rate [50]. The disadvantage of this system is that it does not provide a real-time predictive system that uses sensor data for proactive health monitoring [7].

He *et al.* (2020) proposed a framework that transfers client data into client computers and smartphones using Bluetooth, WiFi, and other LAN technologies once the wearable IoT device has collected client data for 24 hours. The clever will then upload the data to a distant cloud server, where they will apply a machine learning algorithm that has already been taught to diagnose the submitted data. They can attain up to 90% accuracy in this area. However, as the Internet of Things integration was not tested in this work, speed and power consumption are still unknown.

Shaikh *et al.* (2015) used Decision Support in a Java Application using Data Mining Techniques. The system tries to extract hidden knowledge from the database. After determining the probability and in accordance with the probability, pattern matching algorithms will be used to generate the appropriate treatments.

Ganesan *et al.* (2019) developed an effective cloud and IoT-based disease diagnosis model for monitoring, forecasting, and diagnosing heart disease [24]. The UCI Repository dataset and medical sensors were utilized to create an effective framework for predicting cardiac disease, which was also investigated [17]. Furthermore, classification algorithms are utilized to categorize patient data in order to diagnose cardiovascular disease. The heart disease dataset is used to train the classifier, which is subsequently employed by the classification method to detect the presence or absence of heart disease [15]. The trained classifier will evaluate incoming patient data to determine whether or not the patient has heart disease [27]. Khalid Binsalman *et al.* (2018) had used some in healthcare systems, sensor technologies can be beneficial. It is especially beneficial to patients with chronic cardiac disease since it allows for early intervention, which helps to save lives and cut the risk of death in half [20]. Especially if these technologies are used in patient-monitoring systems through the internet. As a result, using sensor technologies, this research presented a useful remote monitoring system for heart disease patients [20].

With rising research in the fields of Internet of Things and machine learning, as well as the growing desire for intelligent and data-driven healthcare ecosystems, Bhat *et al.* (2020) have presented an automatic and real-time medical diagnosis and prediction. The suggested strategy in this research seeks to allay these worries. The interactive, user-friendly environment that combines real-time ECG detection and diagnosis as well as a simple mobile application benefits patients undergoing diagnosis. However, accuracy is the key component of a medical application. A system that is impervious to error overall is produced by deep learning models that can correctly and automatically learn the required characteristics [5].

V Tamilselvi et al. (2020) proposed a system that may be utilized to constantly, efficiently, and remotely monitor a patient's temperature and heart rate. The doctor may remotely monitor the patient's health from anywhere in the globe and provide consultation based on the results, eliminating the need for the patient to visit the hospital's O.P.D. (Outpatient Department). Temperature and heart rate thresholds have been specified. The BLYNK app, which we utilized, sends a notice to the phone whenever one or both of the readings exceed the threshold. In addition, the suggested system is cost efficient due to the low cost of the components employed. It's small in size, light in weight, and convenient to transport with the patient wherever they go. The suggested approach is a logical and acceptable method of providing appropriate help to cardiac patients.[29] developed a system that employs Edge-Fog-Cloud computing to provide a novel smart healthcare paradigm. Data for this proposed model was collected from a number of hardware sensors. To extract cardiac properties from signals, peak amplitude, total harmonic distortion, heart rate, zero crossing rate, entropy, standard deviation, and energy were used. The characteristics of other attributes were obtained in the same manner, by finding their "minimum and maximum mean, standard deviation, kurtosis, and skewness." By improving essential CNN parameters with the CCNN with GSO algorithm [2,] all of these qualities were introduced to the diagnostic system. By improving essential CNN parameters with the CCNN with GSO algorithm[2,] all of these qualities were introduced to the diagnostic system. PSO-CCNN, GWO-CCNN, WOA-CCNN, and DHOA-CCNN were 3.7 percent, 3.7 percent, 3.6 percent, 7.6 percent, 67.9 percent, 48.4 percent, 33 percent, 10.9 percent, and 7.6 percent more precise than PSO-CCNN, GWO-CCNN, WOA-CCNN, and DHOA-CCNN, respectively. As a result, the smart healthcare paradigm with IoT-assisted fog To improve the prediction system's accuracy in detecting cardiac illness, the current model could be enhanced in the future by incorporating more advanced feature selection methods, optimization approaches, and classification algorithms [2].

15.3   Proposed system

Figure 15.3 represents the block diagram of our proposed system.

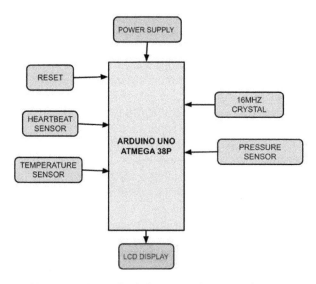

Figure 15.3   Block diagram of proposed system

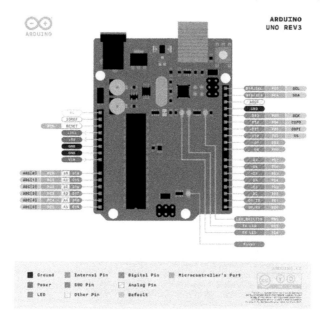

Figure 15.4   Arduino UNO

15.3.1 Arduino UNO

The Arduino UNO [43] uses the ATmega328P microcontroller illustrated in Figure 15.3. In comparison to other boards, such as the Arduino Mega, it is simple to use. The board consists of digital and analog input/output (I/O) pins, shields, and other circuitry [4]. The Arduino UNO contains six analog input pins, fourteen digital pins, a USB connection, a power jack, and an ICSP (In-Circuit Serial Programming) header. It's written in the IDE programming language (Integrated Development Environment). It is applicable both online and offline [30]. The block diagram of our suggested system is shown in Figure 15.4. The hardware requirements are stated below.

The major components of Arduino UNO board are as follows:

- USB connector
- power port
- microcontroller
- analog input pins
- digital pins
- reset switch
- crystal oscillator
- USB interface chip
- TX RX LEDs

Figure 15.5   Heartbeat sensor

15.3.2   Heartbeat sensor

The sound of a person's heartbeat is formed by the contraction or expansion of the valves in his or her heart as they force blood from one area to another. The rate of the heartbeat is measured in beats per minute (BPM), and the pulse is the heartbeat sensed in any artery adjacent to the skin [1].

The heartbeat sensor shown in Figure 15.5 is powered by the photoplethysmography principle. It detects changes in blood volume traveling through any organ of the body, resulting in a change in the intensity of light passing through that organ (vascular region) [1]. In applications that measure heart pulse rate, pulse timing is very crucial. The amount of blood that flows is determined by the rate of heartbeats and blood absorption.

A basic heartbeat sensor consists of a light-emitting diode and a detector, such as a light-detecting resistor or a photodiode. As a result of the heartbeat pulses, the flow of blood to various parts of the body varies [10]. When a light source, such as a led, illuminates tissue, the light either reflects (as in finger tissue) or transmits (as in eye tissue) (earlobe). Some of the light is absorbed by the blood, and the light detector detects the transmitted or reflected light [16]. The blood volume of the tissue determines the amount of light absorbed [16]. The detector produces an electrical signal proportional to the heartbeat rate [34].

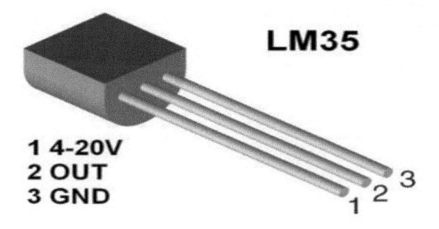

Figure 15.6   Temperature sensor

15.3.3   Temperature sensor

The LM35 series, as illustrated in (Figure 15.6), are precision integrated-circuit temperature devices with a linearly proportional output voltage to temperature in degrees Celsius [10]. Unlike linear temperature sensors calibrated in Kelvin, the LM35 temperature sensor has the advantage of not requiring a sizable constant voltage to be subtracted from the output in order to provide appropriate Centigrade scaling [46].

15.3.4   Pressure sensor

Figure 15.7 shows how a constant-area sensing device in pressure transducers responds to the force generated by fluid pressure. The applied force will cause the diaphragm of the pressure transducer to deflect. The internal diaphragm deflection is detected and transformed into an electrical output [18]. Microprocessors, programmable controllers, computers, and other electronic equipment can therefore monitor pressure [14].

15.3.5 Liquid crystal display (LCD) display (16 × 2)

As shown in Figure 15.8 an LCD 16*2 is a sort of electronic display device that shows data and messages. It shows 32 characters (16*2=32), each made up of 588 (40) Pixel Dots. It has 16 columns and 2 rows, as the name says. As a result, rather than 1,280 [3] the total number of pixels in this LCD is 32 ×40.

The proposed method detects a heart attack by monitoring the heartbeat through the object's internet connection. A heartbeat sensor [30], a Wi-Fi module, and an Arduino board are used in our solution [51]. The heartbeat sensor will begin to detect heartbeat readings after the programme is set, and the human heartbeat will be displayed on the LCD screen [49]. A Wi-Fi module can also be used to

Figure 15.7   Pressure sensor

Figure 15.8   LCD display

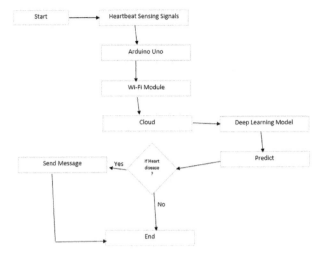

Figure 15.9   Flow diagram

communicate data over the Internet [31]. The device can help determine a person's health by measuring their heart rate and comparing it to a set point [32]. After these constraints are set, the system will begin monitoring the patient's heart rate, and if the heart rate goes over or below the stated limit, the system will alert the user. For this work, we're using an Android app model that will measure a patient's heart rate, monitor it, and deliver an urgent message about the risk of a heart attack [33]. We utilize Deep Learning architecture since it is an artificial neural network (ANN) that allows us to manage the stream by combining Inputs according to trained Weights. As a result, I'm calling for more adaptability in controlling outputs [34]. Using Pre-historic data from the heart disease prediction database and simple ANN, we would create a Deep Learning model. When new data is added to the database, the model should try and predict cardiac disease, update the database, and notify the physician [35].

Figure 15.9 presents the circuit diagram of the proposed system [36].

As shown in (Figure 15.10), the proposed network uses an arduino and the sensors which we use are temperature (LM05), heartbeat, and pressure (MPX4115) sensors [37]. It also has a com port and a terminal connected so by which help us to detect and use the output from the sensors, The Deep learning model is trained with an accuracy of 86.18%, the data which we acquire from the sensors and fed into the Deep learning model and results in an acquired respectively. They also tried training with some machine learning algorithms which we witness an accuracy of 74.3% for both naïve Bayes and logistic regression [38]. Our system works in real-time and the number of sensors deployed is comparatively less, so the accuracy can be increased by adding more sensors and increasing the volume of trained data used to train our model [39].

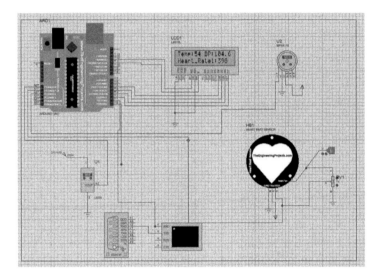

Figure 15.10   Circuit diagram

15.4   Advantages of proposed system

- The accuracy of the system is high.
- The system also tries to detect all the health anomalies of the user.
- The system does not detect heart rates alone but also BP of the victim using pulse rate and body.

15.5   Limitations of proposed system

- Network failure may lead to failure of alerting systems.
- The system uses Bluetooth and the power consumption will be a bit high.
- Power consumption and performance of the system is still unknown.
- The volume of data taken to train is relatively less.

15.6   Results and discussion

The final output of the model is displayed under two separate sections as the sensing section and the predicting section. The results of heart rate, and temperature are displayed in LCD 16*2 displays as shown Figure 15.11.

The results of predicting section are shown in Figure 15.12. If the model detects chance of heart disease based on the sensing results, it prints "chance of Heart Disease," else it prints "Normally Functioning Chance of Heart Disease if Less."

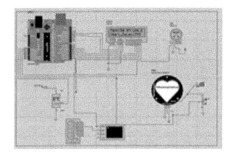

Figure 15.11   Sensing results

15.7   Conclusion

This paper provides a comprehensive study on heart disease diagnosis using a person's heartbeat in the proposed system, the sensor [40] detects heartbeat signals and sends them to the Arduino UNO. The Arduino [41], in conjunction with the WiFi module, sends those signals to the cloud, where they are analyzed and predicted using a deep learning model. The Android application [42] receives an appropriate notification. Because we use artificial neural networks to predict the results, the accuracy is higher. Even though we have improved the accuracy of the predicted results, the network has some flaws. The system functions by sending a heartbeat to a Wi-Fi module linked to a microcontroller [43]. We limited the system's ability to measure heartbeats. In the future we can store all the data in Edge devices and perform further analytics and add the SMS and e-mail module to notify the patients and doctors through our system [44].

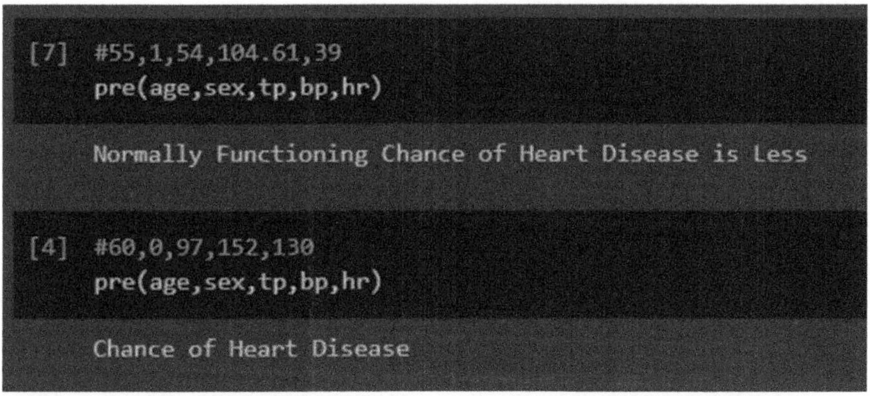

```
[7]  #55,1,54,104.61,39
     pre(age,sex,tp,bp,hr)

     Normally Functioning Chance of Heart Disease is Less


[4]  #60,0,97,152,130
     pre(age,sex,tp,bp,hr)

     Chance of Heart Disease
```

Figure 15.12   Predicting results

References

[1]   Kumar S., Ranjan P., Ramaswami R., Tripathy M.R. 'Resource efficient clustering and next hop knowledge based routing in multiple heterogeneous wireless sensor networks'. *International Journal of Grid and High Performance Computing*. 2017, vol. 9(2), pp. 1–20.

[2]   Sudhakaran S., Kumar S., Ranjan P., *et al.* 'Blockchain-based transparent and secure decentralized algorithm'. *International Conference on Intelligent Computing and Smart Communication 2019. Algorithms for Intelligent Systems*. Springer; 2020.

[3]   Sarangi L., Mohanty M.N., Pattnaik S., Shubham M. 'An intelligent decision support system for cardiac disease detection'. *International Journal Of Control Theory And Applications, International Science Press*. 2015, vol. 8(5), pp. 2137–43.

[4]   Gowrishankar S., Prachita M.Y., Prakash A. "IoT based heart attack detection, heart rate and temperature monitor, international journal of computer applications, (0975 – 8887), volume 170(5)'.2017.

[5]   Aboobacker A., Balamurugan D.S. 'Heartbeat sensing and heart attack detection using internet of things: iot'. *International Journal of Engineering Science and Computing, 6662-6666, Volume 7 Issue No.4, April 2017*. 2017.

[6]   Manisha M., Sindhura V., Ramaya P., Neeraja K. 'IoT on heart attack detection and heart rate monitoring'. *International Journal of Innovation in Engineering and Technology*. 2016, vol. 196.

[7]   Ramesh K., Rao M.C., Subbalakshmi G 'Decision support in heart disease prediction system using naive bayes'. *Indian Journal of Computer Science and Engineering (0976-5166)*. 2020, vol. 2(2), pp. 170–76.

[8]   Patel S Shivam, Chauhan Y 'Heart attack detection and medical attention using motion sensing device- kinect'. *International Journal of Scientific and Research Publication (2250-3153)*. 2019, vol. 4.

[9]   Ashrafuzzaman M.: 'Heart attack detection using smart phone'. *International Journal of Technology Enhancements and Emerging Engineering Research 1*. 2020, pp. 23–27.

[10] Jin B., Che C., Liu Z., Zhang S., Yin X., Wei A.X. 'Predicting the risk of heart failure with EHR sequential data modeling'. *IEEE ACCESS: Practical Innovations, Open Solution, PP. 1-1, 0.1109/ACCESS.2017.2789324.*. 2018.

[11] Javeed A., Zhou S., Yongjian L, *et al.* 'An intelligent learning system based on random search algorithm and optimized random forest model for improved heart disease detection'. *IEEE ACCESS: Practical Innovations, Open Solutions, Vol. 7, Pp. 180235-180243, 2019, Doi: 10.1109/ACCESS.2019.2952107*. 2019.

[12] Sarangi L., Mohanty M.N., Pattnaik S.: 'An intelligent decision support system for cardiac disease detection'. *International Journal of Control Theory and Applications*. 2019, vol. 8(5), pp. 2137–43.

[13] Mamatha Alex P., Shaji S.P. 'Prediction and diagnosis of heart disease patients using data mining technique'. *2019 International Conference on Communication and Signal Processing (ICCSP), Publisher: IEEE, 2019, pp. 0848-0852, doi: 10.1109/ICCSP.2019.8697977*; 2019.

[14] Bahrami B., Shirvani M.H. 'Prediction and diagnosis of heart disease by data mining techniques'. *Journal of Multidisciplinary Engineering Science and Technology (JMEST)*. 2020, vol. 2(2),(3159-0040).

[15] Bhuvaneswari R., Kalaiselvi K. 'Naïve Bayesian classification approach in healthcare applications'. *International Journal of Computer Science and Telecommunication*. 2018, vol. 3(1), pp. 106–12.

[16] Chandra D.P., Deekshatulu B.L., Jabbar M.A 'Cluster based association rule mining for heart attack prediction'. *Journal of Theoretical and Applied Information Technology, 196-201, (1992-8645)*. 2019, vol. 32(2).

[17] Arabasadi Z., Alizadehsani R., Roshanzamir M. 'Computer aided decision making for heart disease detection using hybrid neural network-genetic algorithm'. *Computer methods and programs in biomedicine*. 2017, vol. 141, pp. 19–26.

[18] Amebekar S., Plalnikar R. 'Disease risk prediction by using convolution neural networks'. *IEEE, 2018 Fourth International Conference on Computing Communication Control and Automation (ICCUBEA), 2018, Pp. 1-5, Doi: 10.1109/ICCUBEA.2018.8697423*. 2018.

[19] Ana R., Krishna S. 'IoT based patient monitoring and diagnostic prediction tool using ensemble classifier'. *IEEE, 2017 International Conference on Advances in Computing, Communications and Informatics (ICACCI), 2017, Pp. 1588-1593, Doi: 10.1109/ICACCI.2017.8126068*. 2017.

[20] Gupta A., Yadav S., Shahid S. 'HeartCare: iot based heart disease prediction system'. Presented at 2019 International Conference on Information Technology (ICIT), 88-93, 2019;

[21] Qhe, Maag: 'Heart disease monitoring and predicting by using machine learning based on iot technology'. *UTC from IEEE Xplore*. May 28, 2021.

[22] Shaikh S., Sawant A., Paradkar S., Patil K Electronic recording system-heart disease prediction system *2015 International Conference on Technologies for Sustainable Development (ICTSD*; Mumbai, India, 2015.

[23] M.G 'IoT based heart disease prediction and diagnosis model for healthcare using machine learning models'. *IEEE, 2019 IEEE International Conference on System, Computation, Automation and Networking (ICSCAN), 2019, Pp. 1-5, Doi: 10.1109/ICSCAN.2019.8878850*. 2019.

[24] BinSalman K., Fayoumi A. 'Effective remote monitoring system for heart disease patients'. *2018 IEEE 20th Conference on Business Informatics*; Vienna, Austria; 2018.

[25] Bhat T., Akanksha, Shrikara, Bhat S., T M A real-time iot based arrhythmia classifier using convolutional neural networks *2020 IEEE International Conference on Distributed Computing, VLSI, Electrical Circuits and Robotics (DISCOVER*; Udupi, India, 2020. https://ieeexplore.ieee.org/xpl/mostRecentIssue.jsp?punumber=9278009

[26] Baad P.A. 'IOT based health monitoring system using Arduino'. *Journal of Engineering, Computing and Architecture*. 2020, vol. 10(5).

[27] Raju K.B., Dara S., Vidyarthi A., Gupta V.M., Khan B Smart heart disease prediction system with iot and FOG computing sectors enabled by cascaded deep learning model'.*Computational Intelligence and Neuroscience*. 2022, vol. 2022(5), 1070697.

[28] Kumar S. *Evolution of Software-Defined Networking Foundations for IoT and 5G Mobile Networks*. IGI Publisher; 2020. p. 350.

[29] Kumar S., Ranjan P., Radhakrishnan R., Tripathy M.R. 'Energy efficient multichannel MAC protocol for high traffic applications in heterogeneous wireless sensor networks'. *Recent Advances in Electrical & Electronic Engineering*. 2017, vol. 10(3), pp. 223–32.

[30] Reghu S., Kumar S. 'Development of robust infrastructure in networking to survive a disaster'. *2019 4th International Conference on Information Systems and Computer Networks, ISCON 2019*; Mathura, India; 2019. pp. 250–5.

[31] Kumar S., Cengiz K., Vimal S., Suresh A. 'Energy efficient resource migration based load balance mechanism for high traffic applications iot'. *Wireless Personal Communications*. 2021, vol. 10(3), pp. 1–19.

[32] Kumar S., Cengiz K., Trivedi C.M., *et al.* 'DEMO enterprise ontology with a stochastic approach based on partially observable Markov model for data aggregation and communication in intelligent sensor networks'. *Wireless Personal Communication*. 2022.

[33] Punhani A., Faujdar N., Kumar S. 'Design and evaluation of cubic Torus Network-on-Chip architecture'. *International Journal of Innovative Technology and Exploring Engineering (IJITEE)*. 2019, vol. 8(6), pp. 2278–3075.

[34] Dubey G., Kumar S., Kumar S., Navaney P. 'Extended opinion lexicon and ML-based sentiment analysis of tweets: a novel approach towards accurate classifier'. *International Journal of Computational Vision and Robotics*. 2020, vol. 10(6), pp. 505–21.

[35] Singh P., Bansal A., Kamal A.E., Kumar S. 'Road surface quality monitoring using machine learning algorithm' in Reddy A.N.R., Marla D., Favorskaya M.N., Satapathy S.C. (eds.). *Intelligent Manufacturing and Energy Sustainability. Smart Innovation, Systems and Technologies*. 265. Singapore: Springer; 2022.

[36] Kumar S., Ranjan P., Radhakrishnan R., Tripathy M.R. 'Energy aware distributed protocol for heterogeneous wireless sensor network'. *International Journal of Control and Automation*. 2015, vol. 8(10), pp. 421–30.

[37] Kumar S., Ranjan P., Ramaswami R., Tripathy M.R. 'EMEEDP: enhanced multi-hop energy efficient distributed protocol for heterogeneous wireless sensor network'. *Proceedings - 2015 5th International Conference on Communication Systems and Network Technologies CSNT*; Gwalior, India; 2015. pp. 194–200.

[38] Kumar S., Ranjan P., Ramaswami R. 'Energy optimization in distributed localized wireless sensor networks'. *Proceedings of the International Conference on Issues and Challenges Intelligent Computing Technique (ICICT)*; Ghaziabad, India; 2014.

[39] Chauhan R., Kumar S. 'Packet loss prediction using artificial intelligence unified with big data analytics, Internet of things and cloud computing technologies'. *5th International Conference on Information Systems and Computer Networks (ISCON)*; Mathura, India; 2021. pp. 01–6.

[40] Kumar S., Ranjan P., Ramaswami R., Tripathy M.R. 'A utility maximization approach to MAC layer channel access and forwarding'. *Progress in Electromagnetics Research Symposium*. 2015, vol. 2015, pp. 2363–7.

[41] Kumar S., Ranjan P., Ramaswami R., Tripathy M.R. 'An NS3 implementation of physical layer based on 802.11 for utility maximization of WSN'. *Proceedings - 2015 International Conference on Computational Intelligence and Communication Networks, CICN 2015*; Jabalpur, India; 2016. pp. 79–84.

[42] Sharma A., Awasthi Y., Kumar S. 'The role of Blockchain, AI and IoT for smart road traffic management system'. *Proceedings - 2020 IEEE India Council International Subsections Conference, INDISCON 2020*; Visakhapatnam, India; 2020. pp. 289–96.

[43] Singh P., Bansal A., Kumar S. 'Performance analysis of various information platforms for recognizing the quality of Indian roads'. *Proceedings of the Confluence 2020 - 10th International Conference on Cloud Computing, Data Science and Engineering*; Noida, India; 2020. pp. 63–76.

[44] Kumar S., Ranjan P., Singh P., Tripathy M.R. 'Design and implementation of fault tolerance technique for Internet of things (IoT)'. *Proceedings - 2020 12th International Conference on Computational Intelligence and Communication Networks, CICN 2020*; Bhimtal, India; 2020. pp. 154–9.

Chapter 16

DIAIF: Detection of Interest Flooding using Artificial Intelligence-based Framework in NDN android

P Vimala Rani, Rajkumar[1], Narshimha Malika Arjunan[1], and S Mercy Shalinie[1]

In today's world, information-centric networking (ICN) is a brand-new next-generation network for distributing multimedia content. ICN focuses on sharing content across the network rather than obtaining content from a single fixed server [1]. In-network caching aids in the dissemination of content from the network, and the ICN also includes a number of intrusive security mechanisms. Despite the ICN network's many security measures, several attacks, especially interest flooding attacks (IFA), continue to wreak havoc on the network's distribution capability. In order to address security threats, the literature includes a number of mitigating procedures. However, legitimate users' requests are misclassified as an attack in an emergency circumstance, affecting the network's QoS [2]. In this chapter, Detection of Interest Flooding Attack using Artificial Intelligence Framework (DIAIF) is proposed in ICN. DIAIF seeks to lighten the load on ICN routers by removing the source of the attack without interfering with legitimate user requests. DIAIF depends on router feedback to assign a beneficial value (BV) to each piece of content and to block dangerous users based on the BV. The ICN testbed was designed to assess the proposed DIAIF's performance in terms of QoS during severe flood scenarios, responding with malicious content without interfering with genuine user requests, and identifying the source of attack in a communication scenario.

16.1 Introduction

The distributed denial-of-service (DDoS) is a risky attack that can severely decrease network performance by up to 99 per cent. This attack infected the network with a script named Trin00, which caused the machines to crash severely, and it began on July 22, 1999 [3]. Despite the fact that two decades have passed, Internet security specialists continue to face significant challenges. According to a Kaspersky survey,

[1]Department of Computer Science and Engineering, Thiagarajar College of Engineering, Madurai, India

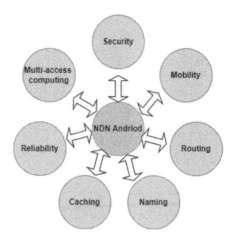

Figure 16.1   Benefits of ICN on application

DDoS attacks have climbed by up to 18 per cent from the year 2021 to today [4]. Similarly, in 2016, Mirai, a botnet that targets 200–300 Internet of Things (IoT) devices and also diverts Domain name system (DNS), creating massive distribution in content distribution, was discovered. GitHub was hit by the greatest enormous attack ever, with 1.3 terabits of bandwidth exploding and bringing the network to its knees. This is due to transmission control protocol (TCP)/ Internet protocols (IP's) lack of built-in security, which causes more collateral harm to the Internet architecture. Many clean slate architectures have been proposed to defend the network against attackers and inefficiency in providing security of today's Internet architecture of TCP/IP, with the information-centric network being the most nominated by the Internet security community in recent years. ICN has built-in features that help you communicate with multimedia content flawlessly. Content store (CS), pending interest table (PIT), and forwarding information base (FIB) are some of the functionalities available. ICN is concentrating on content security rather than end-host security. This built-in security enhancement reduces the danger of security flaws that come with the traditional TCP/IP approach. The in-built components of ICN that make the content distribution process easier are shown in Figure 16.1. Several security solutions for IFA have been identified in the literature [5, 6]. The named data networking (NDN) simulations were used to implement the majority of the security identification and solutions. When attacks are developed in real-time scenarios, however, the simulation results will not adapt. As a result, we propose the ICN testbed in conjunction with NDN functions in order to detect real-time threats using artificial intelligence techniques.

16.2   Background

In this section, the ICN communication model and its components are described in Section 16.2.1, and attack scenario is described in Section 16.2.2.

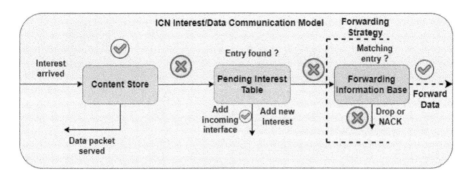

Figure 16.2   ICN interest forwarding process

16.2.1   *ICN communication model*

ICN's material is distributed efficiently using two types of packets: interest and data packets. Each router is made up of three parts: CS, PIT, and FIB. When the router receives the interest packet from the consumers, it first checks the content from CS. If not, it looks up the entry in PIT. If an entry is accessible, it is forwarded to FIB; otherwise, it is added to PIT as a new entry. FIB is in-charge of finding content from the nearest router with choosing multiple next-hop entries. If content is detected on the downstream node, the packet is sent to the user using the PIT entry. Because PIT contains a name for the interface and a user interest packet. Meanwhile, the data packet is saved in CS only if the PIT entry for the same interest packet has more entries. If matching or next-hop address is not found for the interest packet, the router returns the negative acknowledgement (NACK) to consumers. Figure 16.2 shows the ICN interest forwarding model.

16.2.2   *Generating IFA in NDN android*

The IFA is caused by malevolent users who deliberately overload the network with content. The example of IFA in NDN android is shown in Figure 16.3. When a router is overburdened, genuine users' packets are dropped. When the router's PIT is occupied by IFA, the PIT's storage capacity is depleted, and legitimate users' packets are not stored in the PI [7]. Malicious users, on the other side, employ ICN routers to damage the performance of data producers. ICN components are the umbrella under which NDN android operates. The emergency user requests are dropped when IFA is generated in the NDN android service, resulting in a No Route or NACK acknowledgment. With false interest packets, a malicious user sends interest with nonexistent content (now unavailable in the network). PIT will be filled as a result of this fake interest packet, and this packet will remain for a longer time until PIT identifies the relevant data packet [8].

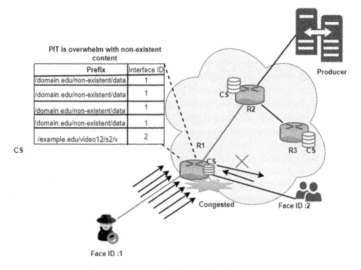

Prefix	Interface ID
/domain.edu/non-existent/data	1
/domain.edu/non-existent/data	1
/domain.edu/non-existent/data	1
/domain.edu/non-existent/data	1
/example.edu/video12/s2/v	2

Figure 16.3   IFA on NDN android

16.3   Proposed methodology: RD Iterative Adaptive Inverse Filtering (RD-IAIF)

In this section, Real-time Detection of Interest Flooding Attack using Artificial Intelligence Framework for NDN multimedia application is presented. RD-IAIF is capable of identifying a number of attack possibilities in NDN, despite the fact that IFA is managing the network by sending significant amounts of interest, which led to the inclusion of the IFA in this study. The IFA generation is mentioned in Section 16.2.2. Before detecting the IFA, the data are collected from the NDN android during the time of attack. The parameters are helpful in the identification of attack that is described as follows:

Packet count: It refers that the count of the same interest packet is received from the total number of content that is received during the time t.

$$\zeta(I) = \frac{\Sigma_{k=1}^{j} n(I_k)}{\Sigma_{r=1}^{j} n(I_r)} \tag{16.1}$$

where $n(I_k)$ is defined as the sum of the number of particular requests for I. $n(I_r)$ is defined as a count of requests that is received by the router.

Variance of packet count: It is the measurement of comparing the relative packet count influence the content distribution of ICN.

$$S^2(I) = \frac{\sum_{k=1}^{N} (I_k - \bar{I})}{N - 1} \tag{16.2}$$

where $\bar{I}$ defines the mean of same interest packet $\bar{I} = \frac{1}{n}\sum_{k=1}^{N} I_k$.

Standard deviation of inter-arrival interest packet: It is the measurement of how inter-arrival of the same interest packet is deviated from the mean.

$$\sigma(I_k) = \sqrt{\frac{1}{N} \sum_{k=1}^{N} (I_k - \bar{I})} \tag{16.3}$$

EWMA: EWMA stands for exponential weighted moving average. It finds the likelihood ratio of same content request in ICN. It is useful to find how the particular content being overruled in time window t. It adds the weight to a content and weight on the past content objects is decreased exponentially. It increases the ratio of a recent data by rejecting the older one. The weigh factor is assigned between 0 and 1.

$$C(t) = \alpha.y(t) + (1 - \alpha) * C(t - 1) \tag{16.4}$$

Satisfaction ratio (γ): It is the ratio of satisfied interest packet from the total packet that is received by the router. During the time of IFA, the satisfaction ratio will be reduced.

$$\Upsilon(r_l^j, t_i) = \sum_{k=0}^{n} \frac{N_{D_k}(t)}{N_{I_k}(t)} \tag{16.5}$$

where N_{D_k} and N_{I_k} are number of data and interest packets belong to j^{th} interface of router (r_l^j) with respect to time (t).

PIT utilization (γ): PIT entries are calculated at each time cycle (t).

$$\rho(r_l, t_i) = \frac{\sum_{k=0}^{n} N_{entries_k}(t)}{N_{size}} \tag{16.6}$$

16.3.1 Attack detection

The Multi Feature(MF)-based Adaptive Neuro-Fuzzy Inference System (ANFIS)-is a attack detection technique on NDN android. The Takagi–Sugeno system is used to model the proposed multi function adaptive neuro-fuzzy inference system (MF-ANFIS), where input is traveled through the multiple layers and output is linear combination weighted average. Figure 16.4 shows the proposed MF-ANFIS model. The sample of Takagi–Sugeno system with two rule set is as follows:

$$\textit{If } x \textit{ is } A_1 \textit{ and } y \textit{ is } B_1 \textit{ then } f_1 = p_1 x + q_1 y + r_1 \tag{16.7}$$
$$\textit{If } x \textit{ is } A_2 \textit{ and } y \textit{ is } B_2 \textit{ then } f_2 = p_2 x + q_2 y + r_2 \tag{16.8}$$

where A_i, B_i are the fuzzy set and p_i, q_i, r_i are the linearly independent output variables. ANFIS contains five layers to process the input to output and nine if-then rules as follows:

Layer 1: All the square input nodes are obtained by the parameters from the whole data stream. The membership function to input node is given in the following equation:

$$O_{1,i} = \mu_{A_i}(x), \ i \in 1, 2, 3; \ O_{1,i} = \mu_{B_{i-3}}(y), \ i \in 1, 2, 3 \tag{16.9}$$

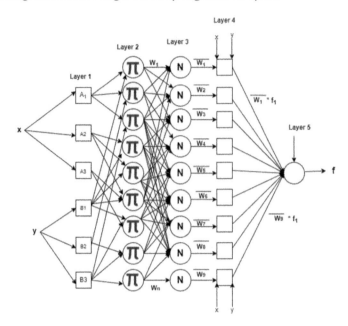

Figure 16.4   List nearest FaceID

Layer 2: In this layer, every node is fixed and it multiplied the product of the input to obtain the output values.

$$O_{2,i} = w_i = \mu_{Ai}(x) * \mu_{Bi-3}(y), \ i \in 1, 2, 3...9 \qquad (16.10)$$

Layer 3: Every node in this layer is considered to be fixed and it does the normalization function.

$$O_{3,i} = \overline{w}_i = \frac{w_i}{w_1 + w_2 + w_3 + ... w_9}, \ i \in 1, 2, 3...9 \qquad (16.11)$$

Layer 4: All square nodes are adaptive. The output of this node is considered to be normalized values.

$$O_{4,i} = \overline{w}_i f_i = w_i.(p_i x + q_i y + r_i), \ i \in 1, 2, 3...9 \qquad (16.12)$$

Layer 5: It sums all incoming single and produces the proper output. All square nodes are adaptive. The output of this node is considered to be normalized values.

$$O_{5,i} = f = \sum_i \overline{w}_i f_i = \frac{\sum_i w_i f_i}{\sum_i}, \ i \in 1, 2, 3...9. \qquad (16.13)$$

16.4   Real-time deployment on emergency applications

The NDN Forwarding Daemon (NFD) is a key component of ICN's content distribution and update provisioning. NFD supports a variety of platforms, including Linux, FreeBSD, Mac OSX, Android, and Raspberry Pi and allows named data communication instead of IP transmission [9]. To facilitate interest/data communication, NFD offers a variety of management protocols. PIT and FIB face lists, as well as removal entries from PIT, CS, and FIB, are all included in the NFD structures. When the router PIT is full, it allows each router to share the notice as "NACK." NFD supports a number of routing protocols that should help with IP over NDN migration.

16.4.1   Communication establishment through NFD

Figure 16.5 shows the usage of NDN android on various enterprises in real-time. In NDN applications, each producer delivers a data packet to the routers with a name prefix. As a result, if the data packet's name prefix is frequently requested, each router keeps it in CS. On the other hand, if customers request the same name prefix, it is immediately shared with them. The NDN forwarders can provide you with the data packet. The following methods can be used to create NDN data packets: Consumer router configuration, prefix announcements,

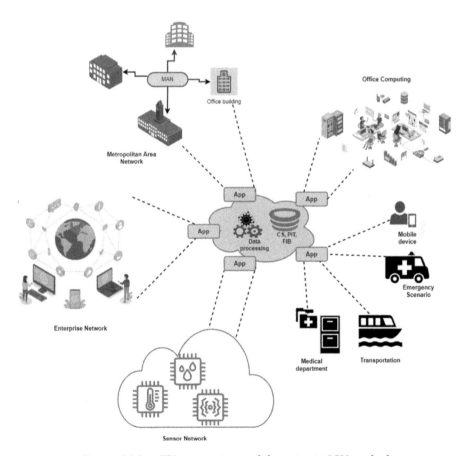

Figure 16.5   IFA generation and detection in ICN testbed

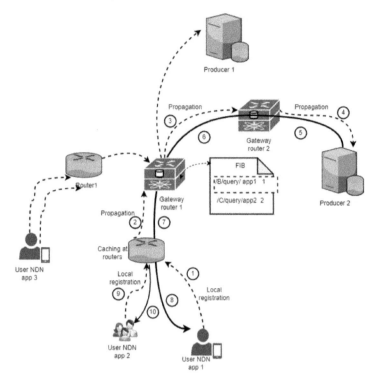

Figure 16.6   IFA generation and detection in ICN testbed

and data discovery tactics are all done manually. The NFD approach with cache for the NDN application is shown in Figure 16.6. The router caches the content when two users request the same prefix name, as shown in step 9 of Figure 16.6. The user of the NDN app can request any type of data to be forwarded to the nearest network. If the content is not available on the local router, it is automatically forwarded to the producer via the gateway router. The FIB is updated for each and every transaction. The local face and name prefix of user app1 are first registered with the local NFD router. Users' names and interfaces are then saved in the local NFD. As a result, the content itself, rather than the location information, is routed to the gateway router. In this method, NDN achieves name-based routing rather than location-based routing.

16.4.2   NDN application on android

The NDN application on android is feasible solution for emergency situations. NFD source code is archived from the GitHub to enable all packages and faces. The NFD allows user to create a face, modify, and delete whenever they want. The NFD syntax for creating face are listed below:

Face creation

Figure 16.7   List nearest FaceID

- nfdc face create[*remote*] < *FACEURI* > [[*persistency*] < *PERSISTENCY* >] [*local* < *FACEURI* >]
- nfdc face create remote udp://education.example.com

Face creation with remote URI

- nfdc face create[*remote*] < *FACEURI* > [[*persistency*] < *PERSISTENCY* >] [*local* < *FACEURI* >]
- nfdc face create remote ether://[07:00:13:02:02:02] local dev://eth4 persistency permanent

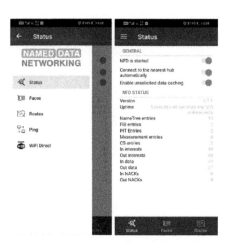

Figure 16.8   User interface on NFD app

Figure 16.9   User chat on NFD app

Congestion-threshold: It creates a face with a congestion marker. [*congestion –*]*marking – interval – INTERVAL >*]

nfdc face create remote udp://education.example.com congestion-marking-interval 100 default-congestion-threshold 65,536

Remove face

It allows the user to remove the face.

nfdc face destroy [*face*]< *FACID|FACEURI* >

nfdc face destroy 300

NFD route list: The route list contains nexthop address and prefix name in FIB. The commands are as follows:

Route list

* nfdc route[*list*[[*nexthop*]< *FACID|FACEURI* >][*origin < ORIGIN >*]]
* nfdc route list nexthop 421

Add route list

* nfdc route add [*prefix*] < *PREFIX* > [*nexthop*] < *FACID|FACEURI*> [*origin < ORIGIN >*]
* nfdc route show prefix /localhost/nfd

Add new route list

Figure 16.10   IFA on NFD app

- nfdc route add [*prefix*] < *PREFIX* > [*nexthop*]< *FACEID|FACEURI* > [*origin* < *ORIGIN* >]
- nfdc route add prefix / nexthop udp://router.example.net

Remove route list

- nfdc route remove [*prefix*]< *PREFIX*> [*nexthop*] < *FACID|FACEURI* > [*origin* < *ORIGIN*>]
- nfdc route remove prefix /ndn nexthop 421 origin static

NFD face is created with nexthop and remote URI for request and response of packets. Figure 16.7 shows the face ID of NDN remote URI. Figure 16.8 shows the updated NDN components after creating the face ID and route list.

We put NFD to the test on two android devices with different compatible models and configurations. NFD tools are also used to configure the producer device. When the gateway router does not have the packet in cache for each test, it sends the request to the producer. When name-based routing is used in the network, the CPU

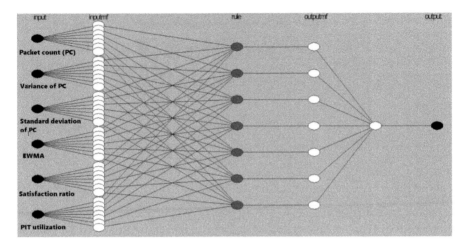

Figure 16.11   User chat on NFD app

use is lowered. Each customer request originates from a 100 MB android handset. The test is run on two android phones: a Samsung phone with 4.0 GB RAM and a Hisilicon Kirin 710 CPU, and a Motorola phone with a 2.1 GHz quad-core CPU.

16.4.3   Attack detection on NFD android using AI

The NDN users can share their information with each other on android NDN. Figure 16.9 shows the sample chat model in NDN.

The transparent content dissemination strategy leads to DDoS attack on NDN application. This DDoS attack on NDN platform is considered to be IFA. . It is partially different from the TCP/IP DDoS attack. Once the IFA is generated from the third party, the content dissemination of NDN platform is disturbed and it leads to "No Route" and NACK notification issues [10]. Figure 16.10 shows the IFA is generated on android NDN. The attacker sends the 1,000/s to ruin the NDN application running process in the communication. MF-ANFIS detects the attack in timely manner that helps to design the NDN communication process more secure. It minimizes the training error between the desired output and actual input. The input of MF-ANFIS is derived from Section 16.3. MF-ANFIS is run on the MATLAB® version 2015a.

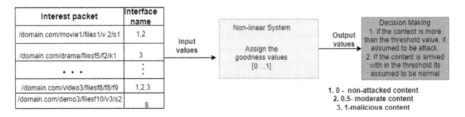

Figure 16.12   User chat on NFD app

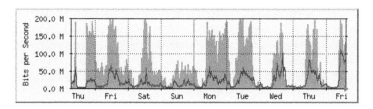

Figure 16.13   CPU consumption on NFD app

The six parameters are given as input to the MF-ANFIS model and it produces one output. Before being fed into the AI model, it must be normalized to [0..1]. In MF-ANFIS gaussmf membership, functions are used to obtain the high accuracy results. The center of gravity functions is used as a defuzzification model. MF-ANFIS uses if-then rules for decision making on android NFD. Figure 16.11 shows the proposed detection model with multiple features. Figure 16.12 shows the MF-ANFIS decision making on NDN android.

During this heavy flooding period, the CPU consumption is considerably high. When a user wants to request or obtain the data from the NDN android, the packets are lost due to the heavy load in the CPU process. With the help of MF-FCM, the CPU load is captured. Figure 16.13 shows the CPU load during the IFA. The "green" line indicates that the traffic has arrived to the network. The "blue" line represents the outbound traffic that is nothing but the router service the packet to the destination.

16.5   Conclusion

In the event of an emergency, the NDN on android provides a far faster response time. The NDN application is vulnerable to a severe attack due to transparent forwarding table updates and name-based routing. During a major flood, the NDN app fails to consider the incoming packet, resulting in significant packet loss in an emergency circumstance. The artificial intelligence-based MF-ANFIS is presented to detect the attack pattern and frequency of the request pattern. MF-ANFIS detects attacks and assists in the discovery of malicious content patterns. As a result, IFA detection is required for real-time applications, and additional research into NDN security challenges pave the path for a healthy and intelligent future.

References

[1]   Antonakakis M., April T., Bailey M., *et al.* 'Understanding the mirai botnet'. *26th USENIX Security Symposium(USENIX Security 17)*; Vancouver, BC; 2017. pp. 1093–110.

[2]   Jose S. 'Global mobile data traffic forecast update, 2016–2021 white paper, index'. *Cisco Visual Networking*. 2017, p. 180.

[3] Dutta N. 'Introduction to Information-Centric Networks. Information Centric Networks (ICN Springer, Cham)'. *Osterweil 2019, 20 years of ddos: a call to action, 2019, arXiv preprint arXiv:1904.02739.* 2021, pp. 1–25.

[4] *Report finds 18% rise in ddos attacks in Q2 2019* . 2019. Available from https://usa.kaspersky.com/about/press-releases/2019_report-finds-18-percent-rise-in-ddos-attacks-in-q2-2019

[5] Khelifi H., Luo S., Nour B. 'Named data networking in vehicular AD hoc networks: state-of-the-art and challenges'. *IEEE Commun Surv. Tutor.* 2019, pp. 320–51.

[6] Nour B., Sharif K., Li F., Wang Y. 'Security and privacy challenges in information-centric wireless Internet of things networks'. *IEEE Secur. Privacy.* 2019, pp. 5–45.

[7] Fang C., Yao H., Wang Z., Wu W., Jin X., Yu F.R. 'A survey of mobile Information-Centric networking: research issues and challenges'. *IEEE Communications Surveys & Tutorials.* 2018, vol. 20(3), pp. 2353–71.

[8] Bouk S.H., Ahmed S.H., Kim D., Park K.-J., Eun Y., Lloret J. 'LAPEL: hop limit based adaptive pit entry lifetime for vehicular named data networks'. *IEEE Transactions on Vehicular Technology.* 2018, vol. 67(7), pp. 5546–57.

[9] Zhang H., Li Y., Zhang Z., Afanasyev A., Zhang L. 'Ndn host model'. *ACM SIGCOMM Computer Communication Review.* 2018, vol. 48(3), pp. 35–41.

[10] Shannigrahi S., Fan C., Partridge C. 'What's in a name? Naming big science data in named data networking'. *Proceedings of the 7th ACM Conference on Information-Centric Networking*; Canada; 2020. pp. 12–22.

Chapter 17

Intelligent and cost-effective mechanism for monitoring road quality using machine learning

Prabhat Singh[1,2], Abhay Bansal[2], Ahmad E Kamal[3], and Sunil Kumar[2]

Nowadays, one of the most significant components of road infrastructure is monitoring road surface conditions, which leads to better driving conditions and reduces the chance of a road accident. Traditional road condition monitoring systems are incapable of gathering real-time information concerning road conditions. In previous generations, road surface condition monitoring was done for fixed roadways and vehicles travelling at a constant pace. Several systems have presented a method for exploiting the sensors installed in automobiles. However, this method will not assist in forecasting the precise placement of potholes, speed bumps, or staggered roads.

As a result, smartphone-based road condition evaluation and navigation are becoming increasingly popular. We propose exploring several machine learning techniques to accurately assess road conditions using accelerometer, gyroscope, and Global Positioning System (GPS) data collected from cellphones. We also recorded footage of the roadways in order to reduce noise in the data. This two-pronged approach to data collection will aid in the exact positioning of potholes, speed bumps, and staggered roads. This method of data collection will aid in the classification of road conditions into numerous features such as roads with smooth surfaces, potholes, speed bumps and staggered highways using machine learning algorithms. machine learning algorithms are used to create characteristics such as smooth roads, potholes, speed breakers, and staggered highways. The user will receive this information via the map, which will classify the various road conditions. Accelerometers and gyroscope sensors will analyze multiple features from all three axes of the sensors in order to produce a more precise location of designated routes. To classify the road conditions, we investigate the performance utilizing support vector machine (SVM), random forest, neural network and deep neural network. As a result, our

[1]ABES Engineering College, Ghaziabad, India
[2]Amity University, Noida, India
[3]IOWA State University, AMES, IA, USA

findings demonstrate that models trained using a dual data gathering strategy will produce more accurate outcomes. Data classification will be substantially more accurate when neural networks, are used. The methods described here can be used on a broader scale to monitor roads for problems that pose a safety concern to commuters and to give maintenance data to appropriate authorities.

17.1 Introduction

Nowadays, roads are the primary resource of infrastructure that provides support for the migration of human beings, goods and logistics, which in turn will develop a strong foundation for social and economic development of a country and inter-connecting city. Apart from this, a sudden increase in volume of vehicles on roads had caused problems such as traffic accidents, traffic jams, and traffic congestion. In the last few years, there had been a sudden rise in the urbanization sector. Due to the increased rates of urbanization, more and more vehicles are being purchased and made available on the road in order to improve the migration of human beings, goods and logistics. As the number of vehicles on the road increases, it in turn will directly increase the traffic congestion, accidents, and pollution.

The Intelligent Traffic and Transportation Management System (TMS) is a better road and traffic management system that integrates data, provides communication and provides access technologies to properly integrate and inform drivers, vehicles and roads in a way that assists people driving the vehicles. TMS's main goal is to use information and communication technology to tackle not only car/bus traffic problems but also economic problems such as ageing, tourism revitalization and long-term economic development of a country.

17.1.1 Definition of TMS

TMS is a new transportation system that uses various new technologies to connect people, roads and vehicles in an information and communication network to solve various traffic and transportation issues such as traffic accidents and congestion. In terms of technology, this is a road or traffic information management system in which road traffic data are gathered and sent to drivers via sensors put along the roadside. The TMS technique provides users with a variety of road traffic applications. The components of TMS are represented in (Figure 17.1).

17.1.2 Issues and challenges faced in TMS

Various issues and challenges are being faced in a road TMS, which are as follows:

1. Shifting of population from rural cities to urban cities:

    In 21st century, the population in urban cities has increased at a very fast rate compared to rural areas. In the year 2019, 56% of the total world

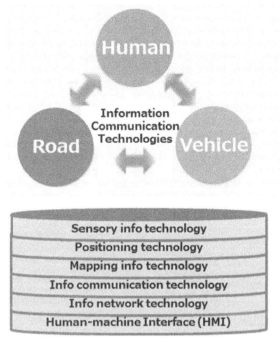

Figure 17.1   Basic components used in TMS

population is living in the urban sector. By the year 2045, UN expects that 76% of the world's entire population will live in cities or the urban sector. Assuming these hypotheses to be correct and the rapid increase in urbanization continues, it is also reasonable to expect that when the count of vehicles increases, other road traffic difficulties occur, such as traffic congestion, traffic accidents and environmental effects. The pictures of traffic congestions in Asian cities are given in (Figure 17.2).

2. Increased population in urban areas needs transportation services:

    As per the rise of population in urban areas, there is a tremendous requirement of transportation facility in terms of road, rail and air. It has been estimated with the rise of passenger traffic by 120–230% by 2045.

3. Increase in demand for transportation service provides sudden increase in CO_2:

    There is an increase in demand for transport in non-OECD countries where passenger traffic is expected to increase by 220–400%. Due to large traffic on roads, CO_2 emissions are expected to increase on the passenger by 30–110%.

Figure 17.2   Examples of traffic congestions in Asian cities

4. Aggravation of traffic safety:

    Traffic safety is one of the major issues nowadays as the requirement and availability of transport are increasing at a very fast rate. Globally, 1 million people have lost their lives and about 50 million got injured due to traffic accidents. Traffic accidents are one of the primary causes of accidents in younger generations nowadays. In detail, mostly, victims of road accidents are pedestrians, bicycle drivers and rickshaw drivers.

5. Aggravation of traffic congestion:

    There is an increasing number of cars in the urban cities, and almost each and every individual is having a car, bike or any other means of transport in urban cities. This rapid increase in turn will give rise to traffic congestion in mega-urban cities.

By 2050, 68% of the world's population will be living in cities, according to the current estimates. This is putting unprecedented stress on what is, in most cases, already ageing facilities including transport infrastructure. Noida is an example of this scenario. It has a growing population, now estimated to be 10 million people, and still growing at around 8.2% compared with the national average of 2.5%.

Year	Total Number of Road Accidents	% Change	Total Numbers of Person Killed	% Change	Total Number of Person Injured	% Change
2014	4,89,400	2.21	1,39,671	4.21	4,93,000	4.41
2015	5,02,321	2.46	1,46,133	4.63	5,00,278	1.38
2016	4,80,652	-4.14	1,50,785	3.18	4,95,294	-1.13
2017	4,64,910	-3.28	1,47,913	-1.9	4,75,274	-4.78
2018	4,67,044	0.46	1,51,417	2.37	4,69,297	-0.33
2019	5,10,000	2.41	1,64,418	2.51	4,88,212	-2.21
2020	5,15,000	3.21	1,68,413	3.12	4,76,298	-2.25

Figure 17.3   Road accidents caused by road conditions in the past 5 years: a comparative analysis

A key feature of the transport system in Noida is the over-reliance on road transport. Rail transport is practically now non-existent putting further pressure on the road network. The road network infrastructure is often in a poor and deplorable state, inadequate to meet needs, and as often lack of funds for maintenance and development. These result in a public transport system with unrestricted access and devoid of standards as well as the enforcement of traffic laws and regulations leading to almost total chaos and anarchy on the roads. According to the National Road Safety Commission between January and February of 2018, there were 2,085 crashes with 366 fatalities. Road safety is thus a major problem. In addition, traditional techniques such as SCOOT loops used in developed countries would not be very effective because of the volume of transport users involved.

According to WHO statistics, road traffic collisions are now one of the main reasons for death worldwide. Road accidents, in particular, took about 1.35 million lives each year (2018). The year wise road accident data is given in (Figure 17.3). According to studies, the majority of vehicle accidents are caused by poor road conditions. As a result, a road surface condition monitoring system is required to increase traffic safety, prevent accidents and safeguard vehicles from damage caused by poor road conditions. Both road management and drivers are interested in gathering enough details on the quality of the road infrastructure. In consolidated ways, monitoring road conditions, expensive and sophisticated equipment such as the specialist accelerometers with data collection systems are employed. These methods are expensive to build and maintain, and they demand a lot of manual labour, which can lead to errors while deploying or collecting data. As a result, new solutions to the country's transportation difficulties must be found, which are low-cost, effective, deployable and scalable.

Due to the growth of population as well as city expansion, there is a rise in traffic as well as the volume due to which there is a deterioration of different transportation infrastructures. Also, the different causes for such destruction are the various effects of bad construction material use, deficiency present in the design of the road, climate change. In combination, all these issues basically result in the appearance of different anomalies in the roads like bumps, potholes, cracks, which can be found in different expressways highways and streets present worldwide.

Not only these anomalies but also illegal construction of the safety breakers is also becoming a threat leading to the deterioration of the road safety. Speed breakers are generally constructed in order to provide safety for the pedestrians in different zones in order to control the limit of speed for the vehicles, which helps in avoiding accidents.

Unnecessarily, a large number of unapproved speed breakers have been installed, many of which are known to not adhere to the actual size set by the NHA.

The speed bumps are very common in the countries like India due to the fact that different signboards like speed limit, stop, yield and so on will not be able to work because of a lack of the traffic to enforcement resources.

This generally happens in the country because of various reasons such as higher speed of the vehicle, negligence of the driver, lesser visibility at night. There are different incidents that have been reported where vehicles such as cars, scooters, motorcycles are much more vulnerable because some speed breakers that are unnoticed may cause them to lose balance and can lead to severe accidents as well as damages.

In the year 2016, India had 300,000 road deaths that is actually double the amount of the estimation by the government that was only 151,000 in accordance to the 2018 global safety report provided by WHO, which basically highlighted the lack of the amount of data on fertility road accidents.

According to the data from the government (Figure 17.4), about 150,000 people have lost their lives in 2017 due to road accidents, which basically means that 17 people die due to road accidents every hour.

The number of deaths accounts for one-third of the overall accidents, which averages roughly 53 every hour.

UP has been hit hardest, followed by Tamil Nadu. Delhi is considered to be one of the safest places for driving considering the various numbers of fatalities that take place.

Different solutions have been considered in order to automatically detect as well as report any kind of anomalies on the road to different government agencies so that the maintenance tasks can be accelerated.

For example, by making the use of different computer vision methods that are based on texture differences as well as shape segmentation in order to identify the potholes. Approaches similar to this like contour information, edges, adopting shape and so on have been considered.

In today's time, the majority of people possess android mobile phones or smartphones that are well equipped with various inbuilt apps such as navigation and Google maps and sensation systems like Gyro Sensor, Accelerometer, Magnetometer and so

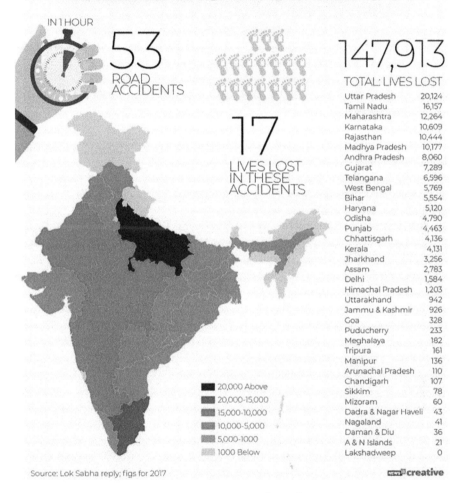

HOW UNSAFE ARE INDIA'S ROADS?

IN 1 HOUR

53 ROAD ACCIDENTS

17 LIVES LOST IN THESE ACCIDENTS

147,913 TOTAL: LIVES LOST

State	Lives Lost
Uttar Pradesh	20,124
Tamil Nadu	16,157
Maharashtra	12,264
Karnataka	10,609
Rajasthan	10,444
Madhya Pradesh	10,177
Andhra Pradesh	8,060
Gujarat	7,289
Telangana	6,596
West Bengal	5,769
Bihar	5,554
Haryana	5,120
Odisha	4,790
Punjab	4,463
Chhattisgarh	4,136
Kerala	4,131
Jharkhand	3,256
Assam	2,783
Delhi	1,584
Himachal Pradesh	1,203
Uttarakhand	942
Jammu & Kashmir	926
Goa	328
Puducherry	233
Meghalaya	182
Tripura	161
Manipur	136
Arunachal Pradesh	110
Chandigarh	107
Sikkim	78
Mizoram	60
Dadra & Nagar Haveli	43
Nagaland	41
Daman & Diu	36
A & N Islands	21
Lakshadweep	0

- 20,000 Above
- 20,000-15,000
- 15,000-10,000
- 10,000-5,000
- 5,000-1000
- 1000 Below

Source: Lok Sabha reply; figs for 2017

creative

Figure 17.4   State-wise road accident analysis

on, are enabled with GPS, and are always connected to the Internet. The technology of smartphones has been adopted in order to tackle such a problem provided its geo-referencing and sensing capabilities.

The accelerometers in smartphones can detect the movement of the device in such a way that if the vehicle comes across any irregular road surface like a bomb or a pothole, the accelerometer will record the occurrence of this event. The major problem then is the identification of the series of continuous readings of the accelerometer when any kind of anomaly occurs. Even though the task of detecting road imperfections with a smartphone is well defined, the organization has been unable to gather much more knowledge and a comprehensive perspective due to a number of issues. It also allows and encourages the development of an Android app that uses the data collected by these sensors in the user's smartphone to warn the user about bumps and poor road conditions.

A literature review of various machine learning algorithms will be discussed in detail in Section 17.2.

17.2   Literature review of machine learning for road condition detection

Detection algorithms are the most differing aspect of the previous work on this topic. Some papers have described machine learning approaches to road quality classification; however, others have opted for different solutions. This subchapter aims to provide an overview of the different feature sets and techniques used in machine learning approaches (Table 17.1).

The Pothole Patrol is a sensor-based programme that monitors the condition of the road surface. It necessitates the integration of particular hardware: an embedded computer running Linux for data processing, a Wi-Fi card for data transmission, an external GPS for localization and a three-axis accelerometer for road surface monitoring are all required for each vehicle. It detects potholes using a machine-learning technique. Microsoft developed Nericell, a system that checks traffic conditions. It necessitates a complex hardware and software configuration. A microphone, GPS and the SparkfunWiTilt accelerometer are among the external sensors used. The technology may mistake smooth, uneven and rocky roads due to the inaccuracy of the detection. Mednis and colleagues proposed a real-time pothole detection system. The system makes use of Android phones with accelerometer sensors and basic algorithms for detecting events from acceleration data. The real positive rate was found to be 90% in the experiments. The system only uses an accelerometer sensor, and data are acquired using specialized hardware, which is one of the work's limitations. A camcorder mounted on the front passenger seat's headrest is used to label the items. Labelling driving data with video, on the other hand, is a time-consuming and error-prone task.

The author describes a technique for detecting potholes. The neural network approach, which has an accuracy of 90–95%, is used to justify the threshold values. Smartphone accelerometers and gyroscopes are utilized to detect surface irregularities using an auditory data tagging method in which a labeler sits behind the driver inside the car and notes everything pertinent he sees or feels. Then, with a 90% accuracy, SVM is employed for detection and categorization of aberrations.

Using a low-cost Kinect sensor, Moazzam *et al.* calculate the volume of a pothole. The use of infrared technology for measurement based on a Kinect sensor is still a novel concept, and more study is needed to reduce error rates. Zhang *et al.*

Table 17.1   Comparison with related research in road surface monitoring

Reference	Smartphone sensors	External hardware	Data labelling	Detection methods
[1]	Not used	Ultrasonic's Sensors, GPS	Not mentioned	Threshold
[2]	Accelerometer, Microphone, GPS	Not used	Not mentioned	Threshold
[3]	Not used	Accelerometer, GPS	Manually	Threshold/ machine learning algorithms
[4]	Accelerometer	Not used	Not mentioned	Threshold
[5]	Accelerometer, GPS	Not used	Video	SVM
[6]	Accelerometer, GPS	Not used	Not mentioned	Threshold/neural network
[7]	Accelerometer, Gyroscope	Not used	Audiovisual	SVM
[8]	Accelerometer, Gyroscope	Not used	Audiovisual	SVM
[9]	Not used	Kinetic sensors	Not mentioned	Three-dimensional (3D) reconstruction
[10]	Not used	Stereo camera images	Not mentioned	Image processing algorithms
[11]	Not used	Camera images	Manually	Three-dimensional (3D) reconstruction
[12]	Not used	Near-infrared camera	Manually	Video processing methods
[13]	GPS, power	Not used	Manually	Threshold on relative roughness
[14]	Accelerometer, GPS	Not used	Not mentioned	Threshold
[15]	Accelerometer, GPS	Not used	Not mentioned	Threshold, the standard deviation of measurements
[16]	Accelerometer	Not used	Not mentioned	Threshold
Road Sense	Accelerometer, Gyroscope, GPS	Not used	Automatic	C4.5 Decision tree

used stereo camera images combined with a disparity calculation methodology to find potholes using image processing methods.

Although, in the general field of pothole detection, camera-based techniques have proven popular, a NIR camera was utilized in a recent study to classify a range of road conditions in the lab and in the field.

Video processing approaches, on the other hand, have the disadvantage of being too computationally expensive for smartphone applications. Vehicles are equipped with an ultrasonic transducer for ultrasonic techniques.

Ultrasonic waves are continuously transmitted onto road surfaces, and anomalies are discovered by measuring the time it takes for them to return. However, an expensive measurement apparatus is necessary to produce highly accurate data. Furthermore, S-Road Assist uses data received from smartphone sensors to detect road surface and traffic situations using threshold-based algorithms.

The standard deviation of readings from mobile-embedded accelerometers is typically a threshold in related studies to detect road irregularities.

Seraj and colleagues employed SVMs with RBF kernels for classification. Time domain, frequency domain and wavelet decomposition were used to extract the characteristics. The signal's frequency-domain representation was created using a Hamming window function FFT approach, and the signal was decomposed using a stationary wavelet transform. The time-domain features included standard deviation, mean, variance, root mean square, peak to peak, mean of absolute values, zero-crossing rate, correlation across all axes, tilt angles, signal magnitude area and waveform duration. Extracted features in the frequency domain included mean frequency, energy of the frequency bands and median frequency. Features extracted from wavelet decomposition included standard deviation, absolute mean, variance and energy for every level of detail. It is also mentioned that experimentations were done with raw signal and demodulated signal data, in order to see which feature sets provide the best detection results. After feature extraction, a two-step classification process was described. All of the windows were processed in the first stage, and those with road abnormalities were sent to the second step. Other classifiers attempted to divide the type of road anomaly present in each window in the second stage. A sliding window with a 66% overlap was employed in the training data, which comprised 3,066 windows. The overall accuracy of detecting serious road irregularities was estimated to be around 90%.

Hoffmann *et al.* [17] categorize their data using machine learning. Direct road surface classification and bump detection-based classification were the two types of road surface classification methodologies used. A road surface was classified as smooth, bumpy or rough using the direct road surface classification method. Features were extracted from GPS and accelerometer data and included: acceleration mean, acceleration variance, and acceleration standard deviation are all variables to consider. In the direct road classification approach, roads were divided into sets of segments. For each segment that needs to be classified, previous segments' features are also taken into account. A feature set optimization was also carried out, with the purpose of finding those features that increase the classification accuracy the most. It was found that speed and inclination confused the classifier or didn't contribute to the learning algorithm. For classification, two machine learning algorithms were used: KNN and Naive Bayesian classifier. In order to test the classifiers on evaluation data, 10-fold cross-validation was used. It was noted that while Naive Bayes and KNN algorithms performed mostly similar, a slight increase was seen with the KNN. However, the overall accuracy of 78% proved to be not satisfactory. In the bump detection-based classification approach, the classifier had to distinguish between a smooth road and a road that has a bump or some other similar anomaly. Here, classification accuracy was a lot better, with an accuracy of around 98%.

Eriksson *et al.* [18] employed signal processing and machine learning to detect and classify a number of different road irregularities. The topic of other undesired abnormalities manifesting in the accelerometer signal, such as abrupt turning or stopping, is discussed in the study. To reject such events, several features, such as speed and filters, such as a high-pass filter, were utilized. The training of the learning algorithm is based on the peak X-axis and Z-axis acceleration values and the instantaneous velocity of the car. To help remove false positives and increase the overall accuracy of correct anomaly detection, the paper describes a process where an anomaly is reported only when several other detectors have also detected an anomaly in the same spot. Overall, the paper concludes that by using training data, which had been carefully examined, the described pothole detection system achieved a false positive rate of 0.2% in controlled experiments.

Smartphones and tablets have grown ubiquitous in today's culture. The worldwide smartphone market has seen a tremendous increase in shipments in recent years [19]. Furthermore, in recent years, mobile internet usage has significantly increased, lately surpassing desktop internet usage on a global scale [20]. Because of the ubiquity of mobile devices and their expanding computational capacity, smartphones are now capable of completing an increasing number of tasks. Mobile applications on platforms like Google Android and Apple iOS can make use of the devices' inherent sensors, allowing for new ways to use these smart gadgets. Sensors can be used for a variety of activities, such as detecting the device's position, or more complicated difficulties, such as sensing human activity [21].

Another key aspect of modern life is road infrastructure. A vast number of individuals use roads on a regular basis, whether driving their own car, riding their bikes, walking, or taking public transportation. Many government services and businesses rely on the road network in some form. A well-maintained and safe road network is beneficial for everyone involved as the rate of motorization continues to rise [22].

Road quality is a reflection of a country's development status and has an impact on travel speeds and safety. There is a major need of evaluation of the quality of roads. The collected data will be forwarded to a self-built server, where an analysis module will calculate and analyze the data in order to generate road condition information. The related previous works revolved around the threshold-based detection techniques, but they were not that much effective as they just detected the damage to roads. Some of the works include the use of fast Fourier transform to get the acceleration information. This research, on the other hand, makes advantage of mobile sensor capabilities as well as social community data collecting. Some works also used spatial–temporal anomalies to detect the damage to the roads. During every action, mobile sensing technology is utilized to identify targeted data utilizing relevant sensing components. This research will use mobile crowd sensing to gather data and develop collective intelligence. This study employs an unsupervised anomaly detection algorithm to aid in the comprehension of typical and aberrant road sections. The sensing components of phones are employed in this paper to capture oscillating amplitude data experienced by a user while driving on a road. Every second, data are gathered and delivered to a self-built analytic server. As a result, in the context of this study, different users traverse the same road and multiple sets of oscillation amplitude data are obtained for the same road. After collection, the server uses an aberration finding algorithm to extract the aberrant information from the data series. The basic goal is to distinguish between typical and aberrant road portions. This work uses an unsupervised anomaly detection approach to model road quality and interpret normal and abnormal road sections. In addition to the analysis of the obtained data and anomaly detection, the Google Maps SDK is employed.

A road monitoring technique was presented to provide security and ease of use to various road users [23]. The major goal of this study is to develop a real-time Android application called Road Sense that uses a tri-axial accelerometer and a gyroscope to automatically forecast road quality. The road position trace will be displayed on a geographic map utilizing GPS, and all recorded workout entries will be saved. It will also provide a depiction of a region's road quality map. The proposed road monitoring system would be created using machine learning, with the C4.5 Decision tree classifier being used to categorize road segments and build the model using training data. The overall result shows a consistent accuracy of 98.6%. Discussion on various road monitoring technologies to predict the road conditions to provide smooth, safe and comfort travel with less damage to vehicles using 27 papers. The literature survey highlights the hardware and software configurations and limitations related to developed applications. The authors highlight the various classification algorithms with the focus to achieve highest accuracy. The framework of the proposed system is divided into two phases:

1. Training phase: Effective features are extracted from specified sorts of road conditions depending on acceleration and rotation around gravity first in the Feature Extraction step. The features are then fed into a classifier model that can do fine-grained identification.

2. Prediction phase: It will detect and identify road conditions by sensing real-time vehicular dynamics. Pre-processing is done on sensor readings after collecting the readings from the accelerometer and gyroscope integrated into the smartphone. The system would next use the learned classifier model to forecast road quality. In this paper, the performance of the system is evaluated in two steps: (a) analytical validation and (b) experimental validation. Analytical validation evaluates the performance of various classifiers using a variety of parameters. The system's practicality is tested in a real-world setting during experimental validation. To obtain the dataset, a drive of about 40 min in length (25 km), and a total of 2,000 samples of data were collected. The author has compared the performance of three classifiers named SVM, Navies Bayes and C4.5 on the scale of various parameters such as

Precision, Recall, ROC area, F-measure, TP rate and FP rate. Overall, the results demonstrate that C4.5 is superior in terms of detection accuracy (98.6%).

[24] The focus is on data from traffic accidents, which is the most fundamental measure of safety without which the scope and nature of road safety cannot be determined. The precision of the data, data keeping and its analysis are all important aspects in making successful use of accident information. As a result, the incident report should be of high quality. If the initial incident report is weak and incomplete, analysis and application of the findings are poor as well. Road accidents are unpredictably unpredictable incidents that require thorough investigation. The heterogeneity problem is a fundamental issue in accident data analysis. Although segmentation can be used to reduce data heterogeneity, there is no assurance that it will produce the most accurate group segmentation, which includes road accidents. The k-means technique is used to suggest a model for analyzing road accident data.

Estimating the count of clusters: Estimating the count is the most difficult part of the clustering method. One of the constraints of this technique is that the value of k must be provided by the user. If the value of k is incorrect, the clustering results may be erroneous. Gap statistics are utilized to circumvent this constraint.

Association rule: This mining is the act of generating a set of rules that define the basic patterns in a data set. The frequency with which attributes of data occur in the data set determines their correlation. The most fundamental prerequisite of cluster analysis is to figure out how many clusters the clustering method will produce. After determining the number of clusters, use the R statistical software to partition the accident data sets using the k-means clustering algorithm. Cluster-based accident variables are determined by a thorough examination of each cluster. Using k to represent clustering and association rules mining methods, this research proposes a method for assessing accident patterns of various types of road accidents. The study looked at accidents that occurred on Maharashtra's roads in 2015 and 2016 [6-9]. K-means clustering finds five categories based on the attribute's accident type, road type, light condition and road attributes (C1–C5). Association rule mining was used to construct rules for each cluster as well as the overall data set. All cluster rules reveal situations relating to incidents within the cluster.

[25]. In paper [25], SVM is used as classification algorithm. The mobile app will first process the data via various algorithms and then will transfer the data to the database by internet. This app produces a sound on pothole detection. With the help of the data, potholes can be categorized as low, medium and high. The paper also shows the technologies and calculation methods used in the model in detail and also shows the settings and results of the experiment. Various research papers are studied by the authors. One of the papers provides them the parameters like speed, Z-peak, etc. which can help in classifying the potholes. One of the research papers uses accelerometer and GPS same as suggested in this paper by the authors. Various designs like Cartel System, Pothole Patrol System, Nericell System, etc. can also be used to detect conditions of road by mobile sensors. The solution is to develop an Android app that collects data. The app can start or stop or save data collection. The file in this paper is saved as .csv format. With the help of accelerometer sensors readings are captured. along with these readings. Accelerometer readings are

also captured. The changes/deviation in accelerometer readings detects the potholes. K-means clustering is used for depicting the pattern. This algorithm clusters data into groups: potholes and non-potholes. After the readings are recorded, script file is then allowed to run on the saved file provided by the android app and labeling is done. Then ML models are used to train the data. Before training, we apply clustering for segregation of pothole and non-pothole. In this paper, accuracy is calculated with various classifiers and SVM proved to provide maximum accuracy of 99.6%.

[26The paper [26] describes that road networks connecting different residences, villages, cities and even countries are becoming key components of contemporary transportation infrastructure. . In the real world, detecting road conditions, which may be separated into four stages, is critical. These are as follows:

- **Manual detection**. Manual measurements have a number of drawbacks, including a high cost, a long time to complete and a low efficiency.
- **Semi-automated detection**. Computers control the mechanical activity, save data in real time and analyze and calculate it at predefined intervals.
- **Automated detection**. Ultrasonic, laser, ground-penetrating radar and other technologies are used to identify roads.
- **Informatization detection**. Communication, network, database and other information technologies are used in road quality testing. Highly developed and shared information technology and information resources can significantly improve test accuracy in any discipline.

A taxi-based mobile sensing system named Pothole Patrol was shown for monitoring and analyzing pavement conditions. Three-axis acceleration sensors, a GPS receiver and a laptop computer with a data aggregation and processing unit are all included in the cab. A more efficient and cost-effective technology for identifying potholes and cracks was devised with laser imaging. It used sensors implanted in cell phones to collect data in cars. The system, for instance, may employ a one-degree-of-freedom vibration model to actively gain a vehicle's competence. Both supervised and unsupervised machine learning methods are used to detect road conditions. Using a simple machine learning methodology and a clustering algorithm, a method for detecting road anomalies was presented for evaluating driving behavior. In the case of potholes and bumps, the average detection rates were determined to be 88.66 and 88.89%, respectively. The crowdsourcing strategy not only lowers costs and improves efficiency but also removes geographical and time constraints, making communication more convenient. The proposed solution of the paper is as follows:

A. **System Model:** Dr. Taguchi employed the Mahalanobis distance (MD) and measurement scale and provided a threshold to identify unknown samples using a combination of MD and signal-to-noise ratio.

B. **Benchmark space:** The window size of flat road data is initially believed to be "h". The flat road sample space has m dimensions, and the sample data is $Xi =$ (Xi1, Xi2, Xim), with the i-th feature's data acquired in the j-th time.

C. **Validation of benchmark Space:** We need to collect some unusual road data to test the validity of the benchmark space Yi = (Yi1, Yi2, · · · , Yim).

D. **Optimization of spatial Features:** In general, the characteristic variables include duplicate information, resulting in a miscalculation and a negative influence on classification outcomes.

Our study took place in Xi'an, where we collected 34,895 records of vehicle traffic data over a period of 15 weeks. We design and then standardize a benchmark space using the detection model validation by computing the correlation matrix and the MD of space by 30 eigenvectors of flat road signal.

17.3   Gaps identified in the literature

After doing the literature survey in detail, the following are the gaps identified in the mentioned research domain:

a. SCOOT Technology can only be used where the traffic flow is very less such as Yamuna Express Way or Agra-Luck now Expressway.

b. In addition to SCOOT, a new technology was developed that is ETSI-G5, which is very expensive as it uses onboard units (OBUs) and roadside units (RSUs) that are placed along with the road infrastructure.

c. Neither SCOOT nor ETSI-G5 talks about the safety of roads. Only monitoring or surveillance of vehicles is done using these technologies. This seems to be providing a costly incomplete solution in terms of all types of traffic flow.

d. In the literature, various road safety techniques have been suggested; however, in maximum cases focus was on the driver's fault for the road accidents.

e. Quality of the roads and accidents due to animals is not being considered in the literature as the factor for road accidents or damages to the vehicles.

f. Study of traffic congestion at traffic lights was not discussed in the literature.

17.4   Proposed methodology

The challenge is to build a low-cost information platform for monitoring traffic flows and to bring that information from different parts of a city together so that it can be analyzed to enable better traffic management routines for mega-cities in low-income countries. The present traffic flow monitoring techniques used in developed countries such as SCOOT cannot cope with the volume of traffic, which would go quickly wear out the SCOOT loops. In addition, newer systems such as ETSI-G5 technology for connected vehicles are very expensive. These systems work by having OBUs and RSUs, which are placed along the road infrastructure. Currently, an OBU and an RSU each cost over US$1,000 . So, the solution being proposed is to use Bluetooth Low Power (BLE) devices. These devices communicate using Bluetooth technology and have a common coverage range of 70–100 m.

Since mobile phones also have Bluetooth interfaces, a lot of apps have been written to take data from the BLE device and use the mobile phone to communicate with a central server or navigational entity. Though what we are proposing does not remove such capability, the system we want to build is not dependent on users having mobile phones. Instead, the BLE device will beacon every few seconds and those beacons with their UUIDs will be picked up by Wi-Fi/BLE gateways. The gateway devices cost £54 each, and this project will buy 50 such gateways. These gateways will then use eight wireless routers, which will be connected to the University of Ghana's communications network. This is an Ethernet network running at 1 Gbps. The information will be sent to a central server, where it will be stored, processed and used to display real-time traffic flows.

The Wi-Fi/BLE gateways will be placed on two very busy roads that border the University of Ghana. The first is called National Highway – four or N4, which runs from north to south along the east side of the Campus. In fact, it forms a direct boundary with the campus for 3.5 km. The second road is called the Haatso-Atomic road and runs from east to west on the north side of the campus and forms a natural campus boundary for 1.5 km. So, in this proposal, we would like to monitor traffic from both roads making this a total of 5 km of road infrastructure that will be monitored. The data gathered will be analyzed to show the traffic flow along these roads. The results will be displayed using a Virtual Network Computing server; hence, the results will be available to all commuters in real time. Information will also be communicated using mobile phones as well as road signage such as overhead road gantries.

Research methodology has been organized into:

1. **Research design**

    The research is exploratory as well as descriptive. The study's associated variables were discovered, and the research problem was specified using an exploratory research methodology. Exploratory research also proposes a conceptual framework that incorporates the pertinent variables. Following that, a descriptive research methodology was employed to empirically test the stated conceptual framework of the study, as well as statistical analysis of the data.

2. **Sampling design**

    The sample for the study of the city of Noida has been selected. We plan to collect the data regarding the roads condition and traffic conditions of the road near the Amity campus. To study will be performed on the road conditions using the sample size of 500 vehicles with BLE devices for communication and sensors like accelerometers embedded with them.

3. **Data collection instruments**

    The basic data collection instruments are the sensor that is embedded in the vehicle.

    1. Accelerometer
    2. Gyro meter
    3. Cameras
    4. GPS

     5. Smartphones with Wi-Fi connectivity
     6. Bluetooth
     7. APP on smartphone for emergency messages

4. **Data collection method**

    The study is based on the survey method of collecting initial information during the research process. Primary data are collected by the researcher himself using the survey method. It is a reliable way to collect the data because the researcher knows where it came from and how it was collected and analyzed.

5. **Statistical techniques**

    The various data cleaning and analysis operations will be performed based on the data collected from the sensors and perform the analysis using statically operations used in the machine learning algorithm. The summarized tentative plan for the same has been described in Figure 17.5.

17.5   Implementation

17.5.1   Flutter-based application

We created a flutter-based android app to collect data. This software uses smartphone sensors to collect sensor data (accelerometer and gyroscope) for potholes and speed bumps (Figure 17.6) . We put a mobile device with an application on the dashboard of the vehicle. The programme puts the obtained data in a Firebase database for machine learning model training when the data gathering operation is done. Regarding the data gathering phase, a machine learning algorithm is trained on the collected dataset to recognize distinct anomalies (potholes, not potholes and speed bumps), and the present position is projected as a pothole, not pothole, or speed bump (Figure 17.7).

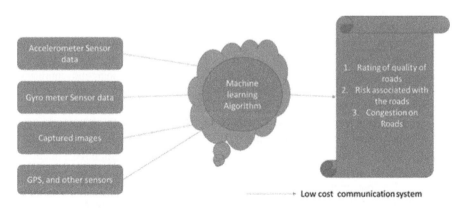

Figure 17.5   *Block diagram of the proposed methodology*

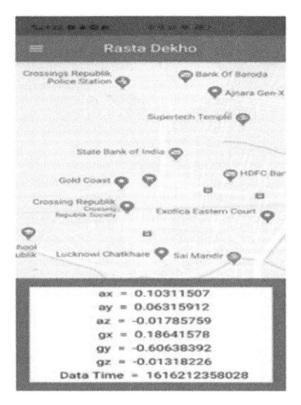

Figure 17.6   Accelerometer and gyroscope sensor reading on a mobile device

17.5.2   Machine learning models

Before training any machine learning algorithm, the gathered data must be pre-processed. To reduce noise from data, which if not eliminated can have an influence on our machine learning model's eventual outputs. The machine learning model will be better at generating predictions if the data we give it is of greater quality. So, in order to execute data pre-processing and data cleaning, we first performed various pre-processing tasks, such as translating timestamp strings into the proper date and time format. We developed statistical characteristics of accelerometer and gyroscope readings for feature extraction and feature engineering, such as mean, min, max and standard deviation for all axes (x, y and z). We standardized data features for algorithms that are sensitive to varying data scales. The volume of the data has an impact on algorithms that use distance-based metrics as part of their implementation.

As can be seen in Figure 17.8, the data we collected were extremely skewed. The dataset's imbalance should be carefully managed since it might have a negative impact on the end outcomes as well as the machine learning models' ultimate interpretation. Dealing with the dataset's imbalance can be done in a number of ways. It is possible that it is not gathering enough data for each class, oversampling the minority class (one in the example above) and undersampling the majority class (0

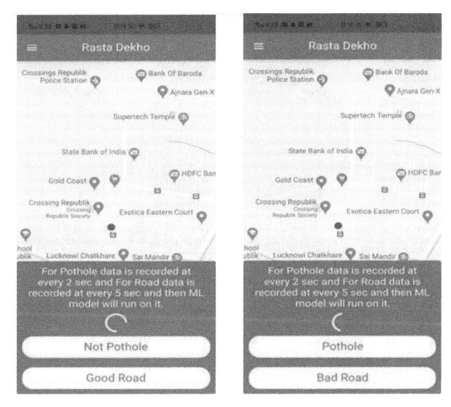

Figure 17.7   (a) and (b) Represent the working model for identifying whether there is no pothole or not a pothole on the road, respectively.

represents the majority class in the above case). We dealt with the problem by adopting stratified cross-validation processes. The entire dataset is divided into numerous folds, with the target distribution remaining the same for each fold. It is called stratified because the folds are made using stratified sampling.

As our initial model, we used logistic regression. The logistic function, commonly known as the sigmoid function, is used to create the simplest basic categorization approach. It is an S-shaped curve that transforms all real numbers to a number between 0 and 1.

The logistic regression model predicts probabilities. It is given by: $Y = 1/(1 + e(-x))$.

The sample logistic regression equation can be modelled as

$$Y = 1/(1 + e(-(b0 + b1*x))).$$

The logistic regression equation's coefficients can be estimated via maximum-likelihood estimation. The second model we built was the k closest neighbours model. KNN is an easy-to-use and develop machine learning algorithm. It is a supervised machine learning technique that may be applied to classification and

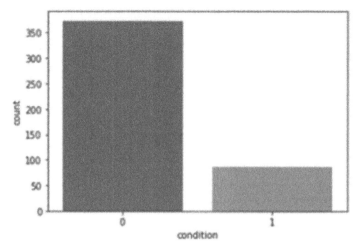

Figure 17.8   Class distribution of Potholes present (1)/absent (0)

regression issues. It is founded on the idea that similar objects are more likely to be located near together, i.e., similar items are kept together as much as possible [5]. The KNN method calculates closeness using several distance metrics such as Minkowski distance, Euclidean distance and Manhattan distance. There is one hyperparameter k in this method that we must choose well in order for our algorithm to perform well on the data. To pick the optimal value of k, we looped over various neighbours in the range of 5–25 in steps of 5, trained the algorithm and then stored the best-performing model. The final model is SVMs. The SVM is a type of super-vised machine learning approach for solving classification and regression issues. In an SVM, each data point is displayed in n-dimensional space, where n is the number of features in the data. We utilize a hyperplane to easily distinguish the classes while categorizing them.

The decision tree classifier is the fourth model. A decision tree is a type of supervised machine learning approach that may be used to solve classification and regression problems. A decision tree is a hierarchical structure consisting of nodes and their connections. There are three types of nodes in a decision tree: root node, internal node, and leaf node. A root node is one that has zero or more outward edges and no incoming edges. A node with exactly one incoming edge and two or more outgoing edges is called an internal node. A leaf node has only one inbound edge and no outward edges. Test attributes are used to analyze and segregate data based on the characteristics of each non-leaf node in a decision tree.

Random forest classifier is the fifth model. Random forest is a supervised machine learning approach for classifying and predicting data. A random forest is a collection of several decision trees that, as the name suggests, create a forest. It uses the ensemble approach. Each decision tree forecasts a distinct class label, and the model's final forecast is determined by the class label that receives the most votes. A random forest model outperforms a decision tree model in the majority of situations due to the low correlation between many decision trees in the model. The model's final prediction is derived using the ensembling approach, which combines many low-correlated decision trees to get a range of forecasts. Uncorrelated models can make more precise forecasts than individual model projections. The reason for this is that in a random forest, each uncorrelated decision tree stops the others from making their own mistakes.

Boosting techniques were also utilized to develop numerous models, including the gradient boosting classifier. It makes use of a boosting method. Boosting is a method of transforming weak pupils into powerful ones. In this situation, the decision tree is a poor learner. Algorithms for boosting exist in a range of shapes and sizes. These algorithms differ from one another in terms of how they transform weak learners into strong learners or how they uncover and correct weak learners' flaws in order to develop strong learners who can more accurately predict data. Adaboost is a boosting method that addresses a poor learner's shortcomings by using adaptive weights or high weight data points. Adaboost starts by creating a decision tree for each observation with the same weights. In succeeding rounds, it adjusts the given weights based on the predictability of a single observation. The data that are more difficult to categorize are given a lower weight, while the data that are simpler to classify are given a higher weight. A gradient boosting machine, on the other hand, addresses the drawbacks of a weak learner by using gradients in the loss function. It uses a progressive, cumulative, and sequential approach to train models. Another algorithm that uses the boosting technique is Xgboost. If the data isn't too tough, it can build an ensemble of linear models and an ensemble of gbtree, which uses a decision tree as the basis estimate. It works by building a base model that predicts the target variable first and then training subsequent models to match the residuals from prior phases. To decrease residuals from previous phases, Xgboost employs a step-by-step strategy.

17.6 Results

As a consequence of our research, we identified a few surprising and fascinating data, indicating that AI approaches may be used to handle the issue of pothole recognition and street condition order. We used a number of AI computations and attempted a variety of proving and boundary modifying processes that we were familiar with to get to our conclusions (Figure 17.9 a, b, c, d).

We trained several other models, such as K nearest neighbours, SVMs, and gradient boosting algorithm, in a similar fashion, and they yielded 91.4, 92, and 92.3% accuracy, respectively. Figure 17.10a,b,c illustrate the results of a comparative examination of models based on F1 Score, precision and recall.

17.6.1 Comparison with the existing models

We completed extensive research on this issue statement of pothole detecting. From data collection through data preprocessing, model training, hyperparameter modification, model selection and monitoring, various intriguing discoveries were

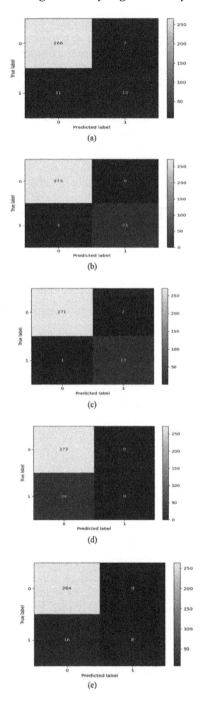

*Figure 17.9   (a) Logistic regression, (b) random forest, (c) XG Boost, (d) KNN,
(e) SVM*

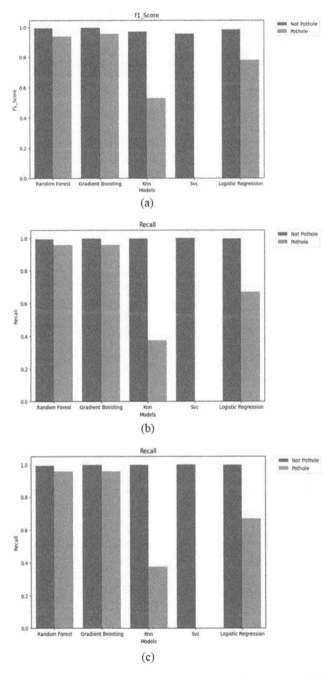

Figure 17.10   *(a) A comparison of models based on the F1 score, (b) precision-based comparative analysis of models, (c) recall-based comparative analysis of models*

discovered as the research progressed. Also, we gathered inspiration from all of the references and used it to replicate their ideas, which we then improved upon to create our own.

A major modification we made as part of our approach was a change in data gathering that we thought would help us obtain a wider range of results from our study. As a result, we used a car rather than a motorcycle, which had previously been employed extensively in other investigations. This technology may be a little more expensive than previous research, but it allows us to obtain more consistent and accurate data from mobile sensors. As a result, our effort in this study meets our expectations in terms of providing us with a high-quality dataset.

In addition, most researchers solely use accelerometers as their major source of research, as evidenced by previous studies. However, in order to offer additional context to the readings supplied by the sensor data, we analyzed the gyroscope reading in addition to the accelerometer reading in this study. We were able to synchronise our accelerometer readings to a global frame of reference thanks to the gyroscope data, regardless of the car's orientation or any other disturbances at the time of data collection.

Last but not least, for our research, we used all three axes of the accelerometer. This indicates that, unlike most previous studies.

17.7   Conclusion and future scope

As a consequence of our study, we produced an android application using flutter. It is used to obtain information from mobile sensors (accelerometer and gyroscope readings). These are speed bumps, not potholes, according to the measurements. Data on numerous roadways were compiled using the programme. After the data have been collected, supervised machine learning techniques are used to process it. Several traditional categorization approaches were applied to the collected data. Traditional classification approaches included SVM, decision tree, and random forest, while modern boosting algorithms included XGboost and CAT boost. There are several problems in our current work that can be solved in future initiatives. The data gathered are significantly skewed. You will be able to finish the task completely if you collect enough samples for each class. The data collection strategy has room for improvement. We just utilized a single Android smartphone to collect data. This can be aided by the use of many mobile devices. Crowd-sensing techniques, on the other hand, can be used to collect and extract road quality data from a large number of users, which is then fed into a parent application for more exact findings.

References

[1]   Pan J., Khan M., Popa S.I, *et al.* 'Proactive vehicle re-routing strategies for congestion avoidance'. *2012 IEEE 8th International Conference on Distributed Computing in Sensor Systems (DCOSS), Publisher: IEEE, Hangzhou, China,*

pp. 265-272, doi: 10.1109/DCOSS.2012.29; New York: IEEE, 2012. pp. 265–72.

[2]   Brennand C.A., de Souza A.M., Maia G., *et al.* 'An intelligent transportation system for detection and control of congested roads in urban centers'. *20th IEEE Symposium on Computers and Communication (ISCC)*, Larnaca; NewYork: IEEE, 6–9 July; 2015. pp. 476–81.

[3]   De Souza A.M., Yokoyama R.S., Maia G., *et al.* 'Real-time path planning to prevent traffic jam through an intelligent transportation system'. *IEEE Symposium on Computers and Communication (ISCC)*, Messina; NewYork: IEEE, 27–30 June; 2016. pp. 726–31.

[4]   De Souza A.M., Yokoyama R.S., Botega L.C., *et al.* 'Scorpion: a solution using cooperative rerouting to prevent congestion and improve traffic condition'. *2015 IEEE International Conference on Computer and Information Technology*, Liverpool; New York: IEEE, 26–28 October; 2015. pp. 497–503.

[5]   Doolan R., Muntean G.M. 'EcoTrec – a novel VANET-based approach to reducing vehicle emissions'. *IEEE Transactions on Intelligent Transportation Systems*. 2016, vol. 99, pp. 1–13.

[6]   Treiber M., Kesting A., Wilson R.E. 'Reconstructing the traffic state by fusion of heterogeneous data'. *Computer-Aided Civil and Infrastructure Engineering*. 2011, vol. 26(6), pp. 408–19.

[7]   Rehborn H., Koller M., Kerner B.: 'Traffic datafusion of vehicle data to detect spatiotemporal congested patterns'. *19th ITS World Congress, Vienna, Austria*; Washington: ITS America, 2012. pp. 1–8.

[8]   Chen N., Xu X. 'Information-fusion method for urban traffic flow based on evidence theory combining with fuzzy rough set'. *Journal of Theoretical and Applied Information Technology*. 2013, vol. 49(2), pp. 560–6.

[9]   Pan J., Pan J., Borcea C P.S. 'Divert: a distributed vehicular traffic re-routing system for congestion avoidance'. *IEEET Mobile Computer*. 2016.

[10] Wang S., Djahel S., McManis J. 'An adaptive and vanets-based next road re-routing system for unexpected urbantraffic congestion avoidance'. *2015 IEEE Vehicular Networking Conference (VNC)*, Columbus, OH; New York: IEEE, 16–18 December; 2015. pp. 196–203.

[11] Madli R., Hebbar S., Pattar P., Golla V. 'Automatic detection and notification of potholes and humps on roads to aid drivers'. *IEEE Sensors Journal*. 2015, vol. 15(8), pp. 4313–18.

[12] Mohan P., Padmanabhan V.N., Ramjee R. 'Nericell: rich monitoring of road and traffic conditions using mobile smartphones'. *Proceedings of 6th ACM Conference Embedded Networks Sensor Systems*; 2011. pp. 323–36.

[13] Eriksson J., Girod L., Hull B., Newton R., Madden S., Balakrishnan H. 'The pothole patrol: using a mobile sensor network for road surface monitoring'. *Proceedings of 6th International Conference on Mobile Systems, Applications, and Services*; 2008. pp. 29–39.

[14] Mednis A., Strazdins G., Zviedris R., Kanonirs G., Selavo L. 'Real time pothole detection using Android smartphones with accelerometers'. *Proceedings*

of International Conference on Distributed Computing in Sensor Systems Workshops; 2011. pp. 1–6.

[15] Perttunen M. 'Distributed road surface condition monitoring using mobile phones'. *Proceedings of International Conference on Ubiquitous Intelligence and Computing*; 2011. pp. 64–78.

[16] Kulkarni A., Mhalgi N., Gurnani S., Giri N. 'Pothole detection system using machine learning on android'. *International Journal of Emerging Technology and Advanced Engineering*. 2014, vol. 4(7), pp. 360–4.

[17] Android Developer page for SensorEvent class. Available from https://developer.android.com/reference/ android/hardware/SensorEvent.html [Accessed 10 May 2017].

[18] Karagiannis G., Altintas O., Ekici E., *et al.* 'Vehicular networking: a survey and tutorial on requirements, architectures, challenges, standards and solutions'. *IEEE Communications Surveys & Tutorials*. 2011, vol. 13(4), pp. 584–616.

[19] Bajpai P. *The evolution of smartphone markets: where growth is going*. 2016. Available from www.nasdaq.com/article/the-evolution-of-smartphone-markets-where-growth-is-going-cm619105 [Accessed 10 May 2017].

[20] StatCounter press release. *Mobile and tablet internet usage exceeds desktop for first time worldwide*. 2016. Available from http://gs.statcounter.com/press/ mobile-and-tablet-internet-usage-exceeds-desktop-for-first-time-worldwide [Accessed 10 May 2017].

[21] Anguita D., Ghio A., Oneto L., Parra X., Reyes-Ortiz J.L. 'Human activity recognition on smartphones using a multiclass hardware-friendly support vector machine'. *International Workshop on Ambient Assisted Living*. Springer Berlin Heidelberg; 2012. pp. 216–23.

[22] Tonde V.P., Jadhav A., Shinde S., Dhoka A., Bablade S. 'Road quality and Ghats complexity analysis using android sensors'. *International Journal of Advanced Research in Computer and Communication Engineering*. 2015, vol. 4(3), pp. 101–4.

[23] Hu S., Su L., Liu H., Wang H., Abdelzaher T.F. 'SmartRoad: smartphone-based crowd sensing for traffic regulator detection and identification'. *ACM Trans. Sensor Netw. 11, 4, Article 55 (July 2015), 27 Pages. DOI: Http:// Dx.DOI.Org/10.1145/2770876*. 2015, vol. 11(4).

[24] Sharma H., Naik S., Jain A., Raman R.K., Reddy R.K., Shet R.B. 'S-road assist: road surface conditions and driving behavior analysis using smartphones'. *Proceedings of International Conference on Connected Vehicles and Expo*; 2015. pp. 291–6.

[25] Kulkarni K., Prashant K.V., Nasikkar S., Ahuja T., Mhetre N. 'Predicting road anomalies using sensors in smartphones'. *Imperial Journal of Interdisciplinary Research*. 2016, vol. 2(6), pp. 219–22.

[26] Li Y., Xue F., Feng L., Qu Z. 'A driving behavior detection system based on a smartphone's built-in sensor'. *International Journal of Communication Systems*. 2017, vol. 30(8), p. e3178.

Chapter 18

Conclusion

Sunil Kumar[1], Glenford Mapp[2], and Korhan Cengiz[3]

18.1 Conclusion

This book presented applications, technologies, challenges, and implementation design models of intelligent networks design by Big Data, Internet of Things, artificial intelligence (AI), and cloud computing approaches in different sectors. Research into real-time fault tolerance, security, and data analytics by addressing significant data volume and velocity measurement are essential in intelligent networks, for example, where different analytical models and AI and machine learning algorithms improve end-to-end performance, efficiency, and quality of service (QoS) [1–10].

The availability of Big Data, AI, cloud computing, low-cost commodity hardware, and new information management and analytic software has produced a unique moment in the history of intelligent networks [11–21]. The convergence of these trends means that we have the capabilities required to analyze unique data sets quickly and cost-effectively. They represent a genuine leap forward and a clear opportunity to realize enormous efficiency, productivity, revenue, and profitability.

This book also discussed issues and challenges that can be addressed and overcome in the future using the new upcoming technologies. The age of intelligent networks is here, and these are truly revolutionary times if business and technology professionals continue to work together and deliver on the promise.

Thank you for taking the time to read this book, and we hope you enjoyed reading it as much as we did write it.

References

[1] Kumar S., Ranjan P., Ramaswami R., Tripathy M.R. 'EMEEDP: enhanced multi-hop energy efficient distributed protocol for heterogeneous wireless sensor network'. *2015 5th International Conference on Communication*

[1]Department of Computer Science & Engineering, Amity University, Uttar Pradesh, India
[2]Department of Computer Science, Middlesex University, UK
[3]Department of Electrical-Electronics Engineering, Trakya University, 22030 Edirne, Turkey

Systems and Network Technologies, CSNT; Gwalior, India, 04-06 Apr; 2015. pp. 194–200.

[2]   Kumar S., Ranjan P., Ramaswami R. 'Energy optimization in distributed localized wireless sensor networks'. *Proceedings of the International Conference on Issues and Challenges Intelligent Computing Technique (ICICT)*; Ghaziabad, India, 07-08 Feb; 2014.

[3]   Chauhan R., Kumar S. 'Packet loss prediction using artificial intelligence unified with big data analytics, Internet of things and cloud computing technologies'. *5th International Conference on Information Systems and Computer Networks (ISCON)*; Mathura, India, 22-23 Oct; 2021. pp. 01–6.

[4]   Sudhakaran S., Kumar S., Ranjan P., Tripathy M.R. 'Blockchain-based transparent and secure decentralized algorithm'. *International Conference on Intelligent Computing and Smart Communication 2019. Algorithms for Intelligent Systems*. Springer; Singapore; 2020.

[5]   Kumar S., Trivedi M.C., Ranjan P., Punhani A. *Evolution of Software-Defined Networking Foundations for IoT and 5G Mobile Networks*. 10. IGI Publisher; 2020. p. 350.

[6]   Kumar S., Ranjan P., Radhakrishnan R., Tripathy M.R. 'Energy efficient multichannel MAC protocol for high traffic applications in heterogeneous wireless sensor networks'. *Recent Advances in Electrical & Electronic Engineering*. 2017, vol. 10(3), pp. 223–32.

[7]   Kumar S., Ranjan P., Ramaswami R., Tripathy M.R. 'Resource efficient clustering and next hop knowledge based routing in multiple heterogeneous wireless sensor networks'. *International Journal of Grid and High Performance Computing*. 2017, vol. 9(2), pp. 1–20.

[8]   Kumar S., Cengiz K., Vimal S., Suresh A. 'Energy efficient resource migration based load balance mechanism for high traffic applications iot'. *Wireless Personal Communications*. 2021, vol. 10(3), pp. 1–14. doi: 10.1007/S11277-021-08269-7.

[9]   Haidar M., Kumar S,. 'Smart healthcare system for biomedical and health care applications using aadhaar and blockchain'. *2021 5th International Conference on Information Systems and Computer Networks, ISCON 2021*; GLA Mathura, 22-23 October 2021; 2022. pp. 1–5.

[10]   Punhani A., Faujdar N., Kumar S. 'Design and evaluation of cubic Torus Network-on-Chip architecture'. *International Journal of Innovative Technology and Exploring Engineering (IJITEE)*. 2019, vol. 8(6), pp. 2278–3075.

[11]   Dubey G., Kumar S., Kumar S., Navaney P. 'Extended opinion lexicon and ML-based sentiment analysis of tweets: a novel approach towards accurate classifier'. *International Journal of Computational Vision and Robotics*. 2020, vol. 10(6), pp. 505–21.

[12]   Singh P., Bansal A., Kamal A.E., Kumar S. 'Road surface quality monitoring using machine learning algorithm' in Reddy A.N.R., Marla D., Favorskaya M.N., Satapathy S.C. (eds.). *Intelligent Manufacturing and Energy Sustainability. Smart Innovation, Systems and Technologies*. 265. Singapore: Springer; 2022.

[13] Kumar S., Ranjan P., Radhakrishnan R., Tripathy M.R. 'Energy aware distributed protocol for heterogeneous wireless sensor network'. *International Journal of Control and Automation*. 2015, vol. 8(10), pp. 421–30.

[14] Kumar S., Ranjan P., Ramaswami R., Tripathy M.R. 'A utility maximization approach to MAC layer channel access and forwarding'. *Progress in Electromagnetics Research Symposium*. 2015, pp. 2363–7.

[15] Kumar S., Ranjan P., Ramaswami R., Tripathy M.R. 'An NS3 implementation of physical layer based on 802.11 for utility maximization of WSN'. *2015 International Conference on Computational Intelligence and Communication Networks*; Jabalpur, India, 12-14 Dec; 2016. pp. 79–84.

[16] Sharma A., Awasthi Y., Kumar S. 'The role of blockchain, AI and IoT for smart road traffic management system'. *2020 IEEE India Council International Subsections Conference, (INDISCON)*; Visakhapatnam, India, 03-04 Oct; 2020. pp. 289–96.

[17] Singh P., Bansal A., Kumar S. 'Performance analysis of various information platforms for recognizing the quality of indian roads'. *Proceedings of the Confluence 2020 - 10th International Conference on Cloud Computing, Data Science and Engineering*; Noida, India, 2020. pp. 63–76.

[18] Kumar S., Ranjan P., Singh P., Tripathy M.R. 'Design and implementation of fault tolerance technique for Internet of things (IoT)'. *2020 12th International Conference on Computational Intelligence and Communication Networks (CICN)*; Bhimtal, India, 25-26 Sep; 2020. pp. 154–9.

[19] Singh P., Bansal A., Kumar S. 'Road monitoring and sensing system using mobile sensors'. *2022 12th International Conference on Cloud Computing, Data Science & Engineering (Confluence)*; Noida, India, IEEE, 2022. pp. 165–70.

[20] Reghu S., Kumar S. 'Development of robust infrastructure in networking to survive a disaster'. *2019 4th International Conference on Information Systems and Computer Networks (ISCON)*; Mathura, India, 21-22 Nov; 2019. pp. 250–5.

[21] Chauhan R., Kumar S. 'Packet loss prediction using artificial intelligence unified with big data analytics, Internet of things and cloud computing technologies'. *5th International Conference on Information Systems and Computer Networks (ISCON)*; Mathura, India, 22-23 Oct; 2021. pp. 1–6.

Index